THE SHENZHEN EXPERIMENT

THE SHENZHEN EXPERIMENT

THE STORY OF CHINA'S INSTANT CITY

JUAN DU

Harvard University Press

Cambridge, Massachusetts
London, England
2020

Printed in Canada

First printing

Library of Congress Cataloging-in-Publication Data

Names: Du, Juan (Author of Shenzhen experiment), author.
Title: The Shenzhen experiment : the story of China's instant city / Juan Du.
Description: Cambridge, Massachusetts : Harvard University Press, [2020] |
Includes bibliographical references and index.
Identifiers: LCCN 2019014447 | ISBN 9780674975286 (alk. paper)
Subjects: LCSH: Shenzhen Shi (China)—History. | Urban renewal—
China—Shenzhen Shi. | City planning—China—Shenzhen Shi. |
Shenzhen Jingji Tequ (Shenzhen Shi, China)
Classification: LCC DS797.32.S446 D815 2020 | DDC 951.2/7—dc23
LC record available at https://lccn.loc.gov/2019014447

Frontispiece: Qing Dynasty depiction of Xin'an County (present-day region includes Shenzhen and Hong Kong), ca. 1685. Walled fort on the left indicates location of the Nantou Ancient City, regional capital ca. 331–1953.

TO SHENZHEN'S PAST AND FUTURE MIGRANTS
IN PURSUIT OF LIVES WORTH LIVING

AND

TO MY PARENTS

CONTENTS

INTRODUCTION

The Myth of Shenzhen

Having missed the last flight out from Shenzhen, I reluctantly stayed the night. During the course of that humid late summer evening, I accidentally stumbled upon an urban scene that I had never encountered in all my previous visits to the city. The experience dramatically changed my perception of Shenzhen and, unbeknownst to me at the time, shaped much of my later professional and academic pursuits, including the writing of this book.

During that summer of 2005, I was flying from Beijing to China's southern city of Shenzhen on a weekly basis. I had visited important sites in the city and spoken with countless city officials and experts. By the end of the summer, all that I had seen and heard led to a convincingly unified story of Shenzhen. Established in 1979 as a special economic zone (SEZ), Shenzhen grew from a "small fishing village" into a sprawling metropolis in mere decades, a modern-day miracle of an instant city. The most representative song from China's early reform era is called "The Story of Spring," and it defined not only Shenzhen, but the spirit of the country during China's Reform and Opening Up:

> The Year of 1979
> That was a spring
> There was an old man
> Drawing a circle by the South China Sea

Mythically building a great city
Miraculously forming a mountain of gold
Shenzhen! Shenzhen!
The Test Pilot of China's Reform and Opening[1]

The "old man" in this popular song is Deng Xiaoping, who is globally credited with having single-handedly pivoted China toward economic reforms. The "circle by the South China Sea" refers to Shenzhen, the iconic city that has come to represent the success of the country's rapid economic turnaround. The images of Deng, reform, wealth, and Shenzhen have been interwoven and embedded into the collective consciousness of China as well as the rest of the world.

Narratives of Shenzhen's history emphasize its meteoric growth, unprecedented in human history: from a rural community with a small indigenous population, Shenzhen became a megacity of over ten million people by the mid-2000s. Fast-forward another ten years, and the city's population today has reached twenty million. The magnitude of Shenzhen's population growth is made all the more impressive by its speed of economic development. From 1980 to 2000, Shenzhen's GDP increased from 0.15 billion to over 200 billion yuan, averaging more than 40 percent increase per year. By 2017, Shenzhen's GDP had grown another tenfold to 2.2 trillion yuan (US $338 billion), finally surpassing Asia's leading financial capital cities of Hong Kong and Singapore. Shenzhen's success has earned it both admiring and disparaging labels, from "miracle city" and "model city" to "instant city" and "generic city." Shenzhen's achievements are often attributed to the power of the centralized state and its modern planning, while the city's reputed lack of history or local characteristics is optimistically theorized as a secret to success, enabling possibilities and the pursuit of the new without an obligation to consider the past. I had shared similar views of Shenzhen before my first visits in the summer of 2005, when I was engaged in curatorial activities to develop a large-scale exhibition marking the city's twenty-fifth anniversary. The exhibition was organized by the municipal government to celebrate Shenzhen and its achievements in city planning and architecture.

My initial visits to Shenzhen were on a schedule aligned with the hustle of the city's development. Mornings were spent on the cross-country flight from China's northern capital to the southern border city. Then came a car ride into the city center on the high-speed parkway that might have been anywhere in China; if not for the Chinese characters on the billboards and toll booth signs, it could have been anywhere in the developed world. In

Overview of Shenzhen's three central districts along the city's main transportation spine, Shennan Boulevard. Viewed from the first urbanized Luohu District toward Futian District, with Nanshan District in the distance.

constant traffic, I was driven along the grand Shennan Boulevard, referred to by some as the "business card of Shenzhen" because it represented the best the city had to offer.[2] Both sides of the boulevard were lined with tall towers—some colorful and postmodern, others sleek and futuristic—set amid carefully tended tropical greenery and flowering plants. My travel routine ended with arrivals at various meeting locations in modern, clean, and mostly new government buildings, office towers, schools, commercial centers, and construction sites. Buildings were under construction all over the city, designed by American, Japanese, Italian, Dutch, and Chinese architects, each more ambitious than the one before. The city is affluent, professional, efficient, sanitized, designed for fast cars and faster people. During the first months of the project, I chose to leave as quickly as possible on the last flight out each day—until I missed it that one summer night.

My local host at the Design Department of the Shenzhen Municipal Planning Bureau had kindly upgraded my accommodation at the Overseas

Chinese Town (OCT), an area popular with tourists eager to visit elaborate theme parks. I decided to go for a late evening walk in the well-lit neighborhood. I passed a guarded entrance to a gated residential compound, a luxury shopping mall dimming its lights for the night, and an Italian restaurant where the employees were putting away canopies and chaise lounges before closing up. Lulled into a more relaxed state at seeing the city closing down for the night, I strolled farther, noticing that the buildings and streets were becoming more compact and less orderly. Making a random turn back in the general direction of the hotel, I found myself in an unexpected open space.

I was in a clearing surrounded by walls of dimly lit buildings, six to seven stories tall and leaning very close to each other. Sparkling bare light bulbs hung on wires that stretched from the sides of the buildings to some poles gathered in the middle of a lively and crowded night market. Steam and smoke floated in the air, rising from pots, pans, woks, grills, steamers, boilers, and small furnaces. All sorts of edibles were on display, from watermelon balls, cantaloupe slices, and caramel-covered tangerines and strawberries to egg noodles, pork dumplings, scallion pancakes, shrimp *shaomai,* and vegetable and meat buns. However, the greatest variety seemed to be offered on the open-flame grills: corn on the cob, eggplant slices, stuffed peppers, mini sausages, half chickens, whole fish, shelled orange mussels, small clams, and heaps of large succulent oysters. From behind the food stalls, the busy vendors cooked, served, and chatted while wiping sweat from their faces. Foldout tables of various sizes and shapes were occupied by people with cold beer bottles and platefuls of hot food. Dozens of young children played in groups. They were laughing, shouting, and running, followed by dogs wagging their tails, adding to the chorus of noise with their barking. I had not seen any children during all my prior visits to Shenzhen, and certainly no street dogs, either. My experience in the night market did not match what I knew of Shenzhen.

When I phoned my local acquaintance the next day at the airport and related my amazing discovery of the mysterious neighborhood, there was a momentary pause on the line followed by her concerned voice: "It is very dangerous there, especially for you as a woman alone at night! That place is called Baishizhou, the worst of Shenzhen's many unfortunate *Chengzhongcun!*" This answer piqued even more questions. *Bai-shi-zhou*—White rock sandbank? *Chengzhongcun*—village in the city? And one of many? Why would there be such large villages in modern Shenzhen, especially in the city center, surrounded by wealthy residential and tourist areas? In the months that I had spent on curatorial work for the city's inaugural Shenzhen Biennale of Urbanism \ Architecture, why had no one mentioned the prevalence of these villages in the city? On my walk back to the hotel from the marketplace that night, I certainly had not felt threatened. Even in the poorly lit alleyways, there were always open shops and people around.

I eventually learned that Shenzhen has over three hundred "villages in the city," or urban villages, which evolved from roughly two thousand former agrarian historic villages. Each of the city's administrative urban villages is composed of varying numbers of former historic, or "natural," villages. The Baishizhou village, where I first stumbled across the night market, is actually composed of five different natural villages. Even more surprising than the number of urban villages in Shenzhen is the number of people living in them. The villages altogether hold nearly half of the city's immense population, mostly living in *nongmin fang,* or "peasant houses," referred to as such because they were built by the former agrarian villagers.[3] There are urban villages in almost all Chinese cities today; however, Shenzhen's urban villages have far greater building and population densities than those in other cities, and they are home to a much larger proportion of the city's total population. Nevertheless, in the 2000s there was a general reluctance in Shenzhen to discuss issues surrounding the urban villages, because this reality would open up cracks in its otherwise polished image as a modern and well-planned city. Earlier in 2005, just a few months before my first visit to Shenzhen, the city had declared a campaign to demolish all urban villages in order to eradicate the city's *du liu,* or "malignant tumors." Full of unplanned population and overlooked history, these neighborhoods simply did not fit into the image of a well-planned "instant city."

THE MYTH OF SHENZHEN

The Shenzhen special economic zone was one of the first initiatives orchestrated as part of China's Reform and Opening Up policy under Deng Xiaoping, paramount leader of the People's Republic of China (PRC) from 1978 to 1989. To transform China's stagnant economy, which had been closed off to the world for decades, reform-minded leaders sought to learn from neighboring free market countries and regions that had achieved economic successes. Deng endorsed the creation of three special economic zones in 1980 as a cautious experiment with market reforms. Shen-

Historic village water well still in use at Baishizhou, in Shenzhen's Overseas Chinese Town (OCT).

zhen was the first, followed by Zhuhai and Shantou. The locations of the SEZs were carefully chosen for their geographic proximity to neighbors with "foreign" market economies that could also be persuaded to become trade partners. The Shenzhen SEZ was adjacent to Hong Kong, while the Zhuhai SEZ was close to Macau, and the Shantou SEZ near Taiwan. Close to "corrupt" foreign elements, the SEZs were separated from the rest of China by secondary military-patrolled borders. Until 2006, passports and visas were necessary to enter the SEZ district of Shenzhen from anywhere in China. The SEZs were instrumental in shaping the central government's reform policies, which would eventually spread across the nation. Encouraging everything from land reform to experimentation with foreign trade entities, these SEZ test cases eventually directed China's drastic transformations since the 1980s. The reforms initiated in the SEZs catapulted China's reemergence onto the world stage.

Shenzhen became a powerful tool in the effort to convince skeptics within Deng's government that market reforms could generate wealth quickly and, therefore, constituted the only way to alleviate China's wide-

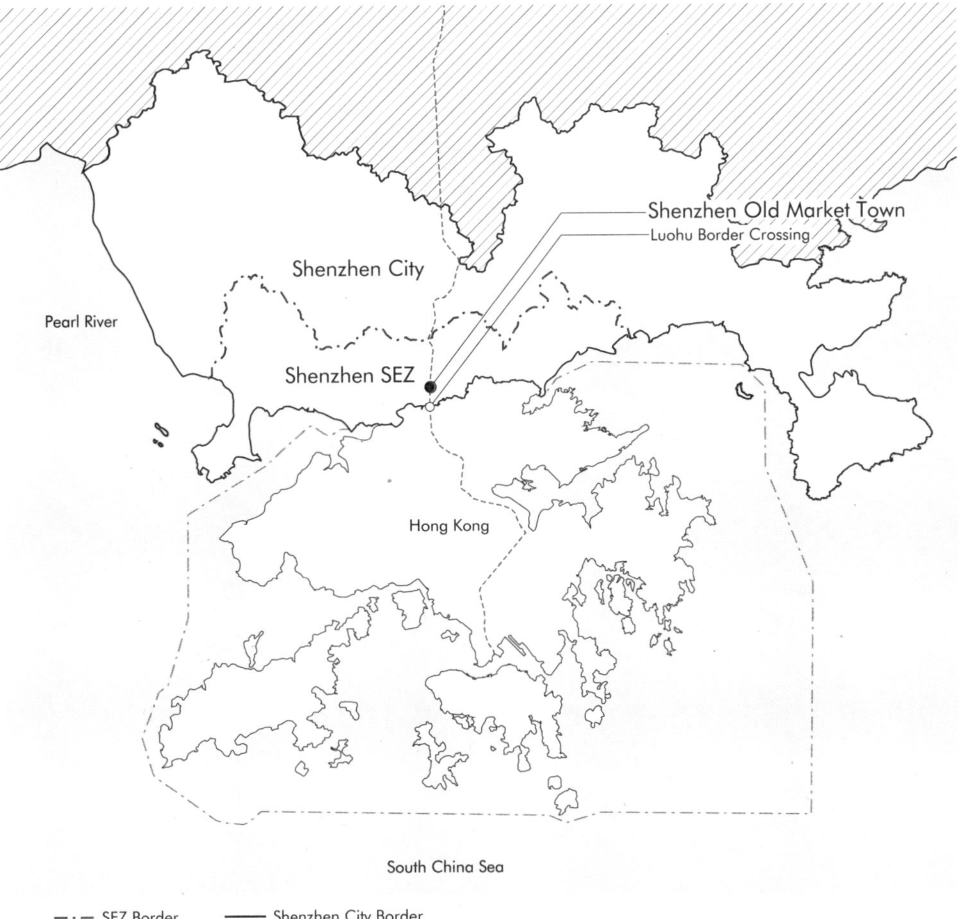

The often-confused "Three Shenzhens": centuries-old Shenzhen Old Market Town (pre-1980 pop. 23,000); 1979 Shenzhen Special Economic Zone (SEZ) (pre-1980 pop. 100,000); and Shenzhen City, inclusive of the SEZ (pre-1980 pop. 300,000).

spread poverty. From the 1980s onward, during Shenzhen's initial years of industrialization as well as its later phase of commercialization, the city's apparent economic success made headlines throughout China. By the year 2000, over eight million migrant workers, both educated and unskilled, had flocked to Shenzhen from all over the country. Ambitious professionals and illiterate laborers alike saw Shenzhen as a land of opportunity. Sensational stories of "mountains of gold" shocked the Chinese populace, impoverished by lack of resources and controlled by austere regulations within a rigid socioeconomic structure.

My original fascination with Shenzhen stemmed from the staggering discrepancies between the city's outward image and the reality that I had come to experience. Academic and journalistic accounts alike tell a remarkably generic story about the reasons for Shenzhen's success, attributing its unprecedented growth and development to the Chinese central government's economic policies and plans across the last forty years. They tell an equally similar story: a tiny and insignificant fishing village from which an instant city arose overnight. The city's sudden emergence in the global economy is so compelling that nearly all local, national, and international reporting on Shenzhen repeats variations of this success story. This story has been reported widely from the *Shenzhen Daily*, the *New York Times*, and *The Guardian*, to the World Bank *Annual Report*. Depending on one's perspective, the story of Shenzhen's founding is either a sacred narrative of economic turnaround or a cliché of rags to riches—either way, it is a story in which an instant city rose from near nothingness.

After more than a decade of scholarly research, architectural projects, and community engagements in the city, I am convinced that this coherent story is less a factual account of the city's evolution than it is a founding myth. In the course of my research, I have been compelled by an increasing sense of urgency to dispel the common misconceptions perpetuated by this myth. The argument of this book is that Shenzhen's growth and development after 1979 should not be attributed solely to the national government's centralized economic policies. In the case of Shenzhen, local negotiations and practices were just as important as—if not more than—national policies and central planning. Likewise, the local geography, history, and culture of the Shenzhen region were just as essential to its evolution as the larger national history for which it became a focal point. The urban form and organization of contemporary Shenzhen are rooted in centuries of complex cultural evolution from earlier settlements—both rural and urban—as well as in events unanticipated at the national level when the ambitious urban experiment to reform Shenzhen, and China more broadly, was initiated in 1979. The Shenzhen SEZ was not simply an experiment, but a critical experiment, meaning one that reflected critically on the problems with China's state of affairs at the time of its initiation. The experiment was controversial, unpopular, and filled with insecurity and uncertainty. The political pathway for China's Reform and Opening Up was far from straightforward or unanimous, and the reforms themselves were not initiated or implemented in a strictly top-down process.

Today, however, the founding myth of Shenzhen is more influential than ever. Outside China, the Shenzhen myth is at times dreaded because it attributes China's stunning economic growth to the actions of a powerful and authoritarian state. Within China, the Shenzhen myth is celebrated as a moral message, one that explains and legitimizes the origin of China's reform policies, which are generally heralded for lifting millions out of poverty. For most of those living in Shenzhen, the myth is sacred, an optimistic mantra that validates their decisions to migrate there, regardless of whether they have made it or are struggling. Whether viewed as a cliché or cherished as an origin story, the Shenzhen myth embodies China's global rise at the turn of the twenty-first century. The myth has become more powerful than any facts about the city.

GLOBALIZATION OF THE SEZ

I am aware of the significance of the Shenzhen myth, and understand that a compelling tale of success often requires the embellishment of kernels of truth. Shenzhen is often referenced in China—and across the world—as a replicable model of city planning and economic development. Implementations of policies derived from the city in the rest of the country have forcefully shaped China as we know it today. After the first batch of SEZs in 1980, China went on to open up fourteen coastal cities in 1984, followed by the southern island Hainan Province in 1988. Shenzhen's "exceptionalism" treatment was rapidly institutionalized into national strategies promoting expedited urban development, with central and provincial governments encouraging the establishment of zones by decentralizing authority to lower administrations at township and county levels.

The Chinese SEZ has also attracted much global attention. While both developed and developing countries around the world have experimented with various forms of zones since the 1960s, most of these—with a few exceptions—have not yielded exemplary results. Shenzhen's success has therefore made the SEZ one of China's most visible foreign policy drivers and sought-after exports, especially in other developing countries. From India to Africa and Latin America, developing countries are looking to China, and specifically to Shenzhen, for ways to achieve rapid economic success while maintaining government control. Forty years ago, China experienced challenges similar to those many developing countries are currently experiencing: lack of infrastructure, outdated modes of industrial production, large surplus rural labor, stagnant local economy, and shortage of investment funding. The idea that Shenzhen became an overnight metropolis, shooting to success from its humble origins as a "small remote fishing village," is incredibly compelling. The rags-to-riches story is irresistibly appealing to governments in China and around the world, especially in developing countries.

Encouraged by the radical application of zones in Shenzhen and other areas of China, zonal strategies have become popular worldwide. Shenzhen is cited in new town planning documents of developed countries, referenced in World Bank reports for developing economies, and courted by various government bodies across the world. China has also promoted the SEZ model globally, most visibly with substantial investments in economic cooperation zones in developing regions.[4] In 2006, there were 3,500 special zones of various types in 130 countries, approximately forty-four times the number in 1975.[5] China's neighboring countries are establishing jointly operated special zones, expecting to learn from the success of Shenzhen. North Korea is founding an area named Rason City, with flexible policies to build a modern port to develop international logistics, trade, tourism, and high-end manufacturing. The North Korean government hopes it will become the country's Shenzhen.[6] Myanmar passed a new special economic zone law, and its port city of Tavoy in the south is looking toward the Shenzhen model. Even in Latin America, a new model of city building, the charter city plan in Honduras, is openly citing Shenzhen as its inspiration. In addition to SEZs inspired by the Chinese experience, Chinese special economic zones have emerged in host countries. Following China's 2001 internationalization policy of Going Out, the 2006 Eleventh Five-Year Plan outlined implementation plans for nineteen Chinese SEZs in other developing countries, with the long-term goal of reaching fifty in total.[7] In Africa, six zones have developed with Chinese government–backed enterprises: one zone each in Zambia, Egypt, Mauritius, and Ethiopia, and two in Nigeria.[8]

Yet while the skyline of Shenzhen could perhaps be repeated elsewhere, the actual operation of Shenzhen is less easily replicated. Indeed, while Shenzhen inspired the creation of additional economic zones in China and around the world, no other SEZ has ever been able to match its unprecedented economic success. And while it may be too soon to evaluate the economic effectiveness and social impact of the newest international zones, it is worrisome that the Shenzhen SEZ model is regarded as a prototype ready for rapid application when its contours are not yet fully understood. The idea that Shenzhen is a replicable model reinforces the assumption that cities can be politically planned and socially engineered from scratch. In fact, national policies based on misconceptions about Shenzhen's developmental history could have devastating consequences in other countries.

SHENZHEN: FOUR MISCONCEPTIONS

This book presents Shenzhen's urbanization and development process as highly specific and extremely complex in terms of its social, cultural, political, geographical, and historical context. Even those responsible for the policy, planning, design, construction, and management of the city may be hard-pressed to state the exact reasons for Shenzhen's exceptional success. I do not pretend to provide a conclusive explanation for Shenzhen's success, but rather aim to offer a critical reflection on a range of assumptions and misconceptions that have shaped narratives of this success. Given Shenzhen's prominence as a global model for economic reform, these misconceptions are due to be revisited and revised. I believe that there are four common categories of misconceptions about this remarkable city: misconceptions surrounding the city's *purpose,* the stretch of *time* relevant to its development, the *place* from which it grew, and the *people* who are part of its story. Because the chapters of this book all address, to varying degrees, each of these four topics—purpose, history, place, and people—in relation to Shenzhen, I will begin by briefly articulating the misconceptions about each one here.

1. Misconception of Purpose: SEZ

The most commonly held view of China's special economic zone policy is that the central government, under Deng Xiaoping's visionary leadership, created it with the goal of turning the country into a globally wealthy and powerful state. This misconception has been perpetuated both in China and abroad. Special economic zones have become synonymous with China's successful centralized economic policies, a perception further promoted by global institutions. According to a publication by the World Bank, "The story of China's economic growth is inextricably linked to the use of 'special economic zones' (SEZs). The transformation of Shenzhen, a small fishing village in the 1970s, into today's city of almost nine million is an illustration of the effectiveness of the SEZ model in the Chinese context."[9] At the other end of the spectrum, those critical of China's recent economic drive also, at times, aggrandize the purpose and impact of the SEZ policy. A paper entitled "The 'Instant City' Coming of Age" offers a typical example of such criticism: "Socioeconomically, while adventurous individual pioneers searching for private fortune or religious freedom built the boomtowns of the old American West, Shenzhen became an instant city as a result of it having been designated as a SEZ—thus its growth was propelled by a purposeful push from a powerful state."[10] However, the goal of China's reforms under Deng was far more modest: it was not to be rich and powerful, but to no longer be poor.

The dire need to lift its people from poverty motivated the country to change. Emerging from the shadows of the Great Famine (1959–1961) and the subsequent decade of the Cultural Revolution (1966–1976), China suffered deep and widespread poverty. The SEZ policy originated as a tentative attempt to experiment with possible ways to alleviate poverty and improve quality of life. While this distinction may seem subtle, the more modest goal of poverty alleviation increased the sense of urgency for China's leaders and gave more agency to its citizens. In turn, the motivations of local governments and individuals played an influential—and as yet, largely unheralded—role in the development of the Shenzhen SEZ. The physical reality of the Shenzhen SEZ was shaped by the purposes of many, not one—from Deng Xiaoping to the tens of millions of migrants who arrived in Shenzhen with little or no resources and began their lives anew.

2. Misconception of Time: 1979

The year 1979 is well established and celebrated as the year in which the city of Shenzhen was founded. Most government documents, scholarly texts, and news articles begin the story of Shenzhen with that particularly important year. Yet it is a misconception to perceive 1979 as the origin point for this story. This popular fallacy conceals the fact that the region's history prior to 1979 significantly impacted the development of modern-day Shenzhen, and obscures the influence of prior historical events on the city today. Shenzhen is not a place without history, as is commonly reported. Rather, Shenzhen has inherited important social networks and industrial traditions from thousands of years of immigration and emigration, political administration, agriculture and aquaculture production, transnational maritime trade, and changing social and political norms, as well as from centuries of reforms in education, culture, trade, and industry. While this book is not a comprehensive history of the city, it does aim to give a necessary historical perspective to Shenzhen's contemporary urbanization. To that end, this book goes as far back as 100 BCE to uncover the forgotten regional history of this strategic location on China's southern coast.

Much of Shenzhen's current spatial organization, social practices, and cultural characteristics can be traced back to its history—both ancient and modern—before 1979. For instance, Chiwan Harbor—located in present-day Nantou Peninsula, Shenzhen's Nanshan District—has a recorded history that dates back to the Tang Dynasty (618–907). Chiwan was one of the most important ports in southern China during the Ming and Qing Dynasties, and the gateway between China and other historic civilizations bound by the South China Sea and beyond. Having been abandoned for a century, Chiwan Harbor was revived with the establishment of the Shekou Industrial Zone and contributed to the rapid development of Shenzhen. To the north of Chiwan Harbor was the Nantou Ancient City: originally an administrative base and military camp during the Tang Dynasty, it grew into the commercial and political capital for a large territory spanning present-day Shenzhen, Hong Kong, Dongguan, Huizhou, Zhuhai, and Macau. Historically, Nantou oversaw an array of political, commercial, and agrarian activities that had a direct impact on the geographical and ecological history of the region; the intricate relationship between Shenzhen and Hong Kong also originates from this shared past. Likewise, the Township and Village Enterprises (TVE), which defined the rural organizational structure of the region for decades prior to 1979, would become some of the most dynamic industrial engines of Shenzhen's economy during the first decade after 1979. The patterns of earlier pre-1979 settlements and industries greatly influenced Shenzhen's later urban form, social organization, and economic production. Much of Shenzhen's current spatial organization, social practices, and cultural characteristics can be traced back to its history, both ancient and modern.

3. Misconception of People: "Thirty Thousand"

There are conflicting reports regarding exactly how many people live in Shenzhen. In 2014, the UK-based *Financial Times* reported ten million: "Since Deng launched his economic reforms in 1979, Shenzhen has changed from a tiny county of thirty thousand people across the border from Hong Kong to a metropolis of ten million with one of the highest per-capita incomes in China."[11] The same year, the *Irish Times* nearly doubled the figure: "The story of Shenzhen's transformation from a fishing village of thirty thousand people across the border from Hong

Kong into a 'special economic zone' and capitalist guinea pig in 1980 into a booming city of eighteen million with the fourth-largest GDP in China is well known."[12] While conflicting population statistics for Chinese cities are prevalent, more problematic here is the erroneous consistency with respect to Shenzhen's reported population. Most media publications and some scholarly papers list "thirty thousand" as the original population prior to Shenzhen's urbanization. However, the actual population inhabiting the 2,020 square kilometers designated as the city of Shenzhen was more than three hundred thousand in the years 1979 and 1980.[13]

The conflicting figures may have arisen owing to different notions of what geographically constituted Shenzhen or what it stood for: the city was split into two territories in 1980, Shenzhen special economic zone in the south and Shenzhen Bao'an County in the north. There were fewer people inside the SEZ, which was a much smaller territory of 327.5 square kilometers, one sixth that of Bao'an County. However, according to official population statistics published by the Shenzhen government, the population even within the Shenzhen SEZ was close to one hundred thousand.[14] Perhaps the "thirty thousand" figure referred to only those living in Shenzhen Zhen, or the Old Shenzhen Market Town, an area of three square kilometers within the SEZ. There were twenty-three thousand people living in this area north of the Hong Kong border; the market town has been an active regional commercial center for centuries.[15] Aside from the matter of statistical inaccuracy, the idea that Shenzhen's pre-1979 population was not material to its urbanization is another misconception. In reality, many overlooked—and in some cases, intentionally omitted—communities and individuals that contributed to its remarkable development. Certain groups of people are entirely unacknowledged in standard accounts of Shenzhen's population explosion. These include the twenty thousand Infrastructure Corps soldiers who arrived in Shenzhen during its first two years (1979–1980) and built many of its towers, roads, and dams, as well as the many inhabitants of "urban villages," former agrarian villages incorporated into the city. Indeed, much of Shenzhen's rapid urbanization and economic growth can be directly attributed to the original villagers who built homes to house the massive influx of migrants. The human dimensions of the city's construction, including the incredible stories of local and regional communities who shaped and were shaped by the Shenzhen SEZ, have yet to be fully narrated.

4. Misconception of Place: "Fishing Village"

Of all the misconceptions propagated by the Shenzhen myth, perhaps the most visual is the "fishing village into metropolis" narrative. The story of a modern, advanced, urban civilization with no memory of its past except a rural seaside hamlet is a powerful modern-day fairy tale. Despite historical records to the contrary, even the Municipal Shenzhen Tourism Board used it as an official tagline for Shenzhen on their website: "Thirty Years Ago, a Peripheral Small Fishing Village." The latest global image of Shenzhen as China's Silicon Valley mythicizes the village-to-future-city narrative even further: "In the space of four decades, Shenzhen has transformed itself from a fishing village into a manufacturing center and now a tech hub—attracting top firms and young talent in sectors including technology, advertising and design."[16] Yet Shenzhen's pre-1979 history included agricultural fields and coastal aquaculture, urban centers and rural settlements. The assumption that the urbanization of Shenzhen is the story of a fishing village erased and replaced by a city that became a center for manufacturing and is now one of technology suggests that the modern metropolis could be anywhere. The sentiment implies that the *placeness* of Shenzhen had little bearing on its development, that the city easily could have been built elsewhere. This book argues, however, that Shenzhen is a unique place with a variety of specific features that contributed to its growth—including a preexisting terrain of farming fields and aquaculture along the coast, a history of significant urban and rural settlements, and numerous unrecognized communities, among them hundreds of thousands of indigenous villagers.

The general notion of urbanization is a process of obsolescence of the rural. Narratives of Shenzhen generally assume that the urban has entirely replaced the rural: the village is no longer, having been erased through the urbanization of rural agriculture, rural land, rural *hukou*, and rural people. However, the physical, social, cultural, and economic characteristics of Shenzhen are not best defined by the obsolescence of villages, but by the empowerment of the rural. Shenzhen's urbanization was tremendously influenced by the transformation and persistence of centuries-old agrarian villages into the current "urban villages" spread across the SEZ, including the Baishizhou village where my own search for the hidden realities of Shenzhen began. But the exceptional physical presence of urban villages in Shenzhen is not a matter of its having more former agrarian villages or indigenous villagers than other Chinese cities. One of the most unique characteristics of Shenzhen's urban village phenomenon is the relatively large sociopolitical influence of the village collectives. The former agrarian community of Huanggang Village, for instance, used community organization, political engagement, economic development, and policy loopholes to participate in the city-making process and leverage its "rural-ness" to the benefit of the villagers. There are currently approximately 350,000 peasant house buildings in the urban villages of Shenzhen.[17] Together, these buildings supply half the city's residential floor area, estimated at 120 million square meters.[18] In some cases, these villages are seen as rent-collecting "parasites" of the city. However, collectively the urban villages of Shenzhen have provided affordable housing in a city that does not have effective social or public housing programs. As elsewhere in China, the few social housing options have strict requirements, and the majority of China's migrant working class is ineligible. Shenzhen's apparent lack of control over the construction and development of the urban villages is not a failure; rather, it is a testimony to the city's strength. The "villages in the city" component of the First Shenzhen Biennale of Urbanism \ Architecture sparked great professional, academic, and public interest, and has become a recurring topic in each ensuing biennial event. Since the 2000s, the urban villages have been gradually transformed from a taboo subject into an important topic for architects, artists, planners, and policy makers in the city and beyond.[19] In addition, increasing attention to urban villages in research and publications about Shenzhen has also disrupted the stereotypical image of the city.[20]

ORGANIZATION OF THIS BOOK

The story of Shenzhen is not the story of a single purpose, but a story of many purposes. Not the story of a single history and a single place, but a collection of varied local histories and local geographies. Not the story of one person or even of one people, but a story of countless individuals. The story of Shenzhen is, in other words, one of pluralities. This book argues that a faithful account of the city's social and material landscape *must* zoom in to the level of the local artifacts, natural features, infrastructures, buildings, animals, and humans that define it. We can learn a great deal more about this remarkable city by moving beyond the centralized plans for—and the standard narratives about—its development, and instead studying the local, informal, and often contradictory ways in which it *actually* developed. This is the collection of stories that the chapters of this book set out to tell, inclusive of the many perspectives and positions, the many conflicts and negotiations, that shaped the evolution of Shenzhen.

To this end, I have organized each chapter of the book around personal histories of different protagonists—all real people—interwoven with the developmental histories of Shenzhen. Each individual included in the book has in some way contributed to the city's urbanization and economic growth, while each one's story reflects the overlooked processes and hidden costs of Shenzhen's urbanization. The words and sentiments of most of these individuals are based either on participant observations and interviews that I have conducted over the years, or on published texts and public records. Those of historical figures, such as Deng Xiaoping, are based on extensive literary research, including critical analyses of government documents, newspaper articles by the Chinese and foreign press, and published biographies in Chinese and English. In addition to the individuals whose perspectives inform each chapter, artifacts—some intangible cultural productions, others constructed physical forms—also help to reveal the realities of Shenzhen. Each chapter is anchored in an artifact that possesses particular meaning to the subject at hand, and each chapter also contains particular pairs of artifacts: song and tour, fort and oyster, tower and nail house, corporate village and slum village. The narrative structure of each chapter aims to reveal the history of Shenzhen through multiple perspectives and individual experiences, generating humanist and material understandings of China's most heterogeneous city. The four parts increasingly zoom in on Shenzhen, descending in scale from the level of the nation, to the region, to the city district, and finally to the neighborhood communities.

By tracing the transformations in individual lives, communities, events, and material landscapes of Shenzhen, this book connects temporal, spatial, social, cultural, political, and economic discourse to present a new portrait of this complex and exceptional city. The Shenzhen experiment offers the world new perspectives on urgent issues such as collaborative governance, cultural continuity, inclusive community, flexible planning, the informal economy, and the rural-urban continuum. This book contends that the most unexpected and valuable insights offered by Shenzhen are those that contrast with generic misconceptions about its development and its success.

PART I

NATIONAL RELEVANCE

1.

SONG FOR "THE STORY OF SPRING"

An overpowering sense of curiosity compelled Jiang Kairu to go south. Leaving behind all that was familiar, he boarded the train for Shenzhen. It was the year 1992.

Leaving his home in rural Heilongjiang, more commonly referred to as the Great Northern Wilderness, Jiang Kairu traveled nearly four thousand kilometers from China's northernmost province bordering Russia to the southernmost border subtropical region. For three days and nights, Jiang was confined to the cheapest compartment of a tightly packed train. Two decades later, the same train route would take less than twenty-four hours via China's modern high-speed rail system; but, in the early 1990s, China's national transportation infrastructure was far from developed and train carriages were notoriously crowded. While enduring the seventy-two-hour journey on a hard seat in the cramped compartment, Jiang listened to passengers' chatter as pop songs broadcast from the train's radio. He raked over burning questions about his destination. With cash hidden in a pocket within his undergarments, carefully sewn by his wife, Jiang was nervous and wary. He had had to borrow the travel fare of two thousand yuan, mostly through the generosity of family and friends. Having recently retired early, at the age of fifty-seven, from his post at a rural township cultural council, he had no official business in Shenzhen. Spending two thousand yuan on a personal trip was a rare extravagance, as it amounted to an entire year's salary for a state employee. This appeared even more peculiar given that he was not visiting family or friends. Jiang just wanted to see Shenzhen with his own eyes.

Jiang Kairu had decided to make this trip only a few months earlier. While reading the *People's Daily* in his small northern Chinese town, he was stunned by a special report titled "Eastern Wind Brings an Eyeful of Spring: A Documentary Report of Comrade Deng Xiaoping's Tour of Shenzhen." The report was full of sensational stories recounting Shenzhen and its transformation from a rural establishment into a miraculous new city: "Eight years ago, this was still a place with paddy fields, fishponds, small paths and low-rise houses. Today in 1992, this place is crisscrossed by wide roads, a block of high-rises towering into the sky and full of modernized flavor. . . . The National Trade Plaza building soars skyward. It is the pride of the Shenzhen people. Shenzhen's builders have set a record, erecting 'one floor every three days'—the symbol of Shenzhen Speed."[1] The report's sensational descriptions of Shenzhen contrasted starkly with Jiang's day-to-day experience, or anyone else's in China at the time.

This reported progress in Shenzhen was even more impressive than what Jiang Kairu had read just a year earlier in the widely distributed official report titled *Shenzhen's Mystery of the Sphinx*.[2] Published in 1991, it detailed Shenzhen's spirited establishment in 1979 and described its decade of instant success. Deng Xiaoping was prominently cited as spearheading the SEZ, and one of his instructions to local party leaders remains memorable: "Set up a special zone on your own! Slash a way out!"[3] Deng's rousing battle cry felt familiar to Jiang Kairu. He had signed up for army training at the age of fifteen and served in the Chinese army for seven years before being discharged to Heilongjiang. Jiang Kairu identified with Deng's language and felt personally connected to China's paramount leader, despite having seen him only in photographs.

Relayed by central and local news outlets throughout the country, reports about Shenzhen were read by most of China's literate population. The shocking impact of Shenzhen's urban image, with its fast-rising tall towers and busy wide boulevards, was pervasive in the tentative early years of China's reforms. Written reports and televised images of the shiny new city ignited massive waves of southern migration. Attracted by the mythical pull of a land of opportunity, these urban migration movements, first triggered by Shenzhen, would come to define China at the turn of the twenty-first century. From the lowest ranks of the working class to the highest seats of administration, adventurous dreamers from every socioeconomic class had a part in building Shenzhen—it is the ultimate city of migration.

UNCERTAIN BEGINNINGS

Shenzhen's magnetic pull was so powerful that it far exceeded all population growth expectations in the decades following its establishment. The city's initial objectives were outlined in the March 1979 "Reply of the State Council on Establishing Shenzhen and Zhuhai Municipality in Guangdong Province," which specified an urban population of one hundred thousand as a short-term target, and a projected population of two hundred thousand to three hundred thousand by the year 2000.[4] However, the establishment of the Shenzhen special economic zone in August 1980 prompted publication of the "Shenzhen City Urban Construction Comprehensive Planning," the city's first official planning document, which revised the projected population by the year 2000 to upwards of five hundred thousand.[5] The 1982 and 1986 Shenzhen Comprehensive Plans revised these figures once again, increasing the projected population to eight hundred thousand and 1.1 million, respectively. Despite these successive adjustments, the actual rate of growth far outpaced the projected increases. By the year 2000, Shenzhen's population had already topped six million, or six times more than the most ambitious planned figures.[6] The discrepancy between projected and actual numbers also meant that the planned provisions for urban infrastructure, including housing, transportation, and social services, were far below customary standards for the number of people. One could argue that the real mystery is how Shenzhen managed not only to avoid downfall but to continue growing into a metropolis of twenty million residents in the 2010s.

Contrary to popular narratives of Shenzhen's top-down establishment and instant success, the reality of the city's evolution is far more complex. Shenzhen's early developmental history was fraught with political oppositions, policy uncertainties, economic setbacks, and vicious cultural criticism. Its development did not follow the central planning process directed by Beijing; rather, in a struggle to thrive, the city inadvertently challenged top-down policies and drastically altered centralized planning. Much of the city's subsequent unexpected exponential growth was enabled through local initiatives, bottom-up ingenuities, and unanticipated or informal urban processes.

Mired in political controversies, economic challenges, and cultural clashes, Shenzhen strove merely to meet expectations and survive in its first decade. The earliest reports on Shenzhen were designed to portray a positive urban image in order to rebut pointed criticisms from some of the country's top leaders. The writing of the 1991 book *Shenzhen's Mystery of the Sphinx* was directed by Li Hao, Shenzhen's mayor from 1985 to 1993, and completed by a team from the Shenzhen Department of Publicity, when the city was subject to tremendous pressure and skepticism expressed by influential members of the central government. Despite all efforts, criticisms of Shenzhen—and of China's reform policies in general—reached such dramatic levels in 1991 that the eighty-seven-year-old Deng Xiaoping was compelled to emerge from the privacy of his retirement to make one of his last rounds of public appearances, in the still-fledgling special economic zones. Deng's 1992 visit to Shenzhen, so charmingly portrayed in the "Eastern Wind Brings an Eyeful of Spring," was actually intended to rally support for the city, and more importantly, to ensure that China's national reforms were continued.

To counter the deep-rooted skepticism of powerful party leaders, narratives of Shenzhen's early success depicted bustling urban scenes that attracted millions of ambitious individuals to drive the city's development forward. The most visible and effective beacon of Shenzhen's success was not its oft-quoted economic statistics, but the image of the city itself. Facilitated by rapid building and infrastructure construction, the mythic mirage city sprouted and flourished from mere rice fields. Reports such as *Shenzhen's Mystery* and "Eastern Wind" are often credited for prompting mass migration to Shenzhen during the early 1990s. Having worked in rural Heilongjiang Province for thirty years, Jiang Kairu was inspired by the sensational image of the city described in the "Eastern Wind" report and compelled to embark on his long journey south to Shenzhen.

Jiang Kairu's story epitomizes the magnetism of Shenzhen's mythic narrative. Yet his story is also an exceptional one, as he would later become the lyricist of the hugely popular song "The Story of Spring," which further mythicized Deng Xiaoping's association with Shenzhen. The song captured a moment in Shenzhen's history, consolidating both a nation's hope and Deng's identity as the creator of an instant city. On the cusp of monumental change, following decades of poverty and stagnation, the "spring" in the title and lyrics of the song symbolized personal and collective hopes for a new beginning. The popular song successfully cemented an urban image of Shenzhen as a land of opportunity and became one of the city's most enduring mythmaking artifacts. Interweaving this mythic account of Shenzhen with an ode to Deng Xiaoping, the song served as the national anthem for China's reforms throughout the 1990s.

Jiang Kairu had no inkling of what the future would bring as he alighted from the packed train carriage on May 13, 1992. Walking slowly away from the train station, he looked around and had a sinking feeling that he was not where he was supposed to be. Tired and groggy from his long journey, Jiang Kairu thought for a moment that he had missed the Shenzhen stop and somehow arrived in Hong Kong. Despite the reports he had read about Shenzhen's urban construction, he was caught off guard by the wide boulevards and scores of shiny office towers. Although he had visited other Chinese cities before, he had seen sights like this only in Hong Kong. The single assurance that he had arrived at his destination was the bold sign above the train station: "*Shen Zhen.*" Jiang was doubly comforted by the fact that the sign reproduced Deng Xiaoping's calligraphic inscription of the city's name, made familiar around the country through newspaper reporting.

THE "SPECIAL" NATURE OF THE SPECIAL ECONOMIC ZONE

No sooner had he arrived in Shenzhen than Jiang resolved that he would stay. Like millions of others drawn to and curious about Shenzhen, he altered his initial plan to just briefly visit the city. However, unlike most other newly arrived migrants seeking work, Jiang was categorized as a "person of three withouts": one who came without a stable job, without a permanent home address in the city, and most crucially, without an urban *hukou,* or household registration. The *hukou* system was established in 1958, when the National People's Congress passed its "Regulations on Household Registration in the People's Republic of China," and still exists today (albeit in a more relaxed form). Every Chinese citizen is assigned a *hukou* tied to the lowest-level administrative unit—city, township, village, etc. Depending on its administrative location, a person's *hukou* is further classified as "agricultural" (rural) or "non-agricultural" (urban). In principle, the *hukou* cannot be transferred from one location to another, and especially not from rural villages to urban centers. This system effectively controlled the internal movements of China's vast population and facilitated the country's planned economy, which rationalized and governed state spending on programs such as education, healthcare, housing, and employment. Migration between cities was even forbidden unless authorized by the government. Through its geographic regulations, this institutionally divisive system unintentionally segregated China's population into two broad socioeconomic classes, with rural *hukou* holders benefiting from considerably fewer opportunities for upward economic or social mobility.

Those born to parents of rural *hukou* inherited this second-class citizen status, which restricted how and where they lived, worked, married, and were buried. Access to agricultural land was possible via the village collective, but the Communist state welfare benefits were not available. Prolonged presence in any city was illegal, and one risked being stopped by the police demanding to see identification papers. Until the early 2000s, those caught without the proper *hukou* were fined and sent to detention centers. A woman who was held in a migrant detention center in Beijing described her experience in 1995 as "hell on earth, much worse than normal prisons. . . . Considering all living conditions, including food, I say that is not a place for a human being."[7] If individuals were unable to provide papers within one month of their detention, they would be deported back to their place of *hukou* registration. Massive "clean-up campaigns" to round up millions of rural migrants for repatriation were carried out in most major Chinese cities, as recently as the 2000s.

Although the central government tightly controlled quotas for legalized migration through temporary residency registration, Shenzhen's flourishing industries attracted a massive influx of people from all over China seeking work opportunities without formal registration. Since these enterprises and factories completely relied on rural workers as a source of cheap labor, both employees and employers took the risks of engaging in informal, and at times unlawful, practices. In order to grow, Shenzhen opened its doors to millions of rural migrants seeking opportunities that would have been impossible elsewhere in China. In addition, the Shenzhen government made considerable efforts to recruit skilled and educated personnel. Individual enterprises even awarded a head-hunting bonus to employees as a recruiting incentive.

In 1984, Shenzhen's municipal government began issuing "Temporary Residence Certificates." This made Shenzhen the first city in China to formally recognize the existence of a "floating population" and, most importantly, to offer legal status to the so-called migrant workers, officially authorizing them to live and work in the city. Over the next decade, this practice was replicated by other city governments in Guangdong Province and other urban centers in China. Shenzhen later initiated additional *hukou* reforms to support certain groups of new arrivals by shortening their waiting period for the Shenzhen urban *hukou*. These reforms included the Blue Chop program, designed to attract well-educated workers, and a point-based system that incorporated additional factors such as home purchases. The successful implementation of these "special" measures encouraged their adoption by other Chinese cities, and eventually inspired ongoing nationwide *hukou* reforms.[8]

Whether out of necessity or collective spirit, time and again Shenzhen paved the way for the rest of the country in changing existing policies and formulating new protocols for working migrants. Shenzhen's successive *hukou* reforms, and more importantly, its open and welcoming approach to newcomers, helped to make its urban culture unique in comparison to other cities in China. While Shenzhen has often been described as a pilot site for China's economic reforms, the city's role in ushering drastic changes to societal norms and expectations is just as often overlooked. In a country where one's social network and cultural identifier were largely based on place of origin, a conversation between two people meeting for the first time often started with "*ni shi na li ren,*" which means not just "where are you from?" but, more literally, "you are a person of what place?" In Shenzhen, the same obligatory question would still be asked, but the verbal exchange would usually include some words of comfort to the new comer: "*Lai le jiu shi Shenzhen ren,*" translated as "Now that you're here, you are a person of Shenzhen." The phrase became the city's unofficial motto, a civic sentiment of citizenship upon arrival. Thus, having arrived in the city, Jiang joined other migrants in the hope of becoming a part of Shenzhen.

THE DIFFERENCE IN MINDSET

On his second day in Shenzhen, Jiang started looking for work, which was no simple task. At fifty-seven years of age, he was decades older than others seeking employment. The average age of the Shenzhen SEZ population in the 1990s was under twenty-five. Shenzhen's population was growing at a rate of half a million every two years.[9] Migrant workers were attracted to the city not only because of its more relaxed attitude toward illegal residency, but also because of certain freedoms it offered in the workplace. Elsewhere at that time, China's planned economy delivered workers lifelong employment in state-owned enterprises commonly called *Danwei*, or the work unit. During the decades of national planned economy prior to the 1980s reform era, state-owned work units were the default form of social organization in Chinese cities. Much more than a job would do, the work units also offered housing and other social services to every employee. Colloquially referred to as the Iron Rice Bowl, jobs within the centrally planned economy ensured lifelong social welfare as part of work unit employment. In addition to salary, the work unit provided housing, medical care, child care, and retirement benefits, covering the entire lifespan of each worker. Upon death, an employee's children would even step into the employment post of the deceased parent. And it did not end there. The work unit was not only the regulator of one's employment, but also the general locus of one's social life. Moving house, attending school, getting married, having children . . . any such life change required permission from one's work unit. Switching jobs was rare and signified a major change. By breaking away from the work unit system, Shenzhen was able to invent new types of labor contracts that placed responsibilities on both employers and employees. This system, issuing contracts for both short-term and long-term employment, was later adopted throughout the country.[10]

Shenzhen successfully marketed these changes to attract not only rural migrant workers, but also educated and skilled talents from other more developed Chinese cities. During the first decade of the SEZ's existence, educated employees were often reluctant to leave their stable and reputable jobs elsewhere. However, as news of Shenzhen's progress spread, the city swiftly gained a reputation as a place of personal freedom and freewheeling opportunities, encouraging entrepreneurial and ambitious young graduates from China's top universities to descend on the city. Many new arrivals were highly educated, attracted to the city's government agency and elite corporate sectors; most, however, came from rural regions throughout China to seek work in production factories. This characteristic mix continues to the present day, with Shenzhen holding the country's record both for the lowest education level among its migrant workers and also for the highest number of doctoral degree holders.

It was not surprising, then, that at Jiang's first job interview he was asked if he had a diploma. While jobs in other cities were assigned through central planning and lengthy deliberations based on references, employers in Shenzhen sought qualifications. Jiang did not have a diploma; however, he did hand over an award certificate proclaiming him the winner of China's first national song lyrics competition in 1988, selected from a pool of twenty thousand submissions. His interviewer stated that this kind of talent could be just as relevant as a diploma, so Jiang was hired by the Blue Sky Enterprise Art Troupe. Under the terms of his temporary labor contract, Jiang's tasks ranged from cleaning the office to writing newsletters. He was paid only when he worked on an assignment. Even though the salary was low, the job provided Jiang with a foothold in Shenzhen.

Two weeks later, Jiang received the first letter from his wife since he left home. She asked, "What are people of the Special Zone like?" He replied with a humorous rhyme: "During the hottest days the men are in suits and elegant ties; during the coldest days the women show skin in stylish mini-skirts."[11] Influenced by neighboring Hong Kong, many men in Shenzhen wore Western-style suits even in the humid subtropical weather. Their attire was a sign of Shenzhen's developing business culture, and stood in sharp contrast to the so-called Mao suits worn by men and women throughout the rest of China; women's office attire in Shenzhen likewise stood out as unconventional, owing to the amount of skin exposed. These changes took place in Shenzhen at a time when, in many parts of China, fabric shortages made it difficult to obtain basic clothing items. In prereform China from 1955 to 1993, one could not purchase clothing with cash alone; one also needed to provide fabric ration coupons to acquire the allotted amount. In the same way, one could not purchase essential food items such as rice, cooking oil, sugar, and meats without the corresponding food ration coupons. However, in 1984, Shenzhen became an exception as the first city in China to abolish the food coupon system, allowing the purchase of food items with cash. In Shenzhen, suddenly cash could buy anything. And there was plenty of cash visible in Shenzhen. As he later recounted to his wife, Jiang observed a young woman with a large black plastic bag standing in line ahead of him at a bank. Once at the cashier's window, she handed her bank book to the teller to make a withdrawal and, minutes later, stacks of bank notes appeared on the counter. Without any guards around, she casually placed the notes in her plastic bag. The cash amounted to fifty thousand yuan—about twenty years' worth of Jiang's salary at his former civic job. However, Jiang emphasized he was most struck not by Shenzhen's material wealth but by the attitudes of its inhabitants, which contrasted with those elsewhere in China. Jiang reflected on the strangeness of Shenzhen's people in a letter to his wife: "They did not stress modesty, but they did convey self-confidence. They ranked themselves not by seniority, but by the size of share ownership. They sought solutions not from the mayor, but from the market. They placed importance on loss and profit, not on *guanxi* [i.e., connections]. They spared no sweat, but they cherished time. Time was ticking, time was money, and efficiency was life."[12]

THE LETTER FROM HONG KONG

There was a more personal reason why Jiang was impressed by Shenzhen's progress in 1992. He had visited Shenzhen once before in 1979, just after the city of Shenzhen had been established. That had been on a stopover on what would be a life-changing visit to Hong Kong; Jiang had embarked on this journey prompted by a relative's unexpected letter to come for a visit. Communications between Chinese nationals and overseas individuals were strictly monitored, and for the most part illegal in post-1949 China. However, by 1979 there were signs of change.

In March 1979, the Beijing central government announced that Bao'an County in Guangdong Province—a rural region located along China's national border with then British-ruled Hong Kong—would be transformed into the city of Shenzhen. With an administrative area of 2,020 square kilometers, covering the entire former Bao'an County, Shenzhen was to be governed by Guangdong's provincial leaders in its capital city of Guangzhou. The measure was part of a larger governmental effort to prepare Guangdong and Fujian Provinces for international trade. As a result of centuries of international commerce and external migration, the highest percentage of China's overseas expatriates, or *huaqiao,* comes from these two coastal Chinese provinces. In July 1979, it was officially announced that Guangdong and Fujian would promote international economic activities by adopting the Special Policies and Flexible Measures strategy introduced by the central government. As China's commercial and diplomatic relations were mostly limited to other communist states between 1949 and

1979, the central government also recognized the potential benefits of the international diaspora from these two southern provinces: the social capital embedded in past centuries of international trading and emigration could help China to reenter the world economy.

As news of China's opening up spread, many overseas Chinese reached out to their families living in China. Jiang was contacted by a cousin he had never met, the daughter of an uncle residing in Hong Kong. She sent a letter urging him to visit Hong Kong during the *Qingming* festival, as his aunt was also due to visit from the United States at that time.

In order to make the trip, Jiang had to submit his cousin's invitation letter and a lengthy application report to his work unit—the Mao Zedong Thought Dissemination Team of Mulin County. He had lived and worked in the rural regions of this northeastern Chinese province since his discharge from the army in 1958. It took many months for his application to be processed. Jiang later learned that it had been vetted by government departments all the way up to the CPC Central Department for United Front Work. Jiang never knew if this lengthy and complex application process was standard practice or exceptional—his personnel record was flagged for having a "problematic historical background," which may have delayed the process.

Paradoxically, considering where he ended up in life, Jiang was the son of a Nationalist Army general who had trained at the Whampoa Military Academy, the storied institution that trained many of the top leaders in both armies led by Jiang Jieshi (Chiang Kai-Shek)'s Nationalists and Mao's Communist Party. The complex relationship between the two forces is perhaps exemplified by the fact that Jiang's father first fought alongside the Communist army against the Japanese invasion (1931–1945), then fought against the Communist military during the subsequent Chinese Civil War (1945–1949). With the Nationalists' defeat in 1949, most top Nationalist government leaders and military officers, including many of Jiang's family members, fled to Taiwan and the United States.

While Jiang's cousin wrote of a family reunion with his relatives in Hong Kong, the hidden agenda was a reunion between Jiang and his elder sister living in Taiwan. The siblings had had a close relationship growing up. Married to a top officer in the Nationalist air force, Jiang's sister fled with the military to Taiwan in 1949. Meanwhile, Jiang had not seen or heard from his sister for thirty years, not since their painful goodbye in war-torn China.

To his surprise and delight, Jiang's application was finally approved. To get to Hong Kong, Jiang first had to travel for days to reach Shenzhen in order to cross the border. He made a train journey across the country to Luohu Railway Station, the same journey that he would make thirteen years later in 1992. He arrived at nightfall and spent a nervous night in a guesthouse close to the Shenzhen–Hong Kong checkpoint. When he looked out the window the next morning, he realized that the five-story guesthouse was taller than all of the surrounding buildings, which mainly consisted of single- or two-story farmhouses scattered among stretches of rice fields. Instead of swarms of people, he saw a herd of farming buffalos ambling slowly along the muddy paths. Jiang's impression of Shenzhen in 1979 contrasts starkly with his later experience of the city and its progress. Notably, it would also influence his depiction of the city in "The Story of Spring," and so contribute to the broader cultural impression of what had preexisted in Shenzhen.

What Jiang did not see on his first visit, however, were the many large and productive villages, as well as the historic market town of *Shenzhen Xu,* which occupied the area adjacent to the Luohu border crossing. The name of the new Shenzhen city was adopted from this centuries-old regional commercial area. When Jiang visited in 1979, the population of the Shenzhen market town, which extended for roughly ten square kilometers, was approximately thirty thousand.[13] However, this number was often misquoted as the total existing population of the entire Shenzhen city administrative area. In 1979, the actual population of Shenzhen city's 2,020 square kilometers was over 314,100.[14] The mostly rural population was spread throughout the region's diverse geography, from a number of bustling townships to hundreds of productive farming and fishing villages.[15] The villages were important centers of economic activities; they became instrumental during the initial years of Shenzhen's urbanization process. In fact, one of the most overlooked aspects of China's economic reforms is the importance of the countryside in laying the foundations for change and success. The rural reforms in China's countryside during the late 1970s and early 1980s paved the way for China's urban revolution. This process was especially visible in Shenzhen. The southern region in which Shenzhen is situated has served as an especially important social, cultural, and economic center throughout China's long history. The impact of the past regional rural history on Shenzhen's later urban development is most vividly seen through the transformation of former rural villages into highly developed socioeconomic centers, later labeled as "villages in the city," or urban villages.

The population of Shenzhen prior to 1979, the year generally established as the beginning of its urbanization, has been dismissed as culturally and statistically insignificant. Yet this mostly rural population contributed significantly to the city's social, economic, and spatial development. From a numerical perspective, the difference between thirty thousand and three hundred thousand may seem insignificant compared to the tens of millions that later populated Shenzhen. However, this is an example of the dangerous biases that come with explaining the complexities of cities through statistics alone. The discrepancies between the city's planned projections and its eventual urban reality are intrinsically tied to the organization of the preexisting rural population into hundreds of self-motivated village entities, each contributing to Shenzhen's urbanization in unexpected ways. To ignore or trivialize the role played by existing populations and their socioeconomic activities in the region is to participate in one of the biggest misconceptions about Shenzhen's development after 1979.

There are many reasons why retellings of Shenzhen's origin story underplay the impact of its existing population and previous regional history. Owing to socioeconomic prejudice, some regarded the rural population as inconsequential, while others were driven by political motivation to prove the foresight of central planning. As for Jiang Kairu, he may have developed an inadvertent impression that Shenzhen had little to offer, as he crossed rice fields to Luohu Checkpoint, the demarcation between Communist China and the mysteries of capitalist Hong Kong.

THE BEAUTY OF HUMAN NATURE

Jiang's experience in Hong Kong left him with vivid memories. He later recalled crossing a border through a military patrol station and barbed wire fencing: "The most memorable thing on my way out was the barbed wire. Once I passed it I was in the free world."[16] As he sat on the bus that took him from the border to the inner city of Hong Kong, he was stunned by the sights. He marveled at the high-speed roadways and shiny high-rises. He reflected on the contrast between what he was seeing and what he had been trained to think of capitalism. He had been told that all working people in capitalist societies were oppressed and deprived because of the market-driven economy. As a result, in China the pursuit of wealth was deemed unethical and unpatriotic. However, while in Hong Kong waiting at the bus station for a relative, Jiang did not see oppressed workers. Instead, he saw

Luohu Border Crossing between Hong Kong and Shenzhen, ca. 1950s.

colorfully dressed men and women with puffy permed hairstyles. He glimpsed gold jewelry, flashy watches, and large handheld mobile phones. Jiang felt uncomfortable and poor. He was aware of the stares from passersby at his shabby attire. Fortunately, Jiang soon heard his name called out. He immediately felt comforted by hugs and the warmth of family.

Once reunited with his sister at his uncle's home, Jiang found it difficult to express his emotions. His last memory of her was during the final chaos of war in China, as she climbed onto a waiting army plane and gripped his hands tightly, pleading desperately for him to come with her. But fourteen-year-old Jiang decided not to board the plane. Their mother did not want to leave China, so he stayed behind with her and their younger siblings. Seeing his sister again thirty years later in Hong Kong, Jiang was driven by an instinct to explain how he felt in verse. He wrote these words that night:

> Oh my dear loved one, do you remember,
> The curving creek, the waving willow trees
> Around our home?
> We crossed the little bridge bare-footed,
> You holding my hand in yours.
> Oh my dear loved one, do you remember

Mother's back and Mother's bosom
Carrying us day and night,
Rocking us to sleep like a cradle?[17]

Tearfully, Jiang's sister and family marveled at his poetic words. He explained that it was a song rather than a poem: poetry is read with eyes, while lyrics sing to the heart. The immense grief for all the years lost combined with the joy of reunification prompted him to write similar verses each night in his diary. During his fifty-day stay in Hong Kong, he wrote thirty-eight sets of song lyrics. He submitted five to the respectable local journal *Hong Kong Literature,* and they were all accepted and published.

As his visitation period drew to an end, Jiang's family urged him to stay in Hong Kong. At that time, Hong Kong and China had a mutual agreement to allow Chinese migrants to legally remain in Hong Kong by becoming part of the city's developing economic workforce, which was experiencing a boom and was in critical need of cheap labor. This policy continued until October 1980. Jiang's family even found a job for him. To their surprise, however, Jiang insisted on returning home to the Great Northern Wilderness. Once back home, those around him asked the same question: "Why did you choose to return to China?" Jiang's answer was even more unexpected: the Cultural Revolution.

During China's Cultural Revolution (1966–1976), Jiang's problematic historical background meant that he was labeled "Three Counters" (Counter Communist Party, Counter Socialism, and Counter Maoist-Thought). Anyone with ties to noncommunist countries was suspected of being a spy and traitor during the Cultural Revolution. Many were tortured and killed. When the local Red Guards came for Jiang carrying placards marked "Traitor," intending to arrest him, he dressed himself in black, ready to face the mob. However, at the last moment, his work unit supervisor volunteered to take the punishment in Jiang's place. Jiang later insisted that this not only saved his life, but also restored his belief in the "beauty of human nature." Having experienced the darkest moment in modern China's history, Jiang was able to see the kindness of people during the unkindest of times. He chose to return to China because of the gratitude he felt toward the community that protected and sheltered him during the Cultural Revolution. He also greatly appreciated the policy change that allowed the China–Hong Kong border to be reopened, and made this long-awaited reunion with his family abroad possible.

Beginning in March 1979, China's central government implemented a series of policies that took the world by surprise. For many overseas Chinese, it provided hope that such long-awaited family reunions might be realized after decades of separation. Jiang's was one of thousands of families torn apart by the civil war. Between 1947 and 1950, over two million civilians fled the chaos of the war. Most of them were unable to follow the Nationalists to Taiwan, so they illegally crossed Shenzhen's border to British-ruled Hong Kong. Many remained in Hong Kong, while others emigrated to surrounding Asian countries and beyond. The subsequent halt in China's diplomatic relations with most noncommunist countries resulted in no contact or exchanges between Chinese citizens and their loved ones residing abroad, especially those on the renegade island of Taiwan. Thus, Hong Kong became the city of reunion for many. Hong Kong's role as a logistical and economic hub between Communist China and Nationalist Taiwan emerged during the early reform era and continued for more than fifty years. It was not until 2003 that direct chartered flights between Taipei and Shanghai were established. Regular commercial flights started as late as 2009. Tour group visas were first issued in 2008, while individual tourist visas were not granted until 2011.

Jiang was profoundly grateful for China's Open Door policies. This allowed him to reunite with his family after so many years, and the experience had a transformational impact on him. Jiang left Hong Kong in the spring of 1979 a changed man. On his return to China, he submitted the rest of his song lyrics to literary journals and won acceptance for their publication. He started to write more and more songs. In 1988, he wrote the lyrics for "Shouting Out to the Great Northern Wilderness," the words of which were imbued with his love of the land and gratitude for the people. The song was awarded first place, chosen from twelve thousand entries including submissions by many professional musicians and writers.[18] It was this unexpected achievement that later made it possible for Jiang to land his first job in Shenzhen.

DRAWING A CIRCLE BY THE SEA: THE ZONE OF EXCEPTION

Once he had gained some job security, Jiang Kairu began exploring the SEZ whenever he had free time. It was 1992, and he took photos of the landscape to send home to his family: the pristine Shenzhen Bay, the meandering Shenzhen River that separated China from Hong Kong. The national border contiguous with the Shenzhen River was demarcated as part of the 1898 negotiations between the Qing imperial court and the British Crown, which extended Hong Kong to include the northern New Territories. The British originally proposed that the mountain ranges farther north form the new boundary to the British colony.[19] These mountain ranges historically defined the flatter coastal regions of Shenzhen Bay's fishing villages along either side of the Shenzhen River. The Qing court opposed this aggressive proposition, and the two sides settled on the centerline of the Shenzhen River as the border. This border line drawn in the water divided not only national territories, but also village lands, farming fields, and family members. However, in the centuries prior to the 1898 negotiations, interdependent social, economic, and cultural relationships had evolved across both sides of the river, influencing the social, political, and economic development of the region. From dynastic changes after the fall of the Qing Dynasty and imperial rule, to the inception of the Nationalist Republic of China in 1912 and the communist People's Republic of China in 1949, the river remained porous to indigenous villagers who inhabited either side. Even during the most intense political standoffs between China and the rest of the world, locals still crisscrossed the border, exchanging goods, information, technology, and much more. The most critical exchanges of resources were not the result of top-down policies, but were informal and, at times, illegal. Hong Kong's contribution to Shenzhen's urbanization cannot be fully understood without acknowledging this important historical context. While the influence of each city on the other's urbanization and development was governed by formal policies, the greatest impacts were really channeled through familial relationships and informal processes.

Jiang Kairu was particularly fascinated by the northern border of the special economic zone. Living and working inside the SEZ, Jiang was acutely aware of its unique status in contrast with the rural areas of Shenzhen and the rest of the country. Shenzhen's *Er Xian Guan,* or Second Line Border, was a patrolled fence constructed across the full breadth of the city from east to west. Constructed after the SEZ's establishment in 1980, this barbed wire fence had only nine entry and exit checkpoints. Shenzhen's mountain ranges had finally become a border. The Second Line Border followed the peaks and valleys of Shenzhen's natural geography, from the region's tallest, Wutong Mountain, at 944 meters in the west, to the Tanglang mountain range at 430 meters to the east. Along with the Pearl River Estuary to the west, the South China Sea coast to the east, and the Shenzhen River to the south, the border enclosed an area of 327.5 square kilometers, one-sixth of the entire area of Shenzhen city.

Policies and governance inside the SEZ differed vastly from the outer districts of Shenzhen. The border separated the city into two different administrative areas. The SEZ was effectively an island on its own, a fenced-in area of exceptionalism in economy, politics, and culture.

On one of his visits to the Shekou Industrial Zone Museum, Jiang spotted a map with lines in pencil determinedly circling the area that defined the Shenzhen SEZ.[20] This historic map was the result of a 1979 meeting in Beijing between Yuan Geng, vice president of China Merchants Group (and later director of the Shekou Industrial Zone) and Li Xiannian, vice chairman of the Communist Party of China. In the discussion over a map of Hong Kong that included the southern portion of the then-still-rural Bao'an County, Yuan Geng's primary objective was to obtain a site to develop an export processing zone that could accommodate a seaport. The map actually notes multiple possible locations for such a zone, with a few stars marked in Hong Kong and Bao'an. The circled area on the historic map, which confirmed the final location of the industrial zone, was drawn by Li Xiannian in endorsement of Yuan Geng's proposal. The circle encompassed almost half of what was to become the Shenzhen special economic zone, while the Shekou Industrial Zone would be limited to roughly two square kilometers on the Nantou Peninsula. Established by China's central government in January 1979—nearly two years earlier than SEZ—the Shekou Industrial Zone, directed by Yuan Geng, would profoundly impact the development of Shenzhen. When Jiang Kairu wrote home about the special nature of the zone, he noted that "time is money, and efficiency is life," a direct quote from Yuan Geng's famous corporate motto. So different was this sentiment from the cultural norm in China at the time, which equated the mention of money to the ills of capitalism, that the slogan was heavily scorned by those critical of China's market reforms. Despite many controversies, Yuan Geng successfully directed the Shekou Industrial Zone from 1979 to 1992, and became one of Shenzhen's most influential thought leaders. Like many of Shenzhen's earliest leaders, Yuan Geng was from the region and born decades before the establishment of the People's Republic of China in 1949. His education, local knowledge, and subsequent international experience enabled him to make significant contributions to democratizing enterprise and governance.

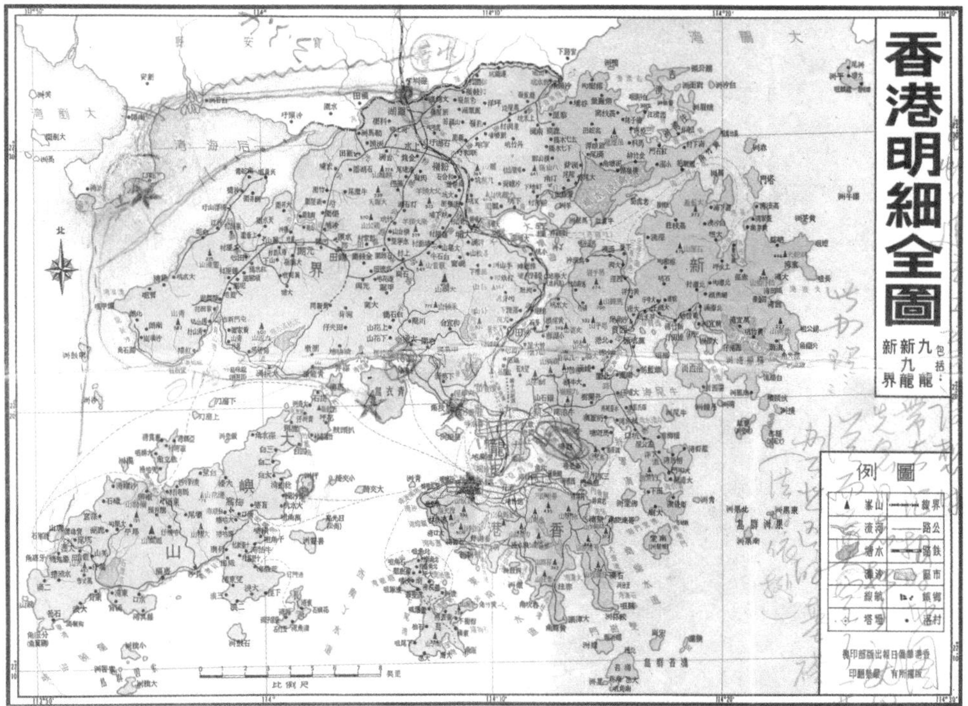

Map used in the deliberation on the location of the Shekou Industrial Zone in 1979. Pencil marks were superseded by the final red circle, containing a red star to indicate a new port. Other red stars on the map reveal other previously considered sites, some located in Hong Kong.

Jiang Kairu was not aware of the whole backstory when he looked at this historic map, but he was nevertheless struck by the significance of his life within a special zone. He commented: "In the past, we viewed the planned economy and the market economy as enemies out to kill each other, unable to get along. Within the circled area, this flourishing development subverted that notion and created a miracle of human civilization. This is the significance of this circle."[21] Jiang's fascination with Deng Xiaoping's push to implement policies in support of the Shenzhen special economic zone, as well as the vivid imagery of a single pencil stroke on a map at the Shekou museum and Shenzhen's own unique geography, would inspire the most memorable line in "The Story of Spring": "There was an old man / who drew a circle / by the South China Sea." The sensational popularity of these few fairytale-like words—Deng Xiaoping as a humble wizard miraculously conjuring up a new city by drawing a "circle by the sea"—became the most popular myth of Shenzhen.

"THE STORY OF SPRING"

On December 12, 1992, Jiang penned the rest of his lyrics to the song that would seal his fate with Shenzhen. The image of Deng Xiaoping "mythically building a great city," expressed in the poem, was inspired by Jiang's experience of the drastic changes to Shenzhen over the span of just thirteen years, including the skyline that shocked him. The "mountain of gold" referred to the stacks of cash notes on the bank counter he glimpsed while waiting in line. For Jiang, "The Story of Spring" celebrated Deng Xiaoping's instrumental efforts in establishing Shenzhen and bringing new hope of a better life for the common man. More importantly and yet little known to the public, the words expressed Jiang's personal appreciation to Deng for encouraging hope after decades of long winters in his own life.

Having composed his song in only a single sitting, Jiang mailed it to the *Shenzhen Special Zone Daily*. Founded in 1982, this daily was the first comprehensive newspaper established by the Shenzhen Municipal Government.[22] It was the most widely read and influential media channel in Shenzhen. Most information and news about Shenzhen's development during the 1980s and 1990s were relayed throughout China after first appearing in the *SSZ Daily*.

Nearly a month later, as Jiang Kairu walked through the gate to his workplace, a young guard called out to tell him that someone with the same name had appeared in the newspaper. The guard could not comprehend that the person in the paper was the same Jiang, a "Person of Three Withouts," who, on the previous day, had carried liquid propane tanks up the stairs with him. Jiang took the newspaper from the guard's hands and was stunned by what he saw. His eyes brimmed with tears as he caught sight of his words to "The Story of Spring" printed in large red lettering.[23]

> The Year of 1979
> That was a spring
> There was a great man
> Drawing a circle by the South China Sea
> Mythically building a great city
> Miraculously forming a mountain of gold
> Shenzhen! Shenzhen!
> The Test Pilot of China's Reform and Opening

The Year of 1984
That was another spring
There was a great man
Inscribing a dictum for Shenzhen
The buffalo cultivating the wasteland striving forward
The giant eagle with wide-spread wings soaring to the sky
Shenzhen! Shenzhen!
The new starting point for China's ascending economy

The Year of 1992
That was yet another spring
There was a great man
Writing a magnificent poem in Shenzhen
Spreading splendor all over China like a spring breeze
Moistening beautiful flowers like springtime rain
Shenzhen! Shenzhen!
China's pioneer ship sailing across the sea

Jiang subsequently went to considerable effort to set his words to music, with the objective of creating a truly remarkable song. He was determined to work with Wang Yougui, an emerging composer in Shenzhen. Aged forty, Wang had left his teaching position at Hunan University to relocate to Shenzhen a few years earlier than Jiang. Born in a Hakka village in Hunan, Wang learned music as a child from his mother, who made him a bamboo flute to play on. A talented flautist, he was accepted by Hunan University and went on to succeed in school. In Shenzhen, his musical compositions gained a local following and sparked Jiang's interest. However, it was nearly two years later before Wang agreed to work on Jiang's song. Wang found the composition a bit unusual, and the wording even more so. Although it was obviously a song in praise of the party leadership, the most common genre of Chinese music, Jiang's tone and choice of words were uncharacteristically informal for a choral tribute to the party leader. Wang's solution was to counterbalance the humble nature of the first two lines by adding an introduction of rousing trumpets and grand percussion, but with a solemn chorus. When the instruments fade, a single clear soprano sings the words in a folklike tune with Hunan dialect–influenced intonations.

In March 1994, Jiang and Wang submitted the song to the Guangdong Youth Song-Writing Contest. To their disappointment, the song did not even make it past the local Shenzhen qualifying round. But, not wanting to concede defeat, they sought the help of another amateur but locally known song writer, Ye Xuquan. Ye was deputy director of the Guangzhou-Shenzhen Water Supply Department, but he also served on the Standing Committee of the Guangdong Youth Federation. He liked the song instantly and suggested condensing the verses while broadening the scope of the song to celebrate the reforms of the entire country rather than just Shenzhen. The amended lyrics included changes from "Shenzhen! Shenzhen! / The test pilot of China's Reform and Opening" to "Ah, China! China! / With new strides full of power and grandeur / You entered a spring of renewed splendor"; from "Mythically building a great city" to "Mythically erecting cities"; and from "There was a great man / Writing a dictum by the seashore of Southern China" to "There was an old man / Writing a poem by the South China Sea." This final version of the lyrics sparked heated debate when it was resubmitted to the competition.[24] The judges were divided in their views. Some felt that the words "an old man" and "drawing a circle" were not serious enough for a patriotic song describing China's great reforms and the country's premier leader, while others felt that the song was a true reflection of the average person's feelings toward the reforms and toward Deng, as it reflected the language of the people. The song went on to win first prize in the competition. Still then, no one predicted that "The Story of Spring" would go on to become such a sensational national success.

THE NATIONAL ANTHEM OF REFORMS

"The Story of Spring" was first aired on television in the winter of 1994, during the broadcast of a Military and Civilian Gala on the state-run China Central Television (CCTV). To Jiang's delight, the song was performed by Dong Wenhua, a singer from the Song and Dance Troupe of the People's Liberation Army. The song, with its folklike score and lyrics, was as such well matched by Dong's formal training to sing the higher octaves of traditional Chinese folk songs. The song's roots in traditional musical culture, combined with the modern national pride in the country's ongoing reforms led by Deng Xiaoping, resonated with both the political government and the general public. The performance garnered Dong Wenhua the top prize in CCTV's Second National Music Television Competition in 1994, and "The Story of Spring" would later become known as her signature song. The success of "The Story of Spring" helped to usher in a new era of pop culture in China, opening the door to other pop singers with military backgrounds into popular music. China's pop culture during the 1990s paradoxically combined patriotic, and often traditional, vernacular elements with new forms of entertainment and media.

In 1994, "The Story of Spring" was also produced as one of China's first music videos. With Dong Wenhua filmed singing on the streets of Shenzhen, the city's newly built iconic urban landmarks were broadcast via television into millions of Chinese living rooms. One scene in the popular music video depicted Dong Wenhua strolling on the sidewalk in front of a large roadside billboard of Deng's portrait. This billboard later became a nationally known symbol of the city. Located on Shenzhen's main avenue (Shennan Boulevard), the billboard was erected in 1992 to commemorate Deng's last visit to the city. The billboard featured a 300-square-meter oil painting of Deng's portrait floating above a mysterious city of towers standing amid the backdrop of a dramatically lit sky. The billboard was updated in 1994 and 1996. The 1996 renovation included the addition of eighteen spotlights and a marble base, and the original narrow sidewalk was expanded to create a small plaza with a landscaped lawn and potted plants.[25] The billboard's new image, one of China's first attempts at large-format digital prints, was a photo portrait of Deng in a similar composition to the previous oil painting. The background featured the actual high-rise buildings of Shenzhen, as a dense modern skyline. However, Deng's declamation to the city and to China was displayed prominently in bold type: "Adhere to the Party's Basic Guideline, One Hundred Years without Change." The plaza in front of the billboard quickly became the city's most popular tourist destination, where people vied to be photographed with Deng and Shenzhen's future skyline.

During the 1990s, the pop music production industry in China grew rapidly in line with an increased acceptance of Western pop culture and the marketization of the television and entertainment industries. TV stations and TV set ownership exploded, reaching almost all urban as well as rural households. By 1997, there were three hundred million television sets in China, compared to three million in 1978. Following decades of strict control and uniformly political-themed music and film, China's nascent new media grew with unprecedented exuberance and freedom. Many music videos produced during this time paired nationalistic or communist revolutionary songs with imported footage of urban settings such

Shenzhen's iconic Deng Xiaoping billboard in 1992, 1994, and 2004. The iterations contained three constant representative elements of Shenzhen: Deng's portrait, his mottos on reforms, and the modern urban image of the evolving skyline.

as the Sydney Opera House and the Empire State Building. Among the more unusual were videos featured bikini-clad women running on beaches to a medley of military marches from decades past. The number of records released in China in the 1990s was ten times greater than that of the previous decade.[26]

"The Story of Spring" reached an even larger audience when Dong Wenhua was selected to perform at CCTV's Spring Festival Gala for the Chinese New Year's Eve celebrations in 1997.[27] Widely viewed across China as well as in Chinese-speaking communities around the world, for decades the CCTV's yearly broadcast of the New Year gala attracted a higher number of viewers than any national variety entertainment show in the world.[28] "The Story of Spring" was the first of many chart toppers by Dong Wenhua, who went on to win multiple national prizes and become one of the most distinguished Chinese singers; in 2007, she performed "The Story of Spring" at New York City's Lincoln Center.[29] The popularity of Jiang's song, both in state media channels and in pop culture, forever entwined two images in the story of China's economic reforms: Deng as a kindly "old man," and the "miracle" of Shenzhen.

FROM THE "SPRING" TO A "NEW ERA"

On February 19, 1997, two weeks after the first national live broadcast of Dong Wenhua's performance of "The Story of Spring" on the eve of the Chinese New Year, Deng Xiaoping passed away at the age of ninety-three from complications relating to late-stage Parkinson's disease. The central government issued orders to all cities to forbid any public farewell events, as per Deng Xiaoping's last directive to the country's top leadership. In a formal letter from his family to his successor, Jiang Zemin, Deng expressed his wishes to minimize any spectacle upon his passing. The letter conveyed five requests: that no ritual funeral ceremony be held; that a memorial service be given only after cremation; that no mourning hall be set up anywhere, including at his family residence; that his corneas be donated and that autopsy of his body be done for medical research; and that his ashes be cast out into the sea.[30] His requests contrasted starkly with the decades-long public display of Mao's embalmed body in the Chairman Mao Memorial Hall at Beijing's Tiananmen Square. Deng was determined to distinguish himself from the persona that his predecessor had created and, by extension, divorce himself from its tragic consequences on China.

Following the news of Deng's passing, an informal memorial emerged in front of the well-known billboard in Shenzhen. The site of celebration became a site of collective mourning, as hundreds of wreaths filled the small plaza under the billboard. Contrary to typical funeral ceremonies in honor of government officials, the wreaths were not bequeathed and signed by fellow government colleagues, but rather quietly laid out by individuals and families. Many of the wreaths and flowers contained written dedications simply stating: "For Xiaoping." The practice of addressing others by first names was, and still is, used only within families or among very close friends. Referring to China's paramount leader by first name as a term of endearment had never occurred before Deng, and has not since. The mourning wreaths grew into small mounds and spilled over the plaza onto the sidewalks. The few policemen discreetly keeping order did not touch the wreaths even when they encroached on the adjacent traffic lanes. City workers carefully cleared the road only late at night, while the plaza filled up again the next day, and for many weeks following.

Shenzhen's collective mourning was further accentuated by the city's preparations for the handover of Hong Kong in July 1997. Deng's negotiations with Margaret Thatcher over the return of Hong Kong had become one of his most celebrated national achievements. He missed this historic event by a matter of months. In commemoration, Shenzhen's Luohu District Cultural Council commissioned Jiang Kairu to compose a ten-song package titled "The Morning of Hong Kong." Yet, so filled with heartache and sorrow over the death of Deng, such a symbolic father figure, Jiang could hardly bear to write any words of celebration. To make matters worse, one of his supervisors ominously commented: "Deng Xiaoping has left. How much longer will 'The Story of Spring' be sung?" This was a direct reference to the political atmosphere in China at the time. Aside from the mourning of Deng, the Chinese felt disquiet and uncertainty regarding the future of the country's reforms. Many in the government believed that China had deviated too far from its founding communist ideologies. In Shenzhen, Deng's passing rendered Hong Kong's return bittersweet and the future of the reformist city uncertain.

Jiang Kairu was deeply anxious about the possibility that China might reverse its course of opening up and reform. Relief only came later in the year in September, when he read Jiang Zemin's public statement in the *People's Daily,* where the new leader of China urged the country to "raise high the great flags of Deng Xiaoping Theory; continue to deepen Reform and Opening."[31] Feeling more assured, Jiang Kairu worked overnight to finish the final song of the package, titled "China Is Fortunate." The title and song lyrics vocalized Jiang's personal sentiment that the country was fortunate to have new leadership to continue the economic reforms that had brought millions out of poverty.

Later retitled "Enter the New Era," this song also became nationally popular and came to define Jiang Zemin as the country's top leader.[32] In 2007, Jiang Kairu composed another song, entitled "The Chinese Dream," in honor of the 17th National People's Congress under the leadership of the new President Hu Jintao. In 2009, during the military parade commemorating the sixtieth anniversary of the PRC's founding, there were fifty-six military formations, thirty-six civic formations, and sixty decorated floats. The centerpiece of the float portion was a four-float arrangement, each of which carried a large framed photo, representing the four generations of modern China's top leadership. First came the portrait of Mao Zedong, accompanied by the song "The East Is Red." Jiang watched the national live broadcast of the parade from his Shenzhen living room as the float carrying Deng Xiaoping's portrait went past accompanied by "The Story of Spring." Jiang Zemin's portrait followed next, as the song "Entering the New Era" played. Hu Jintao's portrait went last, along with the song "Rivers and Mountains," which was not one of Jiang's works. Jiang Kairu was extremely moved and pleased. These accomplishments brought him further recognition, and in 2010 he was named one of "Thirty Outstanding People of Shenzhen" to mark the thirtieth anniversary of the establishment of the Shenzhen special economic zone.

Perhaps the highest praise Jiang received was from the "old man" himself, albeit indirectly. On a spring-like day in January 2002, Jiang met up with Deng Xiaoping's younger sister Deng Xianqun and younger brother Deng Ken. They arranged to meet at Lotus Mountain Park, north of the newly built central business district of Shenzhen. The exact meeting spot was by a large bronze statue of Deng on the peak of a gentle tree-covered hill. This statue in Shenzhen is exceptional, the only one of Deng in China outside his hometown in Sichuan Province. During his lifetime, Deng gave strict orders forbidding any kind of monument in his likeness. However, the state authorized the Shenzhen statue to commemorate Hong Kong's handover in 1997. At the base of the statue on Lotus Mountain, Deng Xianqun instantly recognized Jiang, having previously seen him in photographs, and affectionately called out: "Hey, Story of Spring!" During the meeting, Jiang summoned up the courage to ask a question that had preoccupied him for nearly a decade. "Had Xiaoping heard 'The Story of Spring'?" Deng Ken replied: "He did hear it. Although he never spoke a word about it, he liked to listen to the song, and liked to watch the music video."[33]

BEYOND THE MYTH

"The Story of Spring" is the story of China's reforms, the account of Shenzhen's emergence, and on a personal level, the tale of the twists and turns in Jiang's own life. Jiang Kairu's personal narrative—the tragic division of his family during the civil war just prior to the formation of the People's Republic of China, and the close kinship he maintained with his extended family members in Hong Kong and beyond—reflects just one among hundreds of thousands of cross-border and transnational connections made during this period, particularly by those living in the Shenzhen–Guangdong region. While Shenzhen's rapid growth has benefited, if on a steep learning curve, from its geographic proximity to Hong Kong, the informal and grassroots nature of the investment networks involved have been previously underestimated. During Shenzhen's most difficult initiation decade, the majority of investments in the city were not to set up large corporate or state enterprises, but came in the form of tens of thousands of small-scale workshops and factories. Most of these small-scale businesses were facilitated by financial investments by expatriates in Hong Kong and the rest of the Chinese regional and international diaspora. As well as having the financial desire to exploit business opportunities, many were motivated by kinship and empathy, a desire to help those left behind.

Beyond providing a background to unique cultural artifacts like "The Story of Spring," personal histories like Jiang Kairu's shed light on the secret of Shenzhen's success: the human spirit of the city. The story of Shenzhen is not simply one of reforms and policies; it is a collection of stories of personal struggles and redemptions. Jiang Kairu was enticed by Shenzhen because of its potential for new beginnings, new opportunities to control one's destiny, to shape one's life. This possibility was facilitated not only by economic reforms, but also by sociocultural shifts that altered social standards and cultural norms. As Jiang Kairu noted, it was not wealth that distinguished Shenzhen from the rest of China during the initial decade of the city's development; it was the mindset of the people. The city is a conglomeration of millions of desires, failures, and victories, in pursuit of a better life. Enormous population figures and economic indicators often obscure the human dimension of everyday life in Chinese cities. Shenzhen's most important, yet most overlooked, achievement was its ability to attract motivated and entrepreneurial individuals, the most fundamental component of any city's infrastructure.

In the 1990s it would have been difficult to find a single Chinese person who could not sing a few verses of "The Story of Spring." The sentiments expressed in the song evidently resonated with China's general populace. The image of Deng as a kind elderly man conjuring up a mythic city became permanently engraved in the collective consciousness of the Chinese during the early reform era. Thanks to the song, the widely published reportage, and television broadcasts, Deng is forever entwined with the image of Shenzhen.

The popularity of "The Story of Spring" and other similar myths depicting Shenzhen's origins and instantaneous success obscures a few fundamentals that this book aims to clarify. It is first crucial to grasp the history of the region, decades prior to the city's establishment in 1979, and even centuries prior to the PRC's establishment in 1949. Analyzing the song's history reveals the importance of understanding China's current state of affairs and the reforms within the context of a much longer history. Reading "The Story of Spring" as an homage to a powerful figure would not be complete without learning the related narrative of the extraordinary struggles Jiang Kairu had faced since his youth; in the same way, Shenzhen's story will not be complete until it includes accounts of the city's history prior to 1979.

Deng's reform efforts enabled the creation of Shenzhen; however, in return, the city also facilitated Deng's agenda of nationwide reforms. The apparent speed of construction and economic development in Shenzhen became Deng's most effective evidence, enabling him to refute anyone who challenged the effectiveness of the country's reforms. Despite entwining his identity with the city's, Deng set foot in Shenzhen only twice during his lifetime, and the time he spent there totaled less than a week. The following chapter will detail Deng Xiaoping's 1984 and 1992 visits to Shenzhen, which were the events that inspired Jiang Kairu's popular song. Deng's two short visits to the city greatly impacted Shenzhen's development and, perhaps more significantly, directly contributed to massive sociopolitical changes during China's initial decades of Reform and Opening Up.

2.

THE "SOUTHERN TOURS" THAT CHANGED CHINA

While Deng Xiaoping personified China's momentous reforms post-1979, his visibility was not confined to the domestic stage. Media photographs of Deng donning a cowboy hat at a Texas rodeo in the United States were an international sensation. This was perhaps the first signal in the world's mass media that China was on the brink of change. Deng's goodwill trip during President Jimmy Carter's term in office marked the first visit to the United States by a communist Chinese leader since the founding of the People's Republic of China in 1949. During China's civil war, the United States had backed the Nationalists. When Chiang Kai-shek decamped to Taiwan, the United States government continued to recognize his Republic of China (ROC) as the sole legal government of all China. As a result, no formal diplomatic relations existed between China and the United States between 1949 and 1979, though there were earlier efforts, such as the 1972 Shanghai Communiqué signed by Mao Zedong and Richard Nixon. Facilitated by the Chinese Premier Zhou Enlai and Nixon's aide Henry Kissinger, this less-publicized event laid the foundations for future cooperation between the two countries, while acknowledging continuing disagreements on the subject of Taiwan.

Deng's visit in January 1979 was preceded by the December 1978 joint announcement that the United States and the People's Republic of China (PRC) would establish official diplomatic relations, contingent on the US's withdrawal of diplomatic recognition of Taiwan's ROC. The ensuing US-Sino diplomatic relationship was built upon US acknowledgment of the One-China policy. During Deng's visit, the United States and China signed unprecedented US-Sino cooperation agreements on education, commerce, science, and technology. His formal title at the time was China's vice premier, but both the title and fanfare surrounding his diplomatic mission obscured the fact that the seventy-three-year-old Deng Xiaoping had only been released from military confinement in the winter of 1977.

Just weeks after being freed, Deng Xiaoping left Beijing and traveled south to Guangdong Province accompanied by Marshal Ye Jianying. While together in the provincial capital Guangzhou, Deng and Ye tuned in to reports by anxious provincial leaders describing the devastating effects of the Cultural Revolution in the region. Guangdong Province had been particularly hard hit by various local political struggles and widespread persecution. The most severe problem facing the local government was the abandonment of village communes and farming fields in the "Great Escape to Hong Kong," a phrase coined to describe the successive waves of hundreds of thousands of people illegally crossing the China–Hong Kong border. A recently declassified Guangdong government internal report reveals that between 1954 and 1980 there were 565,000 officially recorded crossing attempts.[1] In Guangzhou, Deng first heard of Shenzhen, an old market town located next to the Hong Kong–China Luohu Border Crossing, and an area most severely impacted by the Great Escape. Ye was particularly anxious about the desolation of the region, not only as deputy chairman of the CCP, defense minister, and marshal of the People's Liberation Army, but as a native of Guangdong who came from a local rural village. Deng came to agree with local Guangdong leaders that alleviating poverty was the only hope for stemming the flow of people across the border to Hong Kong. He famously remarked that military action would not change the situation, and acknowledged that "this is a problem of our policy."[2] The stark contrast in economic wealth between Chinese Guangdong Province and colonial Hong Kong next door loomed clearly. In 1977, the annual income of a village farmer in Hong Kong was one hundred times that of a farmer undertaking the same work on the other side of the border, while the disparity between factory workers in Guangdong and

Hong Kong was even greater. China's isolationist policies and decades of internal political struggles had brought the Chinese economy to a standstill. Escalating illegal migration, the result of political strife and economic poverty, was undoubtedly the trigger that compelled Deng to launch the reforms. In turn, these reforms generated the widespread support that he later received—despite the fact that they represented the absolute reversal of China's long-standing isolationist policy.

Back in Beijing in the winter of 1978, Deng Xiaoping participated in a week-long meeting held in a discreet hotel, along with three hundred of China's highest-level officials. Formally titled the Third Plenary Session of the 11th Central Committee of the Communist Party of China (CPC), and presided over by Mao's appointed successor, Hua Guofeng, this event is widely acknowledged as the historic moment that triggered China's remarkable reforms. Although the session opened on December 18, its agenda and tone had already been set during a month-long Central Working Meeting held from November 10 to December 15. On December 13, as these preparatory meetings drew to a close, Deng Xiaoping made one of his first formal speeches since his return, entitled "Emancipate the Mind, Seek Truth from Facts, Unite and Look Forward."[3] The speech urged fellow members to think more freely, encourage constructive criticism, provide greater autonomy to enterprises and production teams, and protect the democratic rights of workers and farmers. Deng Xiaoping also formally introduced the idea of enabling particular regions to develop "one step ahead" of others, to open up and learn from countries more advanced in science and management methods. Deng read out a list of ten possible locations; the first place he named was Shenzhen.[4]

Following the closure of the Third Plenary Session of the 11th Committee on December 22, 1978, official reports and documents were distributed to all provincial governments for discussion and implementation. While Hua Guofeng retained his title and working role as chairman of the CPC until 1981, by the end of the Third Plenary Session many in the government recognized Deng Xiaoping as the one paving the way for China to enter a new era of social, economic, and political reforms.

Deng's proposed measures were not intended to propel China into a global economic powerhouse. The primary reason for launching national reforms was profound, sweeping, and yet simple: to alleviate deep poverty. However, the government's top leaders did not uniformly support experimentation with market economics and measures such as the special economic zones. Shenzhen was identified as the most visible site for potential experimentation, and Shenzhen's success was also the most effective tool that Deng could wield to convince skeptical government members to put doctrine aside and accept the possibility of an alternative communism that could coexist with a market system, or, in Deng's words, "socialism with Chinese characteristics." The myth of Shenzhen attributed its creation and success to Deng, but Deng himself also needed Shenzhen, equally if not more, to advance his economic and political agenda.

CENTRAL PLANNING AND LOCAL INITIATIVES

The importance of Deng Xiaoping's role in setting out the central government's plan for the SEZ reforms obscured the fact that he did not participate in organizing agendas and operations on the ground. While the central government actively sought out potential market opportunities internationally, the efforts to establish special economic zones in Guangdong combined top-down direction with bottom-up endeavors by local government officials in the region.

The announcement of China's Reform and Opening Up to the outside world was greeted with particular enthusiasm in Guangdong, a region that had already spawned international networks through personal relationships and informal connections with overseas Chinese diaspora.[5] Wu Nansheng, secretary of the Guangdong Communist Party Committee and a native of the province, was especially motivated.[6] Spurred on by widespread poverty in Shantou, his hometown and a former bustling international seaport city, but also keeping in mind the potential advantages of its extensive ties to the outside world, Wu proposed to transform Shantou into an "export processing zone" by attracting investment from members of the city's overseas Chinese diaspora. Wu maintains that this idea did not come from any one individual, but rather was a collective effort generated through discussions with Shantou emigrants who were, by then, wealthy, patriotic businessmen living in Singapore, Taiwan, and Hong Kong.[7] They pointed out to Wu that the key to economic take-off in Singapore and Hong Kong had been their advantages as free ports and processing zones.

By March 1979, Wu Nansheng's idea had received enthusiastic support from Xi Zhongxun, then the chief secretary of the CCP in Guangdong Province, and the father of China's current General Secretary Xi Jinping.[8]

While Xi Zhongxun had only been stationed by the central government in Guangdong for two years, he recognized that the greatest obstacle faced by the provincial leaders was the lack of laborers and farmers following the emptying of villages and cities. The proposal had the potential to stem the exodus of residents as well as improve the regional economy and security. Xi Zhongxun additionally recommended expanding Wu's Shantou export processing zone proposal to cover the entire Guangdong Province. Following internal discussions, the Guangdong provincial leaders decided to first limit the zone to specific locations in Guangdong. In April 1979, Xi Zhongxun presented the Guangdong Proposal to Beijing's central government, suggesting the establishment of export processing zones in Shantou, Zhuhai, and Shenzhen. During his Beijing visit, Xi Zhongxun also requested greater autonomy for the provincial government so that it could experiment with policies geared toward attracting foreign investment and increasing export trade. This was a bold and potentially politically reckless request, especially coming from Guangdong. For decades, and even centuries, this southernmost province of China was criticized in Beijing for exercising "localism," and was therefore closely scrutinized by many in the central government for acts of waywardness. This time in Beijing, Xi Zhongxun's lobbying on behalf of Guangdong's local provincial governance was met with the usual suspicion, as well as unexpected support.

To understand the reasons behind the central government's willingness to consider Guangdong's request for such exceptional treatment, it is necessary to further contextualize the events leading up to the December 1978 Third Plenary Session of the 11th Committee. Over the course of 1978, Premier Hua Guofeng endorsed a group of top government officials to make a series of foreign study trips. The communist leaders traveled to countries in Asia and the West that were more developed and encompassed diverse political systems. It was the first time that many of these leaders realized how backward the Chinese economy and industrial production were, following decades of wars and internal strife. One particularly important tour took place in May 1978, when a high-level delegation led by Vice Premier Gu Mu visited the West European countries of France, Belgium, Denmark, Switzerland, and West Germany. In addition to reports of advanced developments in trade, commerce, and technology, Gu Mu brought back the message that foreign countries, even capitalist ones, were willing to invest and aid in the modernization of

China's industrial production.[9] Gu Mu's report had a profound impact on government discussions the following year, particularly regarding the possibility of reforming China's economic system.[10] However, there were many obstacles to this major change in direction: lack of foreign currency, an outdated industrial base, and limited technical capacity, to mention a few. The central government looked to the countries bordering China for possible guidance. In 1978, in an unprecedented move, Beijing sent a diplomatic delegation to Hong Kong to meet with the British colonial governor Murray MacLehose on the subject of potential economic collaboration.[11] The meeting was productive and, on returning to Beijing, the delegation drafted the "Economic Survey Report of Hong Kong and Macau," which assessed the viability of building production bases for export-oriented activities in rural Bao'an County. However, the only industries under consideration were agricultural production and tourism, and export activities mainly referred to trade with neighboring Hong Kong.

By March 1979, the State Council had approved plans to designate the 2,020 square kilometers comprising rural Bao'an County as the city of Shenzhen, named after the old border market town. The total population in this territory at the time was 358,000, mostly spread throughout two thousand agrarian villages. More concentrated populations could be found in commercial centers such as Shenzhen Old Town, which had a population of thirty thousand. Both the central government's decision to establish the city of Shenzhen and the parallel proposal at the provincial level to establish Shenzhen as a special economic zone were driven by one common purpose: to stop the mass illegal border crossings known as the Great Escape to Hong Kong. The initial plan for Shenzhen city was modest in scale, comprised of new urban development totaling 10.65 square kilometers, and spread among three areas of Bao'an that already existed as regional commercial and industrial centers namely Shenzhen Old Town, Shekou Industrial Zone, and the Shatoujiao commercial area.

The short-term target was to attract a new population of one hundred thousand to Shenzhen SEZ, with an expected increase in population to two hundred thousand or three hundred thousand by the year 2000. The central government's first objective for the SEZ was to generate revenue by expanding the region's light industrial-agricultural production, and the second was to attract visitors from nearby Hong Kong and Macau for scenic tourism. While the second goal may seem contrary to today's commonly perceived image of Shenzhen as a former factory town, the territory's lush mountains and pristine water bodies have been historically renowned for centuries. During this initial phase of centralized planning, with the exception of agricultural production, all industries were required to remain under the operation of state-owned enterprises.

The proposal that Xi Zhongxun presented to the Beijing authorities in April 1979, to set up export processing zones in Guangdong, pushed the boundaries of acceptability much further, inviting direct foreign investment and the development of private enterprises. As mentioned earlier, the proposal received a mixed response: it was criticized by many in the central government, and even the term "export processing zones" sparked objections from a number of Beijing's top CCP members. The term was deemed unacceptable because it is the same terminology used in Taiwan at the time. The alternative expressions "free trade zone" and "trade and export zone" were regarded as too blatantly capitalistic. Although Deng Xiaoping was not present at most of the formal meetings to discuss the Guangdong proposal, he made his support known and, via Vice Premier Gu Mu, offered to solve this dilemma by suggesting adoption of the term "special zone."[12] It had a strong patriotic tone, as it was utilized to designate enclave districts for special administrative and military purposes during China's anti-Japanese war era (1931–1945). In addition, Deng emphasized that while the central Beijing government could not provide substantial funding, it would support Guangdong by granting its local government more autonomy and jurisdiction through the waiving of certain national policies.

After months of deliberation, the Guangdong proposal eventually garnered sufficient support. However, critics of the initiative maintained that it ran counter to communist doctrines, and these voices remained a strong presence in the central government. On July 19, 1979, the Central Committee Document No. 50 was officially issued, granting Guangdong and Fujian Provinces "Special Policy, Flexible Measures" to explore setting up special zones in the cities of Shenzhen and Zhuhai. If successful, these would be followed by zones in Shantou and Xiamen. Vice Premier Gu Mu was charged with leading coordination efforts between the central government and the local provinces. Wu Nansheng, the local initiator from Shantou, was appointed director of the newly formed Guangdong Province Special Zone Office, with the role of leading the planning efforts for all three special zones and the drafting of a special zone ordinance. In December 1979, Wu Nansheng presented a written report to the State

Council, proposing to reduce the ongoing illegal border crossings by boosting the local economy through agricultural production, tourism, and construction of an export processing zone in the Fujian Commune using foreign investment.[13] Wu's report was entitled "An Outline Report on Several Problems Regarding the Establishment of Special Economic Zones in Guangdong." It was the first official appearance of the term "Special Economic Zone" in governmental documents.[14]

FIRST PLANS AND IMMEDIATE CRISIS

Following his appointment as Shenzhen's first mayor and secretary of the Shenzhen CPC in June 1980, Wu Nansheng directed the drafting of the first Shenzhen Urban Construction Comprehensive Master Plan. It was produced by the Guangzhou Planning Institute (planning agencies were yet to be established in Shenzhen) with support from expert advisors from all over China. The plan described its intended outcome as "an industry-led modernized special economic zone with industrial and agricultural production, and to be constructed as a new type of border city."[15] The SEZ was designed to accommodate a service population of three hundred thousand, with a projected total population of six hundred thousand across the 2,020 square kilometers of territory formerly known as Bao'an County; the county was abolished in August 1980, and the territory designated as Shenzhen City. The plan demarcated, for the first time, the special economic zone as an area of 327.5 square kilometers within that territory. The SEZ was situated on the border of Hong Kong, with the Luohu area (named after the border crossing) marked as its center. On August 26, 1980, China's Fifth Standing Committee of the National People's Congress approved the Guangdong Province Special Economic Zone Ordinance for the cities of Shenzhen, Zhuhai, and Shantou. The "Shenzhen Special Economic Zone" was officially a reality.

The making of Shenzhen transformed the territory of Bao'an County at a rate unexperienced in human history. First, the territory was split. The former Bao'an County and its residents were separated into two areas: inside the SEZ, and outside the SEZ. The differences were not so acute, until the subsequent 1982 land nationalization policy that categorized China's land as either urban land owned by the state government, or rural land remaining under the ownership of rural collectives. In the case of Shenzhen, SEZ land continued to be designated as urban and owned by

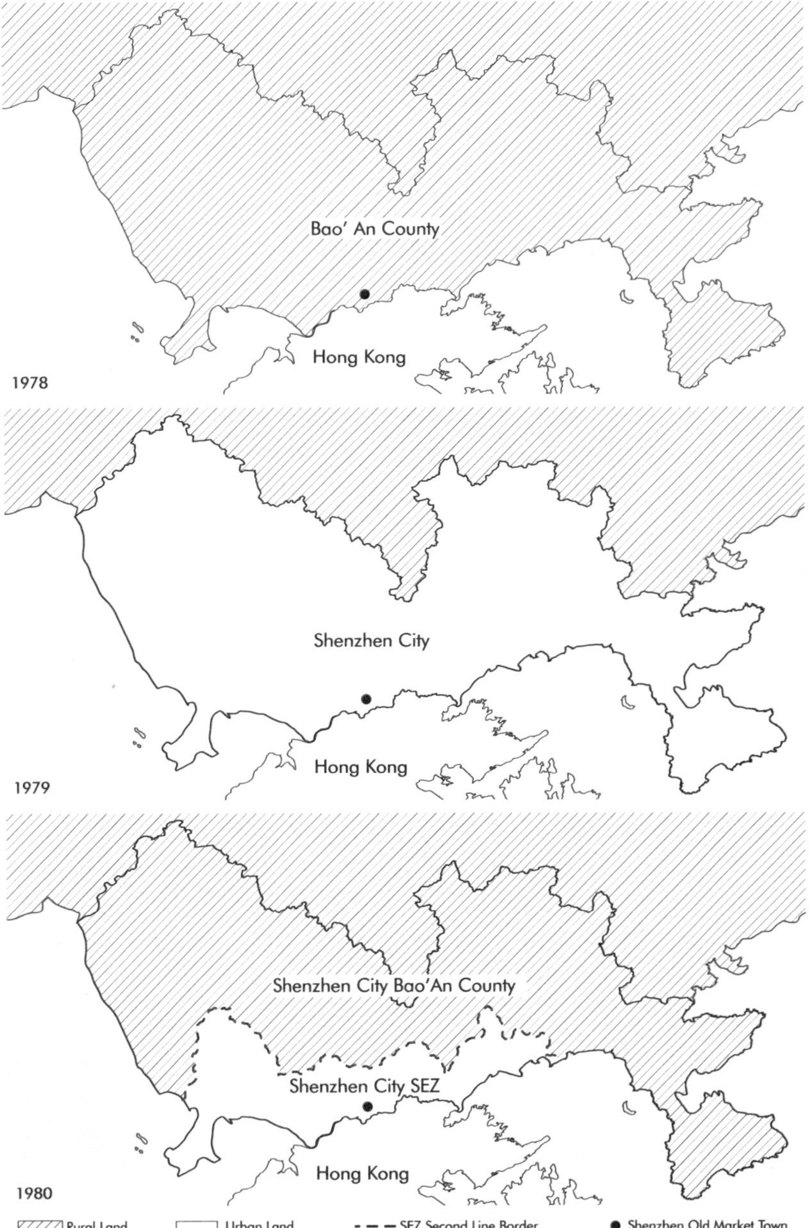

Maps of Shenzhen's early rural-urban administrative changes: the 1978 Rural Bao'an County; the 1979 Establishment of Shenzhen City and cancellation of rural Bao'an; and the 1980 Division of Shenzhen into the SEZ and the reinstated rural Bao'an County.

the government, while land outside the SEZ reverted back to its pre-1980 status as rural. For administrative purposes, the abolished Bao'an County was reinstated in 1982. This time it included only the land outside of the SEZ (i.e., rural land), separated from urban land by a boundary that later became known as the *Er Xian Guan*, or Second Line Border (to distinguish it from the Hong Kong–Shenzhen national border). For centuries, the name Bao'an had referred to the entire territory of what later became today's Shenzhen city. From 1982 onward, the name referred only to the rural areas of Shenzhen outside of the special economic zone.

The 1982 Shenzhen SEZ Master Plan formed a central part of the overall 1982 Shenzhen Special Economic Zone Social and Economic Development Planning strategy, and depicted the SEZ area sandwiched between the southern border of Hong Kong and the northern border of Bao'an County. These influential planning efforts in Shenzhen were led by Liang Xiang, the city's second mayor, who held his office from 1981 to 1985. Liang, a native of Guangdong and seasoned CCP leader, was first appointed by the Guangdong government to Shenzhen's top post of CCP Secretary in March 1981. Under his leadership, the vision for Shenzhen's development was greatly expanded from an industry-oriented processing zone toward a more holistic and fully functioning city. By July 1981, the central government endorsed Liang Xiang's initiatives and announced that Shenzhen would be an "industry-oriented, and concurrently commercial, agricultural, residential, tourist and other multi-functioning comprehensive special economic zone."[16]

With the subsequent establishment of the Shenzhen Municipal Planning Department and Economic Planning Commission, the Shenzhen government produced the 1982 Shenzhen Special Economic Zone Social and Economic Development Plan. Formulation of the new plans occupied the rest of the year: local government officials conducted drafting meetings with national experts in April and consultations with Hong Kong economists and planners in September; finally a finished plan was submitted to the Guangzhou government by December 1982.[17] It is customary for China's city master plans (which outline the general land-use pattern) to be approved by provincial governments; however, owing to its unique status, the SEZ's Master Plan required additional approval by the State Council in Beijing.[18]

The 1982 Shenzhen planning document was more comprehensive in scope than the initial 1980 version. It not only outlined locations for industrial activities, but also designated areas for commercial, residential, civic, and educational functions. In addition, it detailed a more ambitious population projection for Shenzhen: 250,000 by 1985; four hundred thousand by 1990; and eight hundred thousand by the year 2000. However, the centerpiece of the planning document was the elegantly hand-drawn and brightly colored Master Plan map.

The 1982 Master Plan map of the SEZ—the city's imagined future city center—lays out orange-colored residential zones, brown industrial-logistic zones, and green tourism zones, distributed across a yellow background described as "Farming and Forest Land." The red grid denotes a road transportation network stretching from the Nantou Peninsula in the west, via the Luohu border area in the center, to the more isolated areas around Shatoujiao in the eastern areas. The urban form of Shenzhen's city center eventually developed along the west-east spine of the main Shennan Boulevard, which connected the various zones. In the decades that followed, this master plan was credited with the innovation of the so-called Clustered Linear Planning Principle (*dai zhuang zu tuan*), and commended by industry and academia. Indeed, the SEZ's eventual spatial urban development appeared to conform closely to the original spatial planning.[19] However, analysis of the 1982 Master Plan has often neglected the relationship of urban development to the natural geography and built settlements that existed pre-1979. This oversight inflates the impact of the Master Plan while overlooking the geographic and environmental sensitivity of the early planners that contributed to this effort.

Comparing the 1982 Master Plan with a 1960s map of the same region reveals that, while indigenous villages settlements were not noted on the Master Plan, they all neatly fall within the orange-shaded residential zones. Likewise, all the industrial-logistic zones were adjacent to but outside the residential zones, thus avoiding overlap with all the villages. While the distribution of these industrial zones may seem scattered, there was an underlying logic: when the new city government negotiated to purchase land from the local village collectives, financial constraints necessitated that it only expropriate the farming fields surrounding the original village settlements, leaving the villagers with land for self-built housing and self-industrialization. This explains how former farming fields—that is, the land most easily expropriated—became the first industrial-logistic zones. Thus, much of the spatial arrangement on the new Master Plan map could be said to have been born of necessity rather than designed as an ideal urban form. In other words, the locations of the most important industrial and residential clusters within the new city of Shenzhen were

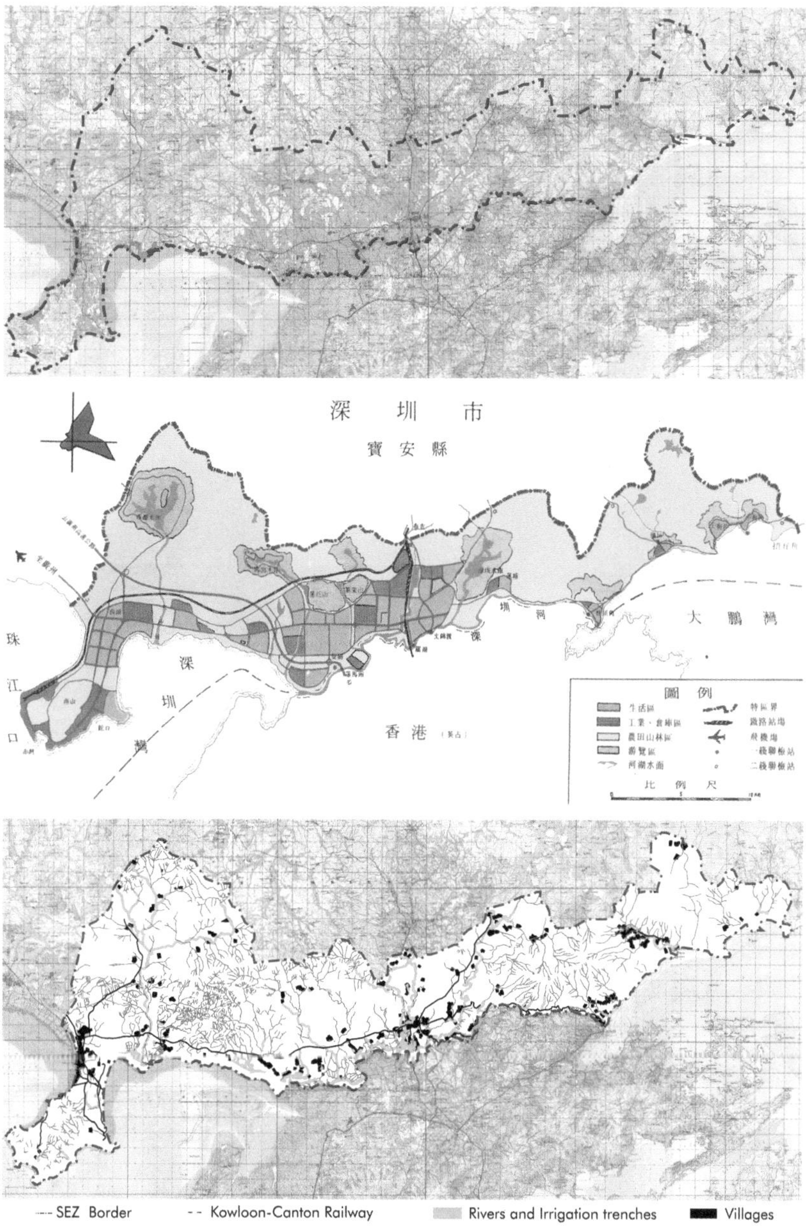

Topographic map of Bao'an County (later Shenzhen) ca. 1950s (*upper*). The First Shenzhen SEZ Master Plan of 1982 (*middle*). Composite map of preexisting villages, waterways, and roads redrawn from the 1950s survey map (*lower*). Comparison of the maps indicates the influence of preexisting man-made and natural geographies on the 1982 Plan, contrary to the view that modern Shenzhen was based on an idealized city plan drawn on a blank slate. Locations of the planned new industrial zones circumvented village areas, and the six newly planned north-south waterways and tourism zones all followed preexisting north-south river bodies.

dictated by the patterns of original village settlements and farming fields. The orange residential zones (rather than the planned brown industrial-logistic zones) would eventually develop into the most densely built-up urban districts of Shenzhen. Embedded in present-day Shenzhen's modern urban pattern lies the hidden original distribution of villages and the lands between them, with the distance from each village center to the periphery of the surrounding farming fields (which were mostly accessible within a day's walk). The spatial development of Shenzhen, the city that would become one of the world's densest urban centers, was unintentionally determined by centuries-old agrarian spatial patterns.

Even the city's most important transportation artery, Shennan Boulevard, closely follows a preexisting country road that was built at the turn of the twentieth century. The original narrow earthen road was formally named Country Road 107, as a part of an old national road system. However, locally it was informally called by its historic name Bao-Shen Road, as it connected the Bao'an Fort in Nantou Old City to the west with Shenzhen Old Market Town to the east, its route linking up various large coastal villages.[20] Furthermore, the 1982 Master Plan depicts several large-scale urban landscape features incorporating the natural and man-made waterways of the region prior to 1979. Abundant with rivers, canals, and marshes, the local geography was dominated by waterways, which provided irrigation for the rice fields and ponds for fisheries. The 1982 Master Plan includes six waterways that originate from a natural reservoir or water dam, which is enclosed by a tourism zone to the north of the industrial-residential zones; these waterways flow southward, discharging into either Shenzhen Bay or the Shenzhen River. The incorporation of existing waterways, farming fields, villages, and transportation networks reflected the early planners' knowledge of and sensitivity to the preexisting natural and man-made geography. The influential Shenzhen origin myth, with its emphasis on the miraculous new city, downplays the impact of the original physical geography and distribution of settlements, as well as environmental considerations by early planners. These elements are continuously overlooked in later accounts of the city's planning history.

In the 1990s, this myth was used to attract workers to Shenzhen; ten years earlier, however, it was part of an effort just to give the city a chance to exist. While city leaders and planners were busy imagining Shenzhen's future, a national storm of anti-reform criticism was raging with cries to close it down. From the outset, both reformers and critics cast Shenzhen

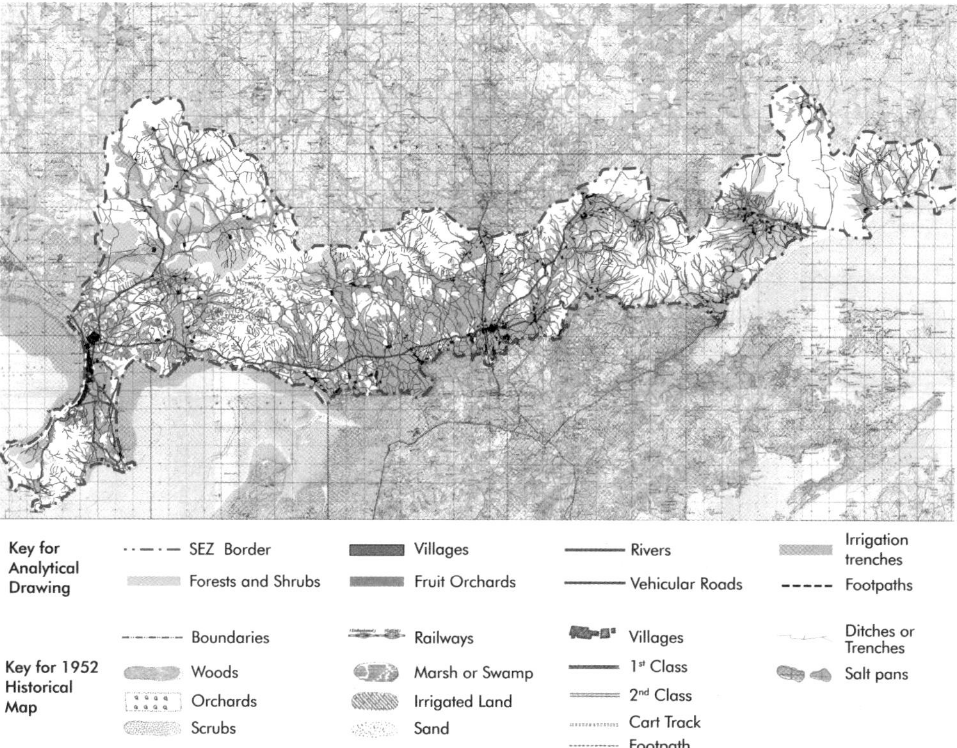

Detailed composite map of preexisting man-made and natural geographies redrawn from 1950s survey map of the present-day Shenzhen. As indicated by the map, the territory was once fully occupied with agricultural and aquacultural productions. These pre-urban spatial, social, cultural, and economic geographies significantly impacted Shenzhen's post-1979 planning and development.

as a symbol of China's Reform and Opening. While its perceived successes were applauded by reform supporters, detractors magnified every perceived problem or failure and used it as an argument against this uncertain path to a new China.

For some, the mere existence of the Shenzhen SEZ was deemed contrary to the doctrines of socialism and communism. Many skeptical of the reform efforts believed that Shenzhen was not only capitalist, but that it was reverting China back to its dark historic periods of foreign invasions and occupation. Many senior CCP members regarded the SEZs as a new form of colonialization, akin to the pre-1949 foreign concessions in China's harbor cities. Returning to Beijing from an inspection of Shenzhen, one elderly statesman lamented: "Other than the Five-Star Red Flag, there are no signs of socialism."[21]

Criticism of the SEZs reached a peak within the CCP in February 1982, during the Guangdong and Fujian provincial meeting. The meeting gathered all top government officials from the two provinces, both of which contained SEZs. It was chaired by one of the strongest critics of the SEZs, Chen Yun, who was the vice chairman of the Communist Party of China and chief secretary of the Central Commission for Discipline Inspection of the CPC. An internal report titled "The Origin of Old China's Colonial Concessions" was distributed in the meeting, and Chen made it the central focus.[22] The report described the newly formed special economic zones as sites of dirty capitalism, rampant corruption, smuggling, money laundering, and worst of all, collusion with enemy foreign powers. The title reflected the report's position on China's SEZs as a shameful and dangerous repetition of the pre-1949 colonial concessions that existed during the imperial and republic periods.

Despite consistent support for the special economic zones by reform-minded officials, many in the central government pressed for policy changes to halt development of the SEZs and associated reforms. As the contents of the government report spread to national and local newspapers, criticism of the special economic zones, especially Shenzhen, intensified throughout 1982 and 1983. Meanwhile, the city struggled on during these crucial start-up years with very little central financial support. In addition, local Shenzhen leaders, particularly Mayor Liang Xiang, were continuously vilified for corruption and money laundering, and blamed for the general perpetuation of the ills of capitalism as well as "betrayal of Communist Party doctrines."[23]

It was common knowledge that Deng Xiaoping's leadership was instrumental in setting up the SEZs as part of a larger push for China's economic reforms. Yet as the Shenzhen debates escalated, he remained largely silent and stayed out of the public eye. Finally, early in 1984 amid mounting complaints, Deng decided to see the SEZs for himself. While this so-called Southern Tour included all three first-generation special economic zones as well as other coastal regions of Guangzhou and Shanghai, the most controversial SEZ took priority. Deng's 1984 tour was his first visit to Shenzhen.

SHENZHEN 1984: INSPECTING URBAN (AND RURAL) REFORMS

On the morning of January 24, 1984, Deng arrived at Guangzhou train station accompanied by Wang Zheng and Yang Shangkun. He was met by

Guangdong provincial leaders at the station, but dismissed their suggestions to take a rest in the more comfortable accommodations Guangzhou had to offer. Instead, he insisted on continuing his journey immediately to Shenzhen, the eye of the storm, stating, "Establishing the special economic zone is the central government's decision, advocated by me. Whether it is successful or not, I need to see it."[24]

As Deng's train pulled into Shenzhen, local officials led by an anxious Mayor Liang Xiang awaited his arrival at the station, uncertain but hopeful for Deng's validation of their local efforts in facing adversity. That afternoon, gathered around a map of Shenzhen in a meeting room at Deng's hotel, Liang Xiang delivered a forty-minute presentation on Shenzhen's progress since 1980. He reported that Shenzhen's industrial and agricultural GDP in 1983 was double that of 1982, and ten times that of 1979. Liang concluded by outlining the various challenges confronting the SEZ, and appealed for further support and guidance. For four years, the local government had weathered shortages in funding, manpower, equipment, and even basic necessities such as water, electricity, and food to accommodate its rapidly increasing population. China's continued poverty during the early 1980s meant there were few national financial resources to support the SEZ efforts. However, the most pivotal challenge had arisen as a result of political uncertainties and criticism. Deng stayed quiet throughout the presentation, and at the end responded to Liang Xiang with mild reserve: "This place is in the middle of development. I took in mind all that you have reported, but I am not going to express any opinions."[25]

Toward late afternoon, Deng was led up to the roof terrace of the newly built twenty-two-story Luohu International Commerce Tower. It was here that Deng saw Shenzhen, with its physical manifestation of his reforms, for the very first time. Luohu New Town District loomed all around him, a busy construction site full of moving cranes and wide boulevards bustling with moving vehicles, bicycles, and pedestrians. Liang Xiang explained that over one hundred tall towers were planned and under construction, which would make Shenzhen the city with the highest concentration of skyscrapers in China. Pointing to an active construction site enclosed by scaffolding and safety nets, Deng asked how tall the building would be. Liang informed him that it was the World Trade Center, destined to be fifty-three stories high and the tallest building in China to date. For the first time since he set foot in Shenzhen, Deng nodded with approval and satisfaction. Years of uncertainty and questions arising from opposing reports were pushed aside, and Deng Xiaoping saw an image of the city that more than satisfied his expectations. As dusk fell, before leaving the tower's roof terrace, Deng Xiaoping said to Liang Xiang: "I have seen it all clearly."[26] The modern towers of Luohu, icons of progress and urbanization, were the physical evidence Deng Xiaoping needed to validate the path of reform for Shenzhen, and for the country.

The next morning, Deng visited China's first 10,000 Yuan Village, named *Yumin Cun,* or Fishermen's Village, on the banks of the Shenzhen River. Perhaps this was the fabled fishing village in the Shenzhen myth. At the village's entrance, Deng was greeted by Wu Baisen, the political leader of the Fishermen's Village—that is, the Communist Party secretary. In Wu's living room, Deng learned that the Fishermen's Village used to be one of the smallest and poorest villages in Shenzhen. Its residents were mostly descendants of Tankas, or the boat people of the South China Sea. With little land, the village's main source of income was from fishing in the nearby sea. However, all that changed in 1979 when Shenzhen city was established, which allowed the village to operate small businesses including restaurants, hotels, and light industry factories funded by Hong Kong investors.[27] With the formation of the special zone, the village set up transportation teams to deliver much-needed concrete and bricks to the hundreds of new construction sites. By 1981, the annual income of each village household exceeded ten thousand yuan. This village was one of the first in China to attain this standard of living.

Stories of the rapid wealth generation in Fishermen's Village often neglect to recognize that the economic dynamism experienced by Shenzhen's villages stemmed not only from the SEZ's urban reform policies, but also from rural reform policies. Like other villages in Shenzhen, the Fishermen's Village was blessed with a unique set of circumstances in that it was a rural land enclave within an urbanized land area. The village collectives were among the earliest participants in Shenzhen's industrialization. One of the first policies issued by the newly founded Shenzhen city government to encourage economic development was, in fact, directed at the villages: "Temporary Regulations on Implementing Special Policies and Flexible Measures in Shenzhen City's Villages." The Shenzhen government extended the provincial and city-level policy directions down to the level of the villages. Enacted in November 1980, the policy encouraged villages to establish "agricultural-industrial-commercial enterprises" for livestock farming, aquaculture, agriculture, sideline industries, commerce, logistics, building industries, processing industries, and tourism.[28] The Shenzhen government applied the usefully ambiguous Special Policies and Flexible Measures doctrine not only to encourage urban reforms, but also to allow the rural village collectives to industrialize. While villages took full advantage of this permission to establish businesses, the city's economy also benefited. Between 1979 and 1980, 426 Hong Kong–Shenzhen cooperation projects were set up in Shenzhen, mostly by village collectives. These joint enterprises generated a revenue of twenty-seven million HKD in 1980 alone.[29] Between 1978 and 1980, the revenue of Shenzhen's village collectives grew by fifteen million RMB.[30]

Remarking on the new two-story house they were sitting in, villager Wu explained it was built together with all the other new houses in the village. The houses were funded and built by the Fishermen's Village Collective in 1982: one-third of the total construction cost had been paid by the village collective, while the remaining two-thirds of each house was paid off in subsequent installments by each household. It was no coincidence that the construction of the Fishermen's Village's new modern housing took place in 1982, the year when China's land nationalization created the two categories of land in the country. In the case of Shenzhen, the land division was not as clear-cut as it first appeared. While all land to the north of the Second Line Border was rural, the land south of the border, inside the SEZ, was not entirely urban. While the SEZ was designated as urban land, there were the hundreds of agricultural and fishing villages inside the special zone. In addition to making the SEZ Second Line Border the division between urban and rural areas of Shenzhen, the 1982 land nationalization also created hundreds of invisible borders surrounding each village settlement inside the SEZ, reservations excluded from centralized urban planning, policies, and social welfare. The villagers inside the Shenzhen SEZ therefore remained rural *hukou* holders, along with those living outside of the SEZ. Each village inside the SEZ became an island of exception in some of the city's most central locations. Thus the city of Shenzhen was split into urban and rural land, and the registered population in Shenzhen was divided into urban *hukou* residents and rural *hukou* residents. The Second Line Border was clear and visible, while the individual borders surrounding the village reservations were socially present but visually invisible. Following the expropriation of agricultural land, each village was left with designated areas of home-based land (HBL) for individual village house construction, and industry development land (IDL) for the village to collectively conduct industrial activities. While the rest of the SEZ land was owned by the government, in villages like the Fishermen's Village, land was collectively owned by all members of the village, and each male villager receives one plot of HBL to build a family home. Villager Wu's house, visited by Deng Xiaoping, was built on his own parcel of HBL.

As Deng Xiaoping rose to leave, Wu Baisen proudly informed him that in 1983 each of his family members had a monthly income of over five hundred yuan. On hearing this, Deng's daughter whispered loudly in his ear that this was more than his salary. Departing from the village, Deng Xiaoping commented to his aides quietly that it would most likely take a "hundred years for all villages in China to reach the same level."[31] This statement was an acknowledgment that most of China's rural villages were still suffering severe poverty in the 1980s. The dramatic transformation of Fishermen's Village and the wealth of its villagers encouraged Deng to continue his push for the nationwide rural reforms that he had first initiated in 1978.

DELAYED VERDICT

On Deng Xiaoping's second day in Shenzhen, he visited an electronics factory located in a new industrial complex comprising a city block along the newly built Shennan Boulevard. Little did anyone know then that this very area would become Huaqiang Bei, the center of the so-called China's Silicon Valley, some twenty years later. Back in 1984, Shenzhen had over sixty electronics enterprises, which together generated a third of Shenzhen's overall industrial revenue.[32] The factory that Deng visited was operated by the Shenzhen Industrial Center of China National Aero-Technology Import & Export Corporation (CATIC). First established in Guangzhou, the Shenzhen CATIC was among the first of Shenzhen's electronic industries.

On the morning before leaving Shenzhen, Deng visited the controversial Shekou Industrial Zone. Located on Shekou Harbor inside the Shenzhen special economic zone, Shekou had been established a year earlier in 1979 as an exceptional industrial zone for reform experimentation. Spanning over two square kilometers, Shekou was the site of some of Shenzhen's, as well as China's, early experimentation with economic reforms. Deng was received by Yuan Geng, the initiator of these reforms and Director of the Shekou Industrial Zone Management Board.[33] The Shekou Industrial Zone experimented with establishing fixed-term labor contracts, floating salary-based bonuses, entrance exams for all administrators and technicians, as well as company leadership selection through anonymous voting. All administrators, including Director Yuan himself, were reviewed on a fixed-term basis through a vote of confidence by the entire workforce. These bold measures had earned Yuan respect in the company and locally, but also countless complaints. The prominently displayed company slogan, "Time is Money; Efficiency is Life," garnered calls by other government leaders for Yuan Geng's dismissal. In keeping with his established refusal to express opinions, Deng did not make any comments following Yuan Geng's report and boarded a Navy gunboat at the Shekou Port for Zhuhai.

Deng stayed in Zhuhai for a similar duration—two and a half days. Before leaving, he was asked to write a calligraphic inscription that translated as: "Zhuhai Special Economic Zone Is Good." This left Zhuhai's leaders feeling encouraged, yet the act greatly disturbed Shenzhen's leaders. Deng had not offered any official comments on Shenzhen. It was upon Mayor Liang Xiang's request days later, on February 1, that Deng wrote "The development and experiences of Shenzhen have proved the correctness of our policy on the establishment of special economic zones," and backdated it to January 26, his last day in Shenzhen.[34] Deng Xiaoping had given the city his stamp of approval, empowering local leaders to continue with their efforts.

Deng continued leaving calligraphic inscriptions during the rest of his tour of the special economic zones. Shenzhen was used as a benchmark for evaluating other locations. In Xiamen, he wrote the words "special economic zone should be done faster and better." At the Shanghai Baoshan Steel Works, Deng compared the speed of construction in Shanghai to a snail's pace, whereas Shenzhen had built "one floor in a few days."[35]

Once back in Beijing, reassured by what he witnessed, especially in Shenzhen, Deng immediately began to initiate reform policies in other regions of China. On February 24, 1984, Deng gave his first speech since returning from his tour. He summarized the experience of his southern tour, and singled out Shenzhen as a blueprint for the speed and the achievements of reform policies. Deng Xiaoping turned the astonishingly rapid construction of the Shenzhen World Trade Center into a metaphor for the speed of economic reform in the special zones:

> This time I went to Shenzhen to take a look; the impression it gave me was one of widespread prosperity and growth. The construction

> speed of Shenzhen is very fast, building one floor every few days and a tall building in no time. The construction crews there are even from the inland provinces. One reason for the high efficiency is the contract system and fairness in administering reward and punishment. Shenzhen's Shekou Industrial Zone is even faster. The reason is they were given a bit of power. They can make their own decisions on expenditure under five million US dollars. Their slogan is "Time is money; efficiency is life."[36]

NATIONAL IMPACT AND LOCAL RESPONSE

In March and April 1984, a series of meetings were held in Beijing to advance further reform policies. By May 4, the central government formally declared fourteen coastal cities, including Shanghai and Guangzhou, as the next sites of economic reforms. In May 1984, the "doors" of Dalian, Qinhuangdao, Tianjin, Yantai, Qingdao, Lianyungang, Nantong, Shanghai, Ningbo, Wenzhou, Fuzhou, Guangzhou, Zhanjiang, and Beihai were opened to foreign investment and trading. At the National Day parade on October 1, 1984, in front of Tiananmen Square, broadcast on national TV all over China, there was a float in the form of Shekou's Ming Hua cruise liner emblazoned with the famous slogan in large bold text: "Time is Money; Efficiency is Life." Formerly used as evidence to denounce Shekou and Yuan Geng for capitalism, the slogan was now celebrated at national level. The State Council released the "Decision of the Central Committee of the Communist Party of China on Economic Reform" document in the same month, signaling to the nation the central government's intention to continue the Reform and Opening Up of China.[37]

Buoyed by the endorsement of Deng Xiaoping, Shenzhen embarked on an ambitious new round of planning. Under the direction of the Mayor's office and the Municipal Planning Department, the Shenzhen Branch of the Chinese Academy of Urban Planning and Design (CAUPD SZ) began work on Shenzhen's Second Master Plan in late 1984. The first step in this new draft involved a detailed survey of the state of urban construction at the time. The 1984 SEZ Survey Map, produced by the CAUPD SZ, revealed that urban development was mainly concentrated in the Luohu District, just north of the Hong Kong border crossing. This was by far the most densely urbanized area of the SEZ, comprised largely of high-rises, and the main focus of Deng Xiaoping's 1984 visit. Prior to 1985, the

Shenzhen SEZ had yet to attract substantial foreign investment and enterprises. The development of the rest of the SEZ—which stretched east and west of the Luohu District city center—was largely left to various individual enterprises, unrestrained by the land use designations of the city master plan. It should be noted that, with the exception of the two large industrial zones of Shangbu and Shekou, the preexisting villages formed some of the most dynamic centers for small-scale industrial activities.

New enthusiasm for Shenzhen's future drove city leaders and planners to develop more concrete plans for the entire SEZ beyond the Luohu District, and the 1984 Master Plan increased the focus area for urban build-up land to 123 square kilometers—25 percent bigger than that of the original 1982 Shenzhen SEZ Master Plan. Given that Luohu District was almost all occupied by new constructions, and in order to facilitate Shenzhen's westward expansion, local leaders decided to move the civic and commercial core of the city from Luohu westward to Futian District. Drafts of the "Shenzhen Special Economic Zone Masterplan 1986–2000" were completed and released by the Municipal Planning Department and CAUPD SZ in 1985. Formal axial planning organized the center of this new Futian District, which would later become the new location of Shenzhen City Hall.

A comparison of the 1982 and 1985 Master Plans clearly shows the city's intention to remold itself from a loose collection of industrial clusters into a comprehensive city. In addition to industrial zones, the second Master Plan specified land uses for commercial, political, educational, and leisure activities, while residential areas were further refined and all connected with an extensive greenbelt-lined road network. The aspiration for a landscaped city reflected the intention to build Shenzhen into a comprehensive city—beyond an industrial production and export zone. It also reflected the influence of Singapore during the early decades of the SEZ. Singapore's manicured green parkways, epitomizing a modern, clean, garden city, shaped the vision of Shenzhen's city leaders, especially Mayor Liang Xiang. Liang's forward-looking vision also included a rapid roadway network that established Shenzhen's future as a car-dependent city, the merits of which might be disputed today. His more admirable measures, however, included setting aside a large land plot for a new Shenzhen University and allocating fifty million RMB, almost half the city's total annual revenue, for its construction and faculty recruitment.[38] This effort designated the education of people as the city's most important investment.

Indeed, while it would have been difficult to predict this outcome at the time, many of the future graduates of Shenzhen University would go on to play significant roles in the technological and economic advancement of the city. Some graduates of the university would generate stunning global impacts, including Tencent's founder Ma Huateng, the most profitable social media organization in the world. Other major civic infrastructure projects incorporated into the new Master Plan included the future Shenzhen Airport, to be located in the former Shajing communes, an area just outside the SEZ; the Guangzhou-Shenzhen Highway; and two additional east-west transportation arteries inside the SEZ, as well as expansion of the previously planned Shen-Nan (Shennan) Boulevard.

The second Shenzhen SEZ Master Plan was refined by the Shenzhen Urban Planning Committee throughout the year, and published in August 1986 as the "Shenzhen Special Economic Zone Master Plan (1986–1990)" to coincide with the release of "Shenzhen's Seventh Five-Year Plan (1986–1990)."[39] According to the published planning document, the Shenzhen SEZ would "be built into a predominantly industrial, export-oriented, multi-functional industrially well-structured, technically advanced, comprehensive economic zone with a high degree of civilization."[40] While the six north-south river-reservoir tourism nature reserves of the 1982 SEZ Master Plan are no longer clearly evident, the 1985 SEZ Master Plan still incorporated the existing natural geography—hills, rivers, forests, and even large lychee orchards—into the urban landscape. The 1985 Master Plan allocated twenty-two public parks and ten tourism areas, all connected by the 140 kilometers of parkways lined with greenery.[41] While not clearly evident from the Master Plan drawing and often overlooked in later descriptions of early planning efforts, many of the designated green areas, public parks, and urban water features were derived from former agrarian fruit orchards, fishing ponds, and river system flood plains. While the Master Plans clearly demonstrate the city's progression from 1982 to 1985, less obvious—and often overlooked—is the significant impact of the preexisting natural and man-made geography on the spatial layout of the new 1985 Master Plan.

Shenzhen's preexisting geography is not the only critical factor that has been underemphasized in the narrative of Shenzhen's formal planning. Another factor was the explosion of unplanned population growth and the lack of housing provisions for this influx of new residents. The population target for the 1982 Shenzhen SEZ Master Plan was set according to

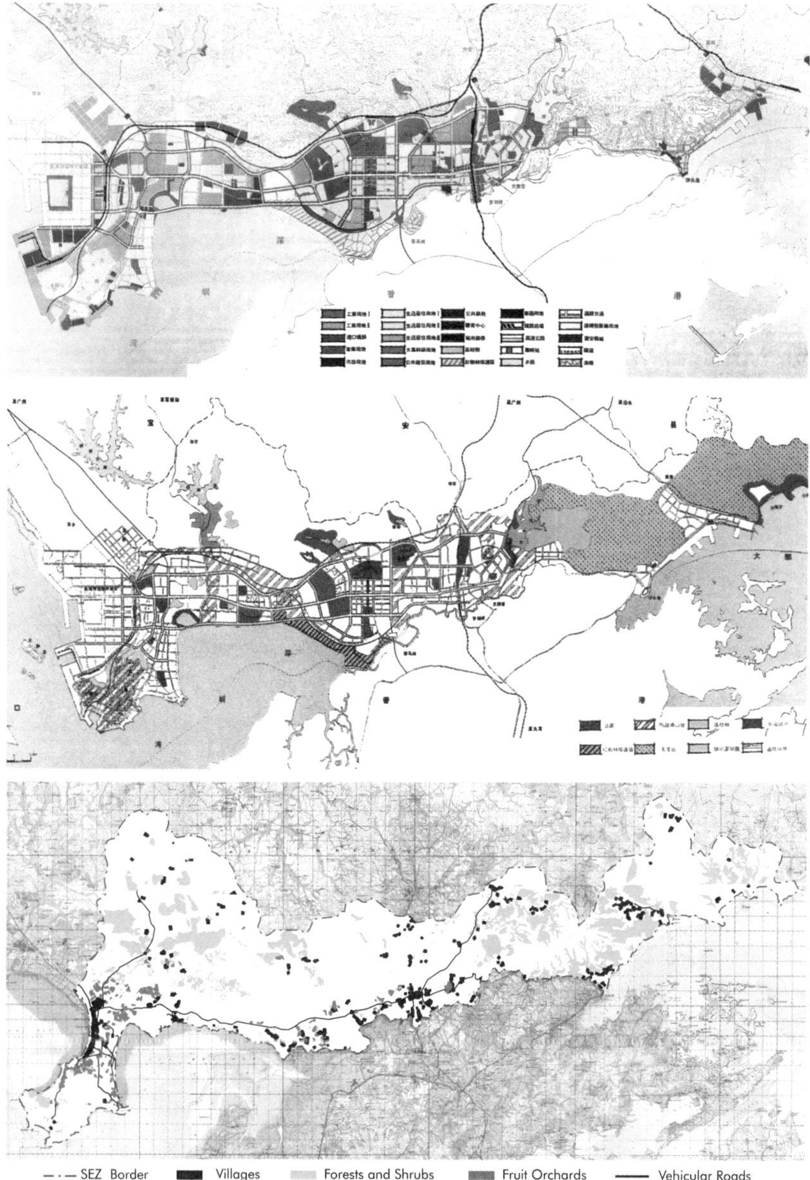

1986 Shenzhen SEZ Master Plan (*above*). 1986 Shenzhen SEZ Urban Greenery Master Plan (*middle*). Composite map of Villages, Roads, Orchards, and Woodlands redrawn from 1950s survey map (*below*). Comparisons of the maps indicate continued influence by the preexisting geographies on Shenzhen's second round of planning. However, the six north-south urban waterways of the first 1982 Master Plan were changed to "Isolation Zones" in the 1986 Plan.

"Shenzhen's Sixth Five-Year Plan." This document anticipated a future population of one million by the year 2000. However, by 1985, Shenzhen's population had already reached 880,000; nearly four hundred thousand of those individuals were unregistered "temporary" residents.[42] While Shenzhen's government officials and planners were aware that they had vastly underestimated the population increase, they were also aware that the central government in Beijing was critical of such uncontrolled growth, especially that attributed to the "temporary" population without urban *hukou* or even registration papers. This explains why the new 1986–1990 Master Plan was obliged to follow the new Seventh Five-Year Plan, and therefore set the new target for the registered population as eight hundred thousand, and for the temporary population as three hundred thousand, by the year 2000.[43] While this Master Plan acknowledged the existence of the temporary population for the first time, it could not blatantly reveal that this segment already made up nearly 50 percent of Shenzhen's population. The stated statistics of the 1986 Master Plan revealed the city's intention to double the registered urban *hukou* population, but curb and reduce the temporary population. However, the reality of Shenzhen's eventual development indicates that increases in the non-registered population consistently outpaced the growth of the registered population, and from 1989 onward unregistered and "temporary" residents accounted for the majority of Shenzhen's total population.[44] Yet the city's formal planning continued in accordance with registered population statistics, which left the majority of Shenzhen's residents without housing and other civic provisions. Considering these conditions, it is perhaps not surprising that former agrarian villages transformed into "urban villages" made up of unplanned housing, which predominantly catered to the working-class members of the unregistered population. In addition to hosting the unplanned population and industries, these village centers also accommodated formal, even state-owned enterprises and associated population, which had also outpaced the city's supply of planned commercial and residential spaces.

Ironically, yet poignantly, some urban villagers even accommodated the city planners themselves. In an internal publication by the Shenzhen Branch of the Chinese Academy of Urban Planning and Design (CAUPD SZ) to mark its 30-year history in Shenzhen, those involved in the early years revealed some humble beginnings. In 1984, CAUPD first started its Shenzhen branch in Yuan Lin New Village, one of Shenzhen's earliest government-built social housing blocks specifically for government workers and civil servants.[45] Given the shortage of office space, the apartments not only served as CAUPD residences, but also as the company's workplace. One planner recalled that the earliest large-format drawings for the 1985 Shenzhen SEZ Master Plans were hand-drawn on two ping-pong tables in one of the apartment units.[46] Within two years, CAUPD Shenzhen had grown from a handful of people to over 100 employees, and could no longer fit within the available units at the housing compound.[47] After months of searching, CAUPD moved to a small six-story building in 1986, this time in the *Laowei,* or old compound, of a former agrarian village. Centrally located inside Shenzhen's Luohu District, this centuries-old village is named Caiwuwei, "Cai's Family Compound." Starting in the early 1980s, the village collective built and operated many new six-story buildings to accommodate the city's growing demand for residential and commercial space. The arrangement of CAUPD's office spaces inside the urban village building was similar to their previous location of the social housing block: the planners and workers lived in the bedrooms and drafted city plans on dining tables in the living rooms. Meanwhile, the ground and second floors of the urban village building were used as laundry rooms by the nearby Caiwuwei Grand Hotel. Built and operated by the village itself since 1984, this hotel was reportedly the first three-star hotel built by rural peasants in China.[48]

Decades later, senior CAUPD planner Zhao Yanqing remarked: "These days, many planners are full of instinctive hatred for urban villages, for the messiness, hazardousness, and disorderliness. However, back then I did not have any of those feelings. A group of young people, thousands of miles away from home, trying to be entrepreneurial in a land of opportunity. That feeling of youthfulness, even within the urban village, was full of passion and vigor."[49] The experience also influenced her professional perspective: "For planners, the experience gained in person is often irreplaceable. In later planning projects, I often faced issues regarding the urban villages. In these cases, my own experience in Caiwuwei Village always helped me to look beyond their disordered appearance, and allowed me to think in the shoes of the people living in the urban villages."[50] The early Shenzhen planners had the unique opportunity to experience a city growing on the basis of necessity and improvisation, rather than on the basis of some ideal plan, which contributed to their relative openness toward the unexpected, unregistered, unregulated, and informal. While the 1986 Shenzhen SEZ Master Plan was designed to accommodate a projected population of 1.1 million, informal reflections by Shenzhen's local planners indicate that they actually designed the transportation system for a population twice the size of the published figure.[51] Nonetheless, population growth in Shenzhen would continue to vastly outstrip even these more ambitious local plans.

CONTINUED CRISIS

While city planners envisioned Shenzhen's grand future from modest living rooms built by former farmers, the city continued to receive intense scrutiny and criticism from many in the central government. By the end of 1985, disapproval no longer focused on the SEZ's anti-socialist and unpatriotic pursuit of capitalism. Instead, criticism shifted to Shenzhen's perceived economic underperformance and especially its failure to become an "export-oriented industrial city." Shenzhen was accused of misrepresenting its success based on economic indicators of export revenue.[52] From 1981 to 1985, the SEZ's total import revenue was 2.3 billion USD, 2.5 times larger than the revenue from its total exports.[53] Reliance on domestic investment, particularly for Shenzhen's large-scale infrastructure and construction projects, was another major concern. Large-scale capital outlay on land and infrastructure development was mainly sourced from domestic banks, state-owned enterprises, and domestic provincial or city-level government departments. For example, in the effort to raise the necessary capital to construct the International Trade Center (Shenzhen's first skyscraper), Mayor Liang Xiang invited provincial leaders from inland China to visit the construction site and offered them floor space in the future tower in exchange for their investment. Once again, this outreach was based on necessity: at the time, China's central government did not have the financial capacity to invest in the SEZ, so the local government had to generate funding from other sources. Some members of the central government saw this as an indication of Shenzhen's failure, that the SEZ was not able to be self-reliant solely on exports and foreign investments. Yao Yilin, China's Vice Premier from 1979 to 1993, delivered a statement that many interpreted as an open threat to the continued existence of the SEZ: "It is impossible for the SEZ's economic development to rely on the country's long-term 'blood transfusion'; now, the 'needle' must be unplugged decisively."[54]

Charges of misrepresentation, corruption, and money laundering were all directed against the Shenzhen SEZ and its local leadership. In addition, mounting criticism of the general hazards associated with China's national economic reforms frequently used Shenzhen SEZ's apparent failure as evidence. Despite support for the reforms from Deng Xiaoping and Gu Mu (now Head of the National Economic and Financial Commission), among others, the critics in the central government successfully forced a change in the direction of national reform policies by the end of 1985. Earlier that year, the central government had moved forward on a series of policies to apply lessons from the SEZs to other locations in China. In February, the State Council had designated the Pearl River Delta, Yangtze River Delta, and Fujian Golden Triangle as Coastal Open Economic Zones.[55] In July, however, Gu Mu reluctantly declared that the original plan to extend SEZ policies to fourteen coastal areas would be scaled back to only four cities: Shanghai, Tianjin, Dalian, and Guangzhou. Meanwhile, the backlash against Shenzhen resulted in severe economic and political repercussions for the city, including the tightening of fiscal credit policies, withdrawal of investments, cancellation of half of its construction projects, and termination of Mayor Liang Xiang's leadership in August 1985.

Fortunately, despite these circumstances, Shenzhen's subsequent Mayor Li Hao (in office 1985–1990) did not reverse the city's developmental direction. Over the next two years, Shenzhen continued to experiment with a series of significant policy changes, including administrative institutional reforms to promote economic competition and land reforms that introduced the transfer of land use rights. Such changes enabled Shenzhen to cultivate China's first post-reform property development market, which infused the city with capital and boosted investor confidence. However, these reforms continued to face attacks and restrictions by political and economic conservatives at multiple levels of governance. The constant oscillation between economic reforms and directives to curb those reforms caused public unease about the government's policies, leading to problems such as consumer price inflation and perceived local government corruption.

By the end of 1987, Shenzhen's export industry performance had exceeded the stringent criteria set by its economic critics in the central government. Reassured by Shenzhen's growth and the stabilizing national economy, which had checked the countrywide inflation of the early 1980s, critics in Beijing's central government were temporarily mollified. By March 1988, many of the SEZ-initiated reform policies were launched in other selected cities. In contrast with the cautious expansion of the previous two years, the new policies were implemented in 293 locations, encompassing a total land area of 426,000 square kilometers and comprising a total of two hundred million people—nearly 20 percent of China's vast population.[56]

As Shenzhen's rapid urbanization continued, the 1986 Shenzhen SEZ Master Plan was modified in December 1988 and released in 1989. The modified Master Plan increased land allotted for urban construction from 123 to 150 square kilometers. Acknowledging the rapid growth of the city's temporary population, the 1989 Master Plan projected a total population of 1.5 million by the year 2000, increasing the projected temporary unregistered population to seven hundred thousand (up from three hundred thousand in the 1986 Master Plan). The "Shenzhen City Urban Development Strategy" was also published in 1989, which described Shenzhen's future as an international city that is "relatively mature in foreign trade, finance and hi-technology; integrates techniques of commerce and industry; outward-looking and multi-functional; well supported by infrastructure; with export-oriented agriculture industry; as well as environmentally attractive."[57] The 1989 strategy document also specified the need to extend planning and development beyond the Second Line Border to the "entire territory" of Shenzhen. However, the implementation of these strategies was delayed by the historic Tiananmen Square incident in June 1989.

During the summer of 1989, public mourning for the passing of the liberal-minded Hu Yaobang inspired thousands of students to gather at Tiananmen Square in protest against China's general state of affairs.[58] Conservatives in the central government blamed the incident on economic and political instabilities created by Deng's reforms. The government's decision to crack down on the student protestors left China in a state of heightened national anxiety and turmoil.[59]

Following the Tiananmen Square incident, China was sanctioned by many Western nations, affecting international trade. Foreign investors began to turn away from China, looking instead to other Southeast Asian countries. Export trade and tourism plummeted as a result. The battle over China's future path—a campaign for market reforms to promote economic advancement on the one hand, and a campaign for the restoration of socialist ideology on the other—continued to rage. The Chinese government was also experiencing tension resulting from European democratic revolutions during this period, leading to the fall of the Berlin Wall in 1989 and subsequent regime changes throughout Eastern Europe. Under the dark cloud of economic recession, political insecurity, and international condemnation, conservatives in the Chinese Communist Party gained momentum, blaming China's troubles on its experimentation with reform and urging a return to isolationism.

On his retirement in November 1989, Deng Xiaoping resigned from all governmental positions and retreated from the public limelight. Over the next two years, he made only two public appearances, one of which was the 1991 Chinese New Year celebration in Shanghai. In this way, Deng hoped to set an example to his generation of political leaders, encouraging them not to interfere with the next generation of governance, headed then by Jiang Zemin. Deng insisted on abolishing the lifelong tenure system that applied to all government leadership positions. However, both Deng and the skeptics of market reform continued to exert opposing influences on the debate about China's future direction. The dissolution of the Soviet Union in December 1991 convinced Chinese conservatives that economic reforms bred dangerous political instability and would cause similar problems in China. Meanwhile, Deng subtly used surrogates and newspaper articles to champion a continued push for economic reforms. His strategy, however, failed to resonate within the government or significantly impact the general public. There was widespread speculation about his health and his political stamina in the struggle to continue shaping China's future. It was during this time that Deng declared his intention to take a "family vacation" in the South.

Details of Deng's four-day visit to Shenzhen in 1992 would be recorded, suppressed, reported, scrutinized, debated, publicized, broadcast, studied, celebrated, and commemorated. The trip would change the social and political atmosphere and ultimately the fate of the Reform and Opening Up of China. The words he spoke, especially during his few days in Shenzhen, became known as his "Southern Talks." These were not planned speeches, however; his words were inspired by the scenes he saw in Shenzhen.

Prior to making the trip, Deng strictly forbade any reporting on it. He was not sure what he would encounter. As he did on his first trip to Shenzhen in 1984, he wanted to see the situation on the ground before commenting on the ongoing reform debate. It had been eight years since his last visit. Was Shenzhen working? Or had it become a den of corruption, as proclaimed by so many?

SHENZHEN IN 1992: RESUSCITATING THE REFORMS

On a cold winter day in late January 1992, Beijing Railway Station was packed with people hurrying home for the Spring Festival. Deng discreetly boarded his special train. The eighty-eight-year-old was accompanied by a few government workers, his wife, his two daughters, and grandchildren. As the train pulled out of Beijing Station, anyone watching would have seen that the destination display on the green train was blank. Meanwhile, the local Shenzhen government received confidential details of Deng's arrival, describing his visit as a family vacation "for a rest in the South." Accompanying the notification was an instruction listing the "Six Nos": no listening to presentations, no accompanied dining, no inscription writing, no journalist interviews, no photography, and no news reporting.[60]

Arriving at the Shenzhen Guest House on the morning of January 19, Deng surprised everyone by requesting to go around the city immediately. From inside a slow-moving car, Deng set eyes again on the busy streets and high-rises of Luohu District center. While the streets of Shenzhen had been predominantly occupied by bicycles during his 1984 visit, they were now filled by fast-moving cars and buses. Already encouraged by what he saw, Deng made a statement to settle the heated debate over Shenzhen's political identity: "From the very outset there were different opinions concerning the establishment of special economic zones, fearing whether this meant practicing capitalism. Shenzhen's reconstruction achievements have expressly answered those having worries of one kind or another. The special zone's surname is 'socialist,' not 'capitalist.'"[61] As his car drove past the modern Luohu Train Station, Deng's daughter Deng Lin pointed toward the façade of the arrival hall, where the sign with "SHENZHEN" in his bold and vigorous calligraphic handwriting was prominently displayed.

The car stopped at the Huanggang Border Crossing Station. Located just across the Shenzhen River from Hong Kong, the station began operation in 1989 and had been designed to handle fifty thousand vehicles and fifty thousand visitors on a daily basis.[62] (The actual volume of traffic at Huanggang Crossing Station would far exceed its intended capacity, significantly impacting Shenzhen's urban form and development.) In 1992, however, the station was processing seven thousand vehicles and two thousand visitors daily.[63] Deng lingered at the junction with the Shenzhen River Bridge, looking across the river border to Hong Kong. Having negotiated the Sino-British Joint Declaration in preparation for Hong Kong's 1997 handover of power to Mainland China, Deng had good reason to engage in some reflective thought by the river.

The most important moment of Deng's 1992 tour was arguably his visit to the World Trade Center. During his previous visit in 1984, Deng had witnessed its development and helped publicize its construction speed of "one floor every three days." At a height of 160 meters (fifty-three stories), double that of the tallest building in China at the time, the tower was a symbol of the enviable "Shenzhen Speed." Another source of pride was its revolving restaurant on the fifty-third floor, which had already hosted international visitors such as Lee Kwan Yew in 1988.[64] Deng was a cherished visitor, and the tower's glass-paneled walls gave him a spectacular view of a dense and thriving city center. The building was surrounded by other high-rises and a forest of cranes at ongoing construction sites. Enthused by the views, Deng permitted Shenzhen's top leader Li Hao to deliver a presentation. Li showed Deng the Shenzhen Special Economic Comprehensive Master Plan and unveiled figures demonstrating Shenzhen's growth in per capita income, from six hundred RMB in 1984 to two thousand RMB in 1991. Following Li's presentation, Deng gave an animated talk that surprised all present. Even his daughter Deng Rong was caught off guard by the spontaneous speech. She later recalled scrambling to borrow a pad of paper from the restaurant staff in order to write down his words.[65] By her account, the elderly Deng was generally quiet during those years, saying few words even in the presence of his family. Yet at the top of the World Trade Center, he spoke continuously for nearly 30 minutes. He made many of his most impassioned and influential statements about the country's future direction at this moment, including the blunt statement: "Failing to adhere to socialism, failing to carry out Reform and Opening Up, failing to develop the economy and improve people's livelihoods can only lead up to a dead end." It was here that he also quipped: "Adhere to the Party's Basic Guideline, one hundred years without change." Pointing to the city's skyline of high-rises, he concluded his address with this statement: "Shenzhen's rapid development was the result of doing solid work, not the outcome of delivering speeches or writing papers." Deng may have been directly rebuking the series of academic papers and articles that had criticized these developments in Shenzhen. By the time he descended to the lobby of the World Trade Center, it was packed with workers and residents who had caught wind of his appearance. While remaining orderly, they gave him round after round of thunderous applause.

Following his visit to the World Trade Center, Deng concluded his Shenzhen tour by examining two of the city's burgeoning industries—electronics and tourism. He stopped at the Shenzhen Advanced Science Technology Group (SAST), located in Futian District's Hongling technology cluster. SAST was known nationally as China's first company to produce compact discs and CD players. Deng was fascinated by the technology involved and probed for information about materials and patent application issues. On the company's factory floor, he stopped to speak with young female migrant workers, inquiring about their native provinces.

During the final days of his visit, Deng relaxed. Outwardly, the trip even began to resemble the family vacation that had been originally announced. Along with his wife, daughters, and grandson, Deng visited the Overseas Chinese Town (OCT) in Shenzhen's Nanshan District. The theme parks at OCT were a major attraction for domestic tourists. During the 1980s and 1990s, tourism became one of the city's largest economic sectors and revenue generators. Deng visited the China Folk Culture Village and Splendid China, where he rode in the battery-operated cars and took family photos in front of miniature replicas of iconic buildings from all over China. The next day, the family was joined by Deng's eldest son, Deng Pufang, as well as China's Premier Yang Shangkun, who also happened to be visiting Shenzhen with his family. Together, they visited the Xianhu Botanical Garden and planted mountain fig trees in the park. This joint family outing was recorded by Yang Shaoming, Yang Shangkun's son, who was also a photographer. His photos of Deng and Yang together at the Botanical Garden appeared in the English edition of the *China Daily*, prior to any formal reporting in China's newspapers on Deng's tour.

Not long after his visit, Deng declared that the speed of development he had witnessed in Shenzhen far exceeded even his own expectations. However, as he left the city on January 23, Deng urged city leaders to push even harder. He wanted Shenzhen to continue to set an example for the rest of China. A later news story described the moments before Deng boarded the ferry for Zhuhai at Shekou Harbor.[66] Shenzhen's party secretary Li Hao thanked Deng for his visit and invited him to return the following Chinese New Year. Deng shook hands and bade formal farewell to all the city leaders present. Reports noted that "Comrade Xiaoping walked a few steps toward the pier. Suddenly he turned back. He looked toward Li Hao and said: 'You all must work faster!'"[67]

SKIRMISHES IN THE PRESS

Only a few journalists were invited to be present during Deng's visit. Initially, the only Shenzhen representative was Chen Xitian, an experienced journalist from the *Shenzhen Special Zone Daily*. Chen was notified of the "strictly confidential assignment" just one day prior to the visit. The call came not from his supervisors at the newspaper, but directly from the Shenzhen Municipal Party Committee Office, along with strict instructions to keep the details a secret, even from his wife. Chen dutifully witnessed and recorded Deng's fateful visit. After the five-day tour, Chen wrote an account of all the talks Deng had given on his trip and handed it to the Municipal Party Committee Office. Along with his supervisor and colleagues, Chen was instructed to continue maintaining strict confidentiality. He anxiously waited as time passed, but from January to mid-March 1992 there were no Chinese media reports of Deng's visit to the South.

However, the Hong Kong press was not subject to such restrictions. By January 22, before Deng had even left Shenzhen, the Hong Kong papers were splashed with headlines about his visit. That same day, the headline in the English-language *South China Morning Post* read: "Deng in Surprise Shenzhen Visit!"[68] On January 23, Deng's presence in Shenzhen was broadcast on Hong Kong's televised news. While Hong Kong newspapers could not be distributed in China at that time, television antennae in many private homes along the southern coast of Guangdong Province picked up the signal. Thus people living outside Shenzhen and Zhuhai soon also found out about Deng's visit and, more importantly, his strongly worded messages.

On January 25, the *South China Morning Post* reported Deng's positive stance on Shenzhen with the headline "Deng's Visit Symbolic of Southern Success."[69] Western newspapers also soon picked up the news of the retired leader's rare public appearance. On February 3, Boston's *The Christian Science Monitor* stated: "Deng's tour sends mixed signals on reform. The Chinese leader lavishes praise on Guangdong reformers, but his vague promises suggest resistance from conservative rivals in Beijing."[70] In Montreal, *The Gazette* offered a more optimistic account in its February 4 issue: "Deng's two-week tour of economically booming southern regions has given a clear signal that Beijing intends to press ahead faster with economic reform."[71] Despite these international reports and the gradual spreading of the news at home, the Beijing-controlled state media cautiously tried to avoid any mention of Deng's visit to Shenzhen. On February 3, Beijing's CCTV broadcast footage of Deng and Yang Shangkun together at government meetings in Shanghai, but made no mention of their presence in Shenzhen or Deng's push for continued reforms.[72]

Most remarkable was the *Asian Wall Street Journal*'s February 5, 1992, report in an article entitled "China: Jiang Affirms Reforms." Prior to

Deng's southern tour, his successor Jiang Zemin has not publicly declared his position on the future direction of China's reforms. The 1992 article reported one of Jiang's first official statements of support for the SEZs in the aftermath of Deng's visit while noting "the comments came a day after senior leader Deng Xiaoping concluded a tour of Special Economic Zones in southern China that have led to market-style reforms. He urged local leaders to borrow good things from capitalism, sending the message he is determined that economic reforms he began in the late 1970s be resumed."[73] Deng's biographer Ezra Vogel also credited Deng's 1992 southern tour with persuading Jiang Zemin to take such a clear position: "From the reports he had received from Zhuhai, Jiang realized that Deng was determined to remove him if he did not boldly promote reform and opening up. Jiang could see from Deng's visit to the South that he had attracted a great deal of support from key leaders in Beijing and from local leaders. Later Jiang acknowledged that by then he had concluded that Deng's views would prevail and that he, Jiang, would be wise to support them."[74]

Between mid-February and mid-March, articles began to appear in China's domestic newspapers supporting the newly adopted agenda of continued economic reforms; an equal number of articles, however, opposed it. Neither side actually referred to Deng's visits to Shenzhen and Zhuhai. Meanwhile, confidential internal government reports summarizing Deng's announcements in Shenzhen started to circulate and gain support within the government. This growing acceptance was facilitated, coincidentally, by improvements in China's economy owing to stabilized inflation and increased export production.[75] During a series of closed-door government meetings in March, Deng's Shenzhen talks were compiled and endorsed as the government's official policy direction.

Back in Shenzhen, journalist Chen spotted an article published in the Guangzhou-based *South Daily*. Entitled "Comrade Xiaoping among People at the Advanced Science Technology Group,"[76] the article hinted at Deng's Shenzhen visit. Not wanting to miss his chance, Chen proceeded to write his own story immediately. He decided to simply present Deng's five-day visit as a running log without commentary, incorporating everything Deng witnessed in Shenzhen and all his remarks along the way. To complete the picture of hope and change, Chen borrowed the title of a composition by the Tang Dynasty poet Li He, "Eastern Wind Brings an Eyeful of Spring." On March 25, he submitted his draft to the Party Committee Office and immediately received approval for its publication, with the added direction "to portray Comrade Xiaoping as a human, not a god." On March 26, the headline "Eastern Wind Brings an Eyeful of Spring: A Documentary Report of Comrade Deng Xiaoping's Tour of Shenzhen" was splashed across the *Shenzhen Special Zone Daily*. Chen emphasized Deng's vitality and enthusiasm. "He looked very healthy, with a pair of bright, piercing eyes, a kindly smiling face, wearing a dark gray jacket and black Western-style trousers. Glowing with health and vigor, he stepped out of the car. After an interval of eight years, he once again set foot on Shenzhen, the hotbed in the forefront of Reform and Opening Up."[77]

Chen's vivid descriptions of Deng's bold advocacy for reform, along with the news of Shenzhen's impressive urbanity, were widely distributed. By March 30, almost all the major Chinese newspapers carried his "Eastern Wind Brings an Eyeful of Spring" report, increasing national knowledge and public support of both Deng's campaign and China's continued reforms. The state newspaper, *People's Daily*, ultimately carried the same report on March 31, 1992, nearly three months after Deng's visit to Shenzhen.

THE SHENZHEN PIVOT

Deng's orations in Shenzhen came to be regarded as conclusive statements, reinforcing his theory of "Socialism with Chinese Characteristics." The "talks" were compiled in the last chapter of the final volume of *Selected Works of Deng Xiaoping*.[78] Deng's words and the imagery of Shenzhen successfully prevented China's return to more orthodox socialist policies, including a centrally planned economy. In a later memoir, Deng Rong commented on her father's final southern tour: "I feel he was lighting a lamp with the political wisdom of an 88-year-old elderly man. It could be the last lamp of his life, but we should say it was also the most brilliant lamp of his life."[79]

By August 1992, China's central government had announced that five inland cities along the Yangtze River, nine cities located on the national border, and all thirty provincial and prefectural capital cities would adopt the same economic policies as the special economic zones.[80] Four chief policy directions were implemented. The first gave "opened cities" greater power to engage in foreign economic cooperation; the second provided support to "open cities" in introducing advanced technology, reforming old industrial enterprises, and developing modernized agriculture; the third initiated incentive policies to attract foreign investment; and the fourth gave "open cities" permission to establish economic and technological development zones.[81] Since the 1949 establishment of the People's Republic of China, the nation's economic growth had been centered on industrialization with highly restricted urbanization. The Reform and Opening Up policies of the 1980s and 1990s marked a pivotal shift away from the previously entrenched socialist governance of China's cities. These reform policies promoted the spread of marketization throughout the country, but *cities* were especially poised to become China's new engines of economic growth. The effects of the robust zonal policy developed during these years can still be seen today: nearly every major city in China has become identified with some type of "economic zone."

Even Chen Yun—Deng's early advocate and subsequent critic—came to accept Shenzhen as a success. Chen Yun's stabilizing efforts through fiscally conservative policies played a major role in reducing instability and easing China's phenomenal transition into a national market economy. Although mystified by Shenzhen, Chen was eventually won over by the city's apparent success. Never having visited any of the special economic zones, Chen declared that he was impressed "with Shenzhen's modern construction and with its great success in increasing export growth at a much faster rate than imports."[82]

The widespread dissemination of reform policies, first established in Shenzhen and later in all other major Chinese cities, drastically changed the structural relationship between China's central government and local municipalities. The accompanying decentralization of economic decision-making also changed the political and social landscape of China. Shenzhen's remarkable physical transformation and its image of modern urbanity set an example for all Chinese cities.

Deng Xiaoping visited Shenzhen only twice in his lifetime. However, in accordance with his belief that the CCP should decentralize authority to local levels, Deng entrusted and empowered local authorities to govern Shenzhen and the other SEZs. The very notion of specialized zones to attract overseas resources was based on a convergence of centralized planning and localized aspirations. Both of Deng's visits to Shenzhen were triggered by national criticism of the country's reforms. The news of his tours, photographs of his visits—and, most importantly, Deng's own words, which were broadcast to the nation—depicted a miraculous modern city full of shiny skyscrapers and wide boulevards, which in turn fueled the public's enthusiasm and aspirations for prosperity. The image of a socially stable Shenzhen also helped persuade skeptics and conservatives of the possibility that other Chinese cities might peacefully transition from a centrally planned socialist economy to a market economy, or, in the famously pragmatic words of Deng, to "socialism with Chinese characteristics." In his biography *Deng Xiaoping and the Transformation of China,* Ezra Vogel describes 1984 as the height of Deng's "Economic Offensive" and the peak of his popular support: "The TV cameras conveying the impressive construction that was taking place in Shenzhen to the rest of China laid the basis for public acceptance of the opening of other coastal areas later in the year."[83] The success of Shenzhen, or at least the successful image of the city, reassured Deng, and turned back the tide of national retreat from reforms.

Shenzhen, without a doubt, played a pivotal role in modern Chinese history. However, the early history of the region that would become Shenzhen in 1979 is less known. This region, located in the southern tip of the country, has witnessed centuries of massive transformations. While Deng Xiaoping was instrumental in shaping the myth of Shenzhen as a new city built on land of previously little significance, there are signs that it was precisely the region's history that motivated much of his determination to reform China. One such sign appears in Vogel's description of Deng Xiaoping's mood as he departed Shenzhen by boat along the Pearl River in 1992: "As the boat passed by the remains of a Qing dynasty customs house, Deng again passed on the essence of his departing message: China had been humiliated by the foreign imperialists, but that era had passed: 'Those who are backward get beaten. . . . We've been poor for thousands of years, but we won't be poor again. If we don't emphasize science, technology, and education, we will be beaten again.'"[84]

Part II of this book embraces the long regional history of Shenzhen, at which Deng's departing message just hinted in 1992. A full understanding of modern Shenzhen is not possible without knowledge of the region's history before 1979, a history that is ignored by most narratives on the city's development. The following chapter begins to excavate this history, uncovering key moments in the region's development from ancient maritime activities to the local commerce of the more "recent" Qing Dynasty. While the city experienced incredible economic and sociopolitical shifts during the 1980s, these shifts have deep connections to both ancient and more recent history—connections that are often hidden in plain sight.

PART II

REGIONAL HISTORY

3.

GATEWAY CITY TO THE SOUTH CHINA SEA

Cai Guangfu was born in 1905, and for much of his youth, he maintained the grounds of a beach-side temple dedicated to Tianhou, the Empress of Heaven. Located on the southern tip of Shenzhen's Shekou Peninsula, the temple was once one of the largest and most revered pilgrimage sites in Southern China. Cai recalled the annual celebration at the temple as a splendid affair:

> People from a radius of hundreds of miles called the Chiwan Tianhou Temple "the Grand Temple." Each year on the day of Tianhou's birth, hundreds of thousands of coastal fishermen from Hong Kong, Macau, Xiangshan, Dongguan, Huiyang, Haifeng, and overseas Chinese from Southeast Asian countries participated in the celebration. With banners fluttering on tens of thousands of vessels and gongs and drums awakening the heavens, the entire harbor bustled with noise and excitement. Such grand celebrations lasted until just before the [1949] liberation.[1]

Tianhou, also known as Mazu, Heavenly Mother, and Goddess of the South China Sea, is worshipped as a guardian of seafarers and anyone that lives on or by the sea. After centuries of Chinese trading and cultural exchange, her following has grown to tens of millions around the world, especially within coastal communities. Tianhou is worshipped by people of various faiths and ethnicities, across national borders and political regimes.[2] There are Tianhou temples all over the world, although the highest concentrations are in Taiwan (over five hundred temples),[3] Hong Kong (over sixty), and Shenzhen (over eleven).[4] Before 1949, however, the Chiwan Tianhou Temple was the epicenter. Here is a description of the Chiwan Temple during the annual pilgrimage:

> Owing to the magnificence of the ancient Chiwan Tianhou Temple, each year inhabitants of Hong Kong and Kowloon, both residing on land and sea, would go there to celebrate Tianhou's birthday, which falls on March 23rd of the lunar calendar. Tens of thousands of boats with colorful banners would be seen on the coast of Kowloon's Yau Ma Tei and Hong Kong's Connaught Road heading for Chiwan.[5]

The sight of the Grand Temple of Tianhou must have been awe-inspiring, particularly when approached from the open sea, with the distant mountain ranges in the background. On the sandy beach before the harbor, crowded with boats of various sizes and styles, the walled temple complex stands out prominently, surrounded on three sides by rising hills topped with flagged forts. From the pier on the beach, visitors come to an open ceremonial gate, followed by an arched stone bridge over a canal, which links the Pond of the Sun to the east and the Pond of the Moon to the west. The front entrance to the walled temple complex, the Gate of the Mountain, opens into the first of three public courtyards, which leads to the front hall, flanked on the east and west by tall incense towers; the second courtyard contains the large main hall, flanked by two side halls to the east and west; and the final courtyard opens into the three-storied back hall, with additional halls to each side. Outside the inner courtyard complex, further structures to the east and west include the drum tower, bell tower, and residence halls. The design and construction of the Chiwan Temple are unusually grand owing to the temple's canonization by its imperial ruler. Only three Tianhou Temples in China received this designation from the imperial court; the other two are in the city of Tianjin and the historic port city of Quanzhou.

The Chiwan Tianhou Temple was reputedly first built during the Song Dynasty (960–1279) at Chiwan Harbor, by then an important seaport.[6] The

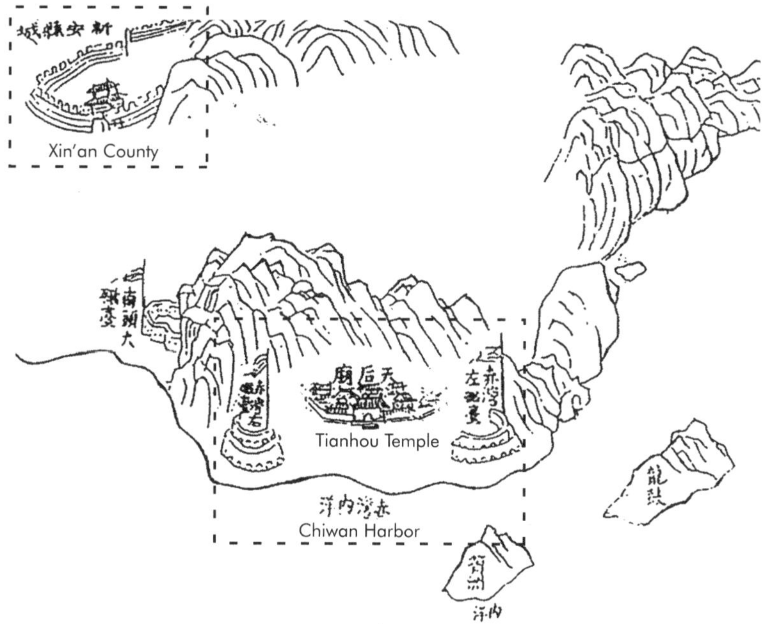

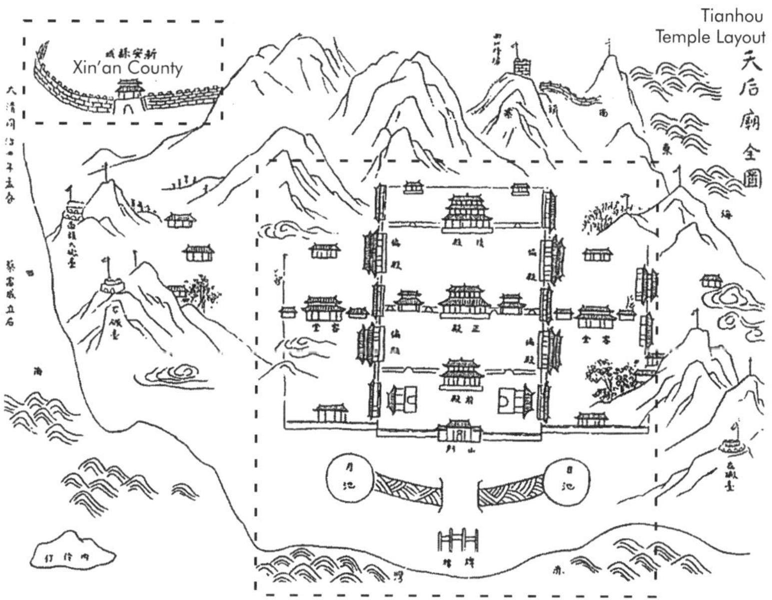

Qing Dynasty depictions of the historically important Chiwan Harbor and Tianhou Temple. A gateway between southern China and the South China Sea since the Tang Dynasty, Chiwan Harbor was left abandoned in the late nineteenth century, and revived for use in 1979 by the Shekou Industrial Zone.

waterway adjacent to Chiwan formed a natural deep sea harbor, making this a strategic location on the seafaring route to and from the Pearl River—the gateway between Southern China and the rest of the world.[7] By the Ming Dynasty (1368–1644), royal orders required all passing imperial court envoys and foreign ships to dock at Chiwan Harbor and conduct worship rituals at the temple.[8] Given its important status, in the subsequent centuries the temple was enlarged by successive local governments and gentry. By the end of the Qing Dynasty (1636–1912), the temple was reported to contain over 120 rooms and ninety-nine portals joined by interconnected complexes and courtyards.[9] The Qing Dynasty's "Record of Rebuilding Chiwan Tianhou Temple" noted its strategic location: "The location of Xin'an's Chiwan Tianhou Temple creates a natural shield for the province, creating a strategic junction to foreign waters, and guarding Humen and Macau, providing protection; forming a convergence between the seas to the east and north as the destination for homebound vessels; foreign ships from Champa, Java, Kmir, and Samboja must come to offer tribute, all must route this way and come ashore. . . . With the garrison stationed at Chiwan, boats and ships form a parade, and horses and carriages proceed continuously like a river."[10]

Facing the open sea at the mouth of the Pearl River and embraced by the foothills of Nanshan, or the Southern Mount, Chiwan's naturally formed deep water harbor served as a strategic port throughout China's extended maritime history. The harbor and adjacent townships and villages played central roles in the regional and national history during the territory's varied political evolutions and cultural transformations. "Xin'an" in the above record refers to Xin'an County, the administrative designation of the territory during China's Qing Dynasty. This contested territory has had many names and jurisdictions dating back to pre-imperial China. During the Qin Dynasty (221–206 BCE), when China's first emperor unified the country, this region was a part of *Nanhai Jun,* or Prefecture of the South Sea. Historical texts and archaeological findings indicate that the area (which formed part of the Nanhai Prefecture), which would later become Shenzhen, was already populous and relatively affluent by the time of the subsequent Han Dynasty (206 BCE–220 CE).[11] Archaeological work in Shenzhen over the past decades has uncovered numerous ancient settlements and burial sites dating as far back as the Neolithic age.[12] In addition to archaeological material, written records describing the region's history from the Han Dynasty onward also exist. The most comprehensive and reliable written records are a few surviving historic *Xianzhi,* or county annals. An important source of historical information in China, these encyclopedic records were compiled by major cities and townships throughout the country. They typically covered topics including historic events, weather, geography, governance and defense, people and culture, buildings and infrastructure, agriculture and commerce, education, and literature. Although the categories may differ between regions—or even between volumes, if they were compiled across multiple generations—all aimed to record the essence of each city. These records were usually initiated by regional governments and scholars and edited over time.

Shenzhen's historical county annals are titled according to the county's past administrative names. The earliest known *Bao'an Annual* documents a historical period of Bao'an County from the Jin Dynasty (265–420), when it spanned a region that included today's Shenzhen, Hong Kong, Zhuhai, and surrounding areas. This is the first document from the imperial period to identify the site that would later become Shenzhen as the region's political and administrative center, with the Bao'an County seat located in an area near today's Nantou Ancient City in Shenzhen. In 2002, seven kilometers north of the historic Chiwan Harbor, an archaeological team excavated a site of 1,600 square meters and found 3,198 cultural relics inside the moat of an ancient fort dating back to the Han Dynasty.[13] The excavated moat was thirty-eight meters wide and contained bricks from East Han (25–220), porcelain from the Three Kingdoms (220–280), and porcelain pottery from East Jin (317–420) and the Southern Dynasty (420–589).[14]

During the Tang Dynasty (618–907), and for the next 750 years, Bao'an County was incorporated in the larger Dongguan County. Therefore, the area's history was documented in later *Dongguan County Annals*. After the Yuan Dynasty fell in 1368, the former Bao'an County was reestablished as Xin'an County and remained intact until the end of China's imperial period in 1912. Most of the past annals from the earlier periods have been lost or are incomplete; the most complete surviving county annals were compiled during the Qing Dynasty. The 1819 edition of the *Xin'an County Annual* is the most commonly referenced for its accuracy and comprehensiveness.[15]

In 1914, three years after the fall of the Qing Dynasty and establishment of the Republic of China, the 1,500-year-old county name Bao'an (meaning "treasured peace") was reinstated. The region retained this name until 1979, when rural Bao'an County was changed to the urban city of Shenzhen.[16] Although it is commonly held that the site of the future Shenzhen contained just "a small *sleepy* fishing village" prior to 1979, Shenzhen's history prior to that fateful moment was much more complicated than this myth suggests. And like the history of many other great cities, it begins with salt.

THE POLITICS OF SALT

At the far end of the Pearl River estuarine system, the western coast of China was, for centuries prior to the urbanization of the 1970s and 1980s, a continuous swath of shallow salt wetlands, home to brine shrimp, fish, and species of local and migratory birds. The unique landscape also protected inland coastal areas from contaminants and sea surges. The subtropical climate and limited rainy season combined with the shallow mudflats along the coast to create natural salt marshes. As the brackish river water mixed with the sea, while the tide flowed in and out, the warm sun evaporated the water, leaving salt crystals for harvesting across acres of easily accessible marshland. It was salt—one of the most sought-after commodities in ancient times—that first drew the attention of northern rulers to the southernmost tip of this South Sea Prefecture. According to a recent report, salt was the oldest industry of both Shenzhen and Hong Kong: "To put the industry in context, there is evidence of the Imperial Salt Monopoly and salt-fields in active use, more than a thousand years before the first mention of Hong Kong's other two ancient industries of incense-wood production and pearl fishing. These salt production activities were also being carried out 1,300 years before the first settlement of any of today's indigenous clans in the area."[17]

Throughout China's long imperial era (2070 BCE–1912 CE), revenues from salt created empires and financed large-scale infrastructure projects from the Great Wall to the Forbidden City. During the Han Dynasty (206–220 CE), under the rule of the ambitious Emperor Wu, salt production and trade first became a unified industry controlled and operated by the imperial court. This imposed state control over the most profitable trades at the time—notably salt, iron, and liquor. The system established a financial and political power structure and allowed Emperor Wu to rule for fifty-four years, one of the longest reigns in China's imperial history.[18] With the arrival of a court-appointed administrator in the Pearl River Delta region, the Panyu Salt Works was established in 100 BCE, one of twenty-eight imperial salt works in the expansive Han Empire.[19] Without conclusive records of salt works in nearby coastal areas, historians have inferred that the salt works located in Shenzhen's Nantou area were the main hub of the Panyu Salt Works.[20]

However, these policies faced strong criticism from influential Confucian scholars at the time. In 81 BCE, six years after the death of Emperor Wu, the new Emperor Zhao invited more than sixty influential Confucian literati to the imperial court to discuss Emperor Wu's political and economic policy with the court officials.

In addition to the debate on state monopoly of trade, there were heated exchanges between Confucian scholars and the court officials on topics such as common law and implementation of order, military defense versus diplomacy, and the objectives of culture and education. The Han Dynasty book *Yan Tie Lun*, or *Discourses on Salt and Iron* contains a record of these discussions. Divided into sixty sections, it meticulously presents the rhetorical arguments, including colorful comments by each side, regarding their opponent's "coarse gowns" and "big and outdated words."[21] Following the two-day debate, imperial control of the liquor industry and the tax on liquor were abolished; however, the imperial government retained control over the salt and iron industries. This tension between intellectual and ideological schools of thought, regarding the purpose of the state, had great impact on the later history of China, including the periods of reforms in the late twentieth century.

During the subsequent and short-lived Three Kingdoms Dynasty (220–280), Emperor Sun Hao set up a Salt Commandant's Office at the Han Dynasty Dongguan salt works and promoted the local administrator to a prefecture commissioner.[22] A walled compound to house the Salt Commandant's Office was constructed at Nantou, and expanded during the Eastern Jin Dynasty (317–420).[23] Begun in the Han Dynasty, China's centralized salt monopoly would last another two thousand years until its abolishment on January 1, 2017.[24]

"SOUTHERN MIGRATION OF THE WELL-DRESSED"

The majority of those living in Nanhai Prefecture prior to the Han Dynasty were descendants of the Bai Yue, an ethnic group who had inhabited the coastal regions of South China since the first millennium BCE. The first migrant settlement in the region was triggered by Emperor Qin Shi Huang's conquest of Bai Yue around 219 to 210 BCE.[25] The migrants included forced settlers during the Qin Dynasty, deployed troops during the Han Dynasty, and failed rebel armies as well as refugees escaping from northern wars during the Jin Dynasties.[26]

The first period of large-scale migration occurred during the Western Jin Dynasty (265–316), when constant warfare in the northern borders and political unrest in the central plains led to an extensive southward movement of the population. In 317, the capital of the Jin Empire was moved from Luoyang to Jiankang (modern-day Nanjing). This marked the first moment in China's history when the political and cultural center of the country moved from the central plains to the southern region. As a result, the Guangdong and Guangxi Provinces received a significant wave of migrants from the North. Among the migrants escaping from the northern wars were affluent landowners and merchants. The relative wealth of these migrants prompted this period of Chinese history to be named "the Southern Migration of the Well-Dressed."[27]

The sudden surge in population and material wealth led to the restructuring of administrative, political, and economic boundaries in China's southern regions. In 331, the Eastern Jin Dynasty's Dongguan Prefecture was carved from the original Nanhai Prefecture, and an administrative center for Dongguan Prefecture and Bao'an County was set up. Dongguan Prefecture covered the southernmost coastal region including Bao'an County (modern-day Shenzhen, Hong Kong, Zhongshan, Zhuhai, Macau), as well as other counties in present-day Dongguan, Panyu, Huiyang, and Huilai.[28] As the capital of Dongguan Prefecture and Bao'an County, the seat of government was built upon the foundations of the earlier walled compound around the Salt Commandant's Office. Being the political and commercial center of Bao'an and five other counties, the compound grew into an urban settlement. The development of the capital, later known as Nantou City, or "City of the Southern Tip," marked the beginning of Nantou as a regional civic center.

Throughout subsequent political and territorial changes, the governmental seat of Bao'an County remained at the site of the future Nantou City. Dongguan Prefecture's administrative center was later moved repeatedly to different areas with each regime change, before it was finally abolished in the Sui Dynasty (581–619). Throughout these various dynastic changes, Nantou City continued to function as the political and administrative center of the region. During the height of the Tang Dynasty (618–907), the southern salt works came to be known and valued throughout China for its high-quality salt and productivity. The Dongguan Salt Works of Bao'an was one of the three largest in China's southern (Lingnan) areas.

Beginning in the middle of the Tang Dynasty, invaders from the northern borders and rebels from the central plains sparked a second large wave of southern migration. During the late Tang Dynasty, under the rule of Emperor Xizhong (873–888), taxes on the salt and iron industries from Bao'an County were exclusively used to cover military expenses involved in quelling the uprisings. However, the increased drive for profit created hardship for the salt works and workers, which led to a decline in salt production.[29]

To revive the industry and encourage production, the Northern Song court (960–1127) introduced remedial policies and improved working conditions for the salt workers. Salt production in Bao'an County reached its height during this time. Between 960 and 1023, salt production had increased more than twenty times. Additional salt works locations were established around the region.[30] During the Northern Song Dynasty, under the rule of Emperor Shenzhong (1067–1085), the resale price of salt was nearly ten times the cost of its procurement. Revenues from salt works became a major source of income for the Song Empire and supported the famed Song currency reforms as well as military defense expenses.[31] Some salt came from deep salt wells in inland areas, but the majority was from the coastal areas.

Increased production from the salt works during the Song Dynasty coincided with one of the highest surges in population growth in the Shenzhen area. Many were descendants of earlier refugee migrants from the late Tang and early Song periods, who had escaped conflicts in China's Central Plains and settled in the Guangdong and Fujian area.[32] In the mid- to late Song Dynasty, these clans mobilized a second-stage move further south, attracted by the growing economy. In 1273, the Mongol invaders defeated the Song army and established the Yuan Dynasty. The Song imperial rulers and their families, along with noblemen clans and their servants, fled the capital city of Lin'an (today's Hangzhou) and embarked on a two-year southward journey. They met with former governor and resistance general Wen Tianxiang in Guangdong in 1277, and continued south to the area of present-day Shenzhen and Hong Kong. The last Song emperor, the seven-year-old Zhao Bing, was crowned while in exile on Hong Kong's Lantau Island in 1278. The remaining Song army mounted military comebacks but lost the final Yashan Naval Battle in 1279. In Hong Kong's Kowloon area, a large stone tablet attributed to "Sung Wong Toi," the Hau Wong Temple, and the burial site of the last Song empress marked these final years in the history of the Song Dynasty. The temple still exists, but the burial site at Kowloon City was destroyed to make way for the building of the Holy Trinity Cathedral in 1890. The young Emperor Zhao Bing's tomb was found in Shenzhen's Chiwan Village next to the harbor. It is the only emperor's tomb located in the South, a solitary exception in

China's history. One of the most enduring records from the end of the Song Dynasty is a poem written by Wen Tianxiang: "Speaking of terror at the Seashore of Terror. Breathing of loneliness on the Ocean of Loneliness. Who in all ages could escape death? The loyal heart shall continue to shine in the annals of history."[33] These lines became one of China's best-known verses, continuously cited by later generations. What is less known is that Wen Tianxiang composed the poem while he was in the Shenzhen area. The Ocean of Loneliness, or *Lingding Yang*, refers to the bay that forms Chiwan Harbor. When Wen Tianxiang was captured after a failed military attack and sent to prison in the Yuan capital, his family members, who had traveled south along with the Song army, remained in the area. The Wen Clan first settled near Shenzhen's Shajing area, eventually growing to over twenty thousand in number, inhabiting many villages in Shenzhen, Hong Kong, and beyond.[34]

Historically referred to as the third and final wave of "Southern Migration of the Well-Dressed," this move included remnants of Song officials and military members, extended royal family, and fallen noblemen clans. They were the first recorded "indigenous Cantonese Clans" of Shenzhen.[35] Many large village settlements in Shenzhen's western and southern coastal areas were established by these groups during the twilight of the Song Dynasty. These areas—presently known as Nanshan, Futian, and Luohu Districts—would later become the site of the special economic zone.

CHIWAN HARBOR AND THE MARITIME SILK ROAD

During the Song Dynasty, the majority of the region's civilian population were coastal salt workers. The areas now occupied by present-day Dongguan, Shenzhen, and Hong Kong incorporated the highest densities of salt works and salt fields in the country.[36] Among the largest were the Dongguan Salt Works (Nantou area), Guide Salt Works (Shajing area), Huangtian Salt Works (Bao'an Airport area), and Hainan Salt Ground (Hong Kong's Lantau Island). The large quantities of salt were loaded onto salt junks and carried up the Pearl River to the Canton Port in Guangzhou. In addition to the salt production tax, there were collection, transportation, and storage tariffs, collected at each stage of handling the goods. As the volume of salt transactions increased, so did the wealth of the port city of Guangzhou.

In addition to salt making and transportation, trade in porcelain thrived along the regional rivers and sea coast. China's maritime activities in the region bordering the South China Sea stretch back to the Qin and Han Dynasties, and surged during the Sui and Tang Dynasties.[37] As navigation and trade expanded in the South China Sea and the Indian Ocean, ships carrying spices from Southeast Asia and Persia reached the Canton Port in Guangzhou. Persian traders reached China by land via the Silk Road from Central Asia; however, seafaring merchants came from Southeast Asia, Arabia, and the East Africa Swahili coast via the South China Sea, along the ancient Maritime Silk Road.[38] Increased international trading activities initiated cultural exchanges in addition to commerce. Sea routes between China and India led to the spread of Buddhism in Guangzhou, and many local temples were quickly established. The Guangzhou Huaisheng Mosque, built in the Tang Dynasty, served the Muslim community in the region.

From the Tang Dynasty onward, all merchant boats bound for Guangzhou were required to pass by the western coast of Shenzhen to avoid the increasingly shallow waters of the Pearl River Estuary. Owing to abundant fresh water supplies in the area, Qianhai Bay, encompassing Nantou, was a popular harbor for merchant ships to stop and replenish. The Tang court established a foreign affairs envoy at Guangzhou, an administrative position designed to regulate the increasing number of maritime trade vessels entering and leaving the Canton Port. In 736, the imperial court established the Tunmen Military Town at Nantou and stationed two thousand soldiers there under the direct command of the military general of southern China.[39] Throughout the Tang and Song Dynasties, Tunmen Town and Chiwan Harbor farther south grew in military and commercial importance.

By the Song Dynasty, China was active in commerce along the ancient Maritime Silk Road. Wreckage discovered in 1987 in the South China Sea was revealed to be a well-preserved Song wooden ship dating back to the early Southern Song Dynasty (1127–1279).[40] Named "Nanhai No. 1," the twenty-two-meter-long ship contained gold and bronze artifacts as well as a full cargo of fine porcelain pottery marked by kiln stamps from renowned makers in present-day Jiangxi and Fujian Provinces. The Shenzhen area served as a major stopover well into the Song and Ming Dynasties (960–1644), as was documented in the county annual's description of the Chiwan Tianhou Temple:

> Chiwan borders the sea, beholding the beauty of Mt. Luofu and Mt. Wutong on the left while overlooking the fortresses of Humen and Longxue on the right. Its land is remarkably stunning; its deity is

mysteriously efficacious. When officials are sent abroad on diplomatic missions or when envoys from Champa (Vietnam), Java, Kmir (Cambodia), and Samboja (Sumatra) come to offer tribute, they all go through the port of Chiwan. During the era of Xuanhe in the Song Dynasty (1119–1125), Imperial Advisor Lu Yundi was on a diplomatic voyage to Korea, when high winds sank many of his ships on the way. The Goddess Tianhou rescued him by bestowing him a giant timber of *nanmu* for his safe crossing. In the eighth year of Yongle (1411), Imperial Envoy Zhang Yuan was sent on a diplomatic mission to Siam. He built a temple at Chiwan. These were the beginnings of the Tianhou Temple at Chiwan.[41]

Imperial Envoy Zhang Yuan was the deputy commander of Zheng He, China's legendary admiral who commanded the world's greatest armada during the Ming Dynasty (1368–1644). Zheng He's expeditions in the South China Sea and the Indian Ocean were financed by the imperial court and ordered by Emperor Zhu Di, who sought to demonstrate authority, establish tributary diplomacy, and facilitate international trade relationships. As the emperor's head eunuch, who first came to the Ming court as a young prisoner, Zheng He was a knowledgeable scholar, a pious follower of Islam and Buddhism, and a formidable military commander.[42]

Zheng He made the first of at least seven voyages in 1405, nearly a century before Vasco da Gama's arrival in West India and Christopher Columbus's North American expedition. The maiden voyage was not completely smooth. According to the Qing Dynasty book *Record of Conferring Imperial Order to the Heavenly Empress,* Zheng He's fleet encountered a strong typhoon in the *Daxingyang* of Guangzhou (waters near Chiwan) and nearly capsized.[43] Zheng prayed to Tianhou to save the lives of those in the fleet, and the storm subsided. Upon his safe return to China at the end of the voyage, Zheng He reported his encounter to the imperial court and received orders to construct the Tianhou Temple. Imperial envoy Zhang Yuan was sent to Chiwan to oversee construction in 1411. In addition to rebuilding the Chiwan Temple in a grander form, the Ming court issued an order requiring all imperial officials to dock and worship at Chiwan before heading out to sea. This made Chiwan an even more important node on the Maritime Silk Road route. Over the course of twenty-eight years, Zheng He made at least seven long-distance voyages across the South China Sea and Indian Ocean, reaching over thirty countries including India, Java, the Malacca Strait, Kenya, and Somalia, and traveling beyond to the Persian Gulf, the Red Sea, and the coast of Africa. Along the way, Zheng He dominated rebels, captured pirates, promoted commerce, and expedited cultural exchange among nations of various languages, ethnicities, and religions.[44] In addition to observing both Buddhism and Islam, Zheng He was also a key figure in the spread of Tianhou worship among common seafarers and at the imperial court. His custom of ceremonial prayer to Tianhou had an impact not only on China, but also on many countries bordering the South China Sea and Indian Ocean. Tianhou temples were erected in many coastal countries, some even with shrines dedicated to Zheng He himself.[45]

LOTUS CITY BY THE FORBIDDEN SEA

Naval defense troops had been stationed in Shenzhen's Nantou area since the Tang Dynasty, and it became an increasingly strategic location during the Song, Yuan, and Ming Dynasties. Over the centuries, the Nantou area grew in size and became an increasingly important center for political governance, trading, and shipping; during the Ming Dynasty, it also became a key site of naval and military command. Large groups of migrants from nearby provinces, including the Zheng Clan from Guangdong, and the Huang, Lin, Zhang, and Su Clans from Fujian, also settled here during the Ming Dynasty.[46] By this time, local industry had diversified to include fisheries, farming, and various service trades for the growing population.

Salt making still thrived as one of the dominant industries. Owing to harsher working conditions, however, many former salt workers turned to production and trade outside the auspices of the salt monopoly, and were referred to as smugglers. During the late Song Dynasty (1173), following failed interventions by the local army, the Guangdong Salt and Tea Commander personally led an imperial troop to arrest "salt smugglers" at Hainan Salt Ground on Hong Kong's Lantau Island. Local salt workers revolted and chased the imperial administrator all the way back to Guangzhou.

The Ming Dynasty's tightening of maritime restrictions corresponded with an increase in piracy and the presence of unfriendly foreign fleets in the South China Sea. Many of the islands around Shenzhen and Hong

Kong were controlled by smugglers and pirates. Many of these pirates—commonly called *Wokou,* or Japanese bandits, by the Ming court—were former Chinese salt workers, fishermen, and soldiers.[47] They often raided coastal salt works, villages, and government shipments.

To protect the coastal regions and the Canton Port in Guangzhou up the Pearl River, in 1394 the Ming court established the Dongguan Defense Garrison to act as the "Defense of Humen and Shield of Guangzhou."[48] The Chiwan Smoke Tower was simultaneously constructed on top of the Southern Mount behind Chiwan Harbor, as a warning system to alert Guangzhou of intruders from the South China Sea. A regional military command was created, with troops headed by a general officer. To accommodate the large population of military officials and their households, as well as numerous service staff, the Song Dynasty Tunmen Walled City was expanded to become the walled city of the Dongguan Defense Garrison.[49] Thus, over the course of a millennium, Nantou City was subject to continuous transformation—from its foundation as the Salt Commandant's Office of the Jin Dynasty in the third century, to the reinforced Dongguan Prefecture and Bao'an County Fort in the fourth century, to the Tang Dynasty Tunmen Military Town (with a commander and two thousand soldiers) in the eighth century, to the Song Dynasty's enlarged Tunmen Walled City, and finally to the Dongguan Defense Garrison in the fourteenth century.

In 1394, the year that the Dongguan Defense Garrison was established, the Dapeng Defense Garrison was constructed at the eastern end of Shenzhen's sea coast. Stationed with military generals and an army of two thousand, the Dapeng Garrison was designed to protect the land and waters along the extent of the southern coast of Guangdong Province. The increase in military personnel created additional demand for agriculture to sustain the community, and specifically for cash crops to subsidize military expenditure. Military-controlled farm operations were formed, and many local villagers were forced to enlist as soldiers and work in the fields.[50]

The Ming Dongguan Defense Garrison was protected by a large fortress wall: approximately two kilometers long and seven meters high, it narrowed from a thickness of seven meters at the base to 3.5 meters at the top.[51] Covered with carved stone, the rammed-earth wall was punctuated with four gates to allow passage via the north, east, west, and south sides. The wall was built to protect the administrative and military operations in the city, not to keep out those living beyond the city. During most of China's

Qing Dynasty Naval Defense Map, demonstrating the strategic location of Xin'an Walled City (above). Qing Dynasty depiction of Xin'an Walled City (below). Locations of the historic wall and civic buildings are still discernable in Shenzhen's Nantou Historic City urban village today.

imperial rule, there were no residential or commercial boundaries dividing cities from countryside.[52] In fact, densely settled villages outside the main south gate formed a continuous urban cluster and gave rise to the folk name "Lotus City" during this period. The fort was located on a slightly raised hill, with gentle ridges, resembling lotus petals, radiating out of the city to the west and north. From the Southern Gate stretched the long stem of the lotus, a string of densely populated villages: Nanshan, Nanyuan, Beitou, Daxin, Chungxia, Guankou, and Yijia, extending all the way down to the South Mount and Chiwan Harbor. These villages supported life inside the fort, with villagers coming and going at will. Residents inside the fort city included not only administrative and military personnel, but also individuals engaged in commerce, crafts, and trade to service villages throughout the county.

During the Ming Dynasty, Nantou City served as a base for administrative governance and military protection, not only for Bao'an County, but for all the waters along the entire southern coast of Guangdong. In 1521, the Provincial Judicial Commissioner Wang Hong stationed at Nantou received orders from the imperial court to expel a Portuguese fleet led by Fernão Peres de Andrade from their occupied island and surrounding waters. Wang Hong led the Ming navy in multiple battles against the Portuguese fleet. He combined traditional Chinese naval tactics of utilizing fire boats with newer technology gleaned from captured Portuguese cannons.[53] The Portuguese sustained heavy damage and casualties in the 1521 Battle of Tunmen and 1522 Battle of Xicaowan, with only a few men managing to escape back to Malacca in October 1521.[54] This was the first military encounter of the sixteenth century between China and the rising Western powers. After a few decades of further negotiations but no further military interaction, the Portuguese government signed an agreement with the Ming court, promising to obey imperial Chinese laws and pay an annual rental levy for the use of Macau Island as a trading base.

With the continued threat of invasions and an escalation in well-organized pirate attacks, Nantou transitioned during the mid-sixteenth century from land-based to water-based military defense. In 1565, the Regional Military Command was restructured as the Nantou Marine Camp with over one hundred battleships and thousands of naval forces. The Nantou Marine Camp also acted as the command center for five other marine camps along the coastal sea of Guangdong. The increase in military power corresponded to a rise in coastal raids by bandits and pirates, which put local villages and townships in a state of constant instability. As the political center of Dongguan County was far from the Nantou coastal area, local residents petitioned the Ming court to establish stronger local administrative power. In 1573, with the support of Provincial Judicial Vice Commissioner Liu Wen, Xin'an County was established to strengthen local governance and increase efficiency in self-defense mobilization.[55] The name Xin'an, "New Safety," was derived from the phrase "Reform the Old and Construct the New; Turn Danger into Safety."[56]

As the new county seat of Xin'an, the Dongguan Defense Garrison fort was once again adapted and strengthened. In 1577, subsidiary fortifications, including three additional fortress towers, were constructed around the east, west, and south gates. With the county's new administrative status came more civic and cultural facilities, including schools, temples, clinics, and markets.[57] Residents of Xin'an County enjoyed a period of relative stability and prosperity. In 1575, the local village clans built a shrine dedicated to Wang Hong and Liu Wen, commemorating the former's triumph against the Portuguese at the Battle of Tunmen and the latter's support for establishing Xin'an County. The Wang-Liu Public Shrine was constructed not inside Nantou City, but south of the city gate in the bustling coastal village of Daxin.

Throughout the late sixteenth and early seventeenth centuries, Ming court administrators and navy commanders stationed at Nantou City continued to combat threats from defector uprisings, peasant rebellions, maritime smugglers, and pillaging pirates. With the fall of the Ming Dynasty and rise of the Qing Dynasty, the Xin'an Marine Camp and Dapeng Marine Camp were reorganized and incorporated into the central Guangdong Navy. The command center of Xin'an Camp remained within Nantou Fort, and the walled city was continuously reinforced. In 1644, the fortress wall surrounding the city was reinforced and increased in height by another two meters.[58]

During the Qing Dynasty, the imperial court continued the policy of *Haijin*, or sea prohibition, and imposed further restrictions on maritime activities. In 1647, to quell anti-Qing rebellions in the region, the court issued "The Imperial Order to Pacify Guangdong Province," which prohibited private boats from navigating near the coast of Guangdong.[59] The order was intended to strengthen the court's military control over the southern coast, but it resulted in the prohibition of all coastal fishing, trade, and shipping activities. Fishing and trading vessels were confiscated and destroyed. By 1656, the ban had been extended from Guangdong to Tianjin and the provinces of Zhejiang, Fujian, Jiangnan, and Shandong, closing off the entire eastern coast of China.[60] The whole country's economy suffered as the coastal salt and fishing industries were abandoned. The

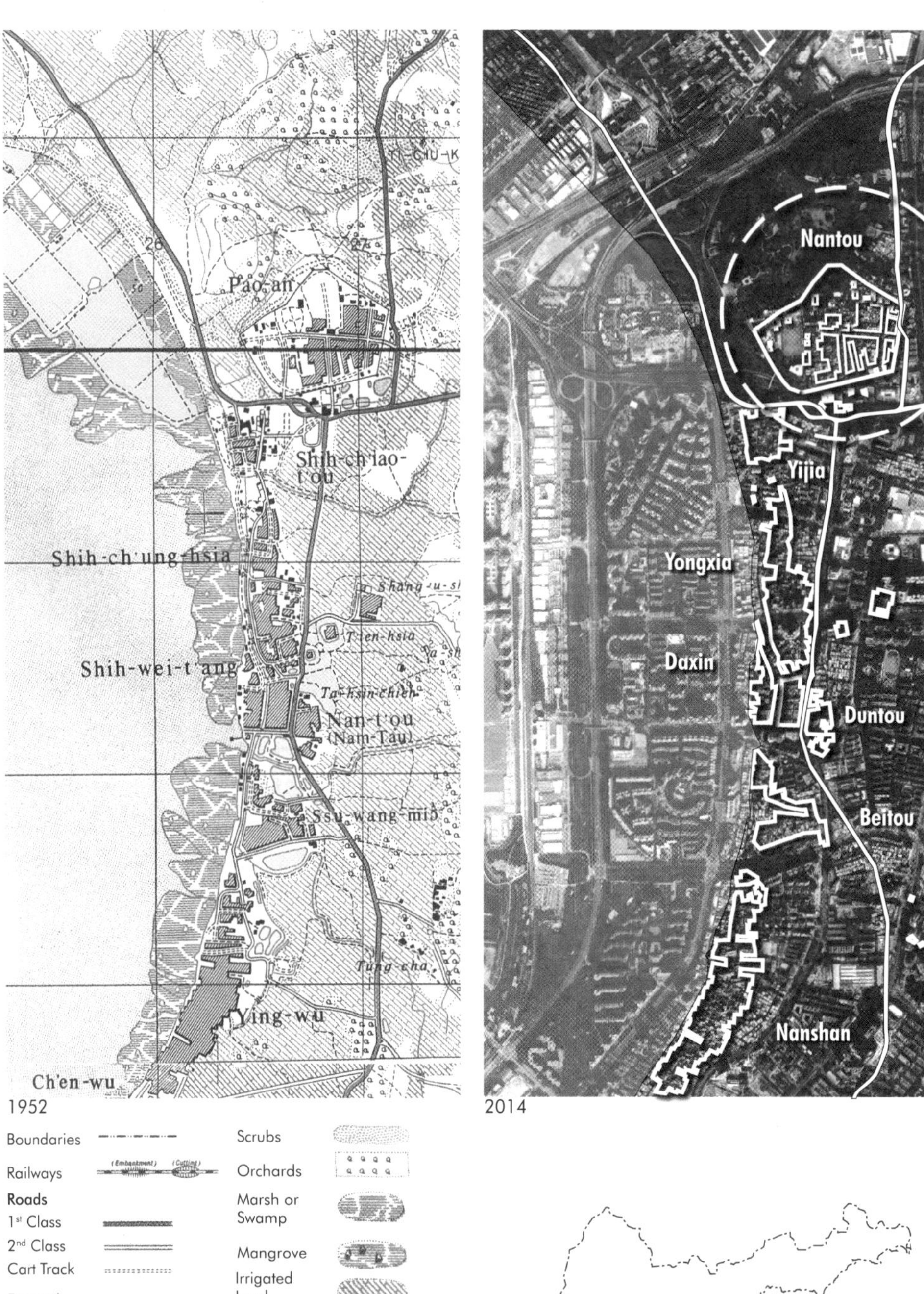

Survey map (1952) compared with satellite image (2014) of Shenzhen's western coastline in today's Nanshan District. Nantou Ancient City in the north, with successive large villages along the former western coast. The former coastal villages are discernable in the satellite image as now land-locked urban villages.

Qing Dynasty marked the final stage in China's progression toward shutting out the world.

In 1661 Zheng Chenggong, an ex-official of the Ming Dynasty and chief general of the anti-Qing movement, took control of the island of Taiwan. He drove off Dutch colonizers in Tainan Town and made Taiwan his command base, from which he continued launching rebellions against the Qing court. To prevent coastal settlers from supporting Zheng, the imperial court ordered the evacuation of all villages and towns within twenty-five kilometers of the coast in Guangdong, Fujian, Zhejiang, and Jiangsu. Two-thirds of Xin'an County—all of present-day Hong Kong and most of Shenzhen—fell within the evacuation zone. To ensure that the region was evacuated, imperial soldiers were sent in. Most of the inhabitants were not aware of the imperial decree until the Qing army arrived, brutally forcing people from their homes, destroying townships, and burning crops to the ground.[61]

As ships were prohibited, those forced out had to make their way to inland regions on foot; many died during the harsh journey. Farmland was scarce in these inland regions, which were less fertile than the coastal regions. Unable to subsist through farming, many families were broken apart. To survive, women and children were sold into servitude while men had to enlist in the Qing army.[62] Nantou City, the surrounding countryside, and the coastal sea were left empty.

"EIGHT NOTES ON REVITALIZATION"

"The young and elderly huddle in pits and gullies; the able-bodied have scattered far and beyond. Seen from above, wild grass and ruins are everywhere. Not even the sound of birds can be heard. There is nothingness."[63] This 1670 account of a desolate landscape was written by Li Kecheng, the newly commissioned Xin'an County magistrate. Originally from China's northern region of Liaodong, he was sent by the Qing imperial court to restore the region after the coastal restrictions were lifted in 1667. Beginning in 1668, indigenous villagers were allowed to return.[64] As many had perished during the forced evacuation process, the return was a slow one. Although coastal fishing and trade were again permitted, many who had suffered from the evictions were eager to leave the country altogether and make a living overseas. Thousands of former fishermen and maritime traders made their own boats and sailed away from China via the South China Sea. The *Haijin* coastal restrictions had inadvertently increased the international diaspora of overseas Chinese. Around half of those who left the region for various Southeast Asian countries never returned, even when the restrictions were lifted.[65] By the time Li Kecheng arrived in 1670, the population of the entire Xin'an County was only three thousand.[66]

Although it had been two years since the relaxation of the coastal restrictions and the reestablishment of Nantou as the administrative center of Xin'an County, the coastal region was still a wasteland when Li Kecheng arrived. Settling at the Magistrate's Hall inside Nantou City, Li Kecheng observed: "The town had been abandoned for such a long time, with no defenses inside or outside."[67] As Li surveyed the region in the following months, he noted that the few who had returned to their old homes had no resources to help them start over. The fishing and salt trades were completely destroyed, and the damaged roads made transportation of goods difficult.[68] Hoping to attract people to the region, Li immediately ordered the provision of farm animals and planting seeds to new settlers. The county government also contributed to the effort, providing funds to repair buildings and encampments without taxation.

In 1671, a powerful hurricane swept through the region and destroyed the nascent efforts to rebuild. To raise morale and attract new settlers, Li Kecheng composed eight poems that capitalized on the historical and cultural heritage of the region. Each of the scenes highlighted a different location in the territory of Xin'an County, conveying the area's cultural and moral values, and interweaving these with the region's natural geography and built heritage. Titled "The Eight Scenes of Xin'an," the poems and accompanying illustrations were disseminated throughout the region:[69]

ONE: "The Splendor of Chiwan"
TWO: "Heavenly Pond of the Wutong Peak"
THREE: "Path of the Beidu Monk"
FOUR: "Aged Trees on Mount Can"
FIVE: "Peach and Plum Blossoms on Mount Lu"
SIX: "Yu Le Village Hot Springs Lake"
SEVEN: "Sweet Waterfall on the Turtle Sea"
EIGHT: "Mirage City at the Dragon Cove"

This opening scene of Chiwan Harbor was an obvious choice for Li Kecheng. He wanted to restore the region's reputation for importance and prosperity. During the Qing Dynasty, the Tianhou Temple at Chiwan

Mid-seventeenth-century Qing Dynasty *Eight Scenes of Xin'an.* Drawings with accompanying poems were disseminated to attract new settlers after decades of natural and military disasters.

gained increasing recognition from the imperial court. Eventually, it became one of only three temples in China to receive imperial recognition. The other two Tianhou Temples were located in Tianjin and Quanzhou, the two most important ports on the Maritime Silk Road route during the

Ming Dynasty. Li Kecheng's poetic description of these port areas, designed to attract newcomers, contrasted starkly with the grim reality of his private records:

> *Ode to the Eight Scenes of Xin'an: Outlining the Beauty of Chiwan*[70]
> Stretching beyond the horizon roll blue waves of ten thousand acres.
> The temple at the entrance to the ocean stabilizes the mountains.
> The grace of this sacred court spreads far and wide like rain and dew.
> Envoys from far-away countries come in great numbers to offer tribute.
> . . .

All the sites referenced by Li Kecheng are in the written records of the *Xin'an County Annals*.[71] Li might have used the *Dongguan County Annals* to gain knowledge of the local culture and heritage. In fact, his inspiration for the "Eight Scenes of Xin'an" came from the "Eight Scenes of Dongguan," a legacy from past magistrates.

Aside from writing the "Eight Scenes of Xin'an," Li Kecheng's main legacy was launching the "Eight Proposals for Revitalization" to attract returnees and new immigrants to the area. The efforts to rebuild the region were extensive: "Encourage reclamation to increase the nation's tax revenue; correct attitude and morality of scholar-bureaucrats in order to revitalize education and cultural inheritance; build the city walls to keep invaders away from the homeland; build raised platforms and military camps for border defense; abolish officials' extra income and encourage donations; prohibit one person's control over all affairs in the village in order to maintain incorruptible rule; strictly implement the Bao-jia system to investigate the treacherous; and check false litigation to pacify the kindhearted people."[72] Li Kecheng's achievements were recorded in the *Kangxi Xin'an County Annals*. In addition to reconstructing buildings, fixing infrastructure, and providing farming equipment, he emphasized the importance of civic order and peaceful resolutions to disputes. The *Annals* indicate that during his tenure as magistrate, the county jail interned fewer prisoners than the norm at that time. He also personally led military efforts to rid the region of the remaining bandits who continued to plunder the villages.

From 1672 onward, Li Kecheng oversaw major repairs to buildings and infrastructure inside Nantou Fort. An expanded central boulevard stretched from the Southern Gate (the fort's main entrance) all the way to the Magistrate's Court on the highest slope in the center of the city. Parallel to this road, five additional north-south streets and three east-west streets formed an orderly grid. He also oversaw the restoration of Xin'an County's farmland: in 1671, one year into his tenure as magistrate, 7,060 acres of farmland were reclaimed, followed by an additional 11,200 acres in 1672; 2,749 acres in 1673; 2,474 acres in 1674; and another 64 acres in 1675.[73] In just five years, most of the region's farmland was restored to arable fields.

The revived economy brought some of the previous settlers back to the region: the Cai Clan returned to their village site of Caiwuwei, and the Zeng Clan returned to their walled village of Dawan Shiju in the Pingshan area.[74] Following the dissolution of the anti-Qing movement in Taiwan in 1683, the coastal restrictions were completely lifted. More migrants from rural areas around the country moved into Xin'an County.

A large number of Hakka clans migrated to Xin'an County during this period, responding to continued efforts by the Qing imperial court to encourage new settlers. The Hakka were originally ethnic Han people who moved to the southern regions between the fourth and tenth centuries, escaping warfare and natural disasters in the Central Plains. They first settled in the border areas between Jiangxi, Fujian, and Guangdong. In the following centuries, they intermarried with the local ethnic minorities, creating a mixed culture and blend of languages. The Hakka culture and language matured and formalized during the Song and Yuan Dynasties. Most of the Hakka clans in present-day Shenzhen and Hong Kong relocated there after the coastal prohibition order was lifted. Hakka people, in particular, were actively encouraged to move to Xin'an County around the end of the seventeenth century.[75] As the coastal areas were already settled by migrant Cantonese clans from Guangdong, Fujian, and Southern Jiangxi, the Hakka clans settled farther inland and in the mountainous areas of Shenzhen and Hong Kong.

As the countryside grew more populous, Nantou City became an increasingly important political, commercial, and cultural center. In 1811 and 1817, court-financed constructions were added to the original street pattern from the Ming Dynasty city layout.[76] The Nantou Fort City became known for its bustling streets and was referred to as the "City of Nine Streets."

According to the *Xin'an County Annals,* the population of Xin'an County in 1632 was 17,871—a number that dwindled to 2,172 following the forced evacuation order in 1668. Spurred by the restoration efforts and encouragement of new migration, the population had grown to 239,112 by 1818.[77] The population growth was greatest among migrant Hakka villagers who originally settled in Guangdong. Large Hakka walled compounds, surrounded by fortresses and defensive moats, were constructed in the northern areas. Some of the compounds accommodated populations of one thousand villagers each. By the end of the Qing Dynasty in the nineteenth century, immigrant Hakka clans amounted to 60 percent of Xin'an County's total population.[78]

EVOLUTIONS AND REVOLUTIONS

By the beginning of the nineteenth century, Nantou City was bustling with shops, administrative halls, temples, shrines, markets, and schools. Just as the city walls and streets had evolved over the generations, many historic buildings inside Nantou City took on new functions. The early sixteenth-century Maritime Defense Hall was converted in 1679 into the Dongguan Headquarters Hall, and in 1801 it was repurposed as the Fenggang Academy.[79] The building's decommission and conversion into an establishment of education and scholarship was initiated by a direct decree from the Qing imperial court. The building complex itself, described in detail in the *Jiaqing Xin'an County Annals,* was quite remarkable:

> The Lecture Hall is located at the center of the compound with a front balcony and a paved path beneath. On the left is the East Hall and on the right, the West Hall. At the front is the gate to the halls, with two ancient ficus trees outside it. A screen wall shields the front of the gate, beyond which is the main entrance, where there is a two-room lodge for the gate keepers. At the rear of the Lecture Hall is the Hall of the Sages, and further back is the Hall of the Stars (with a plaque that reads "The Pavilion of Listening to the Rain," inscribed by Zhang Quan, Director of the Provincial Grain Administration). The sides of the Hall are lined with carved railings, and a total of eight reading rooms are arranged on the left and right of the building. Additional open space behind the building is enclosed with walls.[80]

The imperial rulers' emphasis on education was a legacy passed down through a millennium of dynastic changes, and China's southern regions were particularly committed. The precedent for Li Kecheng's "Eight Scenes of Xin'an" was set by the earlier "Eight Scenes of Dongguan," which included an important scene entitled "Autumn Crossing at the Phoenix Platform," in reference to the public announcement of the winners of the autumn imperial examination at the city's Phoenix Platform. The imperial examination system first emerged in China around 605 CE, during the Sui Dynasty (581–618). Its protocols had matured by the time of the Song Dynasty, and extended into the Qing Dynasty. Regardless of background, those who passed the highest level of the imperial exam, which was presided over by the emperor, were given positions as government administrators. Only scholars who excelled in the imperial exam were eligible for appointment as imperial court officials. The hierarchy of appointments was determined according to individual performance. This is one of the reasons why most of Xin'an's past administrators were able to compose scholarly poetry and emphasized the importance of education. This merit-based examination system, which enabled upward social mobility through scholarship, rather than birthright, was an exceptional institution—not just for China, but for the world as well.

Every village or township in Xin'an County had its own schools or study halls, which taught *Sishu Wujing,* or Four Books and Five Classics, the traditional Confucian canon. It consisted of Confucian texts and ancient classics passed on from the Spring and Autumn Periods (770–476 BCE), allegedly selected and edited by Confucius himself. Those in Xin'an who desired scholarly training past primary level would go to Nantou City to study in one of the academies. The designation "academy" could only be conferred by the imperial court, and a few schools in Nantou City had achieved this distinction. Traditionally influential institutions, the academies had matured during the Song Dynasty's era of artistic and cultural freedom. In a departure from the policy of earlier dynasties, however, the Qing Dynasty permitted the establishment of academies only in major cities, so that it could easily monitor and control them. During the early Qing Dynasty, the government forbade the establishment of new academies altogether, and closely monitored the activities of existing academies, vigilantly seeking to regulate their sociopolitical influence.

The imperial court's support for the Fenggang Academy coincided with the eventual stabilization of the Qing reign. The court followed the historical practice of financially supporting the academies' formation and growth while shaping and controlling their loyalty. The Fenggang Academy went on to become the most influential academy in Xin'an County, offering the highest level of studies available in the region. The principals were carefully selected from a pool of notable scholars, and the institution also specialized in archiving and scholarly editing of publications and manuscripts. The teachers and scholars were entrusted with the important tasks of maintaining and updating the county annals, the tablets of which were stored at the academy for centuries.

Just as Nantou City and the rest of Xin'an County were settling into a period of relative stability, the Opium Wars (1839–1842, 1856–1860) disrupted the region, causing conflicts that lasted for decades. The Qing court in Beijing signed several treaties, in which lands and waters belonging to Xin'an County were ceded to the British in exchange for very little to China; these came to be known in Chinese history as the "Unequal Treaties." After the British victory in the First Opium War (1839–1842), the Qing court ceded the island of Hong Kong to the United Kingdom. Xin'an was recorded to have won "The Battle of Nantou City" in August 1842. The county magistrate Wang Shouren had only five hundred soldiers, but had learned a lesson from Wang Hong during the anti-Portuguese invasion of the sixteenth century. Wang Shouren mobilized thousands of volunteer villagers, who equipped their fishing vessels for battle.[81] With additional military support from the Qing army stationed in nearby Humen, they successfully deterred British naval advancement at the mouth of the Pearl River, next to Chiwan Harbor. However, during the Second Opium War (1856–1860), the Qing imperial court ordered the cession of the Kowloon Peninsula, a territory that belonged to Xin'an County, to the United Kingdom in accordance with "the Sino-British Convention of Peking."

The British colony of Hong Kong consisted of Hong Kong Island and the Kowloon Peninsula for thirty-eight years, expanding with the colonization of Hong Kong's New Territories in 1898. A detailed survey map, published in 1866 by an Italian Catholic missionary stationed in Hong Kong, captured the moment in history. Roman Catholic missionaries were recorded in China as early as the Yuan Dynasty, and Catholic churches flourished in the Ming Dynasty. Entering China at Guangzhou, the missionaries had easy access to China's southern regions farther inland from there. However, Catholicism became so influential that the Qing Emperor Yongzheng (1723–1735) forbade its practice in China. During the British

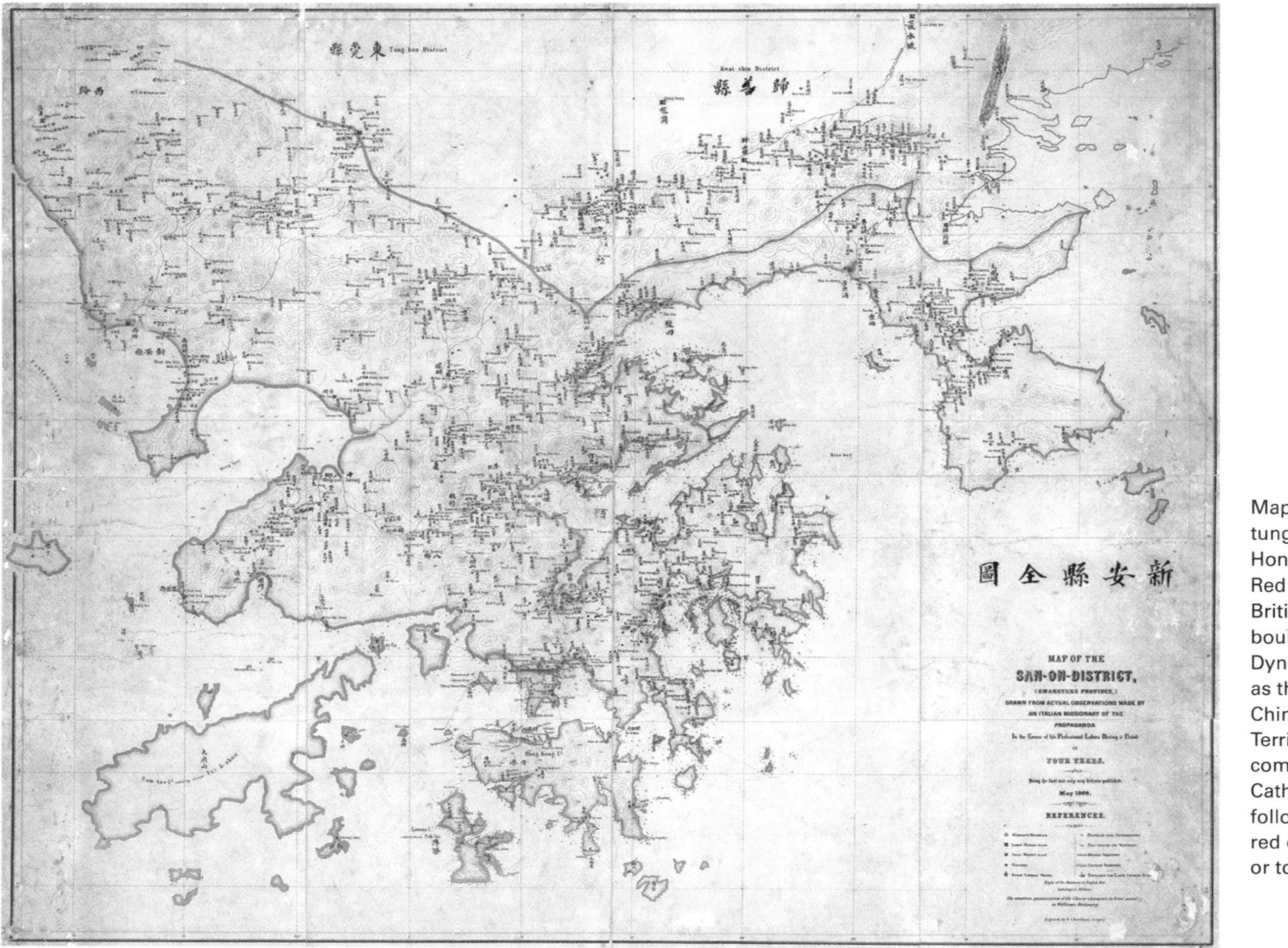

Map of San-On District (Kwangtung Province) of modern-day Hong Kong and Shenzhen, 1866. Red boundaries marked colonial British Hong Kong, while blue boundaries marked Chinese Qing Dynasty Xin'an (San'on) County, as the map was made prior to China's concession of the New Territories. The map was first composed by Hong Kong–based Catholic priests assisted by local followers in both regions; each red dot with text identified village or township settlements.

occupation of Hong Kong Island in 1841, the Roman Catholic Church declared Hong Kong a prefecture apostolic.[82]

The survey for this particular map was conducted from 1862 to 1866. With the help of local Catholic followers, Italian priest Simeone Volonteri, who had come from Milan, and Chinese priest Andreas Leang undertook a detailed field survey of not only British-occupied Hong Kong, but the entire Xin'an County. The map claimed to be "the first and only map hitherto published" of Xin'an, but this is not exactly correct. In 1817, the *Xin'an County Annals* included a county map. However, the 1866 map of the San-On (Xin'an) District was much more detailed and orthographically accurate. With details of topography, water bodies, and township and village settlements, this comprehensive map served both the evangelical mission of the Catholic Church and the military advancements of the British army.

In 1898, territory south of the Shenzhen River in Xin'an County was forcibly leased to the British Empire under the Convention between Great Britain and China Respecting an Extension of Hong Kong Territory, more commonly referred to as the Second Convention of Peking. Qing court officials formally ceded Hong Kong's New Territories to the British from within the magistrate's court in Nantou City.

On June 11, 1898, two days after Qing court representative Li Hongzhang signed the Convention between Great Britain and China Respecting an Extension of Hong Kong Territory, the young Qing Emperor Guangxu and his reform-minded supporters launched the Wuxu Reform Movement. Rejecting the pacifist attitude of influential Qing officials, Emperor Guangxu took a stronger stance against foreign invasions and colonization. The Wuxu Reform Movement pushed for cultural, political, and educational reforms, with the aim of modernizing the sociopolitical institutions of China. However, the movement lasted only 103 days before powerful conservative officials, led by the Empress Dowager Cixi, launched a coup d'état that removed Emperor Guangxu from power.

While the Wuxu Reform Movement was short-lived, it did have an influence on educational reform in China, especially in the southern regions. Nantou's Fenggang Academy adopted a modern curriculum that included natural and social sciences, and embraced progressive thinking, which inevitably impacted later social and political movements. The academy also connected with local village schools, as well as schools in Guangzhou, to create support networks for progressive thinking and future revolutionaries. In 1906, the academy formally changed its name to

Fenggang School. Rejecting the title of "academy," which had been conferred by the Qing imperial court, was a bold move that signaled imminent change.[83]

In 1911, the Wuchang Uprising, led by Guangdong native Dr. Sun Yat-sen, initiated a national movement to overthrow the Qing regime. The Alliance for Democracy led an uprising in the same year, joined by local residents from Xin'an's Longhua. Together, they ousted the local Qing administrators in Nantou City and ended 265 years of Qing imperial rule in Xin'an County. Following the 1911 revolution, a surge in population growth resulted in overcrowding in Nantou, and the south, east, and west walls were demolished. The Nationalist army declared liberation of the entire county in 1914, and Xin'an County was renamed Bao'an County to avoid confusion with another similarly named inland county. The Fenggang School was renamed Bao'an County First Primary School. In 1926, it established a secondary school affiliate by reappropriating the old Confucius Temple near Nantou City's East Gate, renaming it Bao'an No. 1 Middle School.

NANTOU CITY AND THE STRUGGLES OF MODERN CHINA

Nantou did not enjoy stability for long. When Japan invaded China (the Sino-Japanese War, 1931–1945), it soon realized that Xin'an (Shenzhen) served as a midway point for international aid from Hong Kong and Macau to the rest of China via Guangzhou.[84] The Japanese air force first bombed Shenzhen on August 31, 1937, and in November the army took Nantou City, Shenzhen Market Town, and Dapeng Fort, cutting off the last route into China for international aid.

There were more than ten thousand Japanese soldiers stationed across the entire area of Xin'an County, but Nantou was the key base of military occupation. At least two companies of troops were stationed inside the walled city, although the number of soldiers deployed in Nantou reached a few thousand at its height. The military erected tents on the former Qing drill ground outside the fort, and built bunkers within the Nantou Fort area, a few of which can still be found inside Nantou today.[85]

The Japanese army also demolished the Bao'an First Primary School, and used the building materials to construct the Shahe Bridge near Baishizhou Village, to the east of Nantou. The school was relocated to the Wengang Academy building—its original location, which had been vacant since 1800—and renamed the Lotus City Primary School. The Bao'an No. 1 Middle School, housed in the old Confucius Temple, was bombed during an air raid. The Japanese built a 2.5-square-kilometer military airport, with a capacity for thirty aircraft, to the south of Nantou City—today the home of Guimiao and Houhai villages. Many local residents actively resisted the Japanese occupation, as they had done during the initial British occupation of the Hong Kong New Territories. The Japanese army set up an execution ground to the east of Nantou City, within present-day Shenzhen University. More than five hundred civilians were executed at this ground alone. During Japan's seven-year occupation of Nantou, however, a total of twenty-five thousand civilian casualties were reported.[86]

The Nationalists regained control of Nantou in 1945, after the defeat of the Japanese. During this period, the secondary school was rebuilt and re-established as the Nantou Secondary School. The Lotus City Primary School was relocated to Wen Tianxiang Memorial Hall, which had been built in the early nineteenth century by Wen's descendants. On October 16, 1949, toward the end of the Nationalist-Communist Civil War, Nantou was taken by the Communist Liberation Army. The Bao'an County CCP Party Committee and Bao'an County People's Government Headquarters were established inside Nantou. The Lotus City Primary School was renamed Nantou Nine Streets Primary School.[87] After the Battle of Neilingding, fought between the Nationalist and Communist armies in April 1950, the entire territory of Bao'an County came under the control of the Communist army. In May, the Monument to the Liberation of Neilingding Island was built at the South Gate Drill Ground inside Nantou, commemorating this final battle in Bao'an County and the lives lost. In 1917, the population of Xin'an County was estimated to be 287,450. By 1949, the population had fallen to 184,700.[88] Once again, the county, and the nation, began the process of rebuilding.

In 1953, the Bao'an County People's Government was relocated from Nantou Fort eastward to the Caiwuwei area. This marked the end of Nantou City's continuous role as the seat of regional administrative governance. In 1958, Nantou and the surrounding villages formed the "Surpassing England People's Commune." This development took place at the beginning of China's Great Leap Forward (1958–1960), when communes were formed all over the country to serve as the basic governance and organizational structure of people's work and everyday life. In 1959, the commune was split into the Nantou People's Commune, Xixiang People's

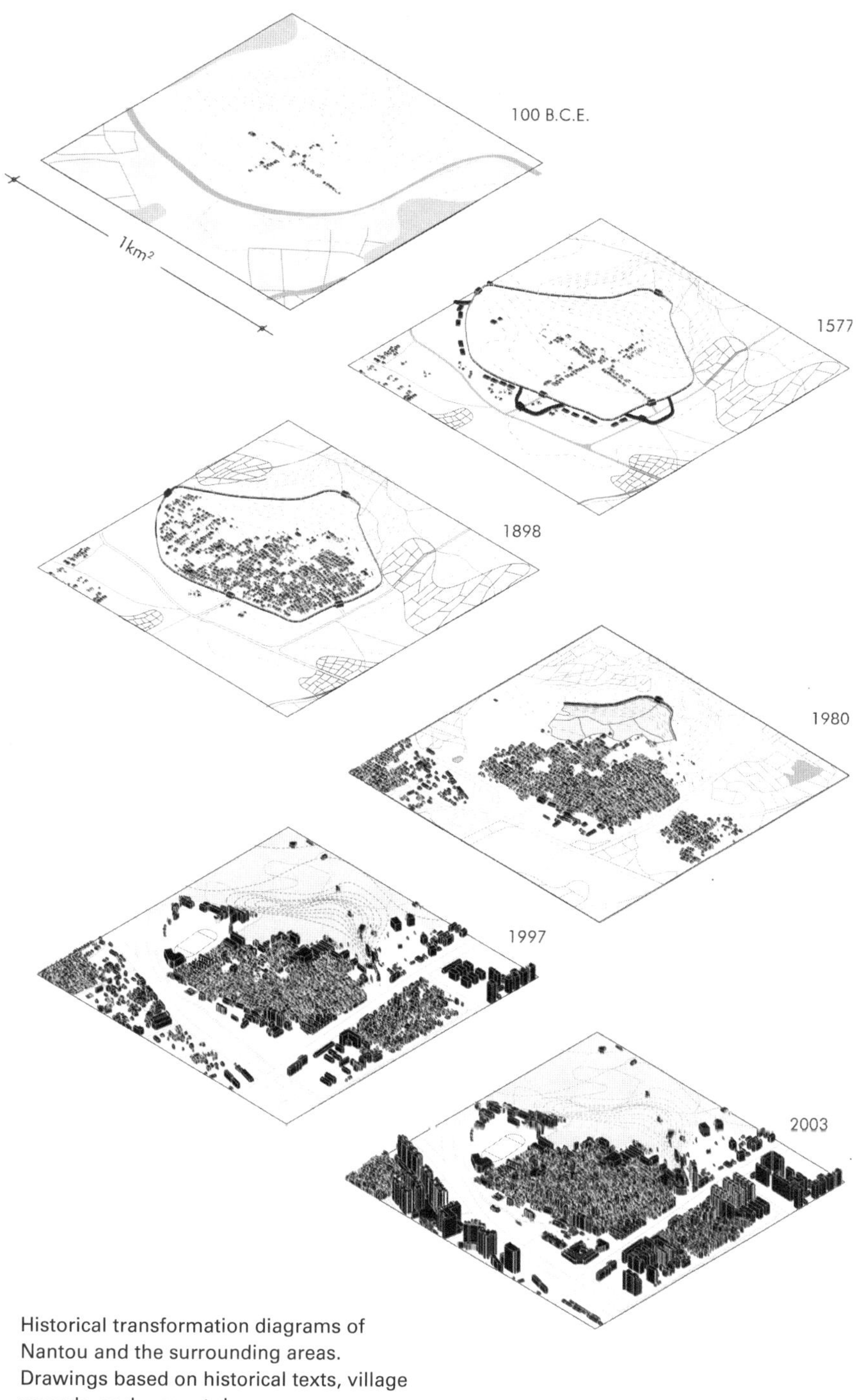

Historical transformation diagrams of Nantou and the surrounding areas. Drawings based on historical texts, village records, and present-day surveys.

Commune, and Xihai People's Commune. In 1963, the Nantou area was restructured into two communes: Nantou Commune and Shekou Aquaculture Commune.[89]

While the lower portions of the original city wall were still recognizable in the 1950s, most segments of the fortress walls were dismantled. The historic Ming and Qing bricks were used to build houses and "backyard furnaces," which produced useless metals during the "Entire Nation Making Steel and Iron" movement in the late 1950s.[90] During the subsequent Cultural Revolution (1966–1976), many historic structures inside Nantou City were demolished. The Taoist Guanyin Temple, the Buddhist Temple, and an ancient pagoda were all considered "dangerous" relics of the past, and so destroyed. Fortunately, a few historic buildings survived these chaotic decades, including the Ming Dynasty South Gate Wall, Wen Tianxiang Memorial (Qing, 1807), Dongguan Commerce Club (Qing, 1868), Guandi Temple (Ming, 1612), and the original Bao'an County Government Centre (Ming, 1573).[91] Many ancient wells remain in Nantou, notably a large Ming Dynasty well that was famously regarded for its sacred water. Located next to the site of the Guanyin Temple, which was destroyed, the well is still in use.

Continuous operation of the Fenggang Academy witnessed two hundred years of history, during which time it had served as the principal center of higher learning in Nantou as well as the wider region. The school's historic and cultural significance lies in its ongoing transformation, which reflected and interacted with the changing political and social climate. Its teachings impacted the historical development of Xin'an (later Bao'an) County by modernizing cultural values, encouraging progressive thinking and scholarly activities, and shaping student movements.

Although most of the buildings lining the streets of Nantou were built in recent decades, the layout of the original nine streets, formed in the Ming Dynasty and reinforced during the Qing Dynasty, is still recognizable. Many of the original houses from the Ming and Qing Dynasties, which were usually organized around a central courtyard and a well, remained until the 1960s and 1970s. This type of courtyard house, known as the Lingnan Bamboo House, had solid wall enclosures on the two long sides, while the two short sides featured doors opening to the streets at opposite ends; the house itself could be anywhere from one to several stories high.[92] Before 1979, the Lingnan Bamboo House was the most residential building type in Shenzhen's urbanized settlements, including Shenzhen

Market Town and Dapeng Fort City. Most of Hong Kong's oldest urbanized neighborhoods also had similar block and street patterns, owing to the length and narrowness of the building plots.

Most of these historic courtyard houses were demolished in the twentieth century to make way for taller edifices. However, many still remain in Nantou and Dapeng. Most of those left in Nantou City are close to its two main streets, which date from the Ming and Qing Dynasties: Magistrate Court Avenue and Archway Main Street. These historic streets have since been renamed Zhongshan Street East and Zhongshan Street South, but are still the most active in Nantou, accommodating nearly a hundred small businesses: barbershops, pharmacies, bookstores, hardware stores, grocers, a post office, telecom centers, restaurants serving cuisine from all over China, and a busy wet market. Although Nantou is no longer a capital city, its long history continues to manifest through its urban life.

REFORMING THE OLD, CONSTRUCTING THE NEW

On February 16, 1979, a speedboat from Hong Kong arrived at the village fishing pier in Nantou's Shekou Aquaculture Commune.[93] The few people onboard worked for the China Merchants Company, a Chinese government-owned enterprise based in Hong Kong. The company was first established in 1872 as the China Merchants Steam Navigation Company, in an effort by the Qing court official Li Hongzhang to engage in modern international shipping, following the First Opium War. It soon established shipping routes to Japan and Southeast Asian countries and became a major shipping company in China during the Qing Dynasty. In 1935, the company was reorganized as the national China Merchants Company under the Nationalist government. After the civil war and the establishment of the People's Republic of China in 1949, China Merchants' Hong Kong office set up a headquarters in British-occupied Hong Kong.

The 1979 visit to the Shekou Aquaculture Commune took place just two weeks after China's central government approved the development of the Shekou Industrial Zone in rural Bao'an County. It also followed Vice Premier Li Xiannian's decision to give Yuan Geng, director of the Hong Kong China Merchants Group, a 2.14-square-kilometer coastal area within a specified section of the territory just north of the Hong Kong–China Border. By July 1979, China Merchants Group had set up a temporary

Satellite image of the current Nantou Ancient City (*opposite*), with discernable Qing Dynasty street patterns and the traces of the long-dismantled city wall, such as the remaining Southern Gate (*above*). The lower portion of the gate dates back to the fourteenth century and is still used as the main entrance to the area, currently an urban village with over thirty thousand residents.

command center in seven old houses purchased from the local villagers.[94] The houses, and the majority of land allocated to the Shekou Industrial Zone, were expropriated from the coastal Shuiwan Village.[95] The houses were among the oldest structures in the village and composed of oyster shells, a sign of local mariculture activities. In exchange, Shuiwan villagers were moved to new two-story houses in a new village compound called the Lychee Garden Community. Shuiwan was the first village in Shenzhen to be redeveloped, and it perhaps gave rise to the popular origin myth of Shenzhen as a "sleepy fishing village."

In the original 1978 proposal by China Merchants Group to the central government, the industrial zone was located on the eastern sea coast of Bao'an County—on the Dapeng Peninsula, the hometown of Yuan Geng.[96] The sixty-two-year-old seasoned executive had a colorful past as an anti-Japanese guerilla fighter, military commander, intelligence agent, civil servant, and school principal in Dapeng. Born in 1917 in Shuibei Village as Ouyang Rushan, he attended the local village school before enrolling at a secondary school in Guangzhou. He went on to enter the Whampoa Military Academy in 1936 at nineteen years old. Returning to his home village after the Japanese invasion in 1937, he became a teacher before joining the underground Communist Party, changing his name to Yuan Geng to avoid any negative impact on his clan members.[97] Born in the area, he knew its long history well. After conducting site visits in various coastal regions, Yuan Geng concluded that the best location was in Nantou's Shekou Commune area, given its natural geography, existing economy, and the availability of water and electricity.[98] Prior to the establishment of Shenzhen, Nantou was the most developed area in Bao'an County. On January 6, 1979, the Chinese State Council received the "Report Regarding the Development of an Industrial Zone in Bao'an by the Hong Kong China Merchants Group," and as stated, Shekou Commune was the first choice of site.

The State Council approved the establishment of Shenzhen City in March 1979, and by October the Shekou Industrial Zone was officially drawn within the proposed boundary of the Shenzhen special economic zone.[99] With funding from independent investors and direct communication to the Beijing central government, Shekou was designated as a special zone within the special zone. This independence gave Yuan Geng room to maneuver, as well as the leverage to generate additional funding for construction and development. As an enterprise, China Merchants Group could not rely on direct funds from the central or local government to develop its operations. Within a year of the company's founding, interest from Hong Kong investors plummeted given the appearance of the Shenzhen SEZ's political instability, which was generated by opponents of Deng's reforms. Yuan Geng urgently searched for alternative investment sources while issuing internal cautions to his management-level employees: "Shekou has only seawater and sludge with no potential for industrial development. Our only choice is to drink the seawater and eat the sand. . . . Do not bring family along, if possible, as there is no need for them to join in the suffering."[100]

From March 1981 to January 1982, Yuan Geng actively lobbied the central government to accept his proposal to construct a deepwater seaport at Shekou for the Ministry of Petroleum. He envisioned the seaport as an infrastructure base for oil exploration in the South China Sea, which would give the fledging Shekou Industrial Zone a much-needed economic boost.[101] The idea of a port base for oil exploration originated at a conference held in Hong Kong in February 1980, on "The Relationship between Hong Kong and South China Energy Development."[102] Attended by representatives from fifteen countries, including the UK, US, Japan, and West Germany, the conference agenda included the possibility of developing petroleum industry support bases in Hong Kong.[103] The meeting took place at the height of the 1980 global oil crisis, first triggered by the Iranian Revolution (1978–1979) that resulted in the establishment of the Islamic Republic.[104] By July 1978, Japan had already signed cooperation agreements with Vietnam to drill for oil in the South China Sea. Soon other oil companies, including Chevron, Shell, and British Petroleum, turned their attention to the world's "second Persian Gulf."[105] Conference attendees expressed unexpected interest in the Shekou Industrial Zone, prompting Yuan Geng to investigate the possibility of building a deepwater seaport to serve as a base for petroleum drilling. While the Ministry of Petroleum and Ministry of Transport, led by the State Council, did take Yuan Geng's proposal seriously, they did not instantly agree that Shenzhen would be the most logical choice for petroleum exploration in the South China Sea, given its limited infrastructure at that time. Therefore, they also reviewed a series of established ports, including Hainan's Sanya Port, Guangdong's Zhanjiang Port, and, notably, ports in Hong Kong and Singapore.[106]

Meanwhile, Yuan Geng and his team diligently gathered evidence to support their proposal. Yuan Geng personally supervised site surveys and found that the optimum location for such a large deepwater port was not within the Shekou Industrial Zone, but at the long-abandoned Chiwan Harbor. In the course of his research, Yuan Geng also reviewed passages from the *Xin'an County Annals* that described Chiwan as the "Gateway of Canton" and "the requested stopover for all ships passing through the Pearl River Estuary." His research also revealed that Chiwan Harbor was considered the major southern seaport in Sun Yat-sen's 1922 "Plan for National Reconstruction," and that after 1949 the PRC's Ministry of Transport also surveyed Chiwan to determine the potential of developing it into the main port for southern China.[107] These past plans obviously had not been realized. Abandoned for nearly a century, the Chiwan Harbor area was still under military patrol in 1981, with restricted civilian access—a reminder of the years of invasions and illegal crossings. The once glorious Tianhou Temple had been reduced to rubble, its richly carved portals and porcelain tiles used as infill for the Shenzhen Water Reservoir in 1960.[108]

Only two "sacred" banyan trees, believed to have been planted with an instruction from Zheng He, remained on the temple grounds. The trees were still adorned with red ribbons, fastened by local villagers praying for Tianhou's protection. The harbor beach was only used as a fishing vessel dock by the remaining twenty-eight village families, who lived in small houses near the coast.[109] After a year-long process of measuring and monitoring the currents, wind, water depth, and overall geology, Yuan Geng and his team concluded that Chiwan would be the best location for a modern port in Shenzhen.

The mayor of Shenzhen at the time, Liang Xiang, also strongly advocated building the port at Chiwan. He pointed out that in addition to supporting an oil industry in the region, a large-capacity port was vital for the overall development of Shenzhen. In 1981, the construction of Shenzhen required 2.4 million tons of building materials, but given the limited capacity of the existing transportation infrastructure, only 1.1 million tons of materials arrived. The reduced supply of materials raised the costs of construction in Shenzhen.[110] Liang Xiang and Yuan Geng had championed the often-opposing interests of the Special Economic Zone and Shekou Industrial Zone, respectively. For the first time, they now collaborated in lobbying for the construction of Chiwan Port.[111]

The proposal for the new port was finally approved in October 1981. Shenzhen's first large-capacity (ten thousand–ton) deepwater bay was completed in June 1983, and the volume of goods flowing into Shenzhen increased rapidly from fifty-five thousand tons to 350,000 tons in 1984.[112] With four additional bays completed by June 1984, the volume of goods entering the region continued to increase to 550,000 tons in 1985, and 920,000 tons in 1986.[113] Chiwan quickly became one of the largest and most efficient ports in the region. In 1990, the smaller Mawan Port was built adjacent to Chiwan, specifically to handle the large quantities of steel, wood, concrete, and other construction materials needed in Shenzhen. In 1994, Hong Kong's Hutchison Whampoa Limited and the Shenzhen Municipal Government codeveloped the Yantian Seaport on the eastern coast of Shenzhen. Yantian, or Salt Field Seaport, was located on the site of a former ancient salt works. By 2003, more than two-thirds of raw materials and more than 40 percent of packaged traded goods (import and export) went through Shenzhen's seaports.[114] In addition, 80–90 percent of Shenzhen's construction materials came in from the seaports, as well as 100 percent of coal, 95 percent of petroleum, and 70 percent of food.

In 2014 alone, Yantian Seaport processed sixty-seven million tons of goods; by comparison, Shekou Seaport managed sixty-four million tons and Chiwan Seaport fifty-three million tons.[115]

In February 1984, British Petroleum became the first foreign petroleum company to set up a base at Chiwan. In September 1985, Shekou Petroleum Base Company (known as Nanyou Department in China) was established within the Shekou Industrial Zone. Soon, more than ten international oil companies, including Amoco and Esso, had established their headquarters in the Chiwan area, employing over three thousand foreign staff brought in from over thirty countries. As the preferred headquarters site for foreign companies in Shenzhen (following the early leads of Carrefour and Walmart), the Nantou-Shekou area went on to host numerous global multinational companies and the largest expatriate community in Shenzhen.[116]

Yuan Geng built the Shekou Industrial Zone into a tremendously successful economic enterprise, and in the process established a model for the development of the rest of Shenzhen. One of his most enduring legacies was the establishment of a democratic local governance structure for this large Shekou enterprise. In 1984, he founded the *Shekou News,* one of the most influential and controversial newspapers in China during the first decade of reform. An article from February 1985, entitled "Time to Pay Attention to Management: Advice to Comrade Yuan Geng," made local and national news. The notion that a top leader like Yuan Geng would openly invite and publicize criticism had jolted the nation. On March 23, the *People's Daily* published the full article with an added title, "Yuan Geng Supports Open Criticism of Himself," and the Xinhua News Agency, China News Service, and CCTV also covered the story that day.[117] The *Shekou News* continued to feature articles such as "Two Teachers Criticized Yuan Geng by Name" and "Only Half of What Yuan Geng Said Was Valid."[118] Prior to its closure in 1989, the *Shekou News* published discussions of issues rarely covered by the public media at the time: law and order, the validity of the *hukou* system, housing affordability, the well-being of rural migrant workers, child labor, and even age and sex discrimination. Both supporters and critics of Yuan Geng often attribute his belief in open debate and introducing foreign business practices into Shekou to "Western" influence, which he experienced while stationed in Hong Kong. However, Yuan Geng revealed an older source of inspiration in a 1984 talk:

> In China's history, the most academically and ideologically active were the Spring and Autumn and Warring States periods when society was undergoing immense reformation. This time of history produced many great thinkers, such as Lao Tzu, Confucius, Mencius, and later Xunzi and Han Fei. They wrote books, gave lectures, and debated with each other, thus bringing about the "contention of a hundred schools of thoughts" in the sphere of learning. Why do we not try to listen to opinions from different schools of thought? . . . With respect to business administration, can we not learn advanced management expertise from foreign enterprises? The answer is positive. Among the factories and enterprises in Shekou are those from Western countries such as Denmark, the UK, and others from Southeast Asia and Hong Kong. It is like a hundred flowers in bloom.[119]

Because the seaports and waterways of Shenzhen played such an important role in the city's rapid construction, industrialization, and urbanization, these classical teachings and debates on the subjects of education and governance have influenced generations of Shenzhen's leaders and residents. Shenzhen's urbanization after 1979 was shaped as much by the region's distant past as by more recent events, and this pre-1979 history is essential to understanding the city's unique cultural, sociopolitical, and geographical contexts.

The momentous transformation of China's cities over the last two decades can make it easy to forget that sweeping reforms unfolded not only in urban centers but throughout networks of villages across the vast countryside. In the story of Shenzhen, as the evolutions of Xin'an and Nantou have shown, the histories of the city and the villages are inextricable. Over centuries of change, one constant theme of the region's history is ongoing reform in pursuit of "Xin An," or renewed peace and stability. The next chapter will reveal the rich history of the Pearl River Valley, tracing the history of oyster cultivation in this region from its ancient beginnings through to modern times. As the transformations of the local villages through the post-1979 urbanization process will demonstrate, the urban revolution in China was preceded by and predicated on the modern rural revolution. Just as the history of fishing and farming activities before 1979 impacted the development of Shenzhen, so too did the urban development of the region greatly transform the rural agriculture and aquaculture practices passed down through many centuries.

4.

OYSTERS OF THE PEARL RIVER DELTA

An extravagant ten-course feast was served in historic Shajing village in 2004, each course featuring exquisitely prepared seafood dishes. In fact, every ingredient featured in the traditional dishes reflected the agricultural geology of the immediate surroundings, many found only at this unique juncture of China's Pearl River. Along with guided tours, historic walks, and traditional performances, this dining extravaganza was part of the 2004 inaugural Shajing Golden Oyster Festival in the Shajing subdistrict, established to celebrate the region's millennial history and success in producing Shajing oysters. The first course on the carefully planned menu was oysters steamed with golden silver garlic, featuring juicy oysters harvested from a unique source: the confluence between a freshwater mountain stream and the South China Sea. To follow were soups with bamboo shoots and mixed dishes containing ingredients from the land, sky, and sea, and delicacies such as Shajing imperial gold oysters—the gold referring to the golden-yellow color of the oysters, which were sundried according to local traditional methods for oyster preservation. But the final dish was not decadent like all the others but a common dish, one prevalent in the area: Shajing oyster congee—a thick rice stew of baby oysters seasoned with salt, ginger, scallions, and black pepper; in contrast to the luxurious courses that preceded it, this concluding course was enjoyed at family dinner tables all across the region.[1]

While oysters today are no longer specifically from this area of Shajing, shellfish continues to be produced in other regions owned and operated by the Shajing villagers. With over eighty square kilometers of mariculture fields yielding seven thousand tons of fresh oysters per year, the centuries-old Shajing oyster industry is still thriving today.[2] Along with the production of electronics and plastic toys, mariculture—especially the harvesting of oysters—today remains a vital industry in Shenzhen's Shajing villages, otherwise known as the Village of Sandy Wells. The Shajing oyster industry is predominantly run by direct descendants of the coastal fishermen who cultivated these oysters for generations. Jointly organized by the Shenzhen Tourism Bureau, the Bao'an District government, and the local Shajing Subdistrict Office, the festival created a sense of celebration in this otherwise quiet suburban area, an hour's drive from Shenzhen's urban center. The once-agrarian village lanes had become streets, thronged with officials, tourists, laborers, and locals. Visitors took guided walking tours through the historic Shajing villages and visited the Jiang Clan Ancestral Hall, a popular highlight. While most villages in the area have ancestral halls, the Jiang Clan Ancestral Hall stands out as one of the best-preserved historic structures constructed of oyster shells. Historic records of the Pearl River region document the use of shells as a building material.[3] So does a nursery rhyme that is still recalled today in Shajing: "There are three treasures in Shajing; oyster meat enters the homes of the rich, oyster soup enters the homes of the ailing, and oyster shells enter the homes of the poor." Records indicate that Europe and the United States (in early colonial towns, such as New Orleans and St. Augustine) also had buildings with walls made from oyster shells.[4] In those cases, however, the oyster shells were fired to form lime, which was used to produce a primitive type of concrete. The shells are visible as aggregates or fragments, but are not intentionally arranged to create any particular visual effect. In this region of China, conversely, the oyster shell walls are visually unique, as the Jiang Clan Ancestral Hall illustrates.

According to local village records, the Jiang Clan Ancestral Hall was originally built on this site by a retired salt works official during the Ming Dynasty (around 1400).[5] The current structure was built during the Qing Dynasty and most recently renovated in 2003.[6] It is composed of three courtyards and three pavilions aligned along a central axis. The roofs are

The Shajing Village Ancestral Hall. Walls were constructed using local oyster shells.

tiled and feature ornately carved details, but the exterior walls surrounding the complex are its most unique characteristic. Bordered by dark-gray bricks and tiles, the walls are comprised of rows of carefully aligned oyster shells. The end of each shell protruded from the wall, and the shells were arranged to form an orderly pattern of horizontal lines from the bottom to the top of each wall. When light reflects from the irregularities in the shells, it creates the illusion of an effervescent glow. Qu Dajun, a well-known Qing Dynasty writer and historian, described this visual effect: "The smooth, lustrous, round surface of a shell's inside is known as the light of the oyster. Villagers use the shells to build a radiant wall. Appearing like the scales of fish, they glow brighter with each rainfall."[7]

Similar oyster shell buildings can be seen outside the Shajing region, scattered throughout historic village sites along the Pearl River Delta.

Those that remain intact are primarily village civic structures. Mysteriously, most of these oyster shell buildings lie in landlocked locations that have not produced oysters for centuries. Their existence can only be explained by the area's natural geological history and its maricultural past. In fact, oysters have not been produced in the Shajing region for nearly thirty years. However, local villagers and tour guides repeatedly assert that while there are no visible oyster ponds in Shajing, and the oysters sold and consumed in Shajing are cultivated elsewhere, the oysters are still authentic Shajing oysters because they are derived from the area's historic oyster seeds and grown using Shajing's unique methods of oyster cultivation. In reality, no oysters have been found in the coastal waters of Shajing, or anywhere in the Pearl River Delta, since the early 1990s. Yet Shajing oysters continue to be one of Shenzhen's major industries, one with a remarkable history dating back over a millennium. The story of the oysters reflects the region's major geological shifts, as well as its tumultuous political regime changes.

OYSTERS, VILLAGES, AND THE PEARL RIVER

Given the momentous transformation of China's cities post-1979, it is perhaps logical to assume that the country's sweeping reforms were rooted in urban centers. However, there were dramatic changes in networks of villages dispersed across China's vast countryside even prior to 1979. Even in the case of the Shenzhen special economic zone—the so-called instant modern city of Shenzhen—the story begins with the villages. Prior to 1978, the vast majority of people in this region lived and worked in rural agricultural regions with deep cultural and ecological histories.

Although frequently described as a "sleepy fishing village" prior to its designation as the city of Shenzhen in 1979, this territory of some two thousand square kilometers accommodated several large townships and hundreds of villages. This region has received numerous municipal names and categorizations over the course of its thousand-year history. From 1914 to 1979, it was called Bao'an County, the land of treasure and peace, and recognized throughout China for its natural beauty and rich culture.[8] The name Shenzhen, meaning "deep water channels," was derived from the name of one of the many townships in Bao'an County: a busy border trading town named Shenzhen Market, which was established at the turn of the nineteenth century.[9]

Scattered throughout the area and supporting these townships were several hundred villages, whose inhabitants cultivated the land and sea for over a thousand years. Until 1978, over 80 percent of the Bao'an County population worked in rice paddies or engaged in related agricultural activities.[10] Consistent with the norms of rural village organization throughout China, each village was typically composed of extended families from one clan with a common family name. In some instances, a village might include a few clans that had developed close-knit relationships through decades of collaborative agricultural work. Despite countless political regime changes and upheaval, including the founding of modern China, the social structures and hierarchies within these villages remained intact, passed on through centuries. The villages each had localized individual histories and identities, and each would have responded differently to such monumental changes. Each village was an insular community, governed by an elected head and a council of representatives, who were usually the village elders. The village head and council oversaw daily life in the village, from deciding when and what crops to plant, to dispensing punishments for offenses and petty crimes. The varying degrees of effective leadership and organizational strength from one village to another would prove to be critical in terms of the instrumental role each village would play in Shenzhen's urbanization, development, and modernization years later. In addition to agricultural production, the Pearl River Delta region was renowned in China for its fisheries and aquaculture. Most of the coastal lands were filled with fish and shrimp ponds. Crops and harvests from the fisheries were exported throughout the Southeast Asia region, mostly channeled through Hong Kong. One of the region's best-known exports was its oysters.

Two millennia before it was home to economic zones and iPhone factories, the Pearl River Delta region was a lush agricultural plain. Commonly referred to as the Land of Fish and Rice, the region is one of the most fertile in Asia, with a subtropical climate, abundant rainfall, and access to irrigation. Encompassing historical urban centers such as Guangzhou and Foshan, the Pearl River Delta has played a pivotal role in the history of Chinese civilization. Many prominent scholars and artists, as well as some of China's most significant political revolutionaries, came from this southernmost region of the country. The region's material wealth and, by extension, its intellectual capital, were in fact made possible by centuries of agricultural, commercial, and, later, industrial activities throughout the extensive waterways. The name Pearl River refers to both the extensive river system, formed by more than two hundred tributaries, and a specific distributary that collects water from three major rivers—the West River, North River, and East River. Spanning 41,700 square kilometers, the delta was formed from the alluvial deposits of these three major rivers where they join the Pearl River before merging with the South China Sea.[11] Constituting more than five thousand kilometers of navigable waterways, these rivers historically provided a natural transport system for shipping and trade that served the entire region.[12] Between the mouth of the Pearl River and the South China Sea, a large estuarine bay is framed by the coasts of Zhuhai, Zhongshang, Guangzhou, Dongguan, and Shenzhen, as well as Hong Kong and Macau. While the term Pearl River Delta does not usually include Hong Kong and Macau, the waters of the Pearl River Estuary unite these cities within a shared marine and socioeconomic ecosystem. The Pearl River basin is 453,700 square kilometers, over ten times larger than the administrative areas of the Pearl River Delta.[13] In addition to spanning Guangdong Province in its entirety, the basin includes Guangxi, Yunnan, and even the border zones of Northern Vietnam. It is a major catchment area for the wider southern China region.

Instigated by the designation of the Shenzhen special economic zone in 1979, industrialization and urbanization spread to the rest of the Pearl River Delta (PRD) region throughout the 1980s and 1990s. In 1994, the Pearl River Delta economic zone was formally established. It currently contributes 10 percent of China's national GDP, its annual production amounting to five hundred million USD. Home to a population of one hundred million, nine interconnected cities (including Shenzhen and Dongguan) sprawl across forty thousand square kilometers of urban and industrial landscape. China's Pearl River Delta region is currently the world's largest urban area, having surpassed Metropolitan Tokyo in 2015.[14] From Christmas ornaments to solar panels, the PRD is today one of the world's largest industrial manufacturing bases. Perhaps more surprising, given that most people know Shenzhen for its factories rather than its fisheries or marine environment, is the fact that the PRD still exports Southern China's celebrated Shajing oysters.

MILLENNIUM OF MARICULTURE AMID SEA CHANGES

Written accounts in the *Records of Linnan* date the consumption and trading of oysters in the Pearl River Delta as far back as the Tang Dynasty

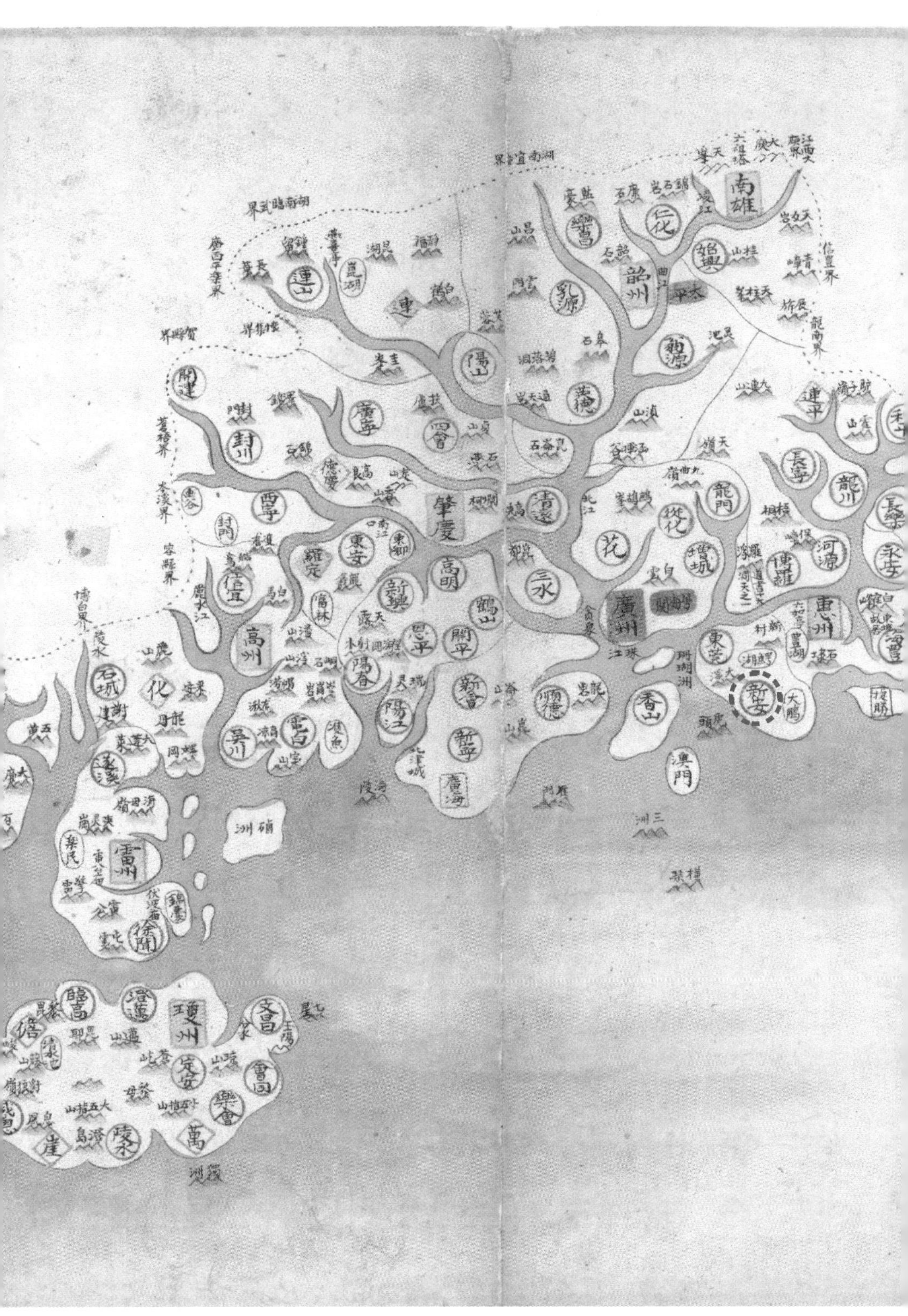

Guangdong Provincial Atlas, 1754, Xin'an County marked in red circle by author.

NASA Earth Observatory images of the Pearl River Delta in 1988 and 2004. With the Shenzhen SEZ as a catalyst in the 1980s, urbanization has spread throughout the region and formed the world's largest metropolitan urban area.

(618–907 CE).[15] Written by Liu Xun, then governor of the region, these records reflect the wonder of a northerner who was sent to this southern region. In these volumes, Liu documented in detail the aspects of local cultures that he found to be strange and noteworthy. The events he recorded and his writing style would influence later historians of the region.

In one chapter, Liu wrote of "sea gypsies" who lived on originally uninhabited islands in the Pearl River close to the southern sea region. They were believed to be descendants of fighters from a failed peasant uprising during the Eastern Jin Dynasty (317–480 CE).[16] The Chinese, and later the British in Hong Kong, used the phrase "sea gypsies" to refer to the Tanka people who continued to live on the waters of the South China Sea until modern times. The Tanka are also referred to as "boat people," made famous by their floating village of boats in the harbors of colonial Hong Kong. According to Liu's records, this tribal community did not live on boats during the Tang Dynasty. Instead, they lived on offshore islands in self-made primitive shelters with oyster shell walls.[17] He also noted that oysters were their main food source, and that they came to the mainland to trade oysters for rice wine at the local village markets.

The mixing of the Pearl River's multiple freshwater outlets with the seawater from the South China Sea downstream creates a constantly changing estuarine environment. This meeting of freshwater from upstream rivers and seawater from the tidal flows produces tidal zones that are subject to changing water levels, temperature, oxygen content, and light levels.[18] For over a millennium, these intertidal zones of the estuary seem to have provided an ideal habitat for the local oyster (a *Crassostrea* species).

While Liu Xun's *Records of Linnan* only document oyster harvesting, a later Northern Song Dynasty (960–1127 CE) poem clearly references oyster culture practices. In "Eating Oysters" the poet Mei Yaochen (1002–1060 CE) vividly contrasts the laborious task of opening oysters with the miniscule reward of eating them.[19] Mei was an influential poet of his time, known for his realistic depictions of everyday life, and is still admired today for his plain use of the spoken language.[20] In the poem, he compares the oyster itself to green silk and liquid jade; the exterior shell is likened to iron rock. The poem's speaker describes the act of prying open the razor-sharp edges of an oyster with a knife, then contrasts the meager reward with heartier fare: lamb shank, beef steak, autumn bass, and winter crabs. The text also depicts the process of oyster cultivation:

Western coast of Shenzhen in the 1930s with coastal oyster fields *(left)* and in the 2000s *(right)*. Continuous reclamation projects since the 1990s have drastically altered the coastlines and marine ecologies of the region.

> As a petty official traveling in the villages by the South China Sea,
> I heard of the delicious Gui Jing oysters.
> Longing for a feast,
> I never expected the toils of prying and boiling before tasting them.
> They are said to grow amid swelling billows,
> attaching themselves onto reefs like the
> mythic turtles carrying the mountains.
> To cultivate them, villagers deploy bamboo cages in shallow waters,
> dropping rocks into the cages along with oyster seedlings.
> Waves lash the rocks as oysters multiply,
> nourished daily by the salty waters.[21]

This text is often cited as the earliest written record of oyster culture in China, and perhaps in the world. Its description of "dropping rocks" and "deploy[ing] bamboo cages," then leaving the oysters to grow over time in the sea, accords with traditional methods of oyster cultivation all over the world. Variations of both methods are still employed today. "Dropping rocks" could refer to placing rocks or tiles with attached oyster larvae, or spat, onto the seabed to be collected later. This is known as the Seabed Culture method. The cultivation of oysters is delicate work, as they are extremely sensitive to their environment. Filtering large volumes of water in order to feed and breathe, the oyster retains phytoplankton, or small fragments of algae, as its food source. Each oyster is able to filter up to fifty gallons of water per day. Water quality, temperature, salinity, speed, pressure, and even light intensity affect the spawning, fertilization, and growth of the oyster. One heavy storm can damage or kill off whole stretches of fragile oyster beds. The fishermen's mastery of oyster culture reflects the advanced knowledge of mariculture in China during the Song Dynasty.

The reference to the fame of "Gui Jing oysters" in the poem's first sentence confirms that these particular oysters and the villagers who cultivated them were already well known in China during the Song Dynasty. The nomenclature "Gui Jing" refers to the origin of the oysters from coastal townships Gui De and Jing Kang, along the eastern banks of the Pearl River. Gui De is the historical name of areas on the western coast of modern-day Dongguan, and Jing Kang refers to a collection of villages along the northwestern coast of modern-day Shenzhen.

The Pearl River Estuary is one of the most complicated in the world, with highly complex and unpredictable distributary bodies.[22] The geological conditions of the Pearl River Delta have always been dynamic, owing to its branching waterway and natural sedimentation. The first major wave of human impact on the region took place between the tenth and thirteenth centuries, when masses of refugees fled to the Pearl River Delta to escape the Mongol invasions in China's northern regions. The migrating population settled along the rivers upstream from the Pearl River, where they constructed villages and began large-scale farming activities. This agricultural development and the resulting deforestation led to soil erosion and increased sand flow, causing escalated sedimentation of the rivers.[23]

Throughout the Yuan Dynasty (1271–1368), these activities drastically changed the geomorphology of the Pearl River Estuary. From 1290 to 1820, the Pearl River Estuary's open water area was reduced by half through newly formed land masses.[24] Stronger river discharge currents and greater sedimentation in the estuary prevented tidal seawater from reaching beyond modern-day Dongguan. By the time of the Ming Dynasty

(1368–1644), the lack of salinity in the waters around Gui De (modern-day Guangzhou and Dongguan) had killed off the oyster population and the associated industry. Therefore Jing Kang, the Shajing area in today's northwest Shenzhen, became the main site of oyster cultivation in the region.

During the Qing Dynasty (1644–1911) oyster farmers in Shajing Village invented the three-zone migratory oyster cultivation method. With knowledge passed down from previous generations, the farmers explored different coastal waters south of their village in order to optimize cultivation. Because of the ever-shifting saline waters, areas farther south were found to be more hospitable to oysters. In addition, the oyster farmers found that, owing to the complex nature of the estuary, different coastal areas had different qualities suitable for the various stages of oyster growth.

During spawning and fertilization, oyster larvae were held in the shallow, calm waters of the Fuyong area—the current site of Shenzhen International Airport. During their growth and development stage, the oysters were attached to clay (later, concrete) tiles and moved to the deeper waters of Shekou (currently Shekou Port) and Houhai (now Shenzhen Bay). During the final stage of maturation and "filling up," the oysters were moved back to the deeper waters surrounding Shajing Village. These waters, fed by more inland streams, had a better food supply for fattening or "filling up" the oysters. Having discovered that oyster growth closely followed seasonal and lunar changes, the villagers carefully calibrated the oyster "migration" to coincide with changing seasons, rainfall events, current shifts, and wind patterns. This laborious work paid off, rewarding the villagers with oysters that were especially large and crisp in taste. The reputation of the oysters from Shajing Village quickly spread. By the time of the mid–Qing Dynasty, the fame of "Gui Jing oysters" celebrated in Mei Yaochen's poem was superseded by Shajing oysters.

This migratory cultivation method, which spread the different phases of oyster growth across the western and southern coasts of Shenzhen, continued throughout the Qing Dynasty. In 1789, as the seawater continued to retreat southward, the Qing court closed the large-scale government saltworks that had operated in this region since 1078.[25] The oyster farmers took over the abandoned salt ponds and converted them into oyster ponds, while the salt-drying fields became oyster-drying fields. The cultivation of oysters expanded rapidly, as former salt workers and even fishermen from nearby villages also joined the oyster trade. By the end of the Qing Dynasty, over ten thousand people were involved in the cultivation and processing of Shajing oysters.[26]

THE RISE AND FALL OF POST-IMPERIAL SHAJING

The oyster cultivation industry in Shajing suffered from the destructive wars and political changes in the first half of the twentieth century as the Qing Dynasty gave way to the Republic of China in 1912. During the nascent era of the Nationalist-led Republic of China, conflicts among warlords raged in the region of the Pearl River Delta. Shajing Village records show that total oyster output fluctuated from year to year, depending on the relative level of peace in the area. By the late 1930s, twenty years after the establishment of the republic, the region had attained a relative level of stability. In 1936, Shajing Village records show that oyster cultivation and processing involved over ten thousand oyster farmers with a fleet of 350 oyster harvesting boats.[27] To reach buyers farther away, oysters were steam cooked then sundried. These preserved products were sold throughout Guangdong Province and the rest of Southern China. Oysters were also exported to Hong Kong and other Southeast Asian regions, although buyers in these export destinations favored uncooked, sundried oysters. The most popular and commonly exported product was bottled oyster sauce, a dark liquid condiment containing oyster extract, which has become a staple ingredient of Southern Chinese cuisine.

By 1938, however, the Japanese invasion of China had brought violence and destruction to the Pearl River Delta. Over three thousand villagers and oyster farmers in Shajing fled. Many were killed, while homes were destroyed and oyster and fishing boats confiscated.[28] According to local records, by 1940 there were only six hundred oyster farmers left in Shajing, a drastic reduction from just four years earlier.[29] While some Shajing villagers continued to grow and harvest oysters, there were further interruptions throughout the seven-year Japanese Occupation. When Japan was finally defeated and withdrew its troops in 1945, the subsequent Civil War between the Nationalist and Communist armies further damaged village life and oyster production. When the war ended in 1949 with the defeat of the Nationalists, there were only ninety-two oyster harvest boats left in Shajing.[30]

With the establishment of the People's Republic of China in 1949, Shajing Village experienced additional sociopolitical changes alongside every other rural village in the country. Most drastically, a series of land reforms were enacted to redistribute privately held land, a practice initiated by the Communist Party in 1927. Before this reform, landowners and wealthy farmers (7 percent of the total population) owned 52 percent of all farmland throughout the country.[31] Just prior to the establishment of the PRC in 1949, 2.3 million square kilometers of land had already been redistributed to 160 million landless peasants in Communist base areas.[32] This practice of "land to the tiller" garnered overwhelming support for the Communist Party from the majority of villagers in China's vast countryside. To initiate these land reforms throughout the rest of the country, the PRC passed the Land Reform Law in 1950, which abolished private land ownership and confiscated assets of the wealthy class such as livestock, furniture, property, and food. The confiscated land and properties were redistributed equally to all local peasants.

By 1950, historic Shajing Village was subdivided into four administrative villages. Each new subvillage was populated by a mix of oyster and rice farmers. At that time, villagers were required to self-identify either as field farmers or oyster farmers. Land farmers received property to till their crops, and oyster farmers collectively held usage rights of the sea along the western coast. Land farmers could keep their own crops, and oyster farmers could keep their own oyster harvest. In 1951, over six thousand villagers chose to be oyster farmers.[33] Each farmer received loans from the central government to assist in revitalizing the devastated industry.

However, by 1953, only half the oyster farmers in the Shajing area remained, owing to the lack of resources among independent producer households (*Dan-gan-hu*). At that time, most of the oyster farmers in Shajing had not yet collectivized to form production cooperatives. This independent household-based production system was generally beneficial in encouraging individual responsibility and motivation to increase output.[34] However, oyster cultivation was traditionally collective work: oyster farmers would work in groups hired by wealthy villagers, using designated boats and collaborating closely for a few intense hours to collect the harvest from the perilous seas. In 1953, records indicate there were 163 individually owned oyster boats in the Shajing area. Those who did not own boats were at a great disadvantage in the new system of individual production.[35] The majority of villagers who left Shajing went to work in the oyster fields of Hong Kong's northern Yuen Long area, where the southward shift in the water's salinity helped to stimulate oyster cultivation.[36] The border between

Communist China and colonial Hong Kong was more tightly controlled than it had been before 1949, but villagers could still cross if they possessed special farming day passes. The oyster farmers who moved south, following the saline water, established a thriving oyster industry in Hong Kong, which continues to the present day.

At the end of 1953, Chen Ganchi from Shajing Village decided to do something about the dwindling number of oyster farmers. He set up Shajing's first cooperative team, which enabled villagers without boats to team up with boat owners.[37] This encouraged oyster farmers to return to a traditionally collaborative cultivation system, but managed under a new economically equitable form of organization. Others followed his lead, and soon many cooperative teams were established in the village. In the ensuing years, Chen Ganchi followed the central government's policy of promoting village cooperatives and helped to combine smaller teams into formal production cooperatives. Chen also led efforts to develop new oyster ponds and cultivation tools. By 1956, the Shajing Oyster Production Cooperative, led by Chen, was cultivating thirteen square kilometers of oyster ponds, employed over 280 oyster boats, and had broken all historical records with respect to oyster output. In 1932, there were as little as two square kilometers of oyster fields left in the Shajing area. By 1957, the total area of oyster field cultivation had reached forty square kilometers.[38] The cooperative was awarded the title "National Model Production Unit" at China's first National Congress of Agricultural Model Workers in 1957. Chen Ganchi represented the organization and was received in Beijing by leaders of the central government, including Mao Zedong, Deng Xiaoping, and Chen Yun.[39]

During the formative years of the PRC, Shajing oysters, along with Fuyong shrimp produced nearby, were directly sourced by the national government. Processed seafood had become a national export, generating desperately needed foreign currency for the central government. Over 70 percent of the Shajing oyster production was exported and, as a result, Shajing became internationally recognized—at least, among nations friendly to the newly formed Communist republic. Delegations from Russia, Japan, and Vietnam came to Shajing to learn from local farmers.[40]

The central government regarded oyster cultivation by Shajing villagers as an important national industry, and requested that Shajing villagers pass on their knowledge and expertise. From 1956 through the early 1960s, Shajing villagers assisted seaside villages along China's southern coast in oyster cultivation. In 1962, villager Chen Mugen was sent to the coastal city of Dalian in Northern China's Liaoning Province.[41] After some initial trial and error, Chen successfully helped develop oyster cultivation along Dalian's Yellow Sea coast within two years.

The Beijing central government also sent Chen Mugen, dubbed China's "Oyster Ambassador" in 1967, to visit Vietnam's Quang Ninh Province at the request of Vietnamese government officials, who were impressed by the reputation of Shajing oysters. Despite the escalating Vietnam War, Chen led a group of Shajing villagers to settle and work in Vietnam's coastal Haiphong Strip under strict surveillance. They established nearly ten viable oyster cultivation sites along Vietnam's eastern coast, stretching from Song Bach Dang in the north to Song Gianh in the south. In 1968, Chen was awarded the Vietnam International Friendship Medal and was received by Ho Chi Minh in Hanoi.[42]

These exercises in "oyster diplomacy," along with other examples of Chinese foreign aid during the 1960s, masked China's horrific natural and man-made disasters at the time. From the Great Leap Forward (1958–1961), which contributed to the Great Famine (1958–1961), to the ensuing internal governmental critiques, which then in part triggered the Cultural Revolution (1966–1976), China endured nearly two decades of upheaval. The destruction and desolation of rural areas during this period was arguably even greater than that of the cities.[43]

With the onset of the Great Leap Forward in 1958, village life in Shajing changed drastically. That year, the villages of Shajing were combined to form the Surpassing America People's Commune. It was one of six People's Communes in Bao'an County. During this time, all agricultural land in China became collectively owned and farmed in accordance with the communist spirit of collective collaboration and equality of benefit.[44] Communes were established throughout China's countryside to govern rural communities, providing social services and infrastructure including high schools, regional hospitals, and large agricultural developments such as river dams. Each commune governed numerous production brigades, which provided basic education, medical clinics, and localized irrigation systems. Under each brigade there were production teams, the smallest unit of rural agricultural organization. In 1961, Bao'an County was reorganized into five district offices, 22 communes, 419 brigades, and 2,847 production teams.[45]

During the years of the Great Leap Forward movement, the fevered pursuit of unrealistic production goals consigned China to chaos. Unscientific production methods, false reporting, local corruption and cover-ups, and illogical organizational shifts had a devastating impact on agricultural production. This culminated in the Great Famine (1958–1961) which eventually led to the death of thirty-to-forty-five million people, mainly in rural villages.[46]

In 1959 Shajing's Surpassing America People's Commune was renamed the Shajing People's Commune. In 1960, it became the Western Sea Peoples' Commune, eventually reverting to the Shajing People's Commune in 1963. These successive organizational changes typified the chaotic disorder during the Great Leap Forward and its aftermath. Villagers in Shajing fared relatively better than their counterparts in Bao'an, and in other regions across China, because they were at least able to draw sustenance from the sea. But oyster production, along with village life, once again was devastated.

THE GREAT ESCAPE TO HONG KONG

By 1963, the administrative structure of Bao'an County was reduced to seventeen people's communes and 165 brigades, owing in part to the region's dwindling production and population. A limerick that became popular during this time goes: "Only three treasures remain in Bao'an, / Flies, Mosquitoes, and Shajing oysters. / Nine of ten families fled to Hong Kong, / Leaving behind empty houses to the old and young."[47]

Locally known as "Escape to Hong Kong,"[48] migration across the border had peaked in the late 1940s during the Nationalist-Communist civil war. The "escapes" resumed amid the national political movements of 1957, which coincided with regional flooding and famine. Tens of thousands of famished farmers fled to Luohu Bridge in Bao'an County, bordering Hong Kong. According to a 1959 internal report by the Bao'an County government office, between 1956 and 1958 there were 20,105 escape attempts, 6,448 by residents of Bao'an County and 13,657 by non-residents.[49]

The situation continued to intensify throughout the disastrous years of the Great Leap Forward. At first, many in Guangdong were able to get by with food packages mailed from extensive kinship networks in Hong Kong and elsewhere. When the government decided to stop the postal service to prevent news of the disaster spreading, the famine worsened and desperation flared. Between April and May 1962, there were a few hundred illegal crossings attempted daily. The Hong Kong authorities caught and repatriated a record 5,620 people on May 23.[50] Between April and July 1962, over one hundred thousand people made it to Hong Kong.[51] While most came from Guangdong Province, there were also "escapees" from twelve other provinces in China. This mass exodus triggered military action on both sides of the border. No longer able to rely solely on Guangdong forces, the central government sent twenty thousand Liberation Army soldiers to the border region. The British Hong Kong government changed its previously relaxed policy on immigration and began repatriating illegal immigrants back to China in 1962. The military response from both sides quieted the border for a few years.

However, the biggest post-1949 "Escape Wave" erupted in the 1970s with the onset of the Cultural Revolution. Echoing past trends, most illegal crossing attempts during the Cultural Revolution and its aftermath were made by farmers, but there were also urban residents, students, workers, "Sent-Down Youth,"[52] soldiers, even local government officials and Communist Party members. On the Hong Kong side of the border, repatriation was suspended in 1968. Beginning in 1974, the Touch Base Policy granted work permit and temporary resident status to those who were not caught by the Hong Kong police at the border and managed to reach an urban area.[53] News of this policy sparked more illegal migration attempts throughout China.

In 1979, there were 119,000 attempted crossings from Guangdong, of which 29,000 succeeded. In Shenzhen there had been 557 crossing attempts, 182 of them successful, by government officials since 1978.[54] Ironically, many of the escapees were in charge of the task forces responsible for the prevention of illegal immigration. According to Hong Kong's Immigration Department records, between 1961 and 1984 there were 629,800 legal immigrants from China, 436,600 illegal immigrants who were granted the right to stay in Hong Kong, and 231,437 illegal immigrants repatriated to China.[55] The 1981 census conducted by the Hong Kong government revealed that three million Hong Kong residents were recent or past immigrants from China,[56] and less than 60 percent of the territory's population was born in Hong Kong.[57]

The escalation of illegal migration directly triggered Deng's decision to launch the reforms and open China's doors. In 1978, during a speech that set the agenda for the CCP Third Plenary Session, Deng first formally announced his idea of enabling particular regions to develop before others.

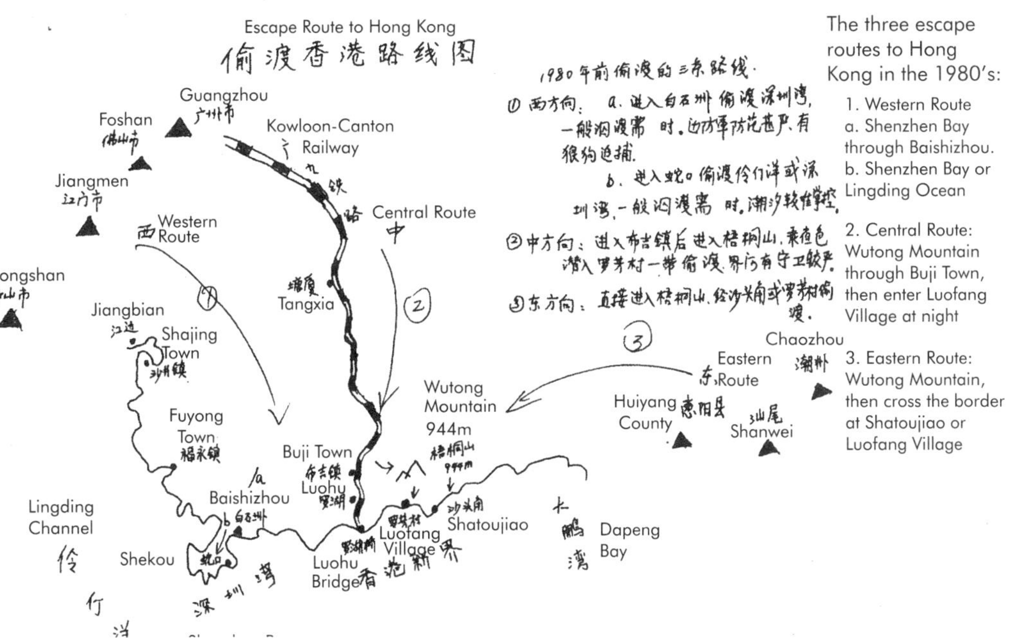

"Escape Routes to Hong Kong" hand drawing by a former "escapee." While many failed, hundreds of thousands from other regions in China reached Hong Kong by crossing the former Bao'an County. Before the 1970s, maps of the region were rare and considered classified for national security reasons.

At one point, he named ten cities that could be possible initial sites. The first one was Shenzhen.

THE RURAL REVOLUTION

When Deng Xiaoping launched his economic reforms, the first target was not the cities but the poverty-stricken villages in China's vast countryside. Two of the most effective reforms were the household responsibility system and the township and village enterprise scheme, both of which ran counter to the central government practices of a planned economy. These two policies initially had far more impact in the villages than in the cities, laying the foundation for China's economic take-off in subsequent decades.[58]

The household responsibility system was intended to encourage agricultural productivity by empowering local villagers through autonomous decision making. This policy was first implemented in rural Anhui Province, a region particularly hard hit by famine, drought, and the chaos of the Cultural Revolution. The province's first party secretary Wan Li was sent from Beijing to Anhui in June 1977, and under his leadership the local government pressed for policies that granted more autonomy to village production teams and individual villagers. In March 1978, Xinhua News Agency announced Wan Li's Implementation of Rural Policies proposal, which allowed production teams to take responsibility for production methods and labor distribution. More importantly, it permitted the farming of surplus "self-reserve land," enabling villagers to generate secondary incomes, in addition to their earnings from working in the village collectives.[59]

Emboldened by the local government's call for reforms and driven by extreme poverty, eighteen men and women from Xiaogang Cun ("village on the small hill") drew up a group agreement to contract a plot of unused land from the village commune and farm it collaboratively. When harvest came, after paying state tax and commune fees, the group was able to keep the surplus produce and profit. After nearly two decades of the People's Commune system, during which the withholding of food or money was deemed an act of counter-communist treason, this seemingly reasonable arrangement had to be conducted in secret. The central government's broad policy did not include any specific guidelines regarding implementation. The villagers were careful to take precautions, having often experienced policies that swung rapidly between extremes. All eighteen swore a blood oath to secrecy, agreeing to collectively raise the young son of the group leader, should it become necessary for the group leader to take the fall.[60] However, when their arrangement was subsequently uncovered by the local government, they were praised instead of punished.[61]

While the Anhui program was widely billed as China's first model of rural reform, local Bao'an County records suggest that just a few months later, in the spring of 1979, two production teams within the Xinqiao Brigade of the Shajing People's Commune had also implemented the responsibility system.[62] For those Shajing villagers who remained behind during the 1970s, life continued under the commune system until 1984. Back in 1966, a new round of state-sponsored rural industrialization under the rubric of "commune and brigade enterprises" was implemented in the region. With the lessons of the Great Leap Forward still fresh, precautions were taken to avoid similar problems, particularly the excessive drain of manpower from the agricultural sector. To counter this possibility, agricultural production was prioritized; all rural industries were tied to agricultural collectives and constantly exhorted to "serve agriculture."[63] The household responsibility system further motivated the populace and led to improved agricultural productivity. In May 1980, Deng Xiaoping publicly announced the economic success of the household responsibility system.[64] On January 1, 1982, the Central Committee of the Communist Party issued a document entitled "Summary of Minutes of the National Conference on Rural Work," which formally promoted the practice and extended it to the whole country.[65] All over China, villagers abandoned more traditional grain farming, such as rice growing, and shifted to higher-revenue produce. By 1983, there were over seven thousand households or work teams in Bao'an County engaged in mariculture and the production of poultry, pork, fruit, and vegetables.[66]

In 1983, People's Communes were abolished and replaced by more than a hundred administrative villages. Each village held a vote to elect its committee members, who served as the local government and managed the collective economy.[67] This type of village organization was largely free from the interventions of municipal bureaucracy. The Shajing People's Commune was remolded into eighteen villages, and local governance was replaced by the new Shajing District Office.[68]

Improvements in production efficiency and villagers' accumulation of disposable income encouraged local collectives to actively participate in the township and village enterprise scheme. By this time, many villagers had gained some form of light industry experience from the commune systems. Industrial enterprises had been established by the socialist communes and production teams since the 1950s. For example, in 1978 there were eight commune and brigade enterprises—a car repair factory, a farm tools factory, an agricultural machinery repair factory, a shipbuilding factory, a bamboo batten–weaving factory, a clothing processing factory, and a non-staple food processing factory—with a combined annual gross output valued at 1.2 million RMB.[69] These factories were exceptions under the centrally planned pre-reform Chinese economic system, where the state owned and operated all industrial and commercial businesses. Prior to 1984, these factories were established and managed by the founding organizations—the commune or production teams, and later the township and villages. When the commune and production team systems were formally abolished, the commune and brigade enterprises were renamed township and village enterprises (TVE).

The most popular and effective business model of the TVE in the Pearl River Delta region was the so-called Sanlaiyibu, which translated to "three imports and one compensation." The term referred to four types of transnational activities: the "three imports" were imported raw materials processing, product manufacturing commensurate with imported samples, and imported parts assembly; while "one compensation" defined the practice of compensation trade, using manufactured products to pay for imported materials and equipment. Promoted by the State Council in July 1978, prior to the establishment of Shenzhen or the special economic zones, Sanlaiyibu was launched in the Pearl River Delta region with the partnership of Hong Kong (and later Taiwan), which provided funding, materials, and technology; the Sanlaiyibu itself provided an abundance of local land, factory space, and cheap labor in the villages.

The first Sanlaiyibu enterprise in Shajing was the Shajing Fuxing Toy Factory. The village provided factory space in modest sheds and employed some villagers to undertake manufacturing jobs. The Hong Kong investor provided raw materials, sample design, machinery, technical management, and order quotas. The villagers were paid for the labor, and the village collective received rental fees for the factory spaces. The village collectives were able to obtain small loans from local banks. Soon Shajing's ancestral hall, warehouses, and farmhouses were all rapidly converted into factory spaces for Sanlaiyibu businesses. By 1983, there were sixty Sanlaiyibu enterprises in Shajing, producing a range of items, including electronics, toys, plastic flowers, computer hardware and accessories, clothing, textiles, leathers, and metal and wood products.[70]

One village in Shajing was particularly prominent during this period of industrialization. In 1982, the Wanfeng Village collective raised around one hundred thousand RMB by auctioning collective assets. With an additional three million RMB loan from the bank, the village built basic infrastructure and established five material-processing factories. In 1983, Wanfeng Village built 250,000 square meters of factory space for light industry production. By August 1984, the annual income of this collective had reached 2.5 million RMB, with fixed assets amounting to twelve million RMB.[71] In May 1985, the village set up the Wanfeng Enterprise Company and became the first village in China to adopt a shareholding system.[72] Of the six million total shares, the Wanfeng Village collective held three million and publicly sold the other three million.[73] Soon other villages in Shajing and throughout Shenzhen followed Wanfeng's precedent and set up shareholding companies. By 1987, Wanfeng Enterprise Company's total shares were valued at forty million RMB. With the capital gained, the village built a 450,000-square-meter factory. Many Hong Kong companies began to establish factory operations in Wanfeng Village. By 1993, it accommodated sixty Sanlaiyibu enterprises, making a variety of products—including computers, telephones, electric fans, recorders, TVs, clothing, and electric toys—for export to the US, Canada, and Southeast Asia.[74]

Figures from 1987 show that seventeen of the eighteen villages in Shajing operated a total of 158 Sanlaiyibu and Foreign Collaborated Enterprises, which had attracted a total of 0.4 billion HK dollars investment from Hong Kong.[75] Across Shenzhen overall, villages played host to more than 3,200 processing trade enterprises by 1988, employing 24,000 factory workers. By this time, the majority of the factory workforce in Shenzhen was no longer made up of original villagers. The relaxation of the *hukou* system in 1984 encouraged the migration of rural laborers to Shenzhen, where they took factory jobs in the TVEs. While their origins were modest, the TVEs became the economic engines of Shenzhen in the 1980s, and later of rural regions all across the country. These village enterprises played a primary role in fueling the eventual "Chinese ascent."[76]

OYSTERS OUTSOURCED

Rapid industrialization created by the numerous Sanlaiyibu enterprises drastically changed the local landscape.[77] While booming village industries brought economic development to the region and wealth to the Shajing villagers, the land, rivers, and coastal sea became polluted. Discharge from the factories caused large-scale water pollution. Sensitive to pollutants, the century-old mangrove forests that lined Shajing's sea coast started to deteriorate. Without the mangrove forests, which acted as natural purifiers, oysters suffered from the environmental change. The oysters that managed to survive were much smaller than those of previous years; the larvae needed longer to mature, and the milky white flesh of the oysters grown closest to the Shajing Village shores began to take on greenish hues. From 1984 onward, yields from the oyster fields along Shenzhen's western coast sharply decreased year by year. By the end of the decade, nearly all the local Shajing oyster cultivation beds had died off. The Shajing oysters had survived thousands of years of sea change caused by geological upheaval, warlord conflicts, the Japanese invasion, Civil War, the Great Famine, and the Cultural Revolution, but not those precipitated by the economic zone.

Despite the growing village industry economy, many oyster farmers were determined not to give up the expertise that had been passed down to them over generations. One such person was Chen Zhaogen, a *Lao Shajing,* or someone born and raised in Shajing and from one of the original village clans. Chen's parents were oyster farmers. He received a local village education, and had worked at the Shajing Fisheries Station since 1962 as an accountant. In the mid-1980s, Chen and a group of villagers explored the possibility of relocating the oyster cultivation areas to other sites that still had the water quality of pre-1979 Shajing. Throughout the 1980s, Chen traveled along the sea coast of the Guangdong and Guangxi Provinces, taking samples to measure indicators such as temperature, salinity, and pollution levels. A few years later, he found a site on the coast of Guangdong's city of Taishan, which had not yet been industrialized. There, the quality of the seawater and its currents was remarkably similar to that of Shajing. The Shajing villagers signed an agreement with the Taishan city government to rent three thousand *mu* of sea area for fifteen years.[78] Following successful cultivation and harvest, the villagers created additional sites in other coastal regions. By insisting that all the oyster larvae came from original Shajing oyster seeds and by utilizing their unique three-zone migratory cultivation method, the villagers were able to transplant the Shajing oyster brand to these off-site locations. These three new oyster-farming sites eventually exceeded the total area occupied by the original Shajing oyster beds, so that, by the end of the 1990s, oyster production here had exceeded Shajing's historical highs. In the mid-1990s, the Shajing oyster farmers finally accepted two hundred million RMB in government compensation and turned over the former oyster ponds along the Shajing coast to industrialization and urban development.[79]

Today the Shajing oyster industry is a large multinational business with investors and operators in Hong Kong, Singapore, and Indonesia.[80] Chen is credited with saving the Shajing oysters from extinction. Nearly eighty years old, Chen is still working in Shajing's oyster industry. He hopes, one day in the near future, to bring oyster cultivation back home. In his own words, Chen expressed his hopes and fears: "The Shajing oyster is a treasure of Shenzhen. I have done everything I could to ensure its continuation. At present, I am still going all out for the cause. In my lifetime, what I fear the most is the destruction of the Shajing oyster by our hands. What I wish to see the most is its healthy survival and prosperity."[81]

Chen had reason to hope for environmental improvements in the Shajing area. In 1998, plans were made to place an area of twenty-four square kilometers along the coast of Shajing under special control, restricting industrial development in order to protect the area from further damage and to conduct remediation measures. This plan was implemented in 2001. Aquaculture activities and coastal reclamation along the entire western coast of Shenzhen had destroyed large areas of native mangroves. When surveyed, the vegetation in this controlled development zone was found to be sparse and lacking in biodiversity: there were only sixty-two families and 187 species of plants in the area. In 2002, the Shenzhen Waterlands Resort was established as an ecotourism site as well as a research and demonstration base for the National High Technology Research and Development Program of China (863 Program).[82] The core ecological remediation testing area was 1.9 square kilometers of "dyke-ponds" built upon the infrastructure of the original fishery ponds. The remodeled dykes forming the ponds were widened and planted with vegetation to form ecosystems that would balance energy input and output.[83] The dyke-pond systems were designed to increase floodwater storage and lower the groundwater table, while optimizing production efficiency and profits.[84] One such example was the mulberry trees that fed silkworms, the droppings of which fed the fish; the organically enriched dredging of the pond was then used as fertilizer for the mulberry trees.[85] In addition, two square kilometers of mangroves were planted, which rapidly improved water quality and helped to increase the quantity and quality of mariculture in the ponds. By 2003, following these ecological remediation programs, plant biodiversity had grown to more than 510 species, and more than thirty species of migratory birds were once again attracted to the area.[86] In recognition of these efforts, the United Nations Environment Program (UNEP) and the Global Environmental Facility (GEF) hosted the second South China Sea Wetlands Working Committee in the resort.[87]

While generations of oyster farmers had already linked the presence of mangroves with healthy oysters, in 2009 the Waterlands Resort collaborated with Guangzhou's Sun Yat-sen University to determine the impact of mangroves on water purification. Researchers tested the level of petroleum hydrocarbon, a common toxic substance in the Pearl River resulting from pollution, in oysters cultivated near different species of mangroves. The university's report demonstrated that hydrocarbon levels in oysters grown with certain species of mangroves could meet national standards for food safety requirements.[88] With these measures and other efforts in environmental remediation around the region, Shajing oysters may migrate home again at some point in the future.

The region's long history cannot be discounted in any narrative of post-1979 Shenzhen, and any understanding of industrialization in the countryside must begin with an understanding of the countryside before industrialization. As the story of the Shajing oysters shows, the past historical agrarian processes impacted Shenzhen's later development. In parallel, the rapid urbanization and industrialization have significantly damaged the region's natural landscape, and continue to do so today. The centuries-long history of Shajing oyster farming also highlights the important and evolving role of villagers in the development of the Shenzhen region. The oyster farmers of Shajing adapted to the rapidly changing environment around them, preserving the reputation and culture of oyster cultivation passed down for generations even as the region moved rapidly in the direction of industrialization and mechanization. The pair of chapters that comprise Part III of the book extend this narrative of rural and urban, village and city, agriculture and industry. It is at times a narrative of confrontation, and at times one of collaboration. Anchored in two symbolic building types of Shenzhen, the tower and the nail house, respectively, these chapters tell the story of the city's urban infrastructure construction from various perspectives of the government, villagers, and developers, all experiencing intense processes of negotiations throughout the process of modernizing Shenzhen.

PART III

CITY CONSTRUCTION

5.

TOWERS BY THE HONG KONG BORDER

Despite the modest expectations he had prior to his arrival, Yang Hongxiang was disappointed when he set his eyes on the dusty surroundings that were to become his home. He did not even bother to lift his camera to take a photo documenting the historic event. In July 1982, he arrived in Shenzhen as a member of the People's Liberation Army Infrastructure Engineering Corps. Requisitioned by Mayor Liang Xiang, the regiments were dispatched to support the newly established municipal government in constructing the Shenzhen special economic zone. As the regiment's designated news journalist, Yang had already read up on the news coverage of Shenzhen, but was nevertheless surprised by the situation on the ground. In undertaking this assignment to document the works of the Infrastructure Corps, he inadvertently became one of the first journalists and photographers to witness the Shenzhen special economic zone.

After failing his college entrance exams in 1978, Yang enlisted in the Chinese military's Engineering Corps. He wanted to learn how to drive, see the world beyond his small home village in Yunnan Province, and experience snow.[1] He was one of three chosen out of the forty applicants from his hometown—the Infrastructure Corps only accepted those with literacy skills and secondary school diplomas. After three months of military boot camp training in Hubei Province, he was sent to a construction team in Shanghai to learn everything from foundation works to bricklaying. He spent his free time reading, writing in his journal, and working on his team's blackboard bulletins. His supervisor soon became aware of his writing skills and encouraged him to write news reports on the work of his regiment. He excelled at these tasks and traveled all over the country, reporting on the regiment's construction work in over forty towns and cities. Since its formation in 1996, the People's Liberation Army (PLA) Infrastructure Engineering Corps had contributed to China's infrastructure construction by building dams, paving roads, and constructing factories and hospitals. It was Zhou Enlai and Deng Xiaoping who first proposed to Mao Zedong the reorganization of the army's construction teams into the Infrastructure Engineering Corps, to "conduct civic works in peacetime and to fight in times of war." With thirty-two divisions and over 490,000 workers, the corps also contributed to ironwork, coal mining, oilfield work, and telecommunications construction, as well as post-disaster relief.[2]

Liang Xiang's request to the central government for infrastructural support in 1980 coincided with Deng Xiaoping's efforts to reduce the size of the PLA, then the world's largest military at six million strong. In 1981, Deng decided to discharge two million soldiers from the Railway Engineering Corps and Infrastructure Engineering Corps over the next four years. The majority were transferred to related government departments under the auspices of the State Council. Hydrological and geological units were reassigned to their respective military regions; the communication corps was transferred to the Communication Department of General Staff.[3] By 1985, Deng had cut another one million military personnel in the PLA by disbanding four military area commands in China's western inland provinces.[4] Yang and his fellow platoon soldiers were envious of those sent to urban centers such as Beijing, or even to smaller cities and townships. Those with connections in the military or government pushed to be transferred to other locations that had incoming work units. In 1982, authorities in the city of Shenzhen could only provide barren plots of land for the new arrivals to set up camp with military-issued tents. There were no housing provisions for them. It is worth remembering that when the municipality of Shenzhen was established in 1979, there were only seven hundred construction workers and three small factories producing concrete and bricks.[5] The twenty thousand Infrastructure Engineering Corps personnel who were relocated there instantly doubled the population living within the special economic zone. In addition to housing, they also had to procure food and water for themselves. Indeed, the lack of basic infrastructure and housing provisions was the very reason that Mayor Liang Xiang had requested additional personnel and equipment from the central government. However, the sudden influx of personnel at first merely exacerbated these issues and acutely demonstrated the city's lack of basic services and infrastructure.

As early as September 1979, on the order of the State Council and the Central Military Commission, a regiment of two thousand Infrastructure Engineering Corps soldiers was dispatched from Anshan in Liaoning Province to the Shenzhen special economic zone. They worked in harsh conditions with limited equipment, while subsisting on rationed water and food, from their first task of dredging the clogged Buji River in 1979 to their first construction project of building the Shenzhen Municipal Complex in 1981. In 1981 the first team of the Shenzhen Infrastructure Corps was assigned to build Shenzhen's first office tower, the Shenzhen headquarters of China's Ministry for Electronics Industry. Led by Ma Chengli, deputy chief of staff of the first regiment in Shenzhen, the team had fourteen months to build a twenty-story, 15,300-square-meter modern office tower in which the government had invested three million yuan. A mammoth construction challenge, this would be both the first tower in Shenzhen and the first tall building project for the construction team. Construction required a 150-meter-tall, three-ton tower crane, which the team had to request from their Liaoning home military unit, three thousand kilometers away. The team studied the technology, conducted experiments, and visited the 114-meter-tall Guangzhou Baiyun Hotel. Built in 1976, the hotel was China's first building over one hundred meters tall. In August 1982, Yang Hongxiang proudly photographed and reported news of the sixty-meter-tall Electronics Tower, completed one month ahead of schedule.[6] Constructed before the widening of Shennan Boulevard, this "First Tower of Shenzhen" still draws attention today, as the only tall building on the street not set back the requisite fifteen to thirty meters.

While constructing the tower and installing modern facilities, the Shenzhen Infrastructure Corps tolerated somewhat primitive living conditions. Unlike Infrastructure Corps units resettled elsewhere in China,

Many of Shenzhen's earliest and most challenging roads, dams, and buildings were constructed by a unique workforce of twenty thousand Infrastructure Corps soldiers sent to Shenzhen during the early 1980s.

Yang and his comrades were not offered shelter in existing military camps or civilian housing developments. Regiments were instead assigned to plots of land scattered throughout the special economic zone, which were temporarily "borrowed" from nearby villages without any expropriation procedures. Yang Hongxiang's regiment was assigned to a plot of land on a gentle hill covered with tall wild grass. There was no plumbing or electricity. They initially relied on small natural springs for drinking water. When these became bug infested, they had to bring in special equipment to dig wells. Located close to the shores of Shenzhen Bay, the brackish well water tasted bitter and salty from the sea. There was just one water truck, which transported drinking water from nearby sources and distributed it to all the regiments stationed in the Shenzhen SEZ.

In addition to food and water shortages, Yang Hongxiang's strongest memory of life in the barracks involved two disastrous incidents in 1983. In July, the small power generator at the camp short-circuited and caused a major fire. Most of the bamboo forest was burned down, along with the twenty-three barracks.[7] Fortunately, the fire broke out during the daytime when the regiment was out working, so they were all safe. On September 9, during a level 12 typhoon, the soldiers were required to assist with preventive measures elsewhere in the city. One soldier, whose wife and child were visiting him at the time, tied a rope around their waists and fastened it to the column of their barracks before leaving. The strong winds carried away the roofs of all the sheds, as well as all the bedding and belongings inside. Even the giant wrought-iron cooking pot used by the cooking team disappeared. When the soldiers returned, they found that luckily no one was hurt. However, for many it was the last straw, and hundreds from Yang's regiment left Shenzhen.

THE HOTEL THAT BROKE THE IRON RICE BOWL

Owing to scarce military funding and lack of building materials, the soldiers built their barracks out of bamboo poles, which were commonly used in construction projects as scaffolding. Using cut bamboo poles as columns and slender stems with leaves to build the walls, they then covered the roofs with oiled felt carpeting. The barracks became known as the Bamboo Forest, a name that is still used today to label the district and subway station in that location.[8]

Some fellow soldiers jokingly nicknamed their barracks the Bamboo Garden Hotel, in reference to the only three-star hotel in Shenzhen at the time. Located in Luohu District, the Bamboo Garden Hotel was notable because of its impact on Shenzhen's economic market reforms. In December 1979, the newly formed Shenzhen municipal government informed Hong Kong of its intention to release a newly drafted document, "The Trade Act of Property Compensation." The act would enable Shenzhen to provide land and factory space to new businesses, with foreign investors providing funds and equipment and sharing future profit with the Shenzhen landowners.[9] The day after this informal notice, Alan Lau arrived at the government's temporary office on a borrowed bicycle—there were still no taxis or bus services beyond the Luohu Bridge border. He would become Shenzhen's first Hong Kong investor. Lau was CEO of Millie's

Group, a Hong Kong–based company, and he also owned one of the most prominent Chinese-language newspapers in Hong Kong at the time, *Tin Tin Daily News*. Surprised by this unexpected and eager investor, the Shenzhen government swiftly reached an agreement with Lau to build a modern hotel. Shenzhen would provide land and labor, and Lau would invest fifteen million Hong Kong dollars, with future profits to be shared. The agreement signed by the Shenzhen Food Services Company and Hong Kong–based Millie's Group on December 21, 1979, was the first Sino-foreign joint venture in Shenzhen, as well as in post-reform China.[10]

However, operations at the Bamboo Garden Hotel had a rocky start upon its completion in 1980. Because of its competitive salaries and its status as a foreign joint venture, the hotel was able to attract experienced employees. However, a clash of cultures soon emerged. Considering it wasteful to clean rooms and launder bedding on a daily basis, the hotel employees fell back to a weekly cleaning schedule, which had been the standard at the state-owned enterprise hotels where they had previously worked. Furthermore, the young female receptionists refused to comply with the hotel's request that they wear makeup, including lipstick, and bow and smile to customers, as these courtesies were seen as capitalistic and demeaning. In March 1980, when the leaders of the Guangzhou Provincial Labor Office held a panel discussion with foreign investors, Lau took the opportunity to voice his concerns: "We Hong Kong businessmen come to Shenzhen to invest, yet you are still using the fixed tenure employment system, where workers hold the Iron Rice Bowl; the workers that I need cannot get in, whereas those I did not want cannot be kicked out. The enterprise lacks vitality. This simply cannot work."[11]

Lau proposed that the hotel establish work contracts with employees, so that both sides had the freedom to end the contract with a one-month advance notice. The recommendation was quickly accepted by the Shenzhen government. By October 1, 1980, the Shenzhen Municipal Labor Bureau had authorized two Sino-foreign (Shenzhen and Hong Kong) joint ventures—the Bamboo Garden Hotel and the Friendship Hotel—to provisionally implement a contract labor system. In November, the Bamboo Garden Hotel became the first work unit in Shenzhen, and in post-reform China, to institute contracts with individual workers. The hotel's subsequent implementation of a variable pay system and floating wages became a national model, studied by Beijing's CPC Central Organization Department.[12]

Barracks of the Infrastructure soldiers after a destructive typhoon in 1983. Owing to limited resources and building materials, most of the soldiers lived in temporary shelters of bamboo structures and straw-mat roofs.

The Bamboo Garden Hotel began a domino effect that cascaded toward the end of the communist Iron Rice Bowl policy in Shenzhen, and eventually all over China. In 1987, the Shenzhen government submitted a draft of the "Labor Regulations of the Shenzhen Special Economic Zone" to the Guangdong Provincial People's Congress. Guangdong not only accepted the proposal, but on August 19, 1988, instituted these labor regulations in special economic zones across Guangdong Province, extending the Shenzhen experiment to the Zhuhai and Shantou economic zones as well.[13] On October 1, 1993, the implementation of the labor regulations of Shenzhen special economic zone paved the way for the 1995 labor law of the People's Republic of China.[14] The labor contract system radically changed China's existing social welfare arrangement, which had been based on work units; therefore, new social security and national pension systems were also implemented in 1995. The director of the Shenzhen Municipal Labor Bureau, Zhang Wenchao, stated, "The labor reform of Shenzhen was started from the Bamboo Garden Hotel."[15] He was present as a staff member at the Guangzhou Labor Office when Alan Lau urged Shenzhen to challenge the status quo.

In describing the significant impact of the labor reform in dismantling the socioeconomic structure of China, Zeng Hongwen, an editor of *Records of Shenzhen Municipal Labor and Social Security*, commented that "the appearance of the labor contract system is like the explosion of an atomic bomb." He added, "The Shenzhen Speed of 'three days one floor' in building the International Trade Center was achieved through action. The Shekou Industrial Zone advocated 'time is money, efficiency is life,' and that was achieved through a few cents extra per cart pulled, not through shouting slogans."[16]

In addition to the Bamboo Garden Hotel, Alan Lau proposed building a commercial residential complex—East Lake Beautiful Garden. The proposal was accepted by the Shenzhen municipal government, which agreed to provide a plot of land of Lau's choosing, while Lau himself agreed to provide funds for the design, construction, and sale of the units in Hong Kong. Negotiating on behalf of the Shenzhen government was Luo Jinxing, the deputy director of Luohu District Construction Headquarters at the time. Luo initially worried that leasing the land was a crime against communist doctrine, until he discovered a precedent in *Collected Works of Lenin:* quoting from Engels' 1872 "The Housing Question," Lenin asserted that "the abolition of property in land is not the abolition of ground rent."[17] Choosing to interpret the quote as permission, Luo drove a hard bargain with Lau, arriving at an agreement that enabled the Shenzhen government to retain 85 percent of the joint venture's future profits.

The 22,680-square-meter plot for the East Lake residential development became the subject of Shenzhen's first Land Lease Agreement, signed on January 1, 1980. It set a precedent for all future land leases in Luohu, and more importantly, gave much-needed confidence to Shenzhen's leaders. The central government in Beijing had provided only thirty million yuan in direct funds for constructing the city of Shenzhen, while development of the initial four square kilometers in Luohu District alone would have required one billion yuan just for basic infrastructure. The success of the East Lake development was a crucial test of whether land speculation could be used to generate much-needed funding to build the city. Lau commissioned a Hong Kong architect to design the residential complex, which featured sixteen apartment buildings, each six to seven stories in height. The design was typical of Hong Kong apartments at the time. When the project plans were unveiled on the Hong Kong Real Estate market, all the units were snapped up off-plan within three days by Hong Kong buyers.[18] This was a shock back in Shenzhen—it was the first time that many had witnessed the phenomenon of speculating on future developments to generate cash. The successful completion of the East Lake Beautiful Garden in 1981 was a milestone, marking China's first commercial residential complex and its first Sino-foreign joint venture real estate project.[19]

CHINA'S TALLEST TOWER CONSTRUCTED AT "SHENZHEN SPEED"

During Shenzhen's early days, the Bamboo Garden Hotel was used to hold official government meetings. In 1981, Liang Xiang invited provincial and city officials from all over China to a special banquet at the hotel. The occasion was the announcement of Shenzhen's proposal to make one of its construction projects, the International Trade Center, into the "Tallest Tower of China." The building's planned height had been increased from thirty-eight stories to fifty-three stories, ostensibly to provide office space in the building to provinces and cities outside Shenzhen. Following the initial pleasantries, Liang Xiang made a surprising admission: "Since this building belongs to everyone, constructing the building is also everyone's business. Shenzhen is not afraid to appear foolish; we don't have enough money to build it, and must depend on your help. Frankly, I invited you here today, for one purpose—'collective funding for construction.'"[20] This was his solution to the Shenzhen government's desperate lack of funding. He invited fellow municipal governments to invest in Shenzhen, providing capital for its construction in exchange for a thirty-year period of use. Provinces and cities from around China could use this building as their headquarters in Shenzhen to promote their own economies. Liang Xiang further enticed local officials with examples: "Jilin's ginseng, Suzhou's embroidery, Beijing's Tongrentang Chinese medicine, Shanghai's light electronics, Dongbei's machinery, Hunan's nonferrous metals . . . all could be brought here to exhibit and sell. This will become an International Trade Center of ten thousand merchants!"[21] This endeavor cemented strong links between Shenzhen and the rest of China's domestic markets, especially during the formative years of the economic zone. With the ad hoc start-up fund and support from the municipal government, ground was broken on the International Trade Center in May 1982. The company in charge of the project was the new state-owned Shenzhen Properties and Resources Development, and the architect was Zhu Zhenhui from Wuhan's Central-South Architectural Design Institute (CSADI).

However, the project continued to face setbacks during the construction process. In 1983, the typhoon that destroyed the Infrastructure Corps' Bamboo Forest barracks also wreaked havoc on the construction site. The city government appointed a new manager of the development company: Ma Chengli, the Infrastructure Corps team leader who led the construction of the Electronics Tower. Utilizing his previous army works and construction experience, he managed to save most of the twenty thousand tons of concrete on site.[22] In addition, he faced the challenge of having to raise additional funds for the project: the city could not provide any more financial assistance, and the banking loans system had yet to be established. Learning from projects like the East Lake residence, Shenzhen Properties built a housing development on a piece of land provided by the city, and sold the units off-plan to raise upfront cash. When a corporate buyer with a steel supply wanted to purchase a property but did not have cash, Ma agreed to trade the property for steel. He sold the steel on the market, and the money was then put toward construction of the tower.[23] Ma explained away the dubious legality of the process with a commonly used phrase that emerged in Shenzhen during this early period: "special solutions for special tasks in the special zone."[24]

News of the ambitious tower construction project spread quickly. It was closely observed by the government and general public, with progress reported in Shenzhen as well as in the Hong Kong press. In order to ensure quality and efficiency, the project team leaders decided to use climbing formwork and slip-form construction for the vertical concrete structure. These methods, which required additional organizational management and a twenty-four-hour continuous site program, had yet to be tested in Mainland China. Several failed attempts initially concerned all parties and the public media. After several trials and under tremendous pressure, the construction team gradually acquired the skills and techniques to meet the challenges of setting, curing, and strengthening the continuously poured-in-place concrete.

Construction of the first floors took around fifteen days per floor, a pace equivalent to that of conventional construction methods. Lacking the proper equipment, however, the team struggled to pour the concrete—2,400 cubic meters for each floor slab of 1,530 square meters—within the prescribed timeframe. After rounds of negotiations with the Shenzhen municipal government and the banks, the project leaders finally obtained sufficient loans to rent four new concrete mixers, a mixing station, a concrete pump, and an additional crane. With the added equipment, the construction team finally achieved the right concrete quality and pouring speed in their fourth round of trials. The workers were motivated by the equipment and the promise of a bonus wage should the tower be completed on time. By the twentieth floor, the construction team had achieved a speed of one floor every six days; from the thirtieth floor onward, they moved at a rate of one floor every three days, giving rise to the popular catchphrase "one floor every three days," which is often cited to illustrate the unique "Shenzhen speed."

Construction of the International Trade Center's final floors coincided with Deng Xiaoping's historic visit to Shenzhen, when he watched its construction from the roof of the twenty-story International Commerce Tower across the street. While the International Commerce Tower made history by hosting Deng in 1984, its construction process had been controversial. When the project started in the summer of 1981, the Guangdong Province Construction Bureau appointed a Guangdong-owned construction company, as was conventional at the time. However, this company repeatedly delayed the construction date while raising the budget three times in one week.[25] Liang Xiang, who had recently taken up his appointment, refused to accept this protocol. Reflecting on the experience of Shekou Industrial Zone, he decided to instigate an open tendering process for engaging the construction company. Eight companies competed in the tender bid, which was won by the First Metallurgical Construction Company from Hubei Province for their demonstrated experience, reasonable budget, and fast pace of construction. The process led to strong opposition from protectionist province offices, and eventually a high-level official from the National Construction Bureau arrived from Beijing to mediate the situation.[26] The bureau insisted that Shenzhen prioritize construction companies based in the home province, in this case Guangdong, and forbid the use of companies from Hong Kong and Macau. Despite this national and provincial pressure, Liang Xiang continued to push ahead with the process of public tendering, extending the opportunity to out-of-province companies and even proactively inviting bids from Hong Kong and Macau.

International Trade Center visited by Shenzhen's second mayor, Liang Xiang, in 1983. Construction of this symbolic tower at "one floor every three days" inspired the now ubiquitous term "Shenzhen Speed."

Shenzhen thus became the first city in China to open its construction market nationally through competitive tendering. This paved the way for the Wuhan-based China Construction Third Engineering Bureau to win the tender for the construction of the International Trade Center in 1982. The company faced considerable pressure to experiment with new technologies, in order to ensure quality and speed of construction and to deliver the project as promised.

The speed of construction, rather than the building's height, was the lightning rod that spread the news of the building's progress throughout China. After witnessing the construction of the building's final floors, Deng often repeated the rate of "one floor every three days" to showcase the instant success of Shenzhen and his market reforms. On March 15, 1984, China's Xinhua News Agency distributed a global press release that highlighted the construction speed of the International Trade Center building in Shenzhen.[27] The International Trade Center was completed on September 4, 1984. At fifty-three floors and 160 meters, it was the tallest building in China. To mark this triumphant occasion, a 160-meter string of bright red firecrackers was hung from the top of the building—when lit, the crackling explosions continued for twenty minutes.[28]

In addition to the building's height, its roof structure—which featured a revolving restaurant—made the International Trade Center an instant icon. The restaurant, central atrium, and lobby escalators were all inspired by the works of American architect and developer John Portman.[29] Indeed, the building bears multiple similarities to the Hyatt Regency designed and developed by Portman in downtown Atlanta. Completed in 1967, that iconic twenty-two-story hotel was defined by its saucer-like top, which contained the revolving restaurant Polaris. In fact, Portman was in the process of constructing the fifty-six-story Marriott Marquis in New York City at the same time that the International Trade Center was being built. The demolition to make way for the Marriott marked the beginning of Times Square's controversial redevelopment, dubbed the Great Theater Massacre of 1982 by its opponents. The top floors (47 to 49) of the completed Marriott were home to a revolving restaurant called the View. At the opening in late 1985, Mayor Ed Koch declared the building to be the center of New York City.

The revolving restaurant atop the International Trade Center in Shenzhen opened a few months before the View, in the spring of 1985. It was instantly the top attraction for domestic and international visitors, including international heads of states, and remained so for many years. One of the first foreign dignitaries to visit the restaurant was Singapore's President Lee Kwan Yew, in September 1985. A month later, United States Vice President George H. W. Bush also visited Shenzhen and stopped at the rooftop restaurant. Shortly after his visit, a Hong Kong news article emphasized Bush's October 15 meeting "with eighty-one-year-old strongman Mr. Deng Xiaoping."[30] Deng would visit the same restaurant nearly seven years later, during his second, and last, tour of Shenzhen in 1992.

SHENZHEN'S FAST RISE AND ABRUPT FALL

George Bush's visit to Shenzhen also made news in the United States. The *New York Times* reported, "Mr. Bush lauded the development in the special economic zone after winding up his six-day visit to China with a flight in a drab-painted US Marine Corps helicopter. He said of Shenzhen: 'It's inspirational. There is a lot of work going on and a lot of work to do. But I am optimistic about its future. [It] looks like there is a lot of potential for a lot of people.'"[31] In addition to touring the city's modern buildings, Bush, accompanied by his wife, Barbara, visited businesses and enterprises. A particular highlight was the first Sino-US joint venture in Shenzhen: a Pepsi Cola plant in Luohu District, built in 1982 using eight million US dollars of investment capital. There, he learned of the company's output-based incentives and bonus wage policies. The local Shenzhen press widely reported Bush's "humorous" comment after he took a sip from a freshly canned product right off the assembly line: "The Pepsi in Shenzhen tastes better than the ones I had in America."[32] The company's policy experimentations also clearly made a strong impression on Bush. The *New York Times* gave the article a provocative headline—"Bush Calls on Soviet to Imitate China"—and quoted him on the subject: "'I'll be honest with you, I'd like to see the Soviets do the same sort of thing, because I think it would be a moderating force,' Mr Bush said. He was referring to China's policies of introducing incentives, competition and foreign investment."[33] This was remarkable at a time when the Soviet Union was a global powerhouse and the US's biggest competitor, while China was still widely seen as an underdeveloped country. However, it is worth remembering that in 1985, the specific market mechanisms Bush described as "China's policies" were in fact only implemented in Shenzhen.

The economic reforms that increased competition, allowed incentives, and opened the market to external enterprises also nudged Shenzhen toward social, cultural, and institutional reforms. The vibrant economy motivated local workers and companies, and also attracted experienced design and construction companies to set up headquarters in Shenzhen. Despite an uphill battle over the lack of infrastructure and shortage of government funding, the first phase of Shenzhen's construction boom reached a peak in the mid-1980s. Urban infrastructure projects including roads, reservoirs, housing, and factories were completed at rapid speed; many of these projects were undertaken by companies that originated from the former Infrastructure Construction Corps. State-owned enterprises in Shenzhen—including several new construction and development companies, reorganized from the former Infrastructure Corps—

struggled to adjust. In 1982 and 1983, the State Council and Central Military Commission in Beijing issued two documents that demobilized the twenty thousand soldiers of the Infrastructure Construction Corps and gave directions for their reorganization and restructuring. Regiments No. 1, No. 16, No. 19, No. 303, and No. 304 were adapted respectively to form the Shenzhen No. 1, No. 2, No. 3, No. 4, and No. 5 Construction Engineering Companies. Regiment No. 302 manned the Shenzhen Municipal Engineering Company. Regiment No. 802 was reorganized as the Shenzhen Mechanical and Electrical Equipment Installation Company. Regiment No. 912 was transferred to the Shenzhen Engineering Geological Investigation Company. In addition, the Temporary Command Hospital of Metallurgical Headquarters and the outpatient department of No. 31 Detachment merged to form the Shenzhen Construction Workers Hospital, later the Shenzhen No. 2 People's Hospital.[34]

Many of the well-educated regiment leaders joined government agencies at a time when Shenzhen was in desperate need of experienced management personnel. Their camaraderie was cemented through this unique bond, creating a trusted network that spanned their varied destinations. These individuals would later play significant roles in the public and private sectors of the city. The majority of former soldiers were channeled into various companies as a result of the reorganization, and this large, disciplined workforce had an immediate and pronounced impact.

In 1980, the floor area under construction in Shenzhen totaled 524,000 square meters, almost double the 293,000 square meters recorded in 1979. This number increased to 969,000 square meters in 1981, leaping to 2,507,000 square meters in 1982 and 3,684,000 square meters in 1983. In 1984, the year of Deng's historic visit, the floor area under construction increased to 6,446,000 square meters, reaching a stunning 10,309,000 square meters the following year.[35] By the summer of 1985, the Shenzhen city government had reviewed and approved 297 high-rise buildings. By 1987, sixty-six towers above one hundred meters had been constructed.[36] The majority of these construction projects were concentrated in Luohu, the first district in the city to be developed.

Shenzhen, along with Mayor Liang Xiang, became the hottest topic of discussion around the country. In the spring of 1985, Liang Xiang was on the cover of the Chinese Communist Party–sponsored journal *Half Moon Dialogue* and nominated as one of the "Top Ten National News Makers." However, criticism mounted alongside the accolades.

Shenzhen had received criticism since the special economic zone was first established in 1980. While Deng's visit in 1984 briefly tempered this criticism, condemnations had reached a crescendo by 1985. During this time, Shenzhen found itself caught in a national tug of war between China's reformers and conservatives. While Deng and Gu Mu led the reformers in the central government, the conservatives were led by the equally respected Chen Yun, head of the national Economic and Financial Commission. Formerly a strong supporter of Deng, who had even led some of the early economic reform efforts in the 1960s, Chen had become increasingly concerned with the reform activities of the 1980s. He publicly criticized the economic reforms, warning of the consequences of national inflation, financial overheating, and ideological corruption. Along with numerous other party elders, Chen went on the attack, citing problems of money laundering, smuggling, and government corruption in the special economic zones. As Shenzhen was the focus of Deng's praise, it was also the target of his opponents' sharpest criticism.[37]

Surprisingly, it was a series of articles published in Hong Kong in 1984 and 1985 that provided supporting evidence to Shenzhen's critics in the central government. Most frequently referenced was a February 1984 report by a Hong Kong–based economist who analyzed the economic data of the SEZ between 1980 and 1984, and deduced that Shenzhen did not meet Gu Mu's initial goal for the SEZ to be "export-oriented" and "foreign investment-oriented." He concluded that

> the prosperity of Shenzhen relies basically on the special economic policies of the special zone, making money in the domestic market with imported goods and merchandise. This runs contrary to the original conception and mandate. If Shenzhen's practice holds an important reference value for the coastal opening cities, it refers mainly to lessons to be learned, rather than experience of success, as well as whether Shenzhen will be able to figure out a real solution in the coming days.[38]

The article emphasized that Shenzhen benefited from central government favoritism and gained wealth at the expense of domestic investment and spending. In addition, the author pointed out that the majority of Shenzhen's yearly revenue was not derived from export-oriented industrial production; rather, it was from speculative investment in real estate and infrastructure construction. This was completely at odds with the socialist ideals of economic productivity at the time. Many similar articles appeared in Hong Kong throughout 1984 and 1985, also raising questions and concerns about Shenzhen's elevation as a successful model of China's economic reforms.

Shenzhen's 1984 infrastructure investment of two billion yuan was defined as "non-industrial," and discredited on the grounds that it was mostly comprised of investments by Chinese state banks and state-owned enterprises, rather than foreign investment. A proposed 40 percent increase in infrastructure projects—435 new projects in total—was cited as further evidence of unbridled and unplanned expansion.[39] Shenzhen's GDP was an astonishing 2.7 billion yuan in 1985, eighteen times that of 1979. In the same year, Shenzhen municipality's total fixed assets investment was 3.3 billion yuan, 83 percent of which was in infrastructure construction.[40] All these figures were suddenly viewed with disappointment, even by the city's own government agencies, because they were predominantly construction-focused.[41]

Senior leaders at various levels of government began to express outrage over the situation in Shenzhen, questioning both the city's success and the general direction of China's economic reforms. Even Deng felt compelled to temper his praise of Shenzhen. On June 29, 1985, when a visiting delegation from Algeria complimented Deng in Beijing for what they had seen on their visit to Shenzhen, he stated, "The special economic zone of Shenzhen is an experiment. We still need to wait and see whether it has taken the right path. Our hope is for it to succeed, but not succeeding is in itself an experience."[42] His comments were published domestically in the *People's Daily* and internationally via the Xinhua News Agency. Deng's description of the Shenzhen SEZ as an experiment that could be abandoned raised further concerns in Shenzhen and reinforced uncertainty over the reforms. Hong Kong's media responded immediately. During the month of July 1985 alone, the *Hong Kong Economic Journal* published twelve articles on the numerous problems in Shenzhen.[43] Even the US edition of the *Wall Street Journal* joined the chorus, with a July 9 article titled "China's Modernization Woes Are Mirrored by Frustrations of Shenzhen Economic Zone."[44]

In the same month, Gu Mu announced that the opening up of coastal areas would be scaled back from fourteen to just four sites: Shanghai, Tianjin, Dalian, and Guangzhou.[45] Speculation that even Deng was giving up on the reforms pushed him to clarify his continued support for the economic zones. In August 1985, he took the opportunity to do so while welcoming another foreign delegation's visit: "Now, I want to confirm two statements: The first is the policy to establish special economic zones is correct; the second is the special economic zone remains an experiment."[46] By the end of 1985, however, even Deng could not contain the mounting opposition to Shenzhen. Liang Xiang was criticized for being overly ambitious and creating an inflated economy that did not faithfully follow the agenda of export-oriented industrial production in the economic zones. While he was allowed to remain as the Shenzhen Communist Party secretary for one more year, Liang Xiang was replaced by Li Hao as the mayor of Shenzhen in August 1985.

The political upheaval in Shenzhen had swift repercussions. Investors had lost confidence in the Shenzhen SEZ, influenced by the avalanche of criticism and speculation about changes in the direction of China's policy. Following the National Congress of the Communist Party of China in 1985, the central government and Guangdong Province reduced allowable credit limits, strengthened foreign currency control, and implemented an export permit system. These policies had a serious impact on economic activities in the Shenzhen SEZ. Restricted industrial activities led to an exodus of factories and businesses, while hotel occupancy rates plummeted, dropping to 20 percent on average, and 40 to 50 percent in the more popular hotels.[47] By the end of 1985, Alan Lau declared bankruptcy of Millie's Group and the Bamboo Garden Hotel. He had to transfer and sell his shares in the Bamboo Garden Hotel as well as the *Tin Tin Daily News* in Hong Kong.[48] Lau did receive some assistance in Hong Kong from Xu Jiatun, the head of the Xinhua News Agency and the de facto top Chinese official in Hong Kong at the time. Xu took out a personal loan of thirty million Hong Kong dollars to give to Alan Lau in order to save the *Tin Tin Daily News*.[49] However, Lau reportedly took the money and absconded to Canada soon afterward. Many other Hong Kong investors withdrew, and enterprises that had invested heavily in the growing China–Hong Kong cross-border commerce took heavy hits. A chain reaction quickly developed, including tightened loan criteria instigated by state-owned banks, and the retreat of capital from inland provinces and Hong Kong investors, all of which led to more canceled construction projects and business ventures. The obvious signs of an imminent economic recession in Shenzhen provided further evidence of the need for drastic intervention and extensive national discussions about the "failure" of the special economic zone as a model for China's reforms.

For all its visibility and symbolism, the tall building became the primary target of the austerity campaign. In 1986, the central government ordered a stop to construction of buildings with heights over eighteen floors in Shenzhen. The order followed a working conference on special economic zones chaired by Gu Mu and held in Shenzhen from December 1985 to January 1986. Representatives from the four SEZs (Shenzhen, Zhuhai, Shantou, and Xiamen), the provincial governments of Guangdong and Fujian, and twenty-nine departments from the State Council attended the meeting. Gu Mu condemned Shenzhen's leadership for focusing only on expansion during the previous year, particularly infrastructure construction, and for not putting enough effort into strengthening management, improving the quality of enterprises and labor, or increasing industrial production.[50] In February 1986, the State Council in Beijing distributed a "Summary of Working Conference on SEZs" throughout the country.[51] Following the conference, the Shenzhen city government cut total infrastructure construction by one third, canceled or suspended 804 projects, and withheld 2.57 billion yuan of infrastructure investment.[52]

The most prominent tower under construction in Shenzhen at the time was the Shenzhen Development Center, which had been set to achieve a record new height in the city. The 186-meter-tall tower was destined to supersede the 160-meter-tall International Trade Center to become the tallest tower in Shenzhen. It was also supposed to be China's first steel composite structure, a departure from the standard concrete construction. Building had already started in 1984; therefore, when the mayor's office issued an order in 1985 to stop work on the project, its lead investor—Shenzhen SEZ Development Company—revealed that more than thirty thousand tons of steel from Japan had already been ordered and the city government would need to reimburse the cost if the project was canceled.[53] The tower was eventually completed in 1990, by which time Beijing and Shanghai already had towers of steel composite structures, which had been initiated at later dates.[54] Despite the delay, the Shenzhen Development Center still became a renowned building in China and set a precedent for other tall buildings in later years.

Between 1985 and 1986, completed building floor areas decreased from 3.2 million to 2.9 million square meters, the first time figures had fallen since 1979. They fell further, to 2.4 million square meters, the following year.[55] The reduction in construction immediately led to unemployment problems. Of the 260,000 temporary workers in Shenzhen, 130,000 left in search of job opportunities elsewhere.[56] Among the hardest hit construction companies were those set up by the former Infrastructure Corps. An article titled "Shenzhen: Pain and Dignity of 20,000" was published in September 1986.[57] Written by a member of the Infrastructure Corps, the report detailed the struggles of some of the construction teams and the sufferings of individual workers. It was reported that construction companies established by the former soldiers had experienced difficulty competing for tender bids. The reasons were mainly their slow adjustment to the newly competitive construction market, as well as the reluctance of former regiment leaders to participate in internal dealings and give kickbacks to middlemen—forms of corruption that exploited the lack of comprehensive regulations in the industry. Construction projects drastically slowed down in 1985, and many construction teams were out of work for months at a time. In the newly formed market system, no work meant no pay or social security. This led to extreme poverty for many of the former soldiers and their families, some of whom resorted to street begging. The report also noted that when Liang Xiang learned of the problems, he immediately tried to assist these companies, ordering government-sponsored construction projects to give them first consideration when bids and competencies were relatively equal. However, it was a few years before the situation improved.

Despite these difficulties, most of the former soldiers, including Yang Hongxiang, felt grateful to Liang Xiang. Yang fondly recalled meeting Liang Xiang at the Shenzhen Opera Theater in September 1983, when Liang hosted the demobilization ceremony of the Infrastructure Engineering Corps: "I did not speak with him, but I was honored to photograph the mayor. He was our savior. We all made our lives in Shenzhen because he wanted us to be here."[58] However, by May 1986, Liang was removed from his final post in Shenzhen as the city's party secretary. At his farewell meeting held on May 22, Liang made a poignant and memorable speech:

> I have worked in Shenzhen for over five years. I feel connection with every blade of grass and every tree, every hill and every stream, but even more with my comrades with whom we worked hard together.

> For that, I am willing to stay here, and settle down here. I constantly care about every achievement of the special economic zone, its every change. I also hope my mayor comrade could issue me a (Shenzhen) *hukou*. In addition, before I go, I want to make my will: after I die my ashes should be placed on Wutong Mountain, I want to face the world, and see the future of China! Just as the great Chilean poet Pablo Neruda wrote: "If I have to live a thousand times, I would like to live in this place; if I have to die a thousand times, I would like to die in this place."[59]

The year of Liang Xiang's departure from the city's government, 1986, was also a watershed moment in Shenzhen given increasing central government monitoring of the city. Shenzhen's local print media directly experienced the repercussions of this conservative retreat from reform. During the early 1980s, Shenzhen's news and literary publications became legendary for their bold articles that directly challenged social and political ideologies—as did the Shenzhen municipal government for allowing such freedom of expression. Shenzhen's public discourse in the press was particularly vibrant because the Publicity Department of the CPC Central Committee in Beijing did not issue instructions or limitations to the experimental Shenzhen economic zone. The less restrictive environment in general enjoyed by China's press media from 1979 to 1989 was referred to as the Golden Decade. Backing Deng's efforts to instigate political institutional reforms, Zhu Houze, head of the Publicity Department of the CPC Central Committee, advocated for China's press to enjoy "Three Loosenings," or "Three *Kuans*": *Kuan Song* (Relaxation), *Kuan Hou* (Generosity), and *Kuan Rong* (Tolerance).[60] Along with the *World Economic Herald* in Shanghai and Yuan Geng's *Shekou News*, the *Shenzhen Youth Daily* was particularly prominent, known for providing a public platform for liberal-minded intellectuals.

The *Shenzhen Youth Daily* targeted the young educated migrants in Shenzhen, but was also widely distributed across the country and therefore influenced urban youth on a national scale. Emboldened by the Shenzhen municipal government's support for freedom of expression, the paper championed the reform of the mind as well as the economy. On September 30, 1986, the entire paper was dedicated to a discussion of reform. Titled "Chinese News Makers Discuss China's 'Sensitive Issues,'" the issue was filled with controversial headlines such as "The Party's Power

Concept Should Be Downplayed," "No Openness in Politics; People Cannot Participate and Supervise," "Pushing the Call for Democracy and Human Rights toward Higher Levels," "Existing System Cultivates Individual Tyranny," as well as a cautionary "How Much Longer Will the Current Tolerant Situation Last?"[61] Just a few days later, the paper published an article entitled "Is the Key to China's Political Institutional Reform a Single Party or Multiple Party System?"[62] On October 21, the paper's most explosive headline appeared: "I Agree with Comrade Xiaoping's Retirement: A Discussion with Comrade Weiying."[63] The article was printed in response to Deng Xiaoping's interview with American journalist Mike Wallace on September 2, for the program *60 Minutes*. While it was not broadcast in China, it was in Hong Kong. Shenzhen residents were able to watch the program, along with other Hong Kong television programs, via homemade antennas jerry-rigged to their building rooftops. The final minutes of the interview highlighted Mike Wallace's characteristic trait of posing tough questions.

> **WALLACE:** Last question. You are number one in China. How long do you intend to continue to be the chief leader and the chief adviser?
>
> **DENG:** I am all for the abolition of life tenure and the institution of a retirement system. As you know, I told the Italian correspondent Oriana Fallaci that my plan was to work until 1985. It's already a year beyond that date. I am now considering when to retire. Personally, I should like to retire soon. However, this is a rather difficult question. It is very hard to persuade the party rank and file and the Chinese people to accept that. I believe if I retire before I die, it will help ensure the continuation of the present policies. It will also be in keeping with my own wishes. However, I need to work harder to talk people around. In the end, as I am a member of the Communist Party, I must obey the decision of the party. I am a citizen of the People's Republic of China, so I must obey the will of the people. I am still hoping that I can succeed in persuading the people to come round to my view.
>
> **WALLACE:** You told Fallaci "until 1985"; what will you tell me?
>
> **DENG:** To be quite frank, I am trying to persuade people to let me retire at the party's Thirteenth National Congress next year. But so far, all I have heard is dissenting voices on all sides.[64]

While the *Shenzhen Youth Daily* article, in essence, agreed with Deng's desire to end the life-long appointment practice for China's top officials, it and the paper itself immediately drew a mix of criticism and support from the public and government officials alike. A week later, in response to a debate on the appropriateness of the paper's decision to publish such seemingly disrespectful commentary, the *Shenzhen Youth Daily* printed another article: "The People Should Have the Right to Discuss the Leader."[65] The paper was never formally reprimanded and continued to garner local government support; however, in early 1987 the Organization Department of the CPC Central Committee ordered its shutdown. Employees at the paper were let go, while the chief editor and deputy editor were forbidden from continuing to work in news journalism.[66]

The closing of the *Shenzhen Youth Daily* was particularly discouraging for Yang Hongxiang; the former resident reporter for the Infrastructure Corps had set his heart on returning to journalism. After the corps was demobilized, twenty-five-year-old Yang immediately began preparing for his college entrance exams, hoping to fulfill the delayed ambitions of his youth. He enrolled in the Shenzhen Municipal Party School's first training course for young cadres, and later obtained a master's degree in economics, graduating in late 1986. Yang's dream job had been to write for the *Shenzhen Youth Daily,* which was no longer in print in 1987. Reluctant to work for any other papers, Yang took up various jobs in real estate development and commerce. Two years later, in August 1988, he finally realized his goal by joining a new monthly magazine called *Shenzhen Youth.* Yang's personal path reflects, once again, the wild swinging of the pendulum between reforms and resistance to reform in Shenzhen and the rest of China.

THE PENDULUM OF REFORM

In February 1987, the State Council distributed the "Summary of Working Conference on Special Economic Zones" with the following disclosure: "Shenzhen exports amounted to 725 million USD, therefore basically achieving a foreign exchange balance. Locally produced industrial goods amounted to 45 percent of total industrial output (processing of orders reached 51%)."[67] Shenzhen had met the central government's goal of focusing its economy mainly on industrial production and export, rather than land and infrastructure development.

While Shenzhen's production and export revenue had met the targets, most believed that the city's new leadership and policies were responsible. Some, however, argued that the previous five years of infrastructure construction had been an essential foundation for this subsequent industrial productivity. In addition, having previously disregarded Shenzhen's small yet prevalent Sanlaiyibu enterprises because they were not high-technology, high-value industries, the city now relied heavily on these enterprises to generate the much-needed export revenue.[68] Toward the end of 1986, Hong Kong suddenly experienced an increased demand for light industry products owing to the increasing strength of the Japanese yen and Taiwanese dollar. Hong Kong businesses all turned to the small joint-venture enterprises in Shenzhen to meet their manufacturing labor needs.

Concurrently across the country, policies of austerity and economic tightening faced such tremendous resistance at provincial and city levels that the central government relented by the end of 1986. Between 1986 and 1988, both Shenzhen and the rest of China experienced readjustments in economic operations and associated policies.[69] Shenzhen continued to experiment with economic reforms as China's national economy reached relative stability. Signals of any changes in policy were picked up quickly by Hong Kong businessmen. In November 1986, Gordon Wu of Hopewell Holdings, who had withdrawn his investments in Shenzhen only a year earlier, announced plans to invest in a power plant as well as the Guangzhou-Shenzhen Highway, later named the Gordon Wu Highway.[70]

On December 15, 1986, Xinhua News Agency released an article titled "Shenzhen Industrial Output Topped the Rankings." It stated that Shenzhen's industrial output in 1986 had exceeded that of commerce and construction, making industrial production the largest sector in the city's economy for the first time. The export rates from industrial output also significantly increased from 1985 onward, amounting to around 50 percent of all foreign exchange export earnings. Both of these benchmarks specifically addressed the two major criticisms of Shenzhen's earlier reform activities that had appeared in the Hong Kong press.[71] In June 1987, Deng declared unconditional support: "I can now say with confidence that our decision to establish special economic zones was not only correct but also successful. All doubts can now be dismissed."[72]

With the pressure now off, Shenzhen actively pursued additional economic and institutional reforms, under the leadership of the more cautiously pragmatic yet reform-minded Mayor Li Hao. Extensive tax reforms, initiated by Liang Xiang in 1983, were implemented in 1985 and 1986. Many of the reforms were centered on the basic institutional unit of China's centrally planned economic system: the state-owned enterprise. These reforms included the manager responsibility system and tenure target responsibility system in 1986, the contract responsibility system in 1987, the horizontal economic union, and the bonus wage by performance scheme. The biggest Iron Bowls had to be broken by instilling mechanisms to ensure accountability, responsibility, and competition.

In 1988, the State Council approved the establishment of a Comprehensive Reform Pilot Area spanning the entire province of Guangdong. Reforms were wide-ranging, extending across sectors such as finance, foreign trade, price controls, wages, real estate, and political governance. The contract responsibility system was expanded to include foreign trade throughout Guangdong Province from 1988 to 1990, and national policies followed suit.[73] The various economic and social links between work and allocation of resources within state enterprises under the centrally planned economy were gradually abandoned. The most significant moment in reforming China's state-owned enterprises took place in 1988, when the central government passed amendments to China's Constitution recognizing the legality of private-owned enterprises. With the earliest precedent set in Shekou nearly a decade before, state enterprises all over China were eventually reformed to become shareholding cooperatives. The state still controlled the majority share, but the restructuring and reorganization measures effectively decentralized economic decision making to all major cities in China.

Economic zones and market reforms once again became a national pursuit. In March 1988, the range of coastal economic open zones was extended to another 140 cities and counties, including Hangzhou, Nanjing, and Shenyang, as well as the Liaodong Peninsula and Jiaodong Peninsula. Hainan Island, originally administered by Guangdong Province, became its own independent province. Liang Xiang, by then sixty-eight years old, was released from banishment and appointed governor of Hainan, the largest special economic zone in China.[74]

Set against this national background, Wang Jingsheng, a former member of the Central Committee of the Communist Youth League, launched *Shenzhen Youth* magazine. In August 1988, Wang arrived in Shenzhen from Beijing with an idealistic agenda to "utilize the magazine as a carrier for cultural construction" in Shenzhen.[75] Yang Hongxiang immediately requested to join the small team of four members, who had set up an office in a borrowed activity room in the Youth League Center with the aid of a small loan from the Communist Youth League of Shenzhen. Less than a year later, the usual growing pains of a start-up enterprise were overtaken by a far bigger challenge: the aftermath of the Tiananmen Square incident on June 4, 1989. Hopes for a revived culture of public debate and freedom of the press were crushed. Public officials and private individuals who had supported the student movement faced criticism and punishment. Liang Xiang, one such supporter, was removed from the governorship of Hainan and exiled from the island, under charges of bribery and corruption. No charges were ever brought, despite an extensive investigation. Liang Xiang passed away, after an illness he contracted during his confinement outside Shenzhen, and his ashes are still waiting to be returned to his beloved Wutong Mountain.

After the Tiananmen Square incident, both Liang Xiang's Hainan special economic zone and Shenzhen were criticized as breeding grounds for ill-intentioned foreign influence and the corruption of China's youth. *Shenzhen Youth* faced severe restrictions and low circulation over the next few years, which wiped out profits to the point that it could not pay its employees. Yang later referred to this period as the "most difficult time in his career."[76] If the Shenzhen crisis of the mid-1980s was based on economic criticism, this second post-1989 crisis was sociopolitical in nature. However, the consequences were similar. State-owned banks tightened their loan criteria, while investors from inland provinces became reluctant to provide capital for growth and development projects, and the city experienced a drastic reduction in infrastructure investments. From 1989 to 1990, investment plummeted by 853 million yuan, more than twice the investment reduction experienced in 1985. The effect on the building industry was immediate. In 1990, the completed building floor area in Shenzhen was only 2.4 million square meters, down by 42.7 percent from the previous year.[77] The ten-month-long downward spiral of the Shenzhen Stock Exchange Market, which only opened in 1991, led to an economic and cultural recession in Shenzhen.

Shenzhen once again found itself at a crossroads, until the spring of 1992 when Deng Xiaoping visited on his "family vacation." In the revolving restaurant atop the International Trade Center, inspired by the urban landscape beyond the expansive glass facade, Deng recited the concluding remark from his 1984 tour: "The development and experience of Shenzhen have proved that our policy of establishing the special economic zones is correct."[78] Following his visit, Deng's warning dictum replaced the previous slogan on the already iconic billboard: "Not Adhering to Socialism, Not Reforming and Opening Up, Not Developing the Economy, and Not Raising People's Standards of Living Can Only Lead to a Dead End." The billboard was just five hundred meters east of the Municipal Government Headquarters Building, at the entrance to the popular public Lychee Park.

By mid-1992, the economic policies pioneered in Shenzhen were extended to twenty cities along the Yangtze River, including cities located at national borders as well as inland areas, impacting twelve provinces. By 2008, 293 cities and counties had opened up and were pursuing similar policies to those in the economic zones, covering 426,000 square kilometers of land and affecting two hundred million people—nearly 20 percent of China's total population.[79]

A NEW RECORD FOR "SHENZHEN SPEED"

After Deng's 1992 visit, a renewed public confidence in China's reforms ushered in new building projects for Shenzhen. Construction of another ambitious tower began on a triangular plot of land off the city's main street, Shennan Boulevard. Located just five hundred meters west of Deng's billboard in the heart of Luohu District, then the city's most coveted location, this site had a particularly important history. Originally belonging to the local Caiwuwei village, the parcel of land incorporated the monument to the anti-Japanese heroes, the People's Plaza of Bao'an County, the historic Yanyi Primary School, and the area's largest open-air farmers' market. The government successfully negotiated the relocation of all these cultural and social landmarks to make way for the construction of the tower. Completed in 1995, the postmodern tower of reflective blue glass—at sixty-nine stories and 384 meters tall, facilitated by two syringe-like antennas—was widely celebrated as the tallest tower in Asia. Formally named Shun Hing Square by its Hong Kong investors, the building is most commonly referred to as the *Di Wang*, or Land King. The nickname arose from the land on which the tower stands, which was even more exceptional than the building itself: this was the first plot of land in China to be openly auctioned to international bidders. Construction at this site marked the beginning of Shenzhen's second spring, a restart after the pause in the city's momentum since 1989.

China's first fixed-term lease of land use rights was granted in Shenzhen on September 9, 1987. The municipal government of Shenzhen signed a lease agreement with the state-owned China Aviation Technology Import and Export Corporation on a 5,300-square-meter plot of land for residential construction in the Shangbu Industrial Zone, for a term of fifty years at the rate of two hundred yuan per square meter.[80] Twenty days later, the city announced a call for tenders for a plot of land nearly ten times bigger, which was zoned for commercial use and located near the Shenzhen–Hong Kong border. Out of nine submissions, the Shenhua Engineering Development Company was awarded the tender based on its offer price and the urban planning design that it had submitted.[81] On December 1, China's first public land auction was held, witnessed by representatives from Beijing's central government, nineteen city mayors, and twenty-eight Hong Kong businessmen and economists. Within seventeen minutes, the 8,588 square meters of land for residential use was sold to the Shenzhen Special Economic Zone Real Estate Company, operated by the Shenzhen Municipality Real Estate Authority. These land transactions in Shenzhen directly triggered a change in the Chinese Constitution, which had previously banned the sale of land. In 1988, the National People's Congress issued an amendment to Article 10 (4) of the Constitution that retained the clause stating that "no organization or individual may encroach, sell, rent or otherwise transfer land illegally," but added a clause stating that "land use rights can be transferred in accordance with the provisions of the law."[82]

The landmark changes in property laws paved the way for China's first international land auction in October 1992. Non-China-based bidders were allowed to enter the auction process, despite the cultural stigma associated with the "colonial concessions" during China's past. The auction received two hundred bids from Chinese and foreign companies, and was won by a joint venture formed by the Shenzhen-based Shum Yip Group and the Hong Kong branch of Japanese development company Kumagai Gumi Co. Ltd—at a price tag of 142 million USD, equivalent to 5,320 yuan per square meter. This gave rise to the building's accolade as the *Diwang Dasha* or "Tower of the Land King."[83] Although it was the tallest tower in Shenzhen yet, it is more renowned for its construction rate, which set a new record for Shenzhen Speed.[84]

Following the successful bid at the October auction, the joint-venture partners launched an international design competition for the tower in December 1992. A US-based architectural firm, K. Y. Cheung Design Associates, won the competition. However, the overall design and construction process was collaboration among multiple local and international contributors. The local design partner was the Shenzhen Municipality Institute of Architectural Design. The structural design was created by UK-based Maunsell Consultants in collaboration with Japan-based Nippon Steel, and the building services work was undertaken by Japan-based Toenec Corporation.[85] The tower's design, structure, building services, and fire safety drawings were quickly completed and submitted to the city authorities for review. In March 1993, the Shenzhen Urban Planning and Lands Bureau made an exception to its normal regulations, allowing site work and foundation construction on the tower to commence while the submitted drawings were still being reviewed.

The construction company contracted to build the tower was the First Construction Engineering Company Limited of the China Construction Third Engineering Bureau, selected for its experience constructing tall buildings in China. More importantly, Bao Guangjian voluntarily returned to Shenzhen from overseas, specifically for the Land King project. He had previously led the construction of both the International Trade Center and the Shenzhen Development Center, the first tower in Shenzhen with a steel composite structure. On April 1, drilling for the foundation piling began ahead of schedule.[86]

Work on the building's 298-meter-tall main structure started in May 1993, and finished in June 1995 with a special topping-off ceremony. The construction team achieved an impressive speed of 2.5 days per floor at the tallest sections of the building, exceeding the three days per floor record set by the International Trade Center. In March 1996, the tower was approved by the city's Buildings and Fire Departments. In October 1996, the first business to open in Land King's building podium was the popular American fast food restaurant, McDonald's. When China's first McDonald's opened in Shenzhen in 1990, the long queues of customers snaked around the city block as far as Shenzhen Old Market Town.[87] Many more international companies soon set up Shenzhen headquarters in the Land King Tower, including technology companies such as IBM and Fujitsu, finance companies such as American International Assurance (AIA), Standard Chartered, and PricewaterhouseCoopers, and other Fortune Global five

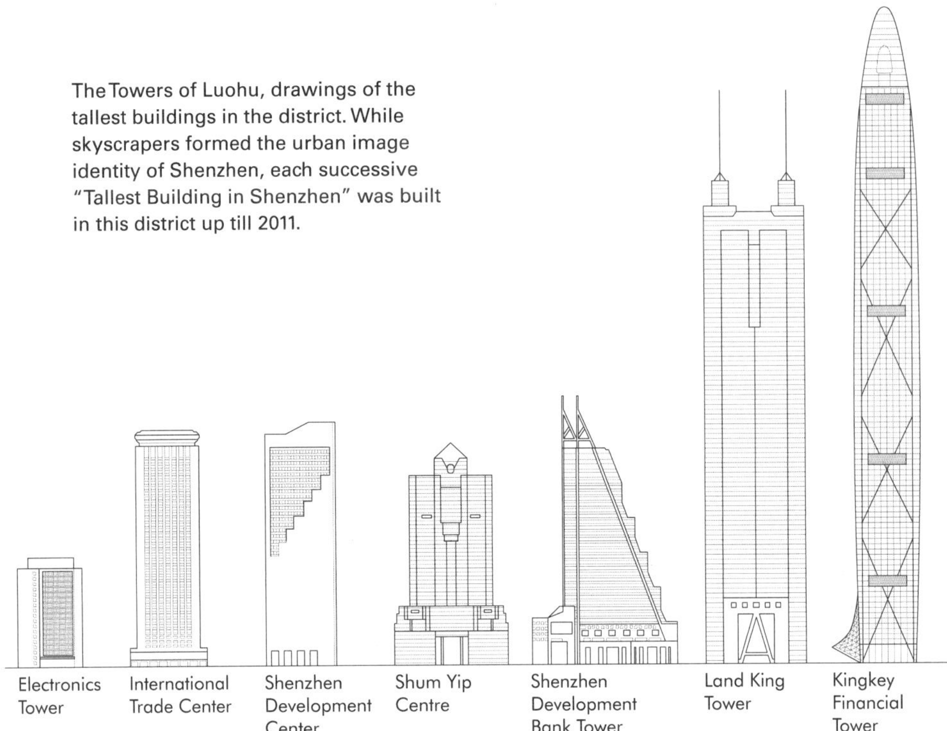

The Towers of Luohu, drawings of the tallest buildings in the district. While skyscrapers formed the urban image identity of Shenzhen, each successive "Tallest Building in Shenzhen" was built in this district up till 2011.

hundred companies.[88] With high-end shopping arcades in the podium, high-end office space in the tower, and an observation deck called the Meridian View Center on the sixty-ninth floor, the Land King continues to define Luohu as the financial district of Shenzhen.

The tall building was first framed as a symbol of economic prowess when Deng praised the International Trade Center in 1984, and this symbolism held throughout subsequent decades in Shenzhen as well as in the rest of the country. By mid-1996, there were 753 tall buildings (over eighteen floors) built or under construction in Shenzhen.[89] The vast majority were within a few street blocks in Luohu District, forming China's first urban cluster of tall buildings. By the end of the 1990s, Shenzhen had twenty-four buildings over one hundred meters tall, and seventeen over 150 meters tall. In order to stand out in the vertical city, new buildings vied to be the tallest.

The race to be the tallest building, and the illusion of the tall building as a symbol of economic dominance, were not unique to Shenzhen. Building the tallest building has been a global obsession ever since the first skyscrapers in Chicago appeared at the end of the nineteenth century.[90] Architectural, technological, and economic developments in the global economy of the 1990s enabled buildings all over the world to reach new heights. The tall building boom in Shenzhen, and soon the rest of China, happened to coincide with this international architectural phenomenon. New records for the tallest building are constantly being set. Just as the 1996 Diwang Commercial Center superseded the 1992 International Trade Center as the tallest in Shenzhen, the 2011 Kingkey Financial Tower beat the Diwang Commercial Center's previous record of 384 meters. Standing at 441.8 meters, the new tower is more commonly called the "KK100," a reference to the development company's name as well as the building's one hundred floors.

The goal to build a new record-setting tower was a symbolic one in the local Luohu District. Such a tower would be its pièce de résistance, cementing the district's image as the financial heart of Shenzhen. The Kingkey Financial Tower project was first initiated in 2003 by a request from the People's Bank to expand their Shenzhen headquarters. Their current facilities were no longer adequate in size to handle their growing business. An open tendering process later that year resulted in the selection of the well-known Shenzhen developer Kingkey Group, founded in 1994 by a former construction worker. Shenzhen's China Urban Planning and Design Institute conducted the initial research, formulated a detailed site analysis, and produced a master plan for the urban zoning, building form, and height. In keeping with the global trend of tall buildings, the tower was intended for mixed use, to contain not only office space but high-end commercial facilities.

The height of the building was important in gaining further government support. In 2006, Kingkey announced its proposal to construct Shenzhen's tallest building; this alone was sufficient to persuade the Shenzhen Planning Bureau to allow the building's height and floor ratio to exceed the city's planning code restrictions. The pressure to deliver the symbolic tower led Kingkey Group and the government to hold an international design competition in 2006. The winner was Sir Terry Farrell, a renowned British architect based in London with projects all around the world, including Hong Kong, where his name is particularly well known. Farrell established an office in the city after winning a 1991 competition for Hong Kong's iconic Victoria Peak Tower.

The completion of Kingkey Tower in late 2011 dominated local and national news, having not only set a new record but also created an updated symbol of prosperity in Shenzhen. The building was celebrated for many of its features: the high-end KK Mall filling the entire four-story podium, the premium office space with special floors specifically designed for stock trading, the six-star St. Regis luxury hotel occupying the seventy-fifth to ninety-fifth floors, and the "sky garden" at the very top of the tower where guests could enjoy a cocktail as well as unparalleled views of the city below and the stars above. The building's simple and elegant form is shaped by its vertically continuous curtainwall facade, which elliptically folds over at the top with a smooth glass roof. Local media and government reports often state that the building's form symbolizes a fountain of wealth and prosperity, springing from the fertile grounds of Shenzhen and cascading down as a waterfall.[91] However, the most lauded feature of KK100 in the media was its height: the new tower was the tallest building in Shenzhen, the third tallest building in China, and the ninth tallest building in the world.

Enthusiasm for the tower's height was not only a Chinese phenomenon. The Western media also highlighted the building's tallness as its distinguishing feature. The UK's popular newspaper *The Guardian* featured KK100 in a 2012 article, entitled "The Tower and the Glory."[92] On the front cover of the February 2012 issue of *Blueprint Magazine,* a leading international architecture publication, the headline was "Terry Farrell KK100 Shenzhen: A Personal Tour of the Tallest Building by a UK Architect," proclaiming yet another record for the building.[93] The cover photo featured a sleek tower rising dramatically above the buildings around it, against the backdrop of an unnaturally purple evening sky. Farrell gave a candid interview, revealing that while KK100 was his first tall "built" building, its design had been conceived years earlier in 1998, for a tower to be built on the then-newly reclaimed land in Hong Kong's Kowloon, facing Victoria Harbor. However, this commission was eventually given to US-based architecture practice KPF. Winning the 2006 Shenzhen competition gave Farrell the chance to revive this design. Architects revisiting past unbuilt designs is nothing unusual; in fact, it is quite a standard practice, even when the new opportunity is in a very different location from the original intended site. KK100's contemporary design, slender and fluid, could answer the call for iconic skyscrapers anywhere in the world. The architect described the project, commenting on the "uniquely community-minded approach to urban regeneration":

> The 3.6-hectare site was previously home to Caiwuwei Village, a dense cluster of tall, tightly-packed village houses that loomed over tiny alleyways and restricted access to sunlight and fresh air. Inadequate municipal servicing contributed to urban decline. The developer began by embracing the villagers as partners, forming with them a joint development company. Village homes were reprovisioned in the form of spacious new flats overlooking Lizhi Park (Lychee Park) and the verdant common space and swimming pool at podium level. Additional apartment buildings provided the villagers with second flats, ensuring their financial security through a steady source of rental income. The arrangement was a win-win for both the developer and the villagers.[94]

In addition to the record-setting skyscraper, the entire KK100 Redevelopment Project also included six new hundred-meter-tall towers for commercial and residential use, totaling 160,000 square meters, over a quarter of the new floor area of the entire project. In addition to the KK100 tower and all the spaces above the commercial podium levels, compensation real estate was provided to the villagers of Caiwuwei, the namesake village of the Caiwuwei Financial Central District Urban Regeneration Planning. This aspect of the project was widely praised in many English-language news reports, which commented on KK100's achievement of "social and cultural sustainability." *The Guardian*'s feature explained how the compensation arrangement further justified the height of KK100: "It's an extraordinary idea: even as China hurtles into capitalism, it does still show remnants of old socialist ideals. Because all of these new towers took up a lot of space, the only way Kingkey could make the kind of money it was looking for—lots—was to build its showcase tower as high as possible."[95]

However, a closer examination of the KK100 negotiation and development process, contextualized within the history of the adjacent Caiwuwei Village, reveals hidden realities that contradict many outward appearances and assumptions, such as the characterization of Kingkey Group as a "generous socialist developer." Located in the midst of Luohu District, the emerging financial and commercial center of Shenzhen, Caiwuwei Village became a focal point for the experience of urban villages during the district's development in the 1990s and 2000s. The private struggles and public battles that beset the Caiwuwei Urban Regeneration project, involving urban villagers, local government officials, and developers like the Kingkey Group, are the focus of the next chapter. The case of Caiwuwei Village shows that the process of urban development in Shenzhen was characterized by competing values—commercial, social, political, and personal—as well as competing visions for the future of the city. And just as tall towers like the Kingkey Financial Tower became the emblem of Shenzhen's advancement, one villager-built peasant house in Caiwuwei Village unexpectedly came to reflect the historical process and resultant conflicts of Shenzhen's urbanization. The voices and emotions of individuals, gaining and losing their foothold in the world's fastest-developing city, offer perhaps the most poignant revelations about this process of urbanization and its costs.

6.

NAIL HOUSE ON "WALL STREET"

In March 2007, an online post titled "Forced Land Acquisition for the Tallest Tower in the South Makes Me Feel Helpless" quickly went viral in Shenzhen, initiating a local—and soon national—media storm. The open letter stated not only the real name and age of its author, but also her address: "My name is Zhang Lianhao, female, sixty years old. My current household residence is at 12 Old Neighborhood, Caiwuwei, in Shenzhen's Luohu District, known as the *dingzi hu* of Shenzhen!"[1]

Dingzi hu, literally meaning nail house or household, refers to the houses of individuals who have refused to move when facing eviction notices from developers or the government. China's nail houses have attracted global attention since dramatic photos of a house stranded in the middle of an active construction site in Chongqing, one of the largest cities in China, appeared in local and international news outlets in early 2007.[2] The owners of the house, a middle-aged couple, had refused the terms of the relocation compensation initially offered by the developer and had not reached an agreement after three years of negotiations. Finally, through local and national media, they waged a successful publicity campaign that garnered widespread public sympathy and pressed the developers and local government to accept the house owners' terms. This was a rare victory in China for individuals protesting big business interests and taking on the complex legal issues of land use and property rights. While not all protesting nail houses in China have been successful, and some have had tragic results, they have acquired quite an online following, with numerous websites and blogs dedicated to the phenomenon.[3] A two-story, life-sized replica of the Chongqing nail house even appeared as an exhibit at the 2010 Venice Biennale, the most prominent international architecture event.[4]

While the 2007 Shenzhen nail house, owned by Zhang Lianhao and her husband, Cai Zhuxiang, also appeared in media profiles showcasing "the coolest nail houses in China," locally it is usually referred to as the "Most Expensive Nail House in China." The monetary compensation Zhang and Cai were demanding was unprecedented, and seen by most as astronomical. However, their demands should be contextualized by the fact that their house was located in the middle of Shenzhen's Caiwuwei Village area, the commercial and financial center of Shenzhen, which was one of the most densely populated and most expensive street blocks in China. Back in 2003, their house was located squarely in the middle of the planned "Wall Street of Shenzhen."[5]

The "Wall Street" project was initiated in 2003, when the People's Bank requested to expand its Shenzhen headquarters because its current facilities were no longer large enough to support its growing business. Because the branch is located adjacent to Caiwuwei Village's Old Neighborhood, the expansion would involve the demolition and resettlement of some village housing. The city government decided to take this as an opportunity to create a more ambitious plan, which became the "Caiwuwei Financial Central District Urban Renewal Masterplan," designed to make Shenzhen even more attractive to multinational finance corporations and major state-owned banks.[6] It was Shenzhen's first major urban renewal project focused on boosting development in the twenty-year-old "old district" of Luohu—but at the expense of the historic Caiwuwei Village. The redevelopment would demolish over one hundred existing residential and commercial village properties owned by 386 village households, impacting roughly two thousand villagers.[7] Zhang Lianhao, her husband, and their two children were among these villagers. They owned their house and the land use rights, which is extremely unusual for residents in China. According to Zhang Lianhao, "in May of 1977 in accordance with a national policy, each village household was allotted land for homestead. We built a house on the land allotted to us and after the reform and opening up of the country, our lives stabilized. However, the good times did not last forever. In 2006, land developers came in the name of remodeling villages in the city to target our village for construction development."[8]

The developer, Kingkey Group, signed on to the project in 2004 and started negotiations with village leaders at the Caiwuwei Village Corporation. After reaching general terms in 2006, the developer started negotiations with individual villagers. At first the majority of the impacted villagers did not agree with the terms offered, and were upset that the village leadership had reached an overall agreement with Kingkey without notifying the villagers first. In her letter, Zhang Lianhao detailed the terms and the reasons for her objections:

> They did not put the villagers' interests first, but rather aimed to profit from land acquisition and sales. The land developers, who had the support of the regional government, flaunted their tough attitude and emphatically expressed their insistence on negotiating with me in a high-handed fashion, stating our property would be acquired at a far lower value than the surrounding properties. The arbitrary terms included "a compensation at the rate of 6,500 yuan per square meter," or "a one-to-one area house of unknown structure and quality to move back into in four years," "no compensation for balcony or roof garden," and "no homestead land compensation." While the surrounding properties were valued at sixteen thousand yuan or higher per square meter, my seven-story single-family house in the solid, bright, beautifully decorated villa style, with permanent land use rights, was valued by the land developers at only three thousand yuan per square meter! My homestead land (usage rights) would be given away for free, without a single penny of compensation! Being just a plain citizen, how can I even think of fighting the government? I just want to be able to live and work in peace. The Communist Party's Reform and Opening Up policies provided me with a happy life, but now this happiness is being destroyed by land developers. Such unfair terms of compensation, how can I accept them?[9]

On September 15, 2006, with the majority of the villagers in support of relocation but without a final agreement on exact terms, the developer's bulldozers started demolition. Soon, the redevelopment site was reduced to bare reddish earth and the few nail houses were left standing alone in a desolate field. Eventually, the developer increased the compensation to twelve thousand yuan per square meter for the ground floor area of each house and offered immediate partial cash compensation. By October 2006, 370 village households had signed the relocation agreement.[10] Zhang and Cai, along with sixteen other "hold-out" families, did not agree to the terms. The Caiwuwei nail houses soon became regarded as "nails" against progress, delaying the entire project. Intensified negotiations continued into early 2007. By March 2007, there were only six nail houses left. Zhang Lianhao experienced coercion and, at times, threats:

> During this time, land developers, district government, subdistrict office, village committee, and task forces were calling upon us nonstop. Even the requisition office under the land bureau had summoned me twice to answer to a ruling, threatening to proceed with forced demolition once the ruling took effect! When they saw I did not give up, they proceeded to harass me: cutting off water and power supply for seven months, blocking traffic passages, disconnecting the telephone line and cable TV. After the developers had put up a wall around the demolition site and placed guards at the gate, they would repeatedly send someone to defecate in the front and back of our house. I called the local police seven times to no avail. Given I am in my sixties with a weak heart, these hurtful acts lead to my frequent loss of consciousness and the need for resuscitation. I am a Chinese citizen protecting my legal rights and trying to lead a peaceful life. Am I wrong in choosing to do so? Do they mean to hound me to death?[11]

It is important to note that from the start of negotiations in 2006 and throughout 2007, Zhang Lianhao and her husband Cai Zhuxiang gave numerous interviews to the local and national media. The Chongqing nail house couple had set a precedent by holding interviews and press conferences, and mounting large TV-friendly slogans on their nail house to attract maximum attention. These practices, conveying the image of the "heroic nail house defender," were emulated by many owners of other nail houses around the country.[12] Zhang and Cai kept the names and contact information of all the journalists in a small notebook and regularly gave them updates, using the press to gain attention and public support against their forced eviction. Zhang went a step further, posting a public letter online in March 2007. Rather than relying on news outlets to translate her message,

The nail house of Caiwuwei in 2007, the last village building standing in the construction site of the Kingkey Tower. The remaining area of the urban village unaffected by the Kingkey construction can be seen on the right side of the photo.

she directly tapped into the tremendous influence of social media with her impassioned online letter. Cai told a reporter that their idea of using the internet came from what they read about the Chongqing nail house online, which encouraged them to ask someone to help them post the open letter.[13]

The internet response was explosive. The online letter was instantly reposted in hundreds of blogs and chatrooms. Thousands of comments, mostly from Shenzhen residents, were swiftly posted in response. These resembled the original letter in zealousness, and displayed a mostly consistent attitude: opposition to Zhang Lianhao. Instead of the sympathy that Zhang and Cai had anticipated, public sentiment gravitated toward criticism and ridicule. One of the responses reads as follows:

> I have always thought indigenous landlords like the owner of this post are the most shameless horde in Shenzhen. They benefited from

Reform and Opening Up and made a fortune from rent that they collected from their dense village housing properties and year-end dividend from collective village property and land use, thus becoming members with vested interests. The pitiful white-collar workers who work day and night ultimately paid their hard-earned money to the landlords. It is just this indigenous horde that gained the benefits but still do not let up. They got rich as a result of reforms and now they turn around to hinder reform and opening up! It is this group of people who did illegal construction and engaged in violent confrontation against the law! The shameless landlord, why doesn't she stop and think, if it wasn't for reform and opening up, would that old building of yours be worth even three thousand yuan? Urban renewal is for the strategic development of Shenzhen. I hope the indigenous understand this truth and that resistance shall be met with harsh punishment! I strongly urge the government to severely punish illegal construction and violent resistance against the law! For those who do not listen to this reasonable advice and insist on having their own way, they deserve to be buried by the bulldozer![14]

The responses revealed several obscured realities of life in Shenzhen. The general public resented the villagers, who were seen by most as slumlords who simply took away their hard-earned wages. Nearly 50 percent of Shenzhen's total population still live in illegal, villager-built houses, similar to the one owned by Zhang and Cai. According to an April 2007 government survey, there were 358,000 local villagers and 350,000 villager-built houses in the city at that time.[15] These houses, the majority of which were illegally constructed, totaled 120 million square meters in floor area.

The story of Zhang Lianhao and her nail house not only sheds light on Shenzhen's rapid urbanization, but also illustrates the complex process whereby the self-financed and illegally built "peasant house" became the most common building block in the city after 1979. That process, however, did not begin in 1979. In fact, the forces that shaped the Shenzhen nail house controversy actually date back to pre-reform China.

THE SENT-DOWN YOUTH OF CAIWUWEI VILLAGE

One important aspect of the Shenzhen nail house debate does not seem to have aroused much interest. In the second line of Zhang Lianhao's public letter, she stated: "I was seventeen years old when I answered the party's call that 'Educated Urban Youth Go and Work in the Mountain Areas and the Countryside.' I came from Guangzhou to the present-day Caiwuwei Village and joined the number-one Red Team to support rural development."[16] In 1964, when Zhang Lianhao left her home city of Guangzhou, she was a teenage girl with a long braid of shiny black hair. In 2007, aged sixty, Zhang still self-identified as a *zhiqing*, or "educated youth"—one of those sent down to the rural countryside to help develop the villages.

The controversial Sent-Down Movement began with the goal of reinforcing rural production while addressing the problem of unemployment in cities; however, it later evolved into a frenzied political campaign that affected nearly every family in the country. This frenzy reached its height during the fervent Up the Mountain and Down to the Countryside Movement, which followed Mao's call on "educated youth to go to the countryside to be reeducated by poor and lower-middle [class] peasants."[17] Between 1968 and 1980, eighteen million urban youths were sent to work in China's undeveloped wilderness and remote mining fields, with the largest number being sent to rural villages.[18] The current Chinese president Xi Jinping spent seven years working in the farming fields of rural Shaanxi. The Sent-Down Movement had an enormous impact on an entire generation, and, along with other hidden consequences of the Cultural Revolution, still haunts China today.

While the majority of the Sent-Down Youth were deployed after 1968, the central government had advocated sending urban youth to villages a decade earlier. From 1958 to 1962, China's Great Famine caused thirty-six million deaths and prevented the birth of another forty million in a country with a population of 650 million at the time.[19] During the 1960s, even the relatively better-off Guangdong Province experienced widespread mass starvation and violence, with even a few reported incidents of cannibalism.[20] In order to escape extreme food shortages and starvation, enormous numbers of villagers in Guangzhou risked their lives to illegally cross the border over to adjacent colonial Hong Kong. In 1961 alone, there were nineteen thousand documented "deserters" in Guangdong.[21] Abandoned farm fields and the lack of agricultural laborers further contributed to the disastrous food shortage throughout the region. As the countryside emptied, the Guangzhou government came under particular pressure to send urban youth to live in rural villages. On September 17, 1964, the city of Guangzhou complied and sent one hundred thousand "unemployed urban youth" between the ages of fifteen and twenty to rural villages throughout the province.[22]

Even though it was less than a day's journey from Zhang Lianhao's home in the city of Guangzhou to Caiwuwei Village, living conditions at Caiwuwei Village were much less comfortable than those in the metropolitan Guangzhou. Zhang Lianhao should have felt some consolation, though: Caiwuwei was more centrally located than other rural villages, being adjacent to the Bao'an County Government Headquarters, which had been relocated from the historic Nantou Fort to Caiwuwei Village in 1957. The village's eastern boundary was marked by the Canton-Kowloon Railway, completed in 1911, and the adjacent *Shenzhen Xu,* a centuries-old market town. The term Shenzhen Xu, or Market of Deep Channels, first appeared in written records in the 1688 *Xin'an County Annals.*[23] The market arose on the site of a squatter camp that first appeared around 1510, occupying a barren field amid villages including Caiwuwei, Luohu, Chikan, Hubei, Xiangxi, Getang, Huangbeiling, Sungang, and Buxin. The squatter camp eventually became known as Nantang Village, and housed migrants with twenty-three different family names, who came from various distant provinces: Shanxi, Shaanxi, Henan, Hebei, Gansu, Anhui, Shandong, Jiangsu, and Jiangxi.[24] Nantang Village grew to nearly three hundred brick houses, arranged along eight east-west and six north-south street grids. Shenzhen Xu's layout was based on these original village streets.[25] By the early Qing Dynasty, Shenzhen Xu was already a thriving trading town. The streets were lined with narrow shophouses, each two or three stories tall, along with eateries, banks, clinics, brothels, and a Buddhist temple. Many villagers from the surrounding areas owned and operated shops in the market town. When the Qing Dynasty government ceded the New Territories region south of Shenzhen River to Great Britain in 1898, Shenzhen Xu became a gateway between China and the rest of the world. The opening of the Canton-Kowloon Railway and the Luohu Railway Station in 1911 introduced even more economic activity to the area. Close proximity to the trading center gave nearby villages access and early exposure to national and international commerce.

Zhang Lianhao heard accounts from the old villagers about the history of Caiwuwei Village, dating even further back than the time of Shenzhen Old Market Town. The villagers were proud of their humble beginnings and their status as one of the largest and oldest villages in the then-rural Bao'an County. Located north of the Shenzhen River and spanning more

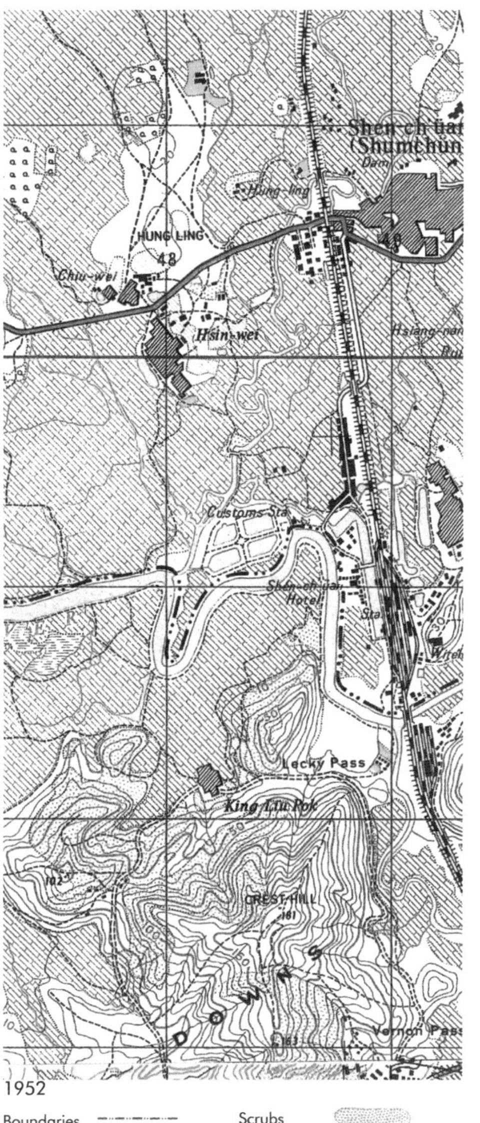

1952

2014

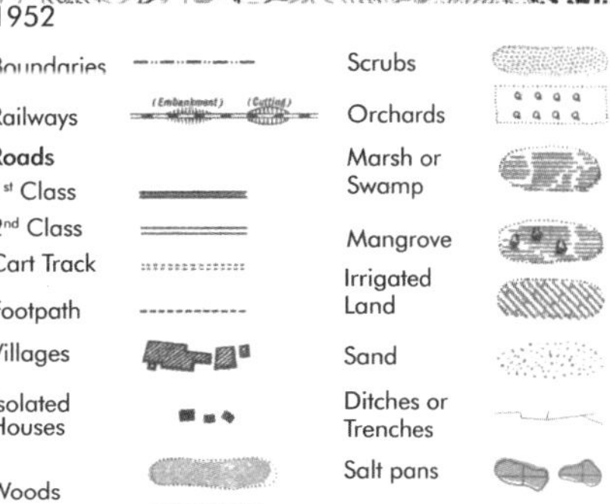

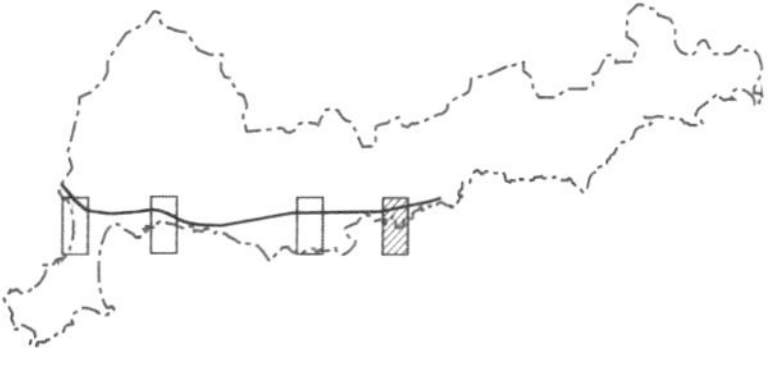

Survey map (1952) compared with satellite image (2014) in Luohu District. Caiwuwei Village is divided by Shennan Boulevard, just as the original village was divided by an early twentieth-century country road that stretched from the Shenzhen Old Town westward to the Nantou Ancient City.

1985 aerial photo of the Caiwuwei village area bisected by the newly expanded Shennan Boulevard. The large clusters of smaller buildings in the center and to the right of the image indicate that Caiwuwei was already the densest urban area in this early period.

than three square kilometers, the village was home to a single clan with the family name Cai. *The Cai Clan Genealogy,* a genealogy account hand-copied by villagers in 1986, asserts that its ancestral history dates back to the Southern Song Dynasty. According to the *Genealogy,* their ancestor Cai An migrated from rural Fujian Province to settle in Guangdong Province's Dongguan area.[26] Some nine generations later, around the fourteenth-century Ming Dynasty, Cai An's descendant Cai Jijuan migrated to the village's modern-day location. Caiwuwei villagers consider the village in Dongguan an ancestral home and still make yearly ritual visits. Cai Jijuan was first hired by the local "Chikan," the Red Cliff Village, to raise their flock of ducks. Eventually, descendants of Cai the Duck Breeder became so populous that a Cai family compound was built.

Chikan Village was officially renamed Caiwuwei, or the "Cai Family Compound," in the early Qing Dynasty. Eventually, as the Cai Clan continued growing, a new settlement called Xinwei was built a little farther south across a dirt path that separated the village from the farm fields. That dirt path later became Shennan Boulevard, the main transport artery of Shenzhen. This area of Laowei (Old Compound) is where Zhang would come to live centuries later, and where she would eventually build her nail house.

While many Sent-Down Youth traveled for weeks across the country, Zhang Lianhao's journey was relatively short. At such a short distance from home compared with her peers, she was able to stay in the village longer than most of the other Sent-Downs. Nearly all these urban youths returned home to their cities when the central government retracted the unpopular policy in 1978. However, Zhang Lianhao stayed, and by the time she became nationally known for the "most expensive Nail House in China," she had lived in Caiwuwei Village for forty-three years.

AN UNUSUAL MARRIAGE

In 1966, the eleven Caiwuwei Village production brigades were reorganized to form three "Red" production teams. Zhang Lianhao was assigned to work on the number-one Red Production Team, where she earned twenty-nine cents per day doing farm work.[27] Caiwuwei offered a more colorful life than other villages in the region, owing to its proximity to the Hong Kong border and its connection with an international network of former villagers who had migrated to other countries in Asia and beyond.

The members of the Caiwuwei diaspora maintained close relationships with one another and their home village for centuries. In 1929, Cai Taihua, a villager who settled in the United States, funded the construction of the first modern school for young pupils in Bao'an County. Located on a campus of six thousand square meters, the school had, in addition to classroom buildings, a library, meeting hall, basketball court, volleyball court, playground, and housing for teaching staff.[28] The school's operation was collectively funded by the village's overseas members. Later migration waves during the twentieth century kept this support going. Today, there are estimated to be 3,500 descendants of the Cai Clan around the world.[29]

In 1961, the village's international community donated funds to purchase a tractor to contribute to agricultural production.[30] Cai Riguang, the village's finance brigade leader, traveled to Hong Kong and brought back a UK-made Ferguson tractor. The eight-thousand-yuan Fergie was one of the more popular tractor models internationally at the time. It was the first mechanized farming vehicle in Bao'an County, and the pride of Caiwuwei Village. As all agricultural land was collectively owned in accordance with the people's commune policies at the time, the tractor was shared by all production teams. The tractor driver, a spirited young villager named Cai Zhuxiang, caught the attention of the young Zhang Lianhao. Cai Zhuxiang relished the attention he received when driving the tractor at top speed on the country roads. A childhood friend recalls Cai as a leader of their boyhood pack, especially after he became the tractor driver: "To be able to drive a tractor at that time would be like driving a Rolls-Royce today—so amazingly impressive!"[31]

After a few years in Caiwuwei Village, Zhang Lianhao made an unusual decision in 1969. Aged twenty-two, she married the nineteen-year-old Cai. The marriage was notable for various reasons. While villagers in China's countryside do marry fairly young, the 1950 Marriage Law of the People's Republic of China stipulates the minimum age at which women can marry is eighteen; for men, it is twenty. A union involving an older bride would normally have been frowned upon by society, and it is a considerable social stigma even today. The marriage was also extraordinary because it united an urban *hukou* holder and a rural *hukou* holder.[32] Even though Zhang was "sent down" to work in the rural countryside, she still held the Guangzhou city registration or *hukou*. Intermarriages between urban and rural *hukou* holders were extremely rare. Furthermore, as a Sent-Down Youth, Zhang Lianhao's marriage to a villager was an exceptional act during a highly exceptional time. Being "sent down" to the villages was deemed a patriotic act, a show of loyalty to the party and the motherland. However, the ultimate patriotic act was to marry a local villager, which proved one's loyalty and commitment to the village. From the late 1960s to the 1970s, local and national papers carried reports of Sent-Down women marrying villagers and hailed them as model examples.[33] While some married villagers as an idealistic declaration, some for companionship, some simply for reprieve from hard labor, there were also numerous reports of women forced into such marriages.[34] However, when interviewed, many of the women "role models" reportedly explained their decision to marry local villagers by citing Mao's words verbatim: "Even with blackened hands and cow dung on the feet, they (the peasants) are still cleaner than the Bourgeois intellectuals."[35]

With the encouragement of national media attention and political campaigning, around forty-three thousand women (0.2 percent of the total "Sent-Down Youth") married local rural *hukou* villagers.[36] Regardless of whether Zhang Lianhao's marriage was an act of patriotism or love, the union between the "Sent-Down" girl from Guangzhou and the village tractor driver was celebrated, and Cai became the envy of other village youth. In the same year they were married, Zhang gave birth to a healthy baby boy. Although not in fear of starvation, the young married couple did not have an easy life. Their combined household income was less than thirty yuan a month. In 1972, the birth of their second child, a baby girl, added to the financial burden. Feeling pressure to make more money, Cai decided to slip away to Hong Kong. Unlike most of the "Escape to Hong Kong" army, Cai found it relatively easy to cross the border by following in the footsteps of many of his village ancestors. Unlike the Iron Curtain surrounding the Soviet Union, the Bamboo Curtain across the Shenzhen River border between Communist China and capitalist Hong Kong was rather porous for local villagers.

It would be more fitting to compare the Shenzhen River border with the Berlin Wall between communist East and capitalist West Germany, as they both separated families. However, the Shenzhen River border also separated properties, owing to the unique history of Caiwuwei and all nearby villages. These villages had farming fields that extended south of Shenzhen Old Market Town, across the Shenzhen River and into Hong Kong's New Territories. The villagers crossed the many shallow and narrow segments of the waterway daily in order to farm their fields. For

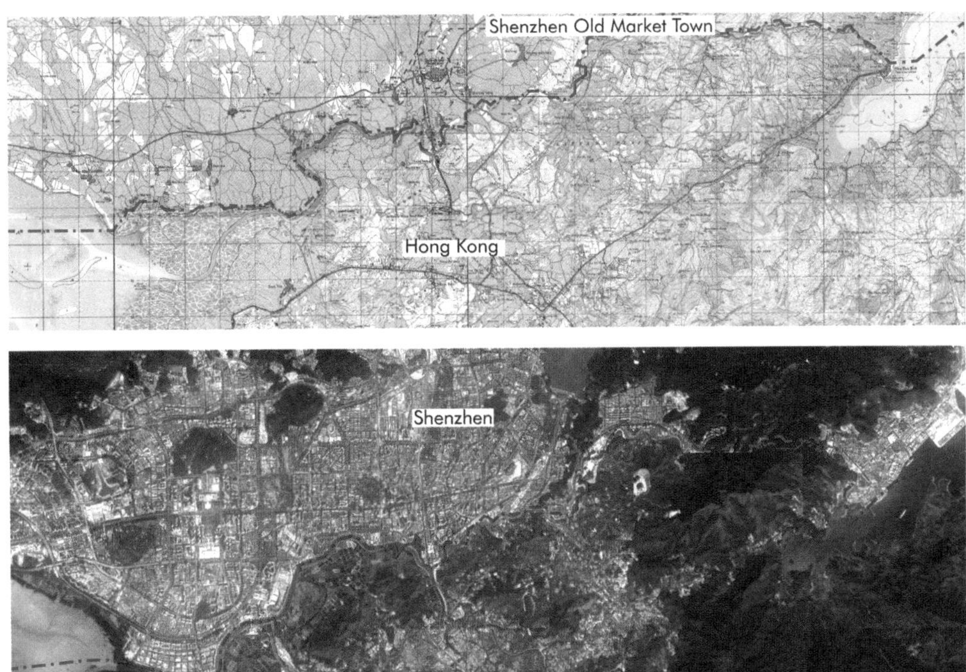

Survey map (1950s) and satellite image (2014) of the Shenzhen and Hong Kong border region along the Shenzhen River. Caiwuwei and other villages in the area once held land and farm fields on both sides of the river.

convenience, some villagers set up village settlements next to their fields. When the Qing government ceded the land south of the Shenzhen River to Great Britain as the New Territories of Hong Kong in 1898, those villagers who had settled south of the river became "Hong Kong villagers." A makeshift border crossing station was set up at Luohu Bridge, which at first was simply a few wood planks. A traditional carved stone bridge was built in the late Qing Dynasty, collectively funded by the nearby villages. Yet farmers in the border region villages seldom bothered to use the crossing station at the bridge. With border patrols watching, many villagers simply nodded in their general direction and waded across the river with farming equipment on their backs or on top of water buffalos. In addition to this connection through farming, many villagers on either side of the Shenzhen River shared common ancestry and often worshipped at the same ancestral hall. Many villagers along the river shared the same clan heritage and family names. For example, several villages on the Hong Kong side bear the family name Chen, the predominant village clan in

Caiwuwei prior to the Cai Clan's ascendancy. The long-established practice of intermarriage between the villagers from either side of the border continued well past 1898. Familiarity with the geographical features of the Shenzhen River and the border regions enabled many villagers in the area to illegally cross the border with ease, particularly during the subsequent years of intense civil and political unrest in China.

By 1949, the Communist-led People's Liberation Army was winning China's civil war against the Nationalist government; consequently, there were periods of tension at the border. The British government worried that the communist government would cross the river to reclaim the New Territories and more. Newspapers in Hong Kong were filled with sensational headlines such as "Communist Army Prepares to Push South." Ultimately under Beijing's command, the Liberation Army halted its southern advancement at the northern part of Shenzhen and chose to avoid further military conflicts. The British–Hong Kong government soon erected wire fencing along the entire southern edge of the Shenzhen River. Both sides stepped up border patrols and maintained a heightened military presence. Despite this drastic political change, villagers on both sides of the river continued their farming activities. However, they were no longer allowed to cross the river wherever they wanted: designated border crossing points were established for each village, and only members from designated villages were given permits to cross.

Even during the height of the Cultural Revolution, the Bao'an Police Department continued to issue cross-border farming certificates to Hong Kong villagers who had ancestral farm fields north of the political border. During those frantic years, in addition to showing the certificates each time they crossed, the Hong Kong villagers also needed to declare their "love for Chairman Mao."[37] Having been inspected repeatedly when crossing the Luohu border in 1971, *New York Times* journalist Seymour Topping described the relative ease with which local villagers proceeded through one of the crossing points: "A narrow railway bridge over a thin, muddy, desultory river separated Lo Wu from Shum Chun [Shenzhen], the station on the Chinese side. Atop the bare hills about us, British observation posts faced out on China. The British Union Jack hung limply in the humid air matched on the other side by the red flag with yellow stars of the People's Republic of China. Local peasants carrying vegetables and live chickens in straw cages and other farm products at the ends of poles across their shoulders seemed to be passing back and forth over the bridge without more than an exchange of nods with the guards."[38]

Thus in 1972, at the height of the Cultural Revolution, Cai Zhuxiang easily crossed the otherwise tightly controlled border. Perhaps given the historical "normalcy" of Cai's "escape," Caiwuwei Village still managed to obtain 125 cross-border farming certificates in 1976, when certification was formally reestablished. The "Cross-Border Farming Certificate" was designed to encourage greater agricultural production. At that time, three types of passes were issued: Cross-Border Horticulture Pass for vegetable and fish farming; Temporary Mariculture Pass for oyster, shrimp, and fish harvesting; and Family Visit Pass. In the late 1980s, the three passes were combined and named the Shenzhen Cross-Border Farming Pass. These passes were issued to individual villagers in around thirty villages neighboring the border.[39] This legal access to both sides of the river brought a series of benefits to the villagers. Not only did it increase the village's arable land and agricultural output, but it also offered access to and knowledge of the more developed Hong Kong. The villagers soon learned to modernize their agricultural methods and increase production. Some villagers took the opportunity of working illegally as day laborers in Hong Kong because the jobs earned them much higher salaries. Many others who crossed the border, like Cai, stayed in Hong Kong. The exodus from these villages became one of the primary motivations for establishing the special economic zone in Shenzhen.

As Cai crossed the border undetected, he was one of those who benefited from Hong Kong's Touch Base Policy, a short-lived Hong Kong governmental policy (1974–1980) that gave residency permits to any illegal immigrant who had family members in Hong Kong and could reach the city center without being caught by Hong Kong's border police. Cai was able to obtain a work permit and the coveted Hong Kong resident status. However, like most other immigrants, he could only find low-wage employment in Hong Kong. He drifted in and out of various jobs, from washing dishes to janitorial service.[40] The highest wages he earned were three hundred yuan a month as a construction worker, ten times more than the average villager north of the border. Cai regularly sent money back to his family in Caiwuwei. However, life for his wife Zhang Lianhao became increasingly difficult.

Left behind in Caiwuwei, Zhang Lianhao did not have a good relationship with the rest of the villagers. She was proud of her Sent-Down Youth status and urban background, but as an outsider and a woman with two young children, she was an easy target for exclusion and scorn. Cai was Zhang's only link to the village's social network of bloodline kinship, and she desperately needed additional income in order to raise two young children. Suddenly in 1979, months prior to the establishment of Shenzhen, money and news from Cai stopped arriving. Life in the village became even more difficult and her status in Caiwuwei more strained. Decades later during the nail house controversy, some villagers speculated that perhaps retaliation underlay Zhang's insistence on holding out for cash compensation rather than relocation housing.[41] Accepting relocated housing as compensation would have meant Zhang's continuing to live with the rest of the villagers, as neighbors within one residential tower.

The villages' centuries-old rural social structure was ill-suited to outsiders like the Sent-Down Youth. In 1976, there were nearly ten thousand reported cases of abuse and 4,970 "unnatural deaths" among Sent-Down urban youths.[42] The majority of reported abuses were directed at women, and most of the charges were of rape. There were also complaints from rural villagers, most of whom viewed the youths as a burden on the villages' limited food and resources. In addition to these complaints in the countryside, there were nationwide protests by the urban youths demanding to be allowed to return to the cities. From 1978 onward, massive resistance was mounted. There were protests in twenty-one provinces, including a demonstration in Shanghai that blocked the city's railroad transportation for twelve hours.[43] By the end of 1980, over 90 percent of the "Sent-Downs" had returned to their home cities. Yet, Zhang did not return to Guangzhou. Despite the disappearance of Cai, she chose to remain in the village with her two young children. Over the next decade, Caiwuwei Village was drastically transformed.

When 327.5 square kilometers of land bordering Hong Kong were designated as the Shenzhen special economic zone in 1980, Caiwuwei found itself surrounded by the political and commercial activities of the new city. The village's land was among the first in Shenzhen to be expropriated by the newly established Shenzhen government. There were no regulated rates of village land compensation; the local government negotiated with each village individually. The first round of government land requisition in Caiwuwei comprised 3.3 square kilometers. At a rate of 4.5 RMB per square meter, the total compensation to the village collective amounted to fifteen million RMB.[44] However, because the newly formed Shenzhen mu-

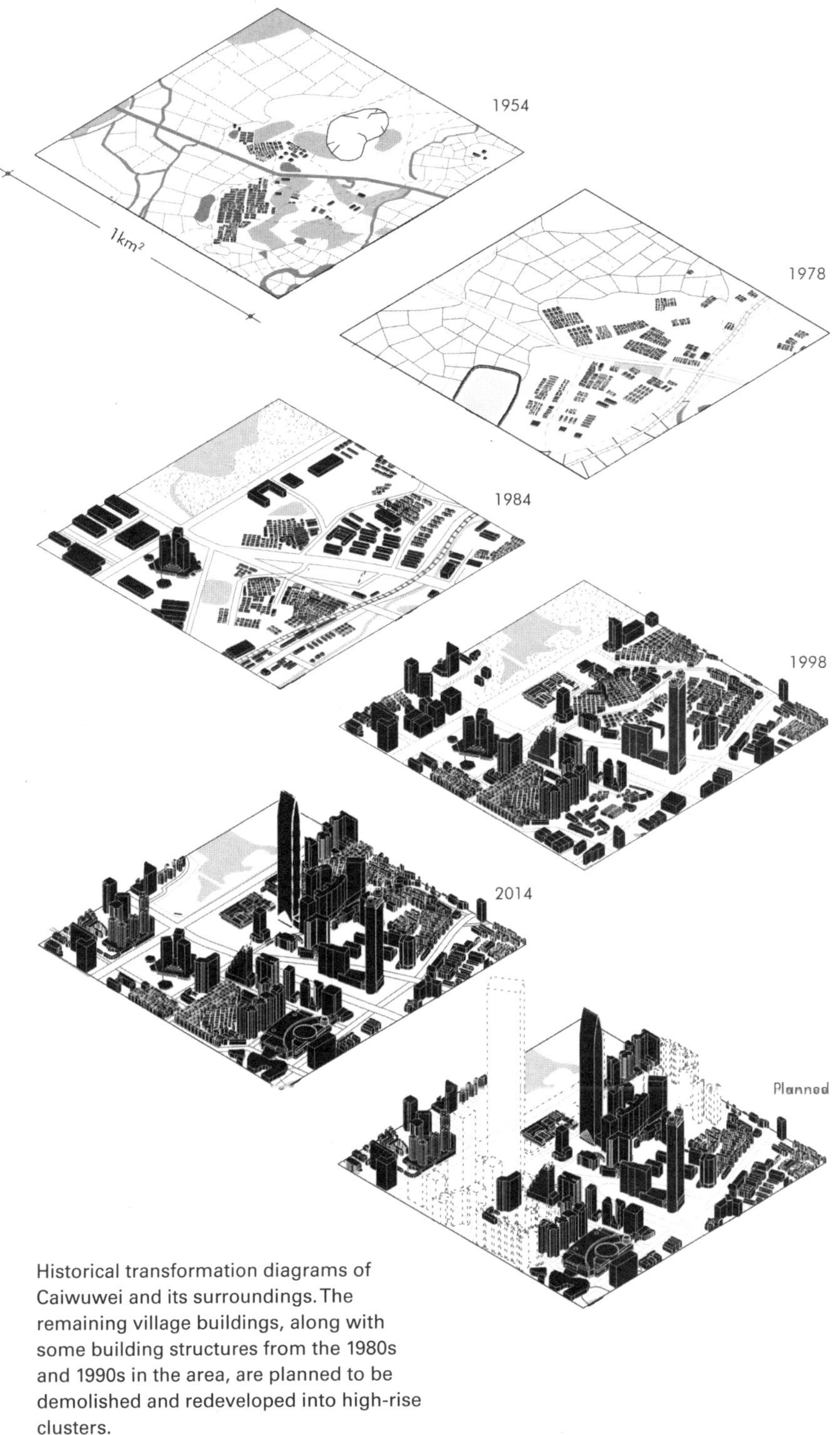

Historical transformation diagrams of Caiwuwei and its surroundings. The remaining village buildings, along with some building structures from the 1980s and 1990s in the area, are planned to be demolished and redeveloped into high-rise clusters.

nicipal government lacked a reserve of funds, the compensation was paid in several installments spanning multiple years. For example, in 1982, the village's large lychee fruit orchard was acquired and modeled into the Lychee Park. Compensation for loss of the land and the lychee trees totaled about one million RMB, and reimbursement to Caiwuwei Village was not settled until a few years later. This was a common strategy used by the Shenzhen government during the early years, raising funds from one area of land development to pay for the next phase of requisitions.

In 1981, SEZ land policy provided that all land in the zone was owned by the state and that enterprises or individuals could only maintain right of use, not ownership.[45] Limited government funding also influenced the policy of keeping villages in place, so that they wouldn't have to be paid for relocation. In 1982, Shenzhen unveiled the first SEZ policy on land use in the villages: "Interim Provisions for Rural Commune Members' Land Use for Housing Construction in Shenzhen SEZ."[46] With this policy, the government reserved the right to expropriate all village land in the future; for the time being, however, it waived the requisition fees for residential areas of villages inside the special economic zone and permitted continued usage of the land by the villages. In addition, each village household became eligible for an additional 150-square-meter plot of home-based land (HBL). Construction of a village home was allowed on each individual HBL plot, provided the building was no larger than eighty square meters in footprint and did not exceed two stories in height. This village policy determined the future land use pattern of all the villages in Shenzhen, as well as the spatial characteristics of future peasant houses in the villages. The gridded pattern of square HBL plots became the foundation for construction of all future village houses, later commonly referred to as "handshake towers."

Following the implementation of this policy, Caiwuwei village leaders designated an area adjacent to the existing village dwelling area for the "new village," divided into square land parcels of 150 square meters each. Allocation of HBL was usually determined by male members of the villages, who were assumed to be heads of each nuclear family. Despite the absence of Cai Zhuxiang, Zhang Lianhao successfully lobbied the village in 1982 for a land parcel on which to build a home for herself and their two children. With money saved from working multiple jobs and from Cai's mailed earnings over the previous years, Zhang managed to build a two-story house in the new village of Caiwuwei. However, her relationship

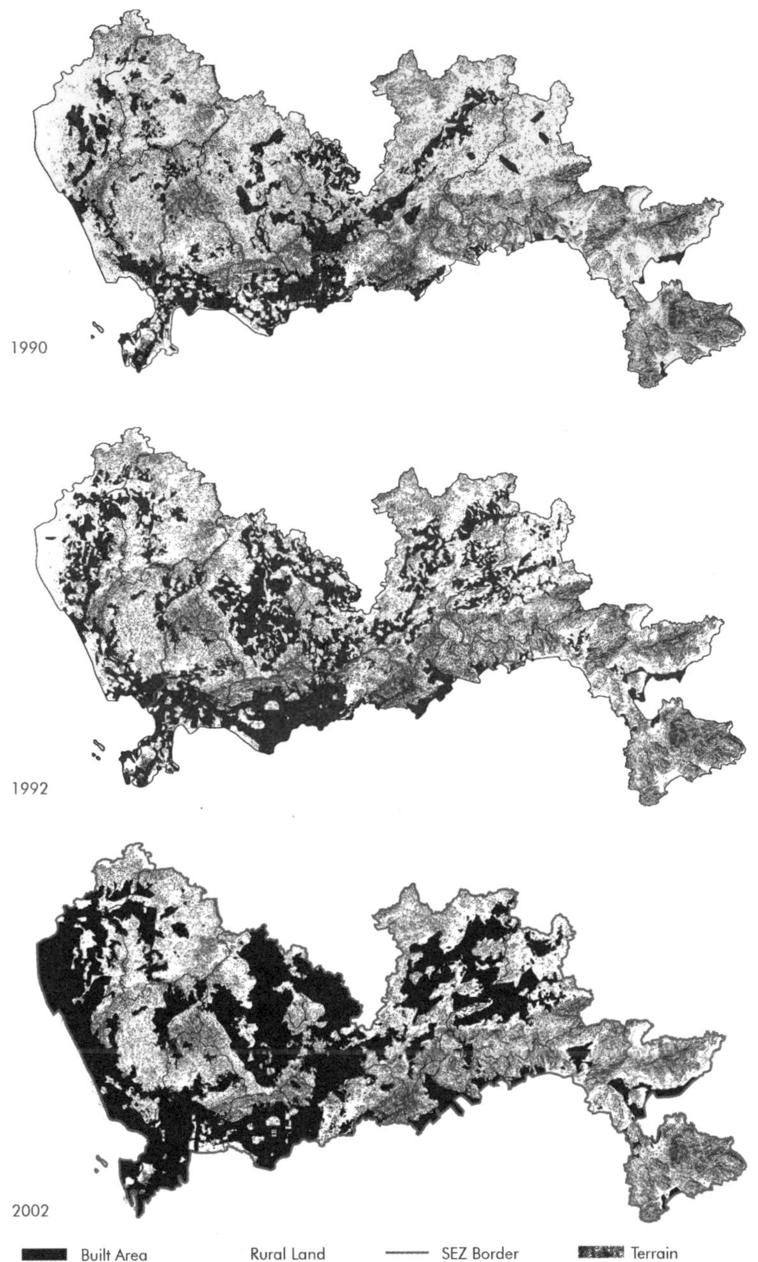

Rural to urban land status changes from 1990 to 1992, and 2002. From 1979 to 1992, except for the remaining villages, land inside the SEZ was designated as urban state-owned land. In 1992, rural land north of the SEZ was also designated as urban, except for the remaining village land. In 2002, all land in Shenzhen was designated as urban; the singular exception was Baishizhou village.

with the villagers did not improve. If anything, she became even more detached, always rushing to leave the village for work early in the morning and returning late at night.[47] While Zhang grew more reserved, the village grew livelier.

VILLAGE INDUSTRIALIZATION IN THE NEW CITY

In November 1984, as the record-setting International Trade Center nearby approached completion, the Caiwuwei Grand Hotel, built by the village, opened its doors for business. The village took advantage of its rapidly urbanizing surroundings by setting up numerous hospitality establishments, including restaurants and hotels. In addition to recognizing existing residential land (old village) and permitting new allocations of home-based land (new village), the 1982 policy also enabled each village to reserve land for collective industrial and commercial use. A village could reserve a total area of fifteen square meters per member of the village commune. Since the villagers no longer had access to agricultural land, it was assumed that each village would have to develop new economic activities to provide income to the village population. The Caiwuwei Grand Hotel was built on the village collective land that had been designated for industrial and commercial use, using 70 percent of the fifteen million yuan paid by the government as compensation for lost village agricultural land. The hotel was the village's first major collective investment. An understated eight-story concrete building in black and white, the hotel stood out among the garish colors and configurations of neighboring buildings. The hotel's one hundred guest suites were fitted with modern hotel amenities, and it soon became known as China's first "peasant-built star-rated hotel."[48] Following this success, the village formed joint ventures with national and international partners to open a series of hotels, upscale restaurants, and clubs in the area.

By the mid-1980s, Caiwuwei also had the largest number of village-operated manufacturing factories in Shenzhen, solidifying its status as the city's leader in village industrialization.[49] Caiwuwei's connections with Hong Kong and early experience of Sanlaiyibu enterprises helped pave the way for this development. The first Sanlaiyibu enterprise in Caiwuwei was a broomstick factory established in 1979, in the Assembly Hall of the Commune. Over the next few years, more than thirty Sanlaiyibu factories were established in the village, producing electronics, furniture, toys, and many other consumer goods. The village's ancestral hall and grain storage warehouses were all adapted as small factory spaces. With the abolition of the people's communes and associated production teams in 1984, the village enterprises provided villagers with necessary jobs and income. The peasants all became factory workers. One of the most successful early village factories was the Times Handbag Company, established in 1982.[50] It was a joint-venture between a then-small Hong Kong–based company, Times Corporation, and Caiwuwei's production team.[51] The Times Corporation sent technical personnel from Hong Kong to train local villagers and provided designs and raw materials. The villagers working on the assembly line were paid wages, while the village collective received rental fees. Profits from sales were retained by the Hong Kong parent company of Times Corporation. The Shenzhen-based Times Handbag became a successful operation and the number of employees grew from the initial fifty local villagers to more than 1,500 workers. The village enterprise had to hire migrant workers from outside Shenzhen. By 1987, the original factory space in mudbrick sheds could no longer house the growing staff. In order to keep the company going, Caiwuwei village leaders agreed to build new factory spaces and dormitories for the enterprise. In 1988, another assembly line was added and the monthly production capacity of Times Handbag reached more than ten thousand pieces, most of which were exported to European and American markets.[52]

Low production costs combined with high profit margins and relatively low risk inspired nearly all Shenzhen's villages, townships, and neighborhoods to run Sanlaiyibu enterprises. These spanned more than thirty different industries such as electronics, textiles, garments, food processing, toys, leather, plastics, crafts, horticulture, aquatic farming, and so on. In 1982, when Shenzhen's state-owned enterprises and formal Sino-foreign joint ventures were just emerging, the city's overall industrial production value stood at 390 million yuan, 70 percent of which came from the thousands of self-organized Sanlaiyibu enterprises.[53] It was during this era that some of the earliest signs indicating the advantages and unexpected influence of small, flexible, bottom-up economic activities at the village level became evident. By 1983, these enterprises had hired more than one hundred thousand migrant workers from other regions, making up more than half Shenzhen's total migrant labor force. The labor-intensive, low technical content, and low-cost nature of the Sanlaiyibu products were criticized for not rivaling the far loftier ambitions of the high-tech, high-value industrial sector in the special economic zone. However, as the village enterprises were less negatively impacted by the reduction in large-scale investments as well as increased restrictions and monitoring, the city would ultimately come to rely heavily on these types of businesses to prop up "export" revenues. It should be noted that these village enterprises greatly benefited not only from the large state-built or state-supported factories in Shenzhen, but also from the extensive civic infrastructure investment and construction that took place between 1980 and 1986—which had been the primary target of Shenzhen's early critics.

By 1988, Shenzhen had more than three thousand Sanlaiyibu enterprises specializing in export processing alone, having signed 3,561 export-processing contracts. Collectively, these enterprises were attracting foreign investment of over one billion USD. By 1990, Shenzhen had formally approved more than eight thousand Sanlaiyibu licenses, with over one billion USD of processing fees paid by the foreign partners of these industries. It was Shenzhen's main source of foreign currency. In 1990, in the still-rural Bao'an County outside the special economic zone, 80 percent of the total annual income came from the processing fees generated by Sanlaiyibu enterprises.[54] During Shenzhen's difficult start-up decade, the village Sanlaiyibu enterprises were the predominant source of industrial production and revenue generation. The proportion of export revenue generated by Sanlaiyibu enterprises eventually decreased to 35 percent by 1996, as the state-supported enterprises and industrial zones matured.[55]

Meanwhile in Caiwuwei village, the abundance of factory jobs both in and around the village attracted thousands of migrant workers. Because there was simply not enough factory-associated dormitory housing for the expanded population, the migrants sought housing in village homes. Zhang Lianhao no longer needed to work multiple low-paid jobs to raise her children and make ends meet. She rented out rooms in her home and was able to finally support her family comfortably from the rental income. Zhang did not receive any news from Cai until 1988.

While in Hong Kong, Cai was persuaded by a friend to leave for an even bigger land of opportunity: America. He was smuggled onto a seafaring ship in the spring of 1979, only to discover on arrival that he was in Latin America. News of the dramatic transformation of his village did not reach Cai Zhuxiang for nearly a decade. He arrived in Ecuador in 1979, when there was no diplomatic relationship between that country and China. In the ensuing years, he married a local woman and they had a son. Working various low-paid jobs in Ecuador, Cai gave up any idea of returning home. A chance meeting with an overseas Chinese resident from Guangdong Province alerted Cai to China's Reform and Opening Up policies and the Shenzhen special economic zone.[56] He got back in touch with Zhang Lianhao in 1988 and returned alone to Shenzhen.

Cai Zhuxiang returned to a thriving village in a booming city. With the increase in output by village factories, all peasant houses were full of rent-paying migrant workers. The high demand for rooms prompted Shenzhen villagers to add multiple floors to their houses. Recognizing this increased demand, in 1986 the government released a "Notice of Further Reinforcement of Rural Villages Planning in Shenzhen SEZ."[57] The policy endorsed an increase of maximum floor height to three stories, with the maximum total area to be capped at 240 square meters for households greater than three persons. Those occupied by less than three were required to maintain the original 150-square-meter limit. However, the increased legal limit was quickly superseded in villages throughout Shenzhen.

From 1987 to 1989, Shenzhen's reform policies effectively privatized land use and the housing market, triggering the city's first major wave of real estate development in the commercial housing sector. State-owned and private enterprises no longer allocated housing to employees as a part of a salary package but provided subsidies to employees to purchase or rent their own homes. This increased the demand for rental housing, especially in the Luohu District, which was becoming the financial and commercial center of Shenzhen. Eager to encourage economic activity, like other local district governments in the SEZ, the Luohu government did not take aggressive action against the rampant illegal construction in the villages of the district. Many villagers built multiple houses, and most of these newly built houses exceeded the original land area and height limitations. In 1990, Zhang and Cai added two more floors to their two-story house, a modest expansion in comparison to those made by their fellow villagers.

The most significant village policy to affect Caiwuwei was the 1992 "Interim Regulations regarding Village Urbanization in Shenzhen SEZ."[58] Implemented following Deng Xiaoping's second visit to Shenzhen, it had a drastic impact on the village collectives and individual villagers.[59] It promoted the urbanization of individual villages, village land, village communities, and village businesses. A separate policy changed the rural *hukou* status that applied to all villagers inside the SEZ to urban *hukou* status. While the villagers retained property rights over their own village-built residential and industrial buildings, all remaining land inside the SEZ, including land occupied by individual villager homes and collective village industries, was expropriated as state-owned urban land. All former village organizations and committees of the 173 villages inside the SEZ were abolished, impacting 450,000 villagers.[60] The collective organizational role played by the former village committee was split across two separate entities. Neighborhood committees were established with government staff to provide sociopolitical leadership, and incorporated companies became responsible for managing the economic activities of the numerous village enterprises.

In 1992, Caiwuwei Village held forty-five meetings and discussions to determine eligibility requirements for membership and other mechanisms for forming incorporated companies. The village's three production teams were turned into three incorporated companies, namely, Golden Dragon, Golden Pond, and Golden China. Village leaders concluded that 1,229 villagers were eligible to own shares.[61] This eligibility was coveted, as Caiwuwei was a financially well-off village in 1992. The net assets of the three newly formed companies were 202 million yuan.[62] Cai Zhuxiang, however, was deemed ineligible, as he had given up his PRC citizenship when he became a permanent resident of Hong Kong in 1984. However, Cai and Zhang still lived relatively comfortably given the rental income from their house full of tenants.

The Shenzhen government took notice of the building activities in all of the villages and attempted to regulate it. In 1992, it introduced bylaws of rental housing in Shenzhen special economic zone. These bylaws required villagers to register rental income and seek formal government approval to rent out their homes, stipulating that "any houses without government's property confirmation cannot be rented."[63] The rental policy was designed to curb illegal construction, of both new buildings and extensions to existing buildings. "Some Provisions for Resolving the Remaining Problems concerning Real Estate Ownership in Shenzhen Special Economic Zone" followed in 1993.[64] The provisions specified four types of land use in the "urban villages": industrial and commercial land use within the legal property boundary, more commonly referred to as the "red line"; industrial and commercial land use surpassing the legal "red line" (which could be registered for property rights after payment of fines);

private housing land use (each household could legally register only one property); and "old village" land that held the historic village structures such as older village houses, traditional squares, temples, and ancestral halls. The regulations were intended to curb illegal construction on village land and establish a method of property registration and standards for fine payment. However, the villagers simply did not recognize or accept the fact that they no longer owned the land occupied by their homes. They continued to believe that industrial-use land in each village belonged to the village collective. Successive regulations failed to curb illegal extensions and construction in urban villages, which only escalated as the years went by.

In 1996, Cai and Zhang followed the trend and demolished their four-story house to construct a new six-story building. Though limited by the size of the land parcel, Cai wanted to build a modern apartment building. He rejected the common practice of incorporating small one-bedroom units and insisted that each floor of the new building consist of a three-bedroom apartment with a large living room, kitchen, and balcony. Having seen similar layouts outside Shenzhen, Cai felt this would "future-proof" their building as compared with other "handshake towers." Even though the three-bedroom layout later proved to generate less rental income than buildings with smaller individual units, Cai and Zhang were proud of their house. Little did anyone know that this building would later become the most expensive nail house in China.

ILLEGAL CONSTRUCTION AND LEGAL REDEVELOPMENT

By the end of the 1990s, hundreds of villages outside the special economic zone also began large-scale illegal construction, building larger and taller buildings at a rate that would far surpass anything inside the SEZ. In 1999, a "Decision by the Standing Committee of Shenzhen People's Congress on Investigating and Punishing Illegal Constructions" was introduced.[65] This was the first time that the local government clarified the definition of "illegal construction" in Shenzhen. According to the policy, illegal construction encompassed all private and collective buildings constructed against planning regulations and without building permits. This announcement, however, led to another surge in illegal construction in villages all over Shenzhen, as the villages feared this was their last chance to build before more specific policies on punishments were established.

From the same land parcel of the village houses rose taller mini towers, mainly six to eight floors but some up to twelve stories, and even taller still in Shenzhen northern suburban areas. These buildings were still called *nongmin fang*, or peasant houses, but they were also nicknamed "handshake towers" and "kissing towers," referring to activities that are possible with one's neighbor in the adjacent building, through the open window, given the narrow space between the buildings.

Zhang Lianhao and Cai Zhuxiang resisted the temptation to build an even taller tower, but even at six stories, their house was still defined as an illegal construction by the 1999 policy. However, a subsequent set of policies introduced in 2002 created a mechanism to legalize their building. The Shenzhen SEZ Provisions for Dealing with Remaining Illegal Private Houses and The Shenzhen SEZ Provisions for Dealing with Remaining Illegal Buildings of the Production Management Type were instituted in 2002, introducing a mechanism for authorizing village-built properties that exceeded the previous legal limits.[66] The penalty amounts were staggered, increasing as the volume and height that exceeded the limits increased. As Cai and Zhang had followed the most fundamental regulation of "one building per household," their modest excess was relatively easy for the government to accept. According to this new set of provisions, Cai and Zhang's house fell into the category of "total architectural area more than 480 square meters but less than six hundred square meters and more than four stories but less than seven stories in height." Their fine would have been a few thousand yuan in order to meet the requirements for rental registration and property rights confirmation. The fines were minor in comparison to the rental income, and the peasant house building boom continued.

While villagers rushed to build housing for rent, developers also rushed in to build commercial real estate on village land. During the first decade of the SEZ, demolition and redevelopment mostly occurred on collectively owned village land and buildings. To make room for the iconic towers of the Luohu financial cluster, such as the Land King Tower, a series of historic buildings in Caiwuwei Village were demolished in 1993, including the Yanyi Elementary School and the Caiwuwei Ancestral Hall. Originally built in 1856 and renovated in 1916, the ancestral hall comprised three courtyards and five pavilions of traditional brick and wood carvings. The building hosted historic events well into the modern era. In August 1924, it was used as the base of the peasant move-

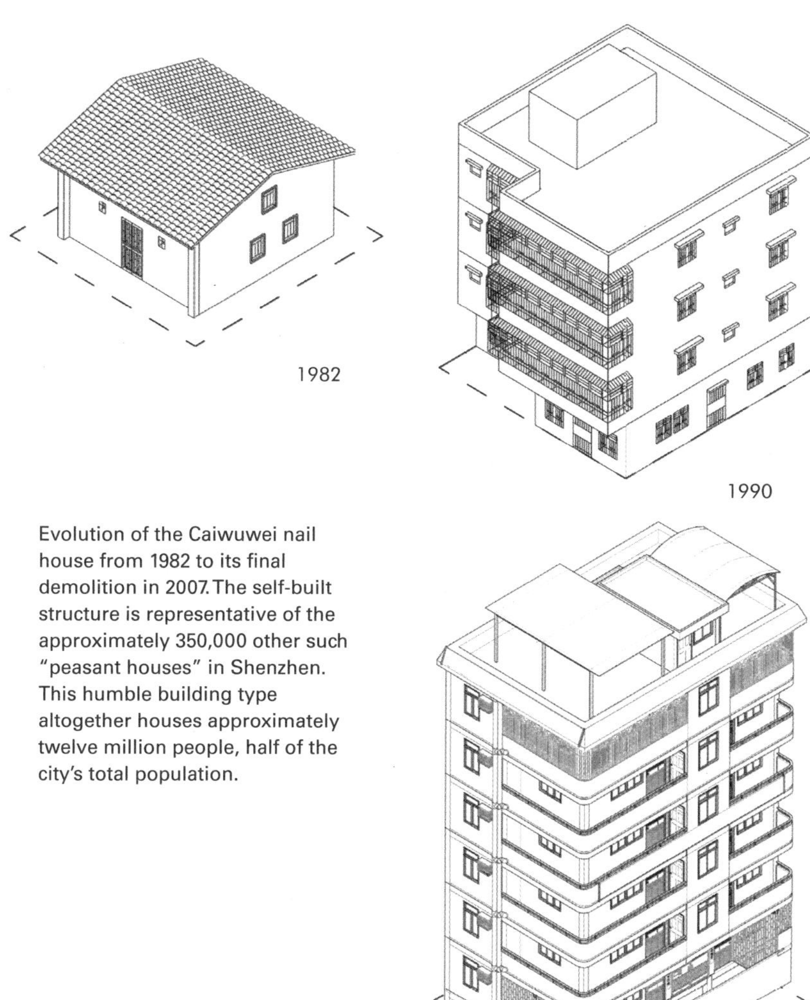

Evolution of the Caiwuwei nail house from 1982 to its final demolition in 2007. The self-built structure is representative of the approximately 350,000 other such "peasant houses" in Shenzhen. This humble building type altogether houses approximately twelve million people, half of the city's total population.

ment against raiding warlords in the region. In 1925, Zhou Enlai, at the time director of the Political Department of Huangpu (Whampoa) Military Academy and concurrently the secretary of the Communist Party's Guangdong-Guangxi Committee, delivered a historic speech in the plaza in front of the ancestral hall, urging villagers of the area to revolt against the local warlord.[67] The demolition of the ancestral hall was the most difficult for the villagers, as it was the ceremonial site and community center of the village.

The first large-scale redevelopment of land occupied by peasant houses was for the construction of Metropolitan Gardens. Approved by the Luohu District government, the development was led and financed by the Shenzhen Palace Property Development Co. Ltd., a company formed primarily for the construction of the Land King Tower, and jointly partnered by the Luohu Zhengyang Investment Development Company and Hong Kong Jianqiao International Development Co. Ltd. The project area of 32,900 square meters was in a prime location adjacent to Shennan Boulevard and was packed full of peasant houses. Negotiations with the villagers started in 1992 and took three long years to complete. According to the final agreement, all affected villagers would receive compensation housing in the future new residential towers in the same location. The compensation package was set at a "ratio of one to one," meaning that villagers would be eligible for new accommodation based on the equivalent size of their peasant house. Metropolitan Gardens was completed in 1999 and comprised six thirty-two-story and hundred-meter-tall residential towers, which offered 1,300 high-end apartment units.[68] This successful development was the precursor to the so-called Caiwuwei model.

CHINA'S MOST EXPENSIVE NAIL HOUSE

The first time Zhang Lianhao and Cai Zhuxiang learned of the relocation plans for their house was when they read about it in the November 11, 2005, edition of the *Shenzhen Special Zone Daily.* The newspaper published the government's "Permit for Housing Demolition and Relocation" for the Caiwuwei Financial Central District Urban Renewal Project. It was news to most of the other villagers, too. Only then did they find out that the head of the Caiwuwei Company had signed an agreement to sell land use rights for the village's 46,000 square meters to Kingkey Group on October 15, 2004.[69] Most of the villagers were angered by this and did not approve the compensation terms set out in the original agreement. Negotiations between villagers, the village company, and the developer came to a standstill until the mayor of Shenzhen, Xu Zongheng, intervened in August 2006.[70]

Village representatives reported to the mayor directly, and articulated four problems: first, the villagers should have been notified prior to the negotiation of the sale agreement; second, there was no guarantee regarding the quality or completion of their future relocation housing; third, 6,500 yuan per square meter was well below the market rate of the surrounding real estate; and lastly, the proposed design of the relocation housing was not suitable for their future needs. With facilitation from the city and district government, new terms were added to the relocation agreement that addressed the villagers' concerns. Kingkey offered an additional three hundred thousand yuan per building; the Luohu District government also added another 360,000 yuan per building, along with increased rental compensation during the entire relocation period until move-in. To provide further insurance and security, the government ordered Kingkey to deposit 450 million yuan into a bank account monitored by the Shenzhen Lands Bureau. Furthermore, the local government promised that, should the developer fail to deliver the future compensation housing, the government would do so instead. Lastly, the government invited a group of village-elected representatives to give input on the layout and design of the compensation properties. By October 23, 2006, 95 percent of the village households had finally signed the new agreement.[71]

Of the sixteen remaining households, Zhang Lianhao and Cai Zhuxiang were the most vocal. As Cai was legally a Hong Kong resident, their case attracted attention not only from local press but from most Hong Kong news outlets too. For reasons only known to them, Zhang and Cai resolutely refused to accept the future compensation housing and demanded cash compensation at the market rate of twelve thousand per square meter, consistent with real estate in the surrounding area. After they rejected Kingkey's increased offer of nine thousand yuan per square meter, Kingkey turned to the Shenzhen Lands Bureau for a verdict. On March 22, 2007, the Lands Bureau ruled in favor of Kingkey and ordered Zhang and Cai to move out of their house in twenty days. The couple swore to remain in their property. On March 29, Zhang posted her public letter online, which ended with the following questions: "In China's modern, civilized and harmonious society, am I right to assume there should not have been such bullying acts of robbery? Are there laws in China to protect me? As a Chinese citizen I am crying out for my basic rights: Who will help me?"[72]

While the unexpected backlash to her article deeply hurt Zhang Lianhao, she soon learned that there was a law to protect her. Zhang's questions were addressed by the landmark passing of the property law of China on March 16, 2007. To take effect on October 1, 2007, China's National Day, the property law was the first law in post-1949 China intended to ensure equal protection to owners of both public and private properties. The passing of the property law was a necessary legal mechanism as the country transitioned from a planned economy to a market economy. In many ways, the 2007 property law was a reversal of China's land reforms in the 1950s, which had turned land ownership from private to public.[73] Similar to eminent domain, however, the Chinese property law does give special powers to the government for expropriation of privately or collectively owned land for public interest.

Cai Zhuxiang bought copies of the published property law booklet and studied it in depth. When the Lands Bureau eviction order was upheld by the Shenzhen municipal government in May, Cai and Zhang sued the Shenzhen government. While Zhang stopped vocalizing their case in public or to the press, Cai continued: "The newly published property law clearly explained the protection of the private resident's property rights. We are protecting the dignity of the civil law. However, the property law does not detail regulations regarding public interest. As a result, in the relocation of Caiwuwei, they say building the financial center is public interest; individual interest must step aside. But I think building a financial center is for commercial interest. They must give me adequate compensation."[74]

Over the following months, the real estate market value surrounding Caiwuwei continued rising to nearly twenty thousand yuan per square meter. With the support of the property law and higher real estate values, Cai and Zhang raised their asking price to eighteen thousand yuan, making the total compensation fourteen million yuan, which is unprecedented in China's recent history of urban renewal.

They may have had the assurance of the new property law, but they did not have public sympathy or local government support. By mid-August, the Shenzhen Luohu District Court reached a ruling and again upheld the original eviction order. Along with two other nail house families remaining on the construction site, Zhang and Cai locked themselves inside their house and braced for the worst. Then on August 18, 2007, the China Ministry of Lands and Resources in Beijing issued a national order to stop all eviction processes across the entire country. Things moved quickly after the serendipitous national order. On September 21, Cai and Zhang signed their relocation agreement with Kingkey Group for twelve million yuan.

On October 22, the developer's construction team demolished the most expensive nail house in China.

Construction on the KK100 tower broke ground on November 11, 2007. By the year's end, Caiwuwei Village's total net assets were estimated to be 68.7 million yuan, its yearly revenue was over 140 million yuan, and its total tax paid to the government was over ten million.[75] The village collective and individual assets had doubled and tripled a few times over, and this process was universally celebrated as a case of sustainable community relocation. The "Caiwuwei model" became the gold standard for future urban village redevelopments in Shenzhen. This precedent gave birth to a new era of power play, in which villagers debated with the government and developers over the progress of subsequent redevelopment projects in Shenzhen. The apparent success of Caiwuwei's redevelopment attracted the attention of other urban villages seeking redevelopment, not only in Shenzhen but across the region. Caiwuwei villagers hosted visitors from villages in both Guangdong Province and the New Territories of Hong Kong.

THE "CAIWUWEI MODEL"

In early 2012, the Caiwuwei Village households that had agreed to the property compensation package moved into their new homes next to KK100, the "Tallest Tower of Shenzhen." The two thousand villagers all moved into their own high-rise tower apartments on top of the commercial-use podiums, surrounded by a private gated fence. Nearly all the village families moved into Block E tower, a thirty-two-story high-rise of spacious three- and four-bedroom apartments, with views of the adjacent Lychee Lake and Park, formerly the village's lychee orchards. Block B was the Caiwuwei Village Corporation Service Apartments, collectively owned by the villagers. Block C was also a residential high-rise, but with small one- and two-bedroom apartments; these were the compensation rental properties for the villagers. And Block D was the Caiwuwei Golden Dragon Company Office Tower: the top floors (eighteen to twenty-nine) were used as offices, while the floors directly below (seven to seventeen) were used as company apartments. The fifth floor of Block D was entirely dedicated to village community facilities, such as tea houses and game rooms. The first four floors of Block D, like all the other blocks, constituted a large podium for retail space rentals above ground, along with a few floors of underground retail and parking space, which quickly filled with luxury cars.

The Caiwuwei Golden Dragon Company owned a total of 62,500 square meters of collective rental property: while the Service Apartments were managed by the Village Collective Corporation, the remaining thirty thousand square meters of mostly high-end retail spaces were all managed by the Kingkey Group. The collectively owned properties together generated a yearly profit of sixty million yuan; prior to redevelopment, the village's collectively owned properties had generated a yearly profit of eighteen million yuan.[76] The successful relocation sparked a round of news reports on Caiwuwei. Its most famous nail house was also dragged back into the limelight. Many were eager to criticize the "foolishness" of Zhang Lianhao and Cai Zhuxiang in demanding eighteen thousand yuan per square meter, which in 2007 was judged to be ridiculously high but seemed absurdly low in 2012. However, the twenty-six thousand working-class tenants who were displaced as a result of the 2007 Caiwuwei redevelopment received almost no media attention except for a brief reference in a Chinese academic journal eight years later.[77] When the villagers returned to their compensation properties in 2012, the market real estate value of their relocation housing had increased to thirty-five thousand yuan per square meter.[78] By 2017, it was sixty-six thousand yuan per square meter.[79] The nail house couple was ridiculed again in the local press, this time for their short-sightedness in not having agreed to compensation real estate. International coverage of the redevelopment project also joined in the commentary:

> Caiwuwei Village was a warren of tenement housing, knocked up quickly to accommodate an exploding population as Shenzhen famously erupted from fishing villages into a megacity of 10 million in the mere three decades since Deng Xiaoping made it China's first special economic zone. Many such neighborhoods still remain, blocks packed so tight that merely a meter often separates them. Caiwuwei was ridden by crime and, unusually, Kingkey offered its residents not only a new flat on-site but a second one to give them a rental income. One couple held out, and parallel to an earlier case in Chongqing, became stranded in the otherwise cleared site in their "Nail House."[80]

However, for the Shenzhen couple—especially for Zhang Lianhao—the initial rejection was not strictly about the unfavorable monetary terms. It was also about distrust of both the developers and the village leadership, who had signed the agreement without consulting all the villagers. In some respects, Zhang's insistence that the negotiated terms disadvantaged "rule followers" like herself, who had built and owned only one peasant house, was proven correct. She contended: "I am not like some of the villagers who are officials or have connections. These people were allotted multiple homesteads and have built multiple houses. They took the lead in signing the agreement because they have other properties to live in. Yet they are brazen enough to say to me sarcastically, 'How can you fight the government?'"[81]

Of the 1,627 total apartments in all the compensation towers, around five hundred were set aside for self-use, and the rest were all quickly snapped up by renters. Each household typically received three to four units; however, there were stories of one family receiving twenty-three rental units.[82] When Zhang Lianhao and Cai Zhuxiang received their financial settlement, it was split into four equal portions. They each took a quarter; the other two portions were given to their son and daughter. Many online posts continued to disapprove of their greed in making such high demands for compensation. In addition, the couple regularly received hoax phone calls from people claiming to be tax collectors, and worse still, death threats. They quickly changed their phone numbers and disappeared from the public eye. When Shenzhen news reporters tracked down Cai Zhuxiang in 2012, they were surprised to discover that he was living with another woman in Shenzhen's suburban district of Buji. Cai and Zhang Lianhao were divorced.[83] Zhang was nowhere to be found. Along with her adopted village and house, it seems that Zhang Lianhao has disappeared.

On July 7, 2012, having benefited from the tremendous wealth generated by the KK100 development, 90 percent of Caiwuwei Village Corporation's shareholders voted in favor of developer Kingkey undertaking an even more ambitious project, which would involve the demolition of 440,000 square meters of the remaining Caiwuwei Village properties. This new round of development would encompass all the areas not yet redeveloped in Caiwuwei, with a gross floor area reaching two million square meters. The project included commercial buildings: two current hotels, three bank headquarters, the Grand Opera House, Caiwuwei Village Corporation's office tower, and school campuses.[84] Throughout 2012, reports of the future design appeared in local newspapers.[85] The design concept was billed as "Street of the Sky and Street of the Earth," a horizontal megastructure that would be suspended over Shennan Boulevard and connect the high-end commercial establishments at either end. The project was expected to take ten years to complete.[86] With the implementation of this latest urban renewal plan, all physical traces of Caiwuwei Village would disappear from the city.

The Luohu District government strongly endorsed the project, which promised to revitalize the old financial industries in Caiwuwei and incorporate an international commercial center, with fifteen million square meters of new space. The project would involve one quarter of the entire district's land area, totaling 8.3 square kilometers. It was proposed that the redevelopment—which spanned 368,000 square meters distributed over forty-seven different land parcels, involving thirty-one property entities or individuals—be subdivided into five areas: the "Golden Triangle" from Dongmen to Southern Renmin Road, Sungang-Qingshui River, Shuibei-Buxin, east of Shennan Boulevard, and Liantang. Altogether, the forty-eight urban renewal projects would cost about one hundred billion yuan.[87]

Luohu District's urban renewal efforts, with the objective of bolstering the area's image as Shenzhen's financial hub, lie at odds with the subsequent relocation of the Shenzhen Stock Exchange out of Luohu, a decision made by the municipal city government. In 2013, the Shenzhen Stock Exchange moved westward to the adjacent Futian District, where it occupied a new tower designed by the Rotterdam-based Office for Metropolitan Architecture. Shenzhen's city hall had moved out of Luohu into Futian District in 2004, initiating Futian's preference over Luohu as the city's political and commercial center. Since then, the city mayor's office and other municipal offices have been housed in Futian's Shenzhen Citizens Center, a massive building designed by New York–based Lee Timchula Architects. These shifts in Shenzhen's urbanization process have had significant implications for villages located in the central districts of Luohu, Futian, and Nanshan. As each of the three central districts transformed, the villages located in these areas also adapted and evolved with varying degrees of socioeconomic success. The urbanization of the formally developed city districts and the informally developed village neighborhoods are relational and deeply intertwined. The next chapter traces the parallel and entwined stories of Futian's Central Business District and Huanggang Village, the centuries-old urban village that found itself at the center of the district's new construction efforts. Huanggang Village leaders played influential roles in the development of the Central Business District area, and Huanggang Village itself was also transformed in the process. The final chapter then turns to Baishizhou Village, a "slum" village in Nanshan, the tourism and educational district of Shenzhen, which reflects a very different set of power dynamics between village leaders, district leaders, and urban developers.

PART IV

DISTRICT TRANSFORMATION

7.

CORPORATE VILLAGE IN THE CENTRAL BUSINESS DISTRICT

The apparent success of the Caiwuwei redevelopment project brought tremendous media coverage and public attention to the developer Chen Hua, founder and chairman of Kingkey Co. Ltd. Kingkey and Chen Hua became known as the pioneers of urban renewal in Shenzhen. The KK100 tower made Kingkey sought-after developers for the redevelopment of urban villages and other old urban neighborhoods. Chen Hua even added KK100's logo, an image of the tower, to his private jet—a Bombardier Challenger 605.[1] Following KK100, Chen successfully invited several international figures to publicize his real estate projects. In 2002, former US president Bill Clinton delivered a speech titled "World Trade Organization and the Chinese Real Estate Economy." He was addressing a VIP audience at the launch event of the Kingkey Bi Hai Yun Tian, a luxury housing estate in the city's affluent Overseas Chinese Town district. Described in Shenzhen as the "Clinton Show," in part owing to his appearance fee of 250,000 USD, the event was both celebrated and satirized in the local and international media.[2] Clinton's appearance generated enormous publicity, prompting Chen Hua to invite other international political figures—including former UK prime ministers John Major and Gordon Brown—to subsequent Kingkey real estate events. Kingkey and Chen Hua became the go-to real estate enterprise for both local government and urban village corporations. In the decades that followed the redevelopment of Caiwuwei Village, the majority of Kingkey's projects were associated with the urban renewal of older neighborhoods. Most of Kingkey's ongoing urban renewal projects concern the redevelopment of urban villages, such as Mumianwan, Shuibei, Changyuan, and Shayi; and more urban village projects are slated to begin in the coming years, including Shangxiawu, Tianxin, Zhuguang, Meifu, and Caiwuwei Phase 2.[3]

In 2012 alone, Kingkey was appointed to embark on urban renewal projects within the districts of Luohu, Nanshan, Bao'an, and Longgang—four of Shenzhen's five administrative districts. The Kingkey projects in those four districts had a total estimated demolition area of 630,900 square meters and would incorporate new development in the realm of three million square meters. In the same year, Chen Hua's name appeared on the *Shenzhen Special Zone Daily*'s honor roll of "30 Practitioners Contributing to the City's Development and Habitats Upgrade," in a special issue marking the thirtieth anniversary of the influential newspaper. Under the title "Chen Hua, Chairman of Kingkey Group: Expanding the Space and Height of a City," the article described Chen's contribution:

> Chen Hua and his Kingkey Group were the first redevelopers to focus on urban villages. They were successful pioneers, who pushed forward the urbanization process of the city. First hailed as the "Big Hero of Urban Renewal in Meilin," then achieving sweeping success with his intervention into the "longstanding, huge, and difficult" redevelopment project of Chiwei community, and later erecting Kingkey 100, the city's urban redevelopment model of success, Kingkey Group is the "Benchmark Enterprise" for Shenzhen's urban renewal.[4]

In addition to Kingkey and its chair, Chen Hua, several other developers featured in the *Shenzhen Special Zone Daily*'s "Top 30 Honor Roll" have business and personal ties to various urban villages. The most intriguing, yet least known, is probably the link between Huanggang Village and Wang Shi. As founder and former chairman of China Vanke Co., Ltd., the world's largest residential property developer, Wang Shi is one of

China's most influential entrepreneurs.[5] The *Special Zone Daily* characterized Wang Shi as "a contemporary entrepreneur holding adamant beliefs and facing the challenges of globalization. . . . In May 1984, Wang Shi founded China Vanke Co. The watershed moment was 2007 when Vanke leapfrogged from 'China's Largest Residential Developer' to 'the World's Largest Real Estate Enterprise in Development Volume.'"[6] Propelled by Wang's near-mythical personal aura as an Everest-climbing and environment-saving trailblazer, China Vanke's genesis in Shenzhen is a source of pride for the city.

However, Wang Shi's account of his early experience as a construction technician on Shenzhen's railroad system from 1978 to 1980 was unfavorable.[7] In his autobiography, *Vanke and I in Twenty Years,* Wang describes how poor his first impressions of Shenzhen were in 1978 and notes that he "was eager to complete the project within the shortest possible time so that I could get far away from Shenzhen that bordered on Hong Kong across a river."[8] Wang's description of Shenzhen in the late 1970s was one of poverty and desperation. The only warm memory of his initial foray into Shenzhen involved an exchange with a villager he called "Cowboy":

> One Sunday morning, a sturdy peasant carried me on the back rack of his reinforced bicycle to Huanggang Village, which lay six kilometers from the North Sungang Railroad Station and one river away from Hong Kong. During the Rural Socialist Education Movement, my father-in-law stayed in the village to observe work in this primary unit. His host happened to be my bicycle-riding host, Zhuang Shunfu (nicknamed "Cowboy"), head of the Huanggang Village.
>
> I followed "Cowboy" into an ordinary house—furnishings a little messy, a black iron wok on the stove using a bellows and firewood for cooking, and a straw rain cape hanging on the wall. "Cowboy" was quiet and spoke such awkward Mandarin that I often misunderstood what he said in our conversation. As for his mother who handled things in the house and his wife who farmed in the fields, I found them even harder to communicate with. At dinner, the two women kept chuckling and placing food in my bowl.[9]

While Wang appreciated the hospitality of Zhuang and his family, the poverty and hopelessness of their village life only reinforced Wang's pessimistic view of the place. Wang Shi had no idea that the "sturdy peasant" and his village would eventually become his conduit to Shenzhen. Often described by others as "a man of few words," Zhuang Shunfu was nicknamed "Cowboy" from a young age. This moniker had no association with the cowboy persona of the American West; it most likely connected with his farm duties as a young boy growing up in Huanggang Village. Zhuang demonstrated maturity and leadership quite early on, and was a village production team leader at the age of twenty-three.[10] Back in 1978 when he carried Wang Shi on his bicycle, Zhuang was not yet the village head; he was a production team leader and leader of the Village Militia Team. While Huanggang's armed village militia followed a proud local tradition, it was common practice for China's villages to employ armed village troops to protect their people, farmland, and livestock. It is documented that Caiwuwei Village, for example, was involved in a number of village turf wars involving hundreds of armed fighters along with the exchange of cannon fire. However, in 1987 Zhuang confessed to Wang that the Huanggang Militia was sparsely manned, as he was the only one left on the team among his old classmates from the village school.[11]

Wang Shi fled Shenzhen in 1980 as soon as his assignment was over, returning to the relative comfort of the more urban Guangzhou. He did not give Shenzhen another thought until a chance visit by "Cowboy" Zhuang:

> Spring 1983 arrived before we knew it. "Cowboy" and his wife came to Guangzhou to visit my parents-in-law, bringing with them freshly caught shrimp, a case of Sunkist oranges and a case of California red apples. "Cowboy" was wearing a light-colored bomber jacket made in Taiwan, his hair much better groomed than before. What amazed me most was Mrs. Cowboy's headful of curly permed hair. When asked where she had her hair done, she just looked down, giggled with a hand over her mouth, and blushed. I wondered what, in three short years, had happened in Shenzhen?[12]

THE HISTORY OF HUANGGANG, VILLAGE OF THE IMPERIAL MOUNT

Wang Shi's surprise and astonishment at Zhuang's Taiwan-made bomber jacket and his wife's fashionable hairstyle were indicative of the clash between their appearance and the norms of daily life in China, outside Shenzhen. Even in Guangzhou, one of China's most cosmopolitan cities, live seafood and fresh fruit were impossible to get, even with money. At that time, regulations governing the planned economy meant that even the basic necessities of food and clothing could not be purchased with cash and were instead rationed through "Flour Stamps," "Meat Stamps," "Fabric Stamps," etc. Both political necessity and cultural norms prescribed the notion that frugality was patriotic and physical conformity reflected one's high moral standards. Images of genderless masses with short cropped hair and uniformly blue Mao jackets epitomized some of the most widely reported impressions by foreign visitors to China throughout the 1980s.

Zhuang's metamorphosis was so remarkable that it ignited Wang Shi's curiosity and ambition. In addition to the sophistication and economic prosperity conveyed by Zhuang and his wife, what struck Wang Shi was the contrast between this image and what he had witnessed in Shenzhen when he left in 1980. What exactly had happened in Shenzhen during those few intervening years? In the experience of Zhuang "Cowboy" Shunfu and his Huanggang Village, it was a drastic change to a village history already highly dramatic.

In his autobiography, Wang Shi mentions that his father-in-law stayed at Zhuang's village home in Huanggang. However, he does not elaborate on the prominence of his father-in-law, Wang Ning, or what his relationship was with Huanggang Village. Wang Ning (1923–2013), an important figure in the Communist government, was already active in the party prior to the founding of the People's Republic of China in 1949. During the 1980s and 1990s, he served as deputy secretary of the CCP Provincial Committee of Guangdong, heading its Political and Legal Affairs Committee.[13] With his experience in the region, Wang Ning played a part in the early decision-making process for the policy outlining of Guangdong Province's special economic zones. His stay in Huanggang and experience with local villagers such as Zhuang Shunfu gave him first-hand knowledge of Huanggang's long agricultural and unique political history. This would have facilitated his approval of reform policies, including the policy that allowed Shenzhen's local villagers to cross the Hong Kong border to carry out daily farming activities.[14]

Residing on the north banks of the Shenzhen River, villagers of Huanggang have fished, farmed, and operated ferry boats along the river since its first settlers, led by Zhuang Run, arrived in 1426 during the Ming Dynasty.[15] Like many of Shenzhen's early settlers (mentioned in Chapter 3), the Zhuang Clan originated from northern Henan Province. They migrated southward during the Tang Dynasty, and later during the South Song Dynasty. The Zhuang Clan's genealogy book recorded the reason for the particular site to be chosen for their new village: "relocated to the country of the Yellow Mount owing to its fertile land."[16] In the Kangxi Period's *Xin'an County Annals* (1688), a chapter on geography refers to Huanggang as the "Yellow Mount Pier," where ferry services operated, taking passengers across the Shenzhen River.[17] The village name was officially changed to "Imperial Mount" after one of the Zhuang descendants ranked first in the national examinations, during the reign of Emperor Qianlong in the Qing Dynasty (1735–1795 CE).[18] In the early Qing period, the villagers built a wall around their settlements and introduced water from a nearby river to form a canal around the wall. Agricultural production in Huanggang Village peaked in the mid-Qing dynasty (1700–1800 CE), when four thousand men farmed fields spanning approximately 3.3 square kilometers.[19] In addition, the village operated forty-three fishing boats and conducted aquaculture production, making Huanggang dried shrimp—a famous regional delicacy. Huanggang Village grew to become a collection of four natural villages: Shangwei (upper court), Xiawei (lower court), Jilong (auspicious dragon), and the namesake Huanggang (Imperial Mount).

Huanggang Village is one of the few historic Ming dynasty villages in Shenzhen still remaining today, despite multiple clearance orders by the imperial government during China's Ming and Qing periods, which sought to abolish Huanggang and other villages so that their crops and fishing boats could not be used by pirates and other seafaring invaders. The imperial army was ordered to burn the villages and farming fields to force all villagers off of the land. Once resettlements were allowed, some persistent villagers returned to settle on their original sites.[20] Generations of descendants of these proud and persistent villagers have played active roles in many historic events in the region. Huanggang is one of the many historic villages that hold this unique history in modern-day Shenzhen as well as Hong Kong. When the Qing government's 1898 Second Convention of Peking conceded all land south of the Shenzhen River to Great Britain, more than one hundred Huanggang villagers refused to recognize this agreement, and led the 1899 Anti-British Uprising with other villagers along the Shenzhen River in order to defend their farmland south of the river. Only the young flag bearer returned alive following defeat by the

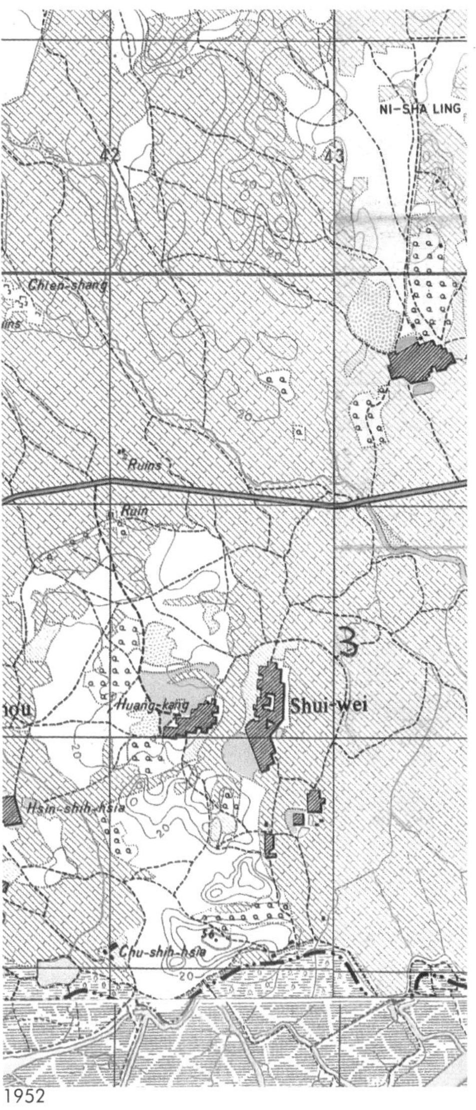

1952

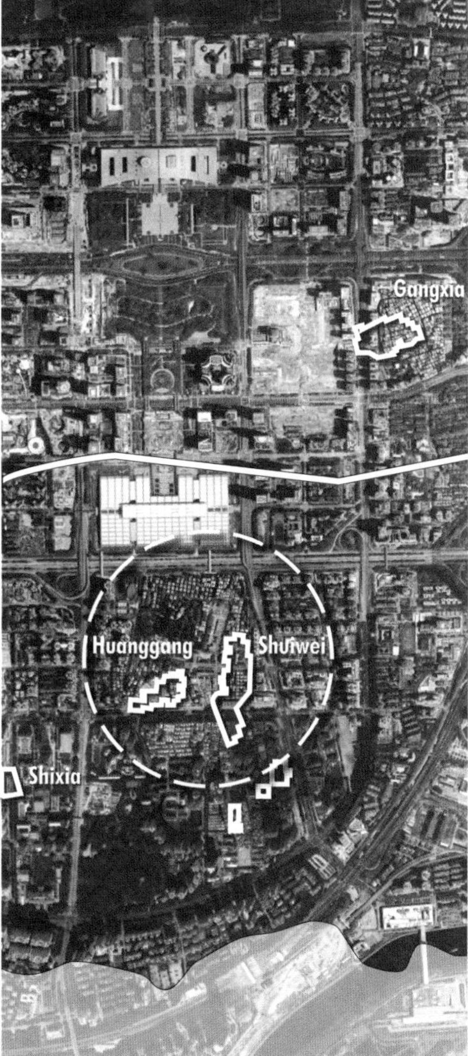

2014

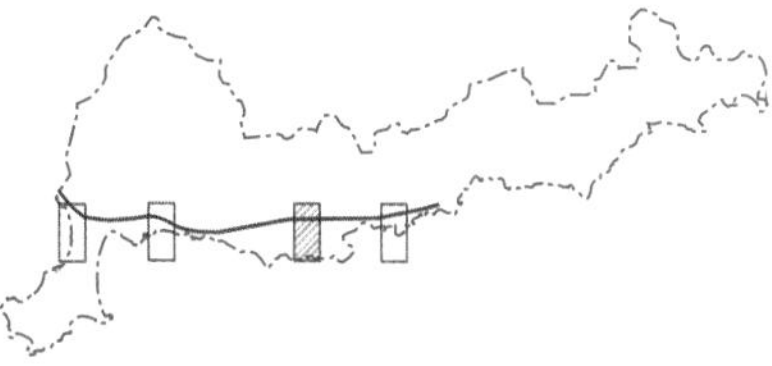

Survey map (1952) compared with satellite image (2014) in Futian District. Huanggang Village found itself to be on the central axis of Shenzhen's new central business district. Taking advantage of its central location as well as its effective village leadership, Huanggang is currently one of the wealthiest urban villages in Shenzhen.

British colonial army.[21] The names of the villagers killed in the uprising were carved into stone tablets, and they were worshipped as heroes in Huanggang's historic Village Ancestral Hall. Built during the Qing Dynasty, the ancestral hall, with its three halls and three courtyards, continued to host remarkable historic events in the twentieth century. In 1925, the Huanggang Ancestral Hall became the headquarters of the Communist Peasant Association and the Peasant Defense Army. While the innermost hall was still devoted to ancestral worship, in 1932 the rest of the complex became the village school, where Communist Party members were disguised as recruited teachers. In 1927, the provincial Communist Party committee set up an underground Communication Center in Huanggang as a liaison point between Communist activists in Hong Kong and Guangzhou. The operation of the communication center was secretly financed by a merchant from nearby Caiwuwei Village, who owned a bank and a jewelry shop in Shenzhen Old Town. The communication center was used to organize guerilla forces and pass military intelligence to the Chinese, as well as other Allied Forces, during the Japanese occupation in the region.[22]

During the Pacific War from 1941 to 1945, Huanggang Village once again served as an underground Communist safe house. Initiated by CCP leader Zhou Enlai and led by the Dongjiang Column, "The Great Rescue" mission smuggled important cultural and political figures with alliances to the Chinese Communists out of Japanese-occupied Hong Kong across the Shenzhen River into China's then-rural Bao'an County.[23] Huanggang Village was one of the most important connection stations for the rescue efforts. The mission rescued over a thousand people, including some British, American, and other Allied Forces personnel fighting the Japanese in the region, many of whom crossed the Shenzhen River under cover of darkness with the help of Huanggang villagers in fishing boats.[24] During the ensuing Communist-Nationalist civil war, Huanggang villagers continued to smuggle weapons, medicines, and other desperately needed provisions from Hong Kong to Communist operations throughout China.[25]

Huanggang Village's strategic contribution was recognized and praised following the Communist victory and establishment of the People's Republic of China in 1949. However, the enduring disasters of the Great Leap Forward (1958–1960) depleted village resources, and Huanggang fell into abject poverty. As a historic and established village, Huanggang experienced much chaos and destruction during the Cultural Revolution (1966–1976). The village's ancestral hall was heavily damaged and the stone tablets of the anti-British village heroes were destroyed. By the late 1970s, most of the able-bodied villagers were smuggled across the border to Hong Kong to seek work. Daily wages in the village production team were as little as one yuan, while in Hong Kong daily wages reached several hundred yuan. The village's farming fields and fish ponds were abandoned, and children were taught to swim from an early age to prepare for crossing the river undetected.[26] Wang Shi's first stay in Shenzhen from 1978 to 1980 was during one of Huanggang Village's historical low points.

THE METAMORPHOSIS OF HUANGGANG VILLAGER AFTER 1979

Thoroughly discouraged, Wang Shi left Shenzhen in 1980. That same year, "Cowboy" Zhuang Shunfu turned thirty years old and faced his first major challenge as a newly elected village leader. Although the Shenzhen special economic zone had been formally established in 1979, the economic turnaround was not immediate and the villages were still organized within the structure of the socialist commune. Faced with continued poverty and eager to participate in the new economy, the better-off subvillage of Shuiwei filed for separation from the rest of the Huanggang Commune. During the separation negotiations, Shuiwei Village elders made a verbal pact with the other three villages: while all assets—including land, people, livestock, and equipment—would be split, the Zhuang Clan Ancestral Hall and the village school inside would remain a shared property with continued support from Shuiwei. This decision recognized the common clan ancestry as well as the remarkable history of the ancestral hall, which was well known to the village elders. Following the withdrawal of Shuiwei from the village commune, the remaining villages faced even greater hardship after handing over ten thousand yuan to Shuiwei. Given these abysmal prospects, Shangwei Village also expressed its intention to separate. Zhuang Shunfu made an impassioned plea to the elders of Shangwei to resist further fractioning Huanggang Village:

> What I most want to say today is, Huanggang is our Huanggang; it belongs to everyone. When Shuiwei and Huanggang split, I was not in charge. I was just the security director, not in a position to approve or disapprove the splitting. But Shangwei, Xiawei, and Jilong have no

> historical precedent for separation; we absolutely cannot split. From now on, no one should ever bring up the matter of Shangwei's desire to split. Allowing it to separate from the team is the one thing I am least willing to do. I think it is not really what you want to do, either. . . . Now, the entire Huanggang is like a large ship. We are all on the same ship together. If this ship overturns, we will all be in the water. Do you want to see the ship being wrecked?[27]

Persuaded by Zhuang Shunfu, Shangwei Village agreed to remain in the commune and even offered a private loan of forty thousand yuan to fund new village businesses that had sprung up as a result of the urban construction surrounding the village. Huanggang villagers went on to provide driving and transportation services to Infrastructure Corps' construction teams. With the implementation of the Household Responsibility System in 1982, Huanggang formed trucking teams that carried sand from the banks of the Shenzhen River to all the construction sites. In addition, another village team was formed to collect refuse from Hong Kong and resell the recyclables—such as old tires and construction waste—in Shenzhen during its initial infrastructure construction boom.[28] Like nearby Caiwuwei Village, Huanggang began to establish numerous light industrial Sanlaiyibu ventures, with Hong Kong relatives as partners and investors. Working together, the Shenzhen villagers and Hong Kong investors managed to create a booming cluster of businesses and lift Huanggang village out of debt. During his visit to Guangzhou in 1983, Zhuang Shunfu described Huanggang's village businesses and large construction projects to an incredulous Wang Shi. Zhuang's account of his life and the drastic changes in Shenzhen made such a strong impression on Wang Shi that he immediately made plans to return to Shenzhen to "restart" his life. When he arrived at the Shenzhen train station, "Cowboy" Zhuang was there to pick him up in a beat-up Japanese car. Wang Shi's first Shenzhen business venture, in 1983, involved importing twenty thousand tons of corn for chicken feed via the newly constructed Chiwan Harbor. In a dramatic twist of fate, he had to rely on Huanggang Village's construction trucks to help him out, fortunately preventing bankruptcy. As a friend, Zhuang Shunfu had bailed him out on more than one occasion. Zhuang took pity on him after the chicken feed near-miss and implored him to join the village recycling business.[29]

In 1984, Zhuang Shunfu became secretary of the Communist Party, Huanggang Branch. As Wang Shi's business ventures in Shenzhen became more firmly established and successful, Huanggang Village also dramatically transitioned. The end of the Commune System in 1983 was officially sanctioned by the State Council document "Notice on the Separation of Governance from the Commune and the Establishment of Township Governments." In 1984, the twenty-four production teams collectively formed Huanggang Industry Limited and received forty million yuan from the Shenzhen government as compensation for village land requisition. Huanggang Village used the funds to set up the Shapuwei Industrial Zone, and the 10,800 square meters of factory facilities soon attracted enterprises such as the Weihuang Knitting Factory and Lilai Electronics Factory.[30] Factory space was in such high demand that Huanggang invested a further nine million yuan to build the Jilong Industrial Zone in 1988. Factories in these two large industrial zones attracted tens of thousands of workers from all over the country. Like the villagers in Caiwuwei, the Huanggang villagers became rent-collecting landlords instead of working in the factories; they rebuilt their two-story village homes into taller and taller rental housing blocks within the footprint of the original buildings. The spaces between these village buildings in Huanggang are relatively wide and airy, unlike those in Caiwuwei. Each village building is set back an equal distance from the street, creating pleasant and airy pedestrian alleyways. This feature was attributed to the relative success of the Huanggang village collective under Zhuang Shunfu's leadership, and to its policy of consistently upgrading the village's civic infrastructure and public amenities.

In 1985, the Huanggang Primary School was moved out of the ancestral hall to a land plot of twenty thousand square meters. An elderly home was built in 1987, and all villagers over the age of fifty-five received a monthly subsidy. In 1988, the Huanggang Kindergarten was built with 1.3 million yuan of collective village funds.[31] The Huanggang Primary School received an upgrade that year, and was given an additional ten thousand square meters of land for a basketball court, as well as a soccer and track field. In 1991, a large complex was built to house an auditorium, a computer lab, a dance studio, and a swimming pool; the addition cost 3.8 million yuan.[32] Besides these physical upgrades, the village set up an initiative to award ten thousand yuan a year to any villager accepted by and enrolled in national or international universities, which was later changed to granting five thousand yuan per semester until graduation to those who completed high school and went on to engage in post-secondary education.[33] In 1992,

1.2 million yuan was invested in computers and learning tools for the village school and community center. Another eight million yuan funded a large library for the village in 1993. In addition, Huanggang Village participated in China's large-scale Project Hope, which had the goal of building schools in impoverished rural regions; the village collective donated to the construction of four schools in such regions as a part of this initiative.[34] Zhuang Shunfu's leadership in prioritizing education was evident both in the construction of facilities and the allocation of scholarships. In addition, he sent his two sons to study finance and design in the US, Canada, and the UK.

The year 1992 was an important one for Huanggang, and for all the other villages within the special economic zone. It was the year in which all remaining land held by the villages received urban status, and the villagers' rural *hukou* was converted to urban *hukou*. In addition, all village enterprises were encouraged to form incorporated companies with the villagers as shareholders. The Shenzhen Huanggang Real Estate Holdings Company Limited was established in 1992, with Zhuang Shunfu as its founding director and CEO. Huanggang's 1,680 villagers, comprising 520 households, all became shareholders in the company. Over the following decade, Huanggang Real Estate Holdings developed major construction projects and established over fifty subsidiary companies specializing in businesses from electronics to garments to chemicals.[35] In 1995, all the villagers in Huanggang moved out of their original village housing blocks into a garden villa-style residential development named Huanggang New Village. The vacated old housing blocks then became entirely occupied by renters. The twenty-two-story Huanggang Tower was the first village-funded real estate project, built in 1997. In addition to accommodating the offices of Huanggang Holdings, the tower contained office space, a hotel, and retail facilities. By 1998, the 300-million-yuan Huanggang development master plan—which had been drawn up back in 1990—was nearly complete.

In 1987, Huanggang Village had commissioned the Shenzhen International Landscape Development Company to formulate the upgrade and development master plans.[36] Subsequently, in 1990, the village commissioned the China Academy of Urban Planning, the same urban planning firm hired by the Shenzhen government for the city's overall master plan. Construction began in 1991. The project created a series of expansive public structures and spaces along an east-west axis, following the orientation of the historic village. A gilded Village Gate in Qing Dynasty style marked the eastern village entrance, leading to a street wide enough for vehicles and lined with modern shopping spaces. The street leads directly to an open space marked by a large bronze sculpture of a big bull leading three smaller bulls. This sculpture was not a reference to the economy's bullish market, but rather a privately acknowledged tribute by the villagers to their respected village leader—none of them would have dared to refer to him as the "Cowboy." The pedestrian space opened onto the Huanggang Cultural Plaza with a large musical fountain in the center, flanked on the north side by a shady grove of palm trees. The south side, meanwhile, featured a European-style clock tower and shopping arcade with a large outdoor LED screen. The axis continued westward with ceremonial steps ending at an expansive raised platform, the location of the stately new Huanggang Ancestral Hall. The original ancestral hall appeared to be abandoned; neither Zhuang nor any of the other Huanggang leaders seemed to invest much historic or sentimental value in it. The newly built ancestral hall was larger and taller, with imperial-style stone pillars of carved flying dragons. The raised area was originally a gentle wooded mount named Zhuzilin, or the Bamboo Forest. Finally, this eclectic collection of civic spaces stood next to the twenty-thousand-square-meter Huanggang Village Park, built in the Southern Scholars Garden style commonly found in China's Zhejiang Province. Unlike the ancestral hall, which is open only to the Huanggang villagers, the lush Huanggang Village Park is open to all: villagers, renters, and the wandering public alike. The park includes a well-stocked koi pond and stone bridges, pavilions with flying roofs, and rock sculptures; and its original function as the village orchard can be seen in the numerous lychee trees throughout the garden space.

Compared to most other urbanized historic villages, Huanggang enjoys an unusually high quality of urban space, services, and maintenance. This difference is most attributable to the village's leadership and the support they enjoy from the villagers, as well as, to a certain degree, the local government. The most typical criticism of the urban villages in Shenzhen, and the rest of China, is that they are *Zang, Luan, Cha,* or "Dirty, Disorderly, and Inferior." Zhuang Shunfu and his leadership team worked hard to make Huanggang a clean and orderly neighborhood, superior not only to other urban villages, but also to most of the urban blocks in Shenzhen's city proper. Huanggang has a generous number of accessible public spaces, including the open plaza with its fountains and lush greeneries. These places, along with the vehicle-accessible streets and pedestrian alleyways,

Inside an alleyway of Huanggang Village, looking north at the adjacent Shenzhen Convention Center on land once occupied by the village industrial zone.

are impeccably maintained by the village company's own sanitation and landscape units. Like other urban villages, Huanggang has a mix of large supermarkets and hundreds of small street-front shops, restaurants, nightclubs, and massage parlors. However, the village company maintains a well-trained and well-equipped security team that preserves law and order in the city as well as the village.

All of Huanggang's public space and facilities construction was funded by the village company, which had accumulated its wealth through the industrial zones and other village enterprises. By 2002, the fixed assets of Huanggang Holdings were valued at 450 million yuan, a quantum leap from the deficit of ten thousand yuan recorded in 1980 and even the three hundred thousand yuan recorded in 1984.[37] In 2000, the two industrial

Beyond the Huanggang Village Ancestral Hall are high-rise residential towers self-developed by its own village corporation.

zones accommodated thirty-eight enterprises and two publicly listed Hong Kong companies. Between them, they employed more than twenty thousand workers, who generated an annual revenue of forty million yuan.[38] The remarkable transformation of Huanggang Village did not escape unnoticed by the city's leadership. In 1998, Zhuang Shunfu was elected vice chairman of the Standing Committee of Futian District People's Congress, an unexpected and extraordinary honor for a former village cowboy.

THE CBD COMES TO HUANGGANG

The stratospheric rise of Zhuang Shunfu's political status, the maturation of Huanggang's village leadership team, and the considerable wealth of

Huanggang Holdings paralleled Shenzhen's transition from an industrial zone to a comprehensive city. In the early 2000s, Huanggang Village found itself at the new spatial center of Shenzhen—the ambitious Central Business District (CBD), which moved the city's political and commercial center from Luohu District westward to the adjacent Futian District. Shenzhen's 1986 master plan had already designated the Futian area as the future Central Business District. In 1989, four planning and architecture offices—the China Urban Planning and Design Institute, Huayi Design Consulting Co. Ltd., the Shenzhen Branch Office of the Architectural Design Institute of Tongji University, and Singapore PACT International Planning Consultants—were commissioned to provide conceptual design for the area. In 1991, based on the various 1989 schemes, a new master plan was prepared by the Architectural Design Institute of Tongji University in collaboration with the Shenzhen Urban Planning and Design Institute (SZUPDI). Land use and street pattern proposals were formally approved in 1992, this time prepared by the Shenzhen Branch of the China Urban Planning and Design Institute (CUPDI). In 1993, a "Detailed Urban Plan" was proposed collaboratively by the CUPDI, the Shenzhen Branch of Wuhan Steel and Iron Group Design Institute, and the Beijing Urban Infrastructure Design Institute. Based on the detailed plan, SZUPDI proposed the "Urban Design for Futian Central District" in 1994.

In 1997, Japanese architect Kisho Kurokawa was appointed to design the CBD's public space system along the district's central axis, with an "Eco-media Axis" concept that would improve the green and public spaces of the area. The American architecture office of Skidmore Owings and Merrill (SOM) was commissioned in 1998 to create a master plan for the office building blocks flanking the central green space, and to provide general guidelines on design implementation. By the end of 1998, six government projects had been started, marking the beginning of the construction phase of the CBD. In the same year, feasibility studies were conducted for the urban renewal of Gangxia Village, located in the CBD diagonally across Shennan Boulevard from the city hall. In 1999, an international design consultation was conducted. Obermeyer Architecture proposed a sunken water system, which was a continuation of Kurokawa's Eco-media Axis scheme. A study was conducted to optimize the proposed urban design for implementation, resulting in the decision to relocate the proposed Shenzhen Convention and Exhibition Center to the plot on the CBD's central axis.

The master plan was based on a classically arranged north-south axis that originates, ceremonially, from the tallest point in Lotus Mountain Park to the northernmost spot in the CBD, occupied by the large bronze statue of the striding Deng Xiaoping. Adjacent to the southern edge of the park, symmetrical land parcels were laid out to accommodate civic buildings such as the Children's Palace, Book City, the Shenzhen Library (completed 1998) designed by Japanese architect Arata Isozaki, and the Shenzhen Modern Art Museum (completed 2017) by German architect Wolf Prix. Farther south from these civic buildings and sitting directly on the central axis was Shenzhen Municipal City Hall; its design was developed from a winning entry by an American practice, John M. Y. Lee / Michael Timchula Architects, in the 1996 international design competition. The Shenzhen municipal government moved from its 1981 location adjacent to Caiwuwei Village to the new Futian CBD in May 2004.

The Shenzhen Convention and Exhibition Center was completed the same year, and it marks the southern end of the north-south central axis defined by the CBD master plan. Funded by the city and designed by the German architectural firm GMP, this enormous structure occupied the entire land parcel of the bustling Huanggang Yuandingtou Industrial Zone. The municipal government acquired the land from Huanggang in 2001, but rather than receiving financial compensation, Huanggang negotiated its sale in exchange for a similar-sized land plot adjacent to the convention center. With the accumulation of capital and rocketing land prices in the Futian area, Huanggang Village sought to engage actively in the city's real estate market.

In 2002, Zhuang Shunfu was elected a deputy to the People's Congress of Guangdong Province. The position carries the political powers to participate not only in decisions concerning the city of Shenzhen, but in higher circles of political leadership at the provincial and national levels. He led Huanggang into a brand-new era, transforming the village as well as the city of Shenzhen.

The village company completed another self-funded project in 2001—Huangxing Towers, a residential complex composed of three twenty-story apartment towers. The company also embarked on phase two of the Huanggang New Village, which included forty-five mid-rise apartment buildings, a new kindergarten, primary school, supermarket, wet market, and a community center.[39] Concurrently, Huanggang collaborated with other real estate developers and private investors to undertake projects such as the three forty-story apartment towers on a Hong Kong–style podium (known collectively as Huangting Caiyuan), the thirty-two-story Huangtingju Tower, two thirty-two-story Guohuang Towers, and two thirty-eight-story Huangdu Towers. By 2004, two more codeveloped projects, both even larger in scale than the tower projects, had also been completed: the Huangda Oriental Garden, consisting of five thirty-two-story towers, and Huangting Century Garden comprised of nine thirty-two-story towers.[40] In addition to these predominantly residential towers, Huanggang codeveloped Huizhan Shidai Center, a fifty-story office tower, in 2004, and self-funded the twenty-story Huangxuan Hotel tower in 2005. Between 1992 and 2007, each Huanggang villager accrued company shares valued at around three hundred thousand yuan.[41]

In 2007, Zhuang Shunfu turned over the directorship of Huanggang Holdings and his position as Huanggang's chief secretary of the Communist Party to his eldest son, Zhuang Chuangyu, who was thirty-three years old, educated in Canada and the UK, and holder of a double degree in business administration and finance.[42] Zhuang Chuangyu continued to forge Huanggang's way into the Shenzhen real estate market. One of the company's next major projects involved the compensated land parcel next to the Convention Center. Huanggang teamed up with one of the largest Shenzhen-based developers, the Excellence Group, which invested in the construction while Huanggang provided the land. American architect Leo A. Daly was hired to design the Excellence-Huanggang Century Center. Completed in 2009, the massive development consisted of four towers surrounding a central open courtyard, with a land area of thirty thousand square meters and four hundred thousand square meters of total floor space. Encased by sleek glass curtain walls, the two tallest towers soar upward to almost three hundred meters in height and accommodate sixty and fifty-seven stories of offices, hotels, serviced apartments, and luxury shopping malls. The development was a spectacular success. In the first two weeks of sales, fifty-six thousand square meters of floor area in the two shorter towers were sold for more than thirty thousand yuan per square meter, instantly generating a revenue of 1.7 billion yuan.[43] The neighborhood of Huanggang Village was recognized as a "Pioneering unit in landscape and garden city development" by the municipal government in 2001,[44] proclaimed to be a national model for "pioneering in civilized community creation" by the Central Commission for Guiding Cultural and Ethical Progress in 2002,[45] and awarded the title of

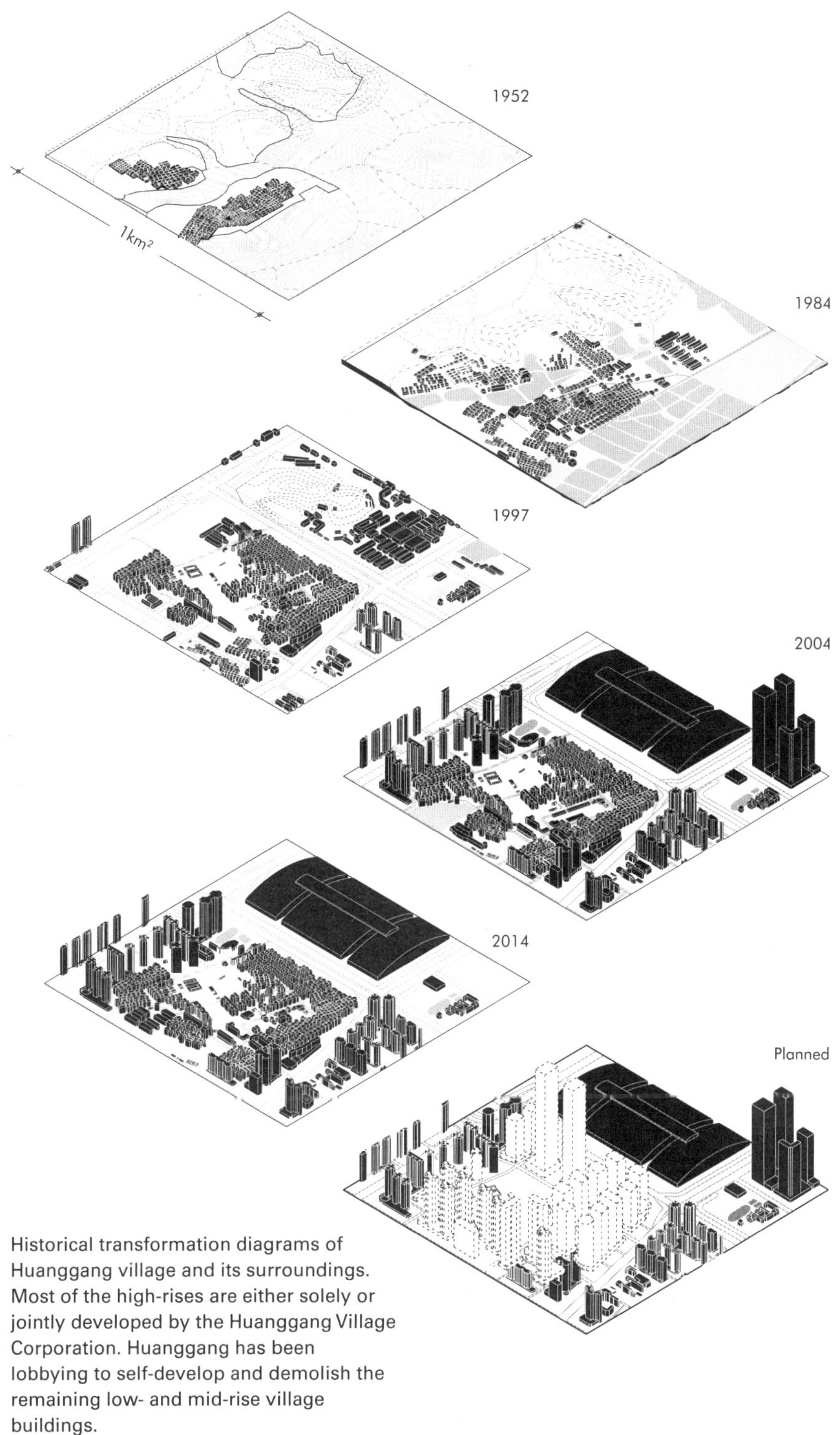

Historical transformation diagrams of Huanggang village and its surroundings. Most of the high-rises are either solely or jointly developed by the Huanggang Village Corporation. Huanggang has been lobbying to self-develop and demolish the remaining low- and mid-rise village buildings.

"Civilized Unit" ten times by the provincial and municipal governments through 2003.[46]

BORDER CROSSINGS AND "SECOND WIVES"

In the year 2002 alone, Huanggang Holdings recorded total assets of 450 million yuan, and each villager of Huanggang received an annual dividend of twenty thousand RMB.[47] In comparison, members of neighboring villages such as Futian, Gangxia, and Shuiwei were allocated, on average, 13,500 yuan per capita.[48] Villages located in outer districts a greater distance from the city center would have only been able to provide each of their members with a couple of thousand yuan annually. This large discrepancy could be attributed to the ability of Huanggang Village's industries and enterprises to adapt to the economic restructuring of Shenzhen. However, shares from the village company were only part of the income received by the original villagers; the majority of the villagers' income came from renting their individual "peasant buildings." For the villagers of Huanggang, many of whom had more than one building each, the income generated from the apartment rentals was several times that of the already generous village company dividends. Rooms and apartments in the "peasant buildings" of Huanggang were in constant demand, and their average rent was among the highest in the city. In addition to the relatively high quality of buildings and public spaces, the village's location directly adjacent to one of the most important Hong Kong–Shenzhen border crossings gave its rental properties an even greater edge over those of its rivals.

The Huanggang Checkpoint first came into operation in December 1989, catering to vehicular traffic between the newly established Shenzhen special economic zone and colonial Hong Kong.[49] The checkpoint is named for Huanggang Village, which is just to the north of the port of entry, and for the old Huanggang river crossing. The bridge spanned the Shenzhen River just south of Huanggang Village, extending into Hong Kong's most northern suburban territories. In 1991, the border facilities were expanded to encompass pedestrian crossing operations. During Deng Xiaoping's legendary 1992 tour of Shenzhen, his stop-off at the foot of the Huanggang bridge crossing made headlines in both the local and Hong Kong press. Back then, no one imagined that this barren location surrounding the century-old ferry crossing would eventually become Asia's largest freight and pedestrian port of entry.

By the year 2000, 68 percent of all Shenzhen–Hong Kong cross-border traffic (cars and lorries) passed through Huanggang Checkpoint, an average of 20,810 vehicles per day.[50] Individual passenger crossings amounted to 11 percent of the city's total, equivalent to over ten million for the year and 29,938 per day.[51] In December 2002, China's State Council formed a joint panel composed of members from eight ministries and commissions to conduct a study to validate the establishment of a twenty-four-hour national border customs point between Shenzhen and Hong Kong.[52] This would be China's first twenty-four-hour border crossing. It took little over a month for the panel to reach a decision and by midnight of January 27, 2003, the twenty-four-hour Huanggang Checkpoint was in operation. The opening was timed just before the Chinese Lunar New Year, when travel between the Shenzhen–Hong Kong border reached peak levels. The decision to open the Huanggang Checkpoint round-the-clock, unlike the oldest Shenzhen–Hong Kong crossing at Luohu, aligned with Shenzhen's eastward urban development and the shift of the city's political and administrative center from the old city center of Luohu District to the new Central Business District of Futian District.

The real estate development boom in surrounding urban villages, such as Huanggang, was a consequence of this shift in the city's focal point, as well as of the border checkpoint's strategic location. In addition, businesses—including hotels, restaurants, night clubs, and massage parlors—mushroomed along the border areas to cater to cross-border activities, mainly targeting Hong Kong tradesmen. With thousands of factories and plants built in Shenzhen, the Huanggang Checkpoint became a primary node for the transportation of goods and services in and out of China. The freight transport and logistics sector grew rapidly and became a major business enterprise for many Hong Kong companies. Hong Kong truck drivers would drive empty trucks north across the border, spend a few days in Shenzhen, and return with a cargo full of goods for export through Hong Kong. Most of the drivers made multiple trips every week into Shenzhen.

The continued economic disparity between Hong Kong and Shenzhen throughout the 1990s was astronomical, as evidenced by a comparison of wages earned by Hong Kong freight lorry drivers and wages earned by the general working class in Shenzhen. Many lorry drivers figured out that their monthly expenses on hotel lodging and meals in Shenzhen came to more than the monthly rent of an apartment in the city together with a live-in girlfriend or, in most cases, mistress. As most of the drivers were married, the women whom they paid for cleaning, cooking, and sexual services were colloquially referred to as *er-nai,* or second wife. Prior to China's abolition of polygamous marriage in 1950, this term described the first concubine married into the household following the *da-nai,* or first wife. For most Hong Kong men and young Mainland women with this arrangement, the preferred rental apartment location was in the urban villages around the checkpoints of Luohu and Huanggang. A number of these urban villages became informally known as "Second Wife Village."

The dark reality of the "second wife" phenomenon remained a taboo subject for many years in the news media of Shenzhen and of China more broadly. This sensitive, and illegal, arrangement existed in many large Chinese cities such as Shanghai and Guangzhou. The men were usually wealthy businessmen from Hong Kong or Taiwan, and the women were mostly young migrants from China's rural countryside who had originally sought factory jobs in the big cities. The first extensive press coverage of this issue in Shenzhen was published by the *Hong Kong Commercial Daily* in April 2001 and titled "Record of the Life of 'Second Wives': An Undercover Reporter's Peep into 'Hidden Mistresses in Golden Chambers.'"[53] The article was written by Tu Qiao, a Mainland Chinese journalist with a reputation for writing investigative reports on the plights of marginalized impoverished groups, such as China's rarely discussed AIDS patients. In January 2001, taking on the guise of a recently abandoned second wife looking for a new husband, she rented a small apartment in "Village X on the banks of the Shenzhen River." In her reports, she listed the "second wife villages" near the Huanggang Checkpoint as "Yu-X Village, Huang-X Village, Huang-X New Village, and Shui-X Village."[54] Anxiously aware of her deception yet determined to shed light on this issue, she befriended many young women and gained insight into this peculiar yet painfully pragmatic arrangement between second wives and their Hong Kong husbands.

Tu Qiao's article generated considerable local attention, as it touched a raw nerve in Hong Kong and Shenzhen. In 2002 alone, forty-two thousand court cases involving Hong Kong men and their second wives were tried by the Higher People's Court of Guangdong Province, resulting in forty-seven convictions of bigamy.[55] However, Tu Qiao's 2001 report was not published in Mainland China until June 2004, in an article in a Beijing literary magazine titled "My 60 Days and Nights in Shenzhen's Second

Wife Village."[56] This time, her report was picked up by numerous national and local Shenzhen news organizations and went viral in online media. In late 2004, Tu Qiao published a book called *Bitter Marriages,* which offered a full account of her experiences in a bid to escalate public attention and intervention on the issue:

> I have been to the homes of *ernai* (mistresses), underground horse races, and underground Majiong centers. I even had blind dates and accompanied hysterical women wanting to find their husbands. Through these experiences, I truly became part of their social circles so that they could expose their own wounds to me, and they truthfully told me their poignant stories. I won their trust and witnessed the real life of the *ernai.* When I got to know them better, I could sense the helplessness and weakness of those marginalized women.[57]

The phenomenon was finally exposed in China's news media, yet neither the articles nor Tu Qiao's book make any mention of the name of the actual village where she spent those two months. Many other news features and reports also exercised similar restraint. One published report, which described the efforts of a group of "ex-second wives" in Shenzhen, who had established a small organization offering assistance to other "sisters" living in the same urban village, referred to this village as "Huang-X Village."[58] However, with increasing public and media attention from the late 2000s onward, many villages in Shenzhen's Luohu and Futian areas were publicly named by the local press as "second wife villages." Huanggang Village, which usually appeared in the local media for its exemplary economic and community service achievements, was exposed in the regional and national press on account of assertions that over half of its tenant population were "second wives."[59] Huanggang Village was the principal location highlighted in a 2011 article by the Spanish newspaper *ABC* titled "*La Ciudad de Las Segundas Esposas,*" or "The City of the Second Wives."[60]

"AN ERA OF MERGING WITH THE CBD"

Zhuang "Cowboy" Shunfu and other village leaders never publicly addressed Huanggang's label as a "second wife village." When inquiries were made about the village's tenant demographics, they stated that all the original villagers had entrusted rental operations to second parties; therefore, they had little control over the subletting of the properties.[61] Huanggang's shadow population of "second wives" inevitably began to diminish with the onset of the Asian financial crisis after 1997. With the downturn of the Hong Kong market, the devaluation of the Hong Kong dollar against the Chinese yuan, industry restructuring and relocation to more rural locations, and less income disparity between Shenzhen and Hong Kong, Hong Kong's border-crossing population saw their purchasing power drastically decline. Hong Kong truck drivers discovered that their income could no longer stretch to pay for monthly apartment rentals and dedicated mistresses.[62] Soon after, Huanggang Village's tenants shifted: the falling numbers of "second wives" were replaced by workers from the newly constructed office towers, hotels, and luxury shopping centers surrounding the village. Despite the ups and downs of the financial market, apartments in Huanggang Village's "peasant buildings" continued to command the highest rents among all urban villages in Shenzhen.[63] Other non-village residential apartment blocks in the vicinity could not compete with Huanggang's high-quality facilities and public spaces. The open secret that Huanggang was one of the largest "second wife villages" did not tarnish its polished public and physical image. Any periodic reports in the local press of illegal activities, such as prostitution, drugs, and smuggling, were played down by the village leadership, who continued to pursue additional village urban redevelopment and design projects.[64]

Huanggang Village and Shenzhen city's ambitions for urban development had followed parallel trajectories, but dramatically collided in 2007. As the city's Central Business District reached maturity in terms of built development, the Shenzhen Mayor's Office and the Urban Planning Bureau began deliberating a potential southward extension of the CBD's central axis. The original Shenzhen CBD master plan's site boundary was just north of Huanggang, marked by the mammoth 280,000-square-meter Shenzhen Convention Center that formed the ceremonial central axis. By 2007, the central axis that stretched from city hall in the north to the Convention Center was filled with grand plazas and vast ceremonial and green spaces. However, being bisected by four major highways, the central zones of the axis were not utilized or even easily accessible to pedestrians or vehicles. In 2008, a competition to resolve this issue was won by the Rotterdam-based Office for Metropolitan Architecture (OMA) in collaboration with the Shenzhen-based architectural office Urbanus.[65]

However, their proposal for an underground connection system named Crystal Island went unrealized. Instead, the city intended to continue the central axis by creating more grand open spaces south of the Convention Center, made up of several large urban blocks continuing all the way to the Shenzhen River at the border. These urban blocks all sat on land owned by Huanggang Village, and the proposed open spaces would require the demolition of a third of the village buildings. The Shenzhen Urban Planning Bureau, supported by the Mayor's Office, began to draft the 2007 "Shenzhen CBD Huanggang District Redevelopment Plan." That same year, Huanggang was conveniently listed as one of the forty-five villages officially designated for planned overall redevelopment. This was spelled out in the document "2007 Shenzhen Urban Villages (Old Villages) Redevelopment Annual Plan," prepared by the Shenzhen municipal government.[66] The implication of "overall redevelopment" was that following reconstruction, the new units constructed on former urban village land would be released onto the open market, thereby further bridging the administrative gap between urban village land and municipal land.[67]

While the leaders of the Huanggang Village corporation welcomed the government's proposal to redevelop the area, they opposed the plan to extend the axis by creating vast open spaces through the central zone of the village. Taking a proactive stance, Zhuang Shunfu once again commissioned the Shenzhen branch of the China Urban Planning Institute to design a new master plan for Huanggang's future development, titling it "An Era of Merging with the CBD."[68] Bolstered by the successful groundbreaking that marked the construction of the Excellence-Huanggang Century Center in 2007, the Huanggang leadership proposed that two interconnected two-hundred-meter-tall towers should be built on the northernmost edge of the village, directly on the central axis. The twin towers possessed a striking similarity to the Petronas twin towers in Kuala Lumpur. With the exception of the village's central plaza, public garden, and ancestral hall, all other buildings in the Huanggang master plan were earmarked to be demolished and replaced by commercial and residential skyscrapers. Huanggang objected to the city's master plan not because it would demolish and urbanize the village, but rather because the planned development did not maximize new construction to make the village sufficiently more urban and integrated with the rest of the central business district. Huanggang leaders were no longer content to give land to the city and merely adjacent to its center—they wanted Huanggang to be the city center.

The Shenzhen Planning Bureau found Huanggang's counter-proposal unsatisfactory. The two parties disagreed on how to extend the city's central axis, and faced the challenge of negotiating control of the city's most precious commodity—land—in the most expensive central areas of Shenzhen. To address this challenge, the Shenzhen Planning Bureau launched an international design consultation competition for the Shenzhen CBD Huanggang Area Redevelopment Project, which encompassed fifty hectares, twenty-three of which were owned and managed by the Huanggang Village Collective. The Hong Kong–based architecture office IDU won the competition with a proposal to extend the ceremonial central axis at ground level on a larger spatial scale, thus enabling the contested ground space of Huanggang Village to remain active with mid-rise buildings and bustling commercial activities.[69] Between 2007 and 2009, IDU further developed the proposal into a master plan in close collaboration with both the Urban Design Department of the Planning Bureau and Huanggang Village leaders. Huanggang Village leaders were satisfied with a few key features of the master plan, which incorporated their requested FAR (floor area ratio) for new construction, as well as a phased demolition and construction program that would allow the village corporation to finance the construction with minimal support from outside developers. However, Huanggang Village leaders objected to other features in the IDU proposal, including its provision for transitional affordable housing, the mixed mid-rise clusters along with high-rise towers, and the absence of the Petronas-like twin towers. This process made it clear that while Huanggang Village valued the economic potential of the future development, it was also self-conscious of its own perceived image. The village's century-old history could be retained in the form of the preserved ancestral halls and proposed village museum, but its twenty-year history as an "urban village" was regarded by the leadership as a stain on its record, which had to be completely removed and replaced by shiny new skyscrapers.

With continuous negotiations and adjustments, the master plan passed through the Planning Bureau and the Vice Mayor's Office for Urban Development, reaching Shenzhen Mayor's Office in early 2009. Finally, in March, the "Shenzhen CBD Huanggang District Redevelopment Plan" was to be presented to Mayor Xu Zongheng in the largest presentation room in the Planning Bureau. The Huanggang plan was just one of several projects to be presented to the mayor, and the presentation itself was supposed to be a matter of procedure. The scheduled five-minute presentation was delivered by a designated official, while the designers responsible for the proposal were relegated to the back of the room and only permitted to observe. However, the official had barely begun the presentation when several Huanggang Village leaders, led by Zhuang Shunfu, entered the room. When they saw Zhuang, Shenzhen city's top leaders—directors, deputy mayors, and Mayor Xu—stood up as a gesture of acknowledgment and greeting. Zhuang Shunfu and Huanggang Village, although in certain ways exceptional among urban villages, contradict the perception that China's governance structure is uniformly top-down, particularly in the case of Shenzhen. Although urban village leaders often occupied influential positions locally, all of Shenzhen's official government workers and leaders were "parachuted" into the city. These leaders tried to establish good working relationships with those who held local power and influence, such as real estate tycoons, corporate heads, and village leaders. Zhuang Shunfu was all three, and more. The "Shenzhen CBD Huanggang District Redevelopment Plan" was later cast aside for years as a consequence of changing city leadership. Compared with the rather short-lived political careers of city leaders such as Shenzhen's successive mayors, political positions of the local village leaders are often more secure.

THE MODEL VILLAGE IN THE MODEL CITY

Despite the occasional whiff of political scandal and the periodic media exposure of illicit activities, Huanggang Village's image as a successful and exemplary urban village continues. Huanggang's accolades include being named Shenzhen's "Model Civilized Community" in 2004[70] and Guangdong Province's "'Six-Excellences' Safe and Harmonious Community" in 2006.[71] By 2007, Huanggang had received more than five national awards espousing its virtues as an exemplary demonstration community.[72] Honors like this are unusual for an urban village not only in Shenzhen, but anywhere in China. However, Huanggang's highest achievement in terms of national recognition was perhaps Premier Wen Jiabao's visit to Shenzhen for the thirtieth anniversary of its founding in August 2010. Wen's visit to Shenzhen and appearance in Huanggang was reminiscent of Deng's Southern Tour and his stopover in Fishermen's Village in 1992.

The well-orchestrated visit was extensively covered and publicized by local, regional, and national news outlets:

> Since the establishment of the Shenzhen special economic zone thirty years ago, people's living quality has risen to a new level. In the early morning on August 21st, Wen Jiabao came to the Huanggang community in the district next to Hong Kong. This community, which thirty years ago was only a fishing village, has now been built with lots of high-rise buildings and a big population. When you enter the community, you can see fountain water dancing with music and residents playing Tai Chi and soft ball in the square; you will be impressed by this harmonious image. . . . Then Wen Jiabao went into the home of a local resident, Zhuang Zhizhong, and chatted with his family, asking about the population, income, and other domestic issues. Zhuang Zhizhong told the premier that his ancestors were all Huanggang villagers and since the Reform and Open policy, life has been better and better.[73]

In addition, there was much news coverage featuring the exchange of words between Premier Wen and former village secretary Zhuang Shunfu. The *People's Daily* reported the following:

> Then the former village secretary Zhuang Shunfu, sitting next to the premier, said, "Over thirty years ago many Huanggang villagers illegally emigrated to Hong Kong. But the Reform and Opening Up policy and the establishment of the special economic zone have brought about earth-shaking changes to the village." He said, "During the thirty years in the special economic zone, we have also experienced a trilogy of development." "What trilogy?" Wen asked with great interest. "First it was the change from a rural village to part of a city in 1992. Second, we have moved from processing to service industry. And lastly, the construction of a modern international community means that we can completely change our destiny and rebuild a new age of passion."[74]

The *Shenzhen Special Zone Daily* further recounted the conversation between Zhuang and Wen Jiabao:

> Zhuang: "We are no longer young now and we need the youth to take charge. There are already two overseas returnees among the five

> forming the board of directors of the joint-stock company; one of them returned from the United Kingdom and is the chairman, and the other returned from the United States and serves as the general manager. These young people are better educated with stronger capabilities than us."
>
> Wen: "As well educated as they are, nevertheless it was you, the older generation, who laid the foundations. The fact that 40 percent of the directors are overseas returnees means we can already say you are moving toward internationalization, which is the third stage in the trilogy."
>
> What Premier Wen said made everyone laugh.[75]

It is perhaps worth noting that the "chairman" from the UK referenced is Zhuang Chuangyu and the "general manager" from the US is his brother, Zhuang Chuangjian, the two sons of Zhuang "Cowboy" Shunfu. As with many organizations in China, the seemingly international and modernized management team is still very much an extension of the traditional, even feudal, practices of China's past.

However, Huanggang's colorful "past" shows signs of selective memory. In 2013, the village devised a new five-year master plan titled "The Years of Service Industry Development." The aim of the plan was to make service industries the village's development priority and to upgrade those that already existed. Business consultants were commissioned to gradually eliminate low value–added industries within the village, and to propose a strategic plan for business development.[76] The Jilong Qiongli Old Village House, the oldest tiled single-story house in Huanggang Village (which was renovated as a result of this plan), went on to become the "first village museum in China."[77]

This planning phase did not escape some controversy; in this case, it was not over the reemergence of the Petronas-like twin towers, but over the proposed demolition of the original Zhuang Clan Ancestral Hall. The Qianlong Period Qing Dynasty complex, with its series of three halls and three courtyards, had not been used by Huanggang Village since the construction of the grand new ancestral hall in 1995. The old complex, adjacent to a recently established trash dump and recycling facility, was neglected and poorly maintained. However, some historians and conservationists criticized the plan to demolish it and replace it with a cluster of commercial towers. The response by Zhuang Shunfu, on behalf of Huanggang Village, defended the new development plans. He insisted that the old ancestral hall no longer had any value since the new ancestral hall had replaced it in both function and importance. He argued that those who called for preservation of the old hall were using this as an excuse, and really just did not want to see the continued urban integration and economic development of Huanggang Village.[78] In light of Shenzhen's decade-long, city-wide campaign of urban village demolition and redevelopment, Huanggang Village was hailed as a shining example by local government officials, who wished that all urban villages were as progressive.

The urban village featured in the next chapter, Nanshan District's Baishizhou Village, has a very different history and reputation from Huanggang Village. Among all urban villages located in the central districts of Luohu, Futian, and Nanshan, the Administrative Urban Village of Baishizhou Village is the largest in terms of resident population, the densest in terms of building density, and yet the poorest in terms of the village corporation company's economic capacity. An administrative village could hold one or more "natural villages," normally referring to the smaller units of each historically clan-based village. In Shenzhen, there are around three hundred administrative urban village, but these could be further demarcated into nearly two thousand natural villages. Baishizhou usually refers to the administrative village that is composed of five "natural" villages, altogether holding a population of over 150,000 people. Baishizhou is the name of the village organization, which, unlike its counterpart in Huanggang, was not able to offer indigenous villagers the benefits of land rentals to industries during the first phase of Shenzhen's industrialization. Restricted by complications over its urban / rural designations, Baishizhou Village also could not participate in the later phase of real estate development. The stark contrast between Huanggang and Baishizhou demonstrates the nuance and complexity with which the Shenzhen SEZ policies unfolded at the local level. Each urban village in Shenzhen has a unique story to tell. Baishizhou's saga is perhaps the most complex and layered of them all.

8.

"SLUM" IN THE HIGH-TECH GARDEN CITY

Shenzhen's urban villages hold economic power and political status unparalleled elsewhere in China; however, there are vast differences among the 318 urban villages that remain in Shenzhen.[1] While Huanggang is on one end of the spectrum of wealth, on the other end is an urban village cluster known as Baishizhou, or Village of the White Rock Isle.

Baishizhou is commonly known in Shenzhen as the city's poorest, dirtiest, and biggest urban village. It also has the most inhabitants, as well as the highest building and population density, of any urban village in Shenzhen. Roughly two hundred thousand people are crammed into a neighborhood of 2,477 walk-up peasant houses, lined mostly with dark, damp, and refuse-scattered alleyways. Owing to land ownership contestations, the villagers of Baishizhou have not been able to profit from selling property to developers in the way that members of other villages have done. For seventy-two-year-old Chi, as for many Baishizhou villagers, collecting rent from his building has been his only source of income to both raise a family and save for old age.[2] The village company has not been able to generate any collective income for the villagers or the maintenance of public spaces, infrastructure, and general law and order in Baishizhou. Unlike Huanggang, which receives far more positive press coverage than negative, Baishizhou is the subject of frequent local news reports featuring robberies, gangs, assaults, and sensational stories—such as a story about Hong Kong mob bosses hiding out in the village's maze-like shadowy structures. As a result, Baishizhou has the lowest rent of all seventy-two urban villages in the central districts within the original boundaries of the SEZ.[3] Yet, astonishingly, Baishizhou is located in the heart of Nanshan District, an area known for education and technology.

Shenzhen's ambitious public- and private-sector investment in new technology has impressed global observers in recent years. *Bloomberg* reported that in 2015, three billion USD were invested in the city's R&D from state and private capital, almost 6 percent of the city's GDP.[4] *The Guardian* estimated that Shenzhen productions took up 25 percent of the global mobile phone shipment market, and called Shenzhen a "technological nirvana" for hackers and entrepreneurs.[5] A 2017 *New York Times* article on China's growth in technology highlighted two globally competitive companies:

> The technology world's $400 billion-and-up club—long a group of exclusively American names like Apple, Google, Facebook, Microsoft, and Amazon—needs to make room for two Chinese members. The Alibaba Group and Tencent Holdings, Chinese companies that dominate their home market, have rocketed this year to become global investor darlings. They are now among the world's most highly valued public companies, each of them twice as valuable as tech stalwarts such as Intel, Cisco and IBM.[6]

The article did not mention that both Alibaba's International Operation Headquarters and Tencent's home base are located in Shenzhen, and specifically in the Nanshan District. Tencent Holdings Ltd, "the only company other than Facebook to have a social network with more than one billion users," had its humble beginnings not far from Baishizhou in the Shenzhen Science and Industry Park. First established in 1985 by the fledging SEZ government under Mayor Liang Xiang, the industrial zone was renamed the Shenzhen Science and Technology Industrial Park in 1996 and expanded to its current size of 11.5 square kilometers. By 1999, the industries inside the Shenzhen Science and Technology Industrial Park were producing products with a value of 25 billion yuan, 85 percent of Shenzhen's total digital and electronic industries. In addition to local companies, the park also attracted national enterprises such as Huawei, ZTE, and Lenovo, as well as international companies including IBM, Philips, and Compaq.[7] By 2015, the Technology Park hosted 7,675 registered industrial and commercial enterprises and achieved a gross industrial output value of 515.3 billion yuan, 9.6 percent of the city's total GDP. Numerous new hardware technology enterprises from this area also went global, such as the Royole Corporation, which produced ultra-thin full-color flexible displays of 0.01mm and was named the best exhibitor by Reuters in the 2016 Consumer Electronics Show. In the same year, *San Francisco Business Times* named Royole the winner of its Tech and Innovation competition, the only entry from the global hardware industry.[8] The technology enterprise DJI, which invented the Phantom Series consumer drones, was also a global success. DJI's annual revenue reached six billion yuan within ten years and took up 70 percent of the global market.[9]

The Technology Park is located adjacent to Shenzhen University, the oldest and largest university in the city, first established in 1983 by Mayor Liang Xiang, with half of the SEZ's governmental budget.[10] The university became well known for its computer sciences programs, with the most famous alumnus to date being Ma Huateng. After graduating in 1993, Ma founded Tencent in 1998 with four others, three of whom were his classmates from the university. The Technology Park just south of the university was a natural choice for these young scientists and entrepreneurs.

Shenzhen University and the Technology Park are located just to the west of Baishizhou Village, connected by Shennan Boulevard and separated by Shahe, or Sandy River, which runs into Shenzhen Bay. To the east of Baishizhou is the lushly landscaped Overseas Chinese Town (OCT). Filled with theme parks and luxury residential developments, OCT is another source of pride for Shenzhen.

Theme parks in the OCT—with such names as "Splendid China," "Window of the World," and "Chinese Folk Culture Village"—have been Shenzhen's largest tourist attractions. Visitors from across the country come to see the miniature versions of the Potala Palace and Eiffel Tower, hear Yunnan folk songs and drums, and stay at OCT luxury hotels, all linked by a raised rail system, the first of its kind in China. The well-planned tourist path ensures efficient transportation and carefully avoids Baishizhou, which is in most places separated from the OCT's gated compounds by a tall, well-guarded wall and blocked from view with landscaping. One portion of the separation wall that lines the Window of the World theme park is disguised by a landscaped hillside, on top of which stands a five-meter-tall statue of Christ the Redeemer with open arms, in imitation of the iconic thirty-meter-tall Christ the Redeemer atop the Corcovado Mountain in Brazil's Rio de Janeiro. The Shenzhen statue's arms open toward the theme park, while his back is turned to the masses of Baishizhou. The OCT's northern section also features a luxury gated community, Portofino, modeled after the idyllic seaside township on the Italian Riviera. The pastel-colored villas, high-end restaurants and bars, cobbled piazza, and medieval bell tower are all scattered around a natural spring-fed lagoon named Swan Lake. It is perhaps not surprising that the villas in Portofino are the most expensive residential property in Shenzhen. Portofino is separated from Baishizhou by a tall concrete wall topped with barbed wire, but even this physical division is not as sharp as the economic divide between the two communities.

The economic polarization of Nanshan District, and of Shenzhen, is vividly reflected in the density differentiation at this location. In the well-landscaped 4.8 square kilometers of the OCT resides a population of thirty-five thousand, with a total building floor space of approximately two million square meters. The 7.4 square kilometers of Baishizhou feature 2,477 individual "peasant houses," mostly self-built, totaling close to 2.1 million square meters.[11] Yet the staggering number of renters—over 150,000 individuals—renders Baishizhou's population density more than forty times that of the OCT, and fifty-six times the average population density in Shenzhen overall.[12] These are relatively conservative estimates; some estimates of Baishizhou's rental population are well above two hundred thousand, accounting for many unregistered and undocumented residents. This would make Baishizhou more populous than the largest favela in Brazil, Rio de Janeiro's Rocinha, where the estimated population is 180,000, more than double that of the governmental census.[13]

Owing to cheap rent and large supply, rooms in Baishizhou peasant houses are often a starting point for new migrants to Shenzhen. There is even a well-cited localism asserting that every individual who lives in Shenzhen has at one time or another lived in Baishizhou.[14] Certainly it is one of the most often-discussed urban villages in blogs and online comments. One comment posted by "Hu Ping" summarized the social and psychological separation between Baishizhou and the rest of the city:

"When I first arrived in Shenzhen, I lived in Baishizhou for three months. It stirs my memory, every time I go past the village, of those days that I was fresh to the city and struggled without thinking too much. For those who live outside Baishizhou, looking at the village is a kind of satisfaction, but for those who live inside Baishizhou, looking out is a goal."[15]

VOLUNTARY EXODUS TO THE SHAHE FARM

Before the post-1979 mass migration to the Shenzhen SEZ, Baishizhou had been a destination of immigrants and refugees for centuries. Baishizhou Village was originally right on the coast, although shorelines have been pushed farther south because of several rounds of land reclamation into Shenzhen Bay since 1979. Modern narratives of the village's origins often date the earliest settlement at Baishizhou to a Qing Dynasty habitat named Village of the Ten Thousand Families.[16] Historical records and maps on the ancient salt production of Xin'an County reference a settlement camp at the White Rock Port in the Ming Dynasty. Named after a large white rock on the hillside facing the sea, the White Rock Port was one of the few sites set up in Xin'an County for the imperial salt trade, and the one nearest to the regional capital of Nantou Fort.[17]

The village settlement's unusual name, "Ten Thousand Families," indicates that, unlike traditional agrarian villages, it was not occupied by a single-family clan. This name, and the presence of many different family groups, might be explained by the village's military and commercial origins. Records show that during the Qing Dynasty, this village protested the imperial court's policies and was wiped out by the military. The site was later resettled by a migrant Wu family, who named it Baishi Village and allowed other migrant families of both Canton and Hakka origins to set up village settlements nearby. The Canton clan of Zheng set up Huatang Village (later named Xintang); the Hakka clans of Chen, Zhong, and Zheng started the Shangbaishi Village; and additional Hakka clans of Chen, Zheng, and Zhang set up the Xiabaishi Village. Since the Qing Dynasty, these migrant settlers have farmed, fished, and cultivated oysters together in this coastal region.

In 1957, the Guangdong provincial government received an order from the State Council to develop non-staple food crop production in the region.[18] In 1959, Guangdong established the Shahe Farm, to be managed by the Foshan Bureau of Agriculture and Reclamation, on a rural area

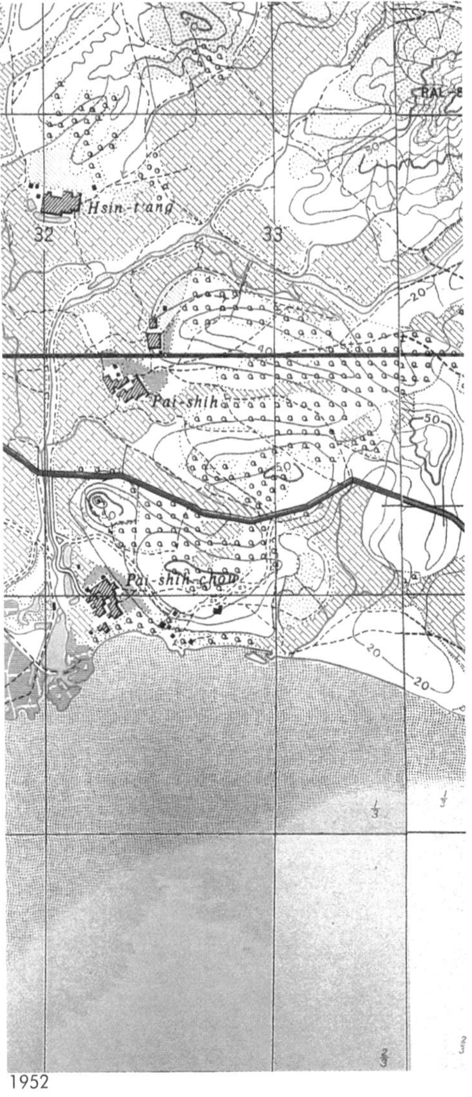

1952

Boundaries		Scrubs	
Railways	(Embankment) (Cutting)	Orchards	
Roads		Marsh or Swamp	
1st Class			
2nd Class		Mangrove	
Cart Track		Irrigated Land	
Footpath			
Villages		Sand	
Isolated Houses		Ditches or Trenches	
Woods		Salt pans	

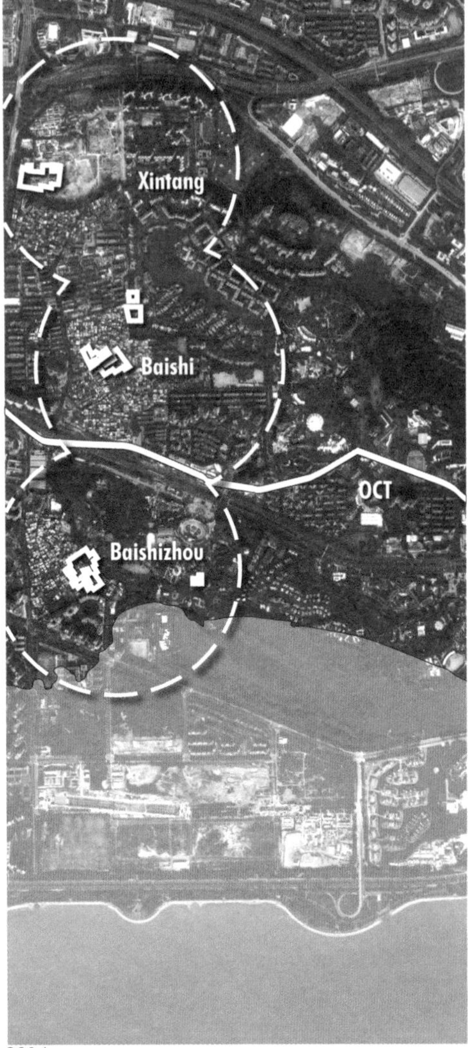

2014

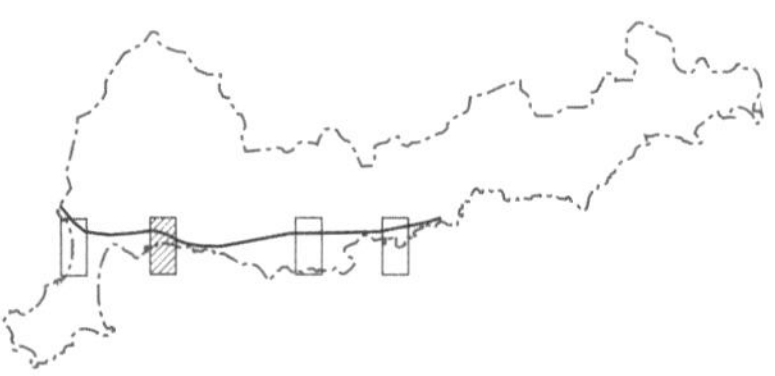

Survey map (1952) compared with satellite image (2014) in Nanshan District. In addition to the three historic villages indicated on the 1950s map, two more villages were relocated here in the 1950s; the five villages are collectively referred to as Baishizhou. The dense urban village fabric contrasts with the adjacent Overseas Chinese Town developments of luxury villages and theme parks.

spanning twelve square kilometers in Bao'an County, including all of the Baishizhou villages. As the villages became a state-owned farm, the villagers were converted from rural peasant status to workers in a state-owned enterprise in 1960. Over that year, the villagers of Tangtou Village migrated to this area from northern Bao'an County, thus becoming the last migrant village to join Baishizhou. From this time forward, Baishizhou came to refer to all five villages in this location: the original Baishizhou, and the later Shangbaishi, Xiabaishi, Xintang, and Tangtou.

That year, fifteen-year-old Chi moved to Baishizhou along with nearly five hundred Tangtou villagers, all extended family members of the Chi Clan.[19] A year later in 1959, two government workers started to frequently visit the original Tangtou Village, a centuries-old Hakka village at the foothills of Yangtai Mountain, the tallest peak in northern Bao'an County. Chi came from a modest village home, and school was a luxury his family could not afford. However, he was unhappy working as a shepherd herding the village's livestock and receiving reprimands from his work team leader. He often argued with his stepfather about his desire to attend school. He wanted to attend the First Lower Level Secondary School of Bao'an County (today's Nantou Secondary School), in Nantou Fort, the county seat of Bao'an at the time. His family finally relented when Chi promised that he would pay the school fees by lumbering firewood in the hills surrounding the village. Chi went into the hills to gather firewood each weekend, cutting and carrying as much as he could on his back. On Mondays, he walked the twenty kilometers of mountainous roads to Nantou Fort to sell the wood in the market; he used the money to pay for one week's school and boarding fees.

During a visit home from school, Chi glimpsed the two government workers in the village. He was surprised to see strangers there on a weekend. But he was even more astonished when the government workers came to his home to tell his parents that his family would have to move. The five-hundred-year-old Tangtou Village would soon be flooded and submerged under the newly planned Tiegang Water Reservoir. This construction occurred during the height of the national Learning from Dazhai movement, which encouraged large infrastructure projects throughout the country with the goal of dramatically increasing agricultural production. In Bao'an, the government decided that the Tiegang Water Reservoir would be a good demonstration project, as its construction would ensure irrigation supply for the important farming areas of Xixiang and Shajing.

Some farmlands and villages, including Tangtou, would have to be sacrificed for the greater good and submerged within the dammed area. The Tangtou villagers were devastated, for they had lived in the Shiyan area of Bao'an for generations. They were proud of their village, their farmland, the beautiful mountains, and the celebrated hot springs hidden in the mountain lakes, which constituted one of the original "Eight Scenes of Xin'an," famous since the Qing Dynasty.[20] Being Hakka families, they also had deep cultural and psychological connections to the mountains. But to stay was not an option. The villagers were given a choice, however, of where to build their next homeland: Caiwuwei Village, where they would grow flowers and raise goldfish to sell across the adjacent border with Hong Kong; or the newly established state-owned Shahe Farm, where they could continue farming.

Chi, along with other village youths, wanted to go to Caiwuwei. It was not necessarily because they would rather farm goldfish than land; it was the prospect of Hong Kong itself. Located right next to the Luohu border crossing, Caiwuwei was thought to be the easiest place from which to smuggle goods and people across the border into Hong Kong. However, the village elders held the opposing view. If they went to Shahe Farm and labored in the rice fields, they would become state workers receiving monthly wages. This was an opportunity to escape the hardship of peasanthood, which their ancestors had endured for centuries. Rather than praying for a decent harvest to feed their families each season, they would receive fifteen RMB a month. While not exorbitant, the farm's wage was many times that of their Shiyan Commune. To confirm their thoughts, the village elders sent a few scouts to the Shahe Farm to investigate. Their report back was enthusiastic. The farm was vast, at nearly thirteen square kilometers. Even though there were already four other villages, each Tangtou family was promised plenty of land to farm.

With their collective decision made, the Tangtou villagers learned that not everyone could go to Shahe Farm. Those interested had to apply and be approved after a rigorous background check. Former landowners, "rich peasants," counter-revolutionaries, "bad elements," and "Rightists," commonly known as the "black five categories," could not go.[21] In addition, as Shahe Farm is located just across Shenzhen Bay from Hong Kong, those who had attempted to smuggle across the border were also blacklisted from relocating to the farm. By 1960, 486 men, women, and children of sixty-eight families were approved for relocation to Shahe Farm. Nearly half of the village had to stay behind and be settled in another location in the Yangtai Mountains. Chi's mother and stepfather were cleared to go. However, the fourteen-year-old Chi was asked whether he would go or stay behind with the family of his biological father, who had passed away when Chi was a toddler. Chi's mother remarried when he was still very young, so he had always lived with his mother and stepfather. But both families lived in the same village, and he saw his biological grandparents and family members every day. Moving from the ancestral land of Tangtou to the new land of Shahe Farm marked a formal and final rupture with the past. Chi decided to leave Tangtou.

In 1960, Chi and his family arrived at Shahe Farm, where they encountered a newly leveled muddy field that was to become the new Tangtou Village. Owing to the extreme shortage of building materials during the Great Leap Forward, the promised new housing on the ten thousand square meters of land designated for the resettlement was not yet built. The villagers were dispersed among the other four villages of Baishizhou, to be hosted by various homes or to settle in any available vacant building. Chi's family moved into an empty field house next to a piece of farmland. Disappointed but not able to return home because of the imminent flooding of the old Tangtou, the villagers took matters into their own hands. They dismantled their old village homes, transported the salvaged building material to Shahe Farm, and built their village housing in a manner and layout similar to that of their old village. The new village complex was constructed with thick rammed earth walls and layered tile roofs, and consisted of ten rows of single-story buildings divided by a central pathway.

Facing national instability from the Great Famine (1959–1961) and tensions with neighboring countries, China took measures to strengthen border regions, including increased naval defense. In 1962, the Guangzhou Military Area Command took over the management of coastal Bao'an County, including Shahe Farm.[22] That same year, Chi and his family moved into one of the ninety-two units of the row-house complex. After all the families were settled, the extra units were devoted to collective use, including storage. The hastily built sewage pits and drains located in the communal open areas would occasionally clog with heavy rain, so collective repair efforts were frequently needed. However, just as in their old village compound, the open spaces in between the rows became shared spaces for vegetable drying, potted plants, children's play, and adults' relaxation after meals. There was a large open space reserved in front of all the row houses. This space was used to dry seasonal harvests and hold village gatherings. Wells were dug and each shared with two to three neighboring households, while a larger circular well adjacent to the open space provided the community with a public water supply. Over time, the Tangtou villagers became accustomed to the row houses and their new village. For occasional ancestral worshipping they might still visit what was left of their old village, but for the most part, this was now their home. The Tangtou Village complex is an exceptional sight in this southern coastal region of the SEZ. While sometimes mistakenly generalized years later as "socialist housing blocks," the spatial layout and architectural structures of Tangtou Village's row houses resemble the traditional village plan found commonly in the northern mountainous areas of Shenzhen.

Being one of the few Tangtou villagers with some secondary education, Chi was given work as the village bookkeeper. Of course, he still had to do farm work in the field alongside others from the various villages of Baishizhou. That is where Chi met a girl from another Hakka clan of the adjacent Xiabaishi Village. They were soon married and lived together with Chi's family at the Tangtou Village compound. Life was difficult, but like other villagers, Chi's family raised some pigs to supplement their food supply and meager income. This was allowed under the national policies of Three Self's and One Contract (1960–1963), namely self-retained land, self-run markets, self-responsibility for profits and losses, and contract farming practices that fixed output quotas on a household basis. These measures were prohibited during the initial establishment of the People's Communes, but Liu Shaoqi and his lieutenant at the time—Deng Xiaoping—championed them in response to the widespread famine in China's rural areas. However, by 1963, Mao Zedong had denounced these policies on the grounds that they promoted capitalism and threatened the socialist rural collective economy. The socialist Four Cleanups Movement was launched to educate the rural masses of China's countryside to "cleanse" political, economic, organizational, and ideological corruption. Rural villages, factories, mines, and other enterprises were ordered to investigate and punish anti-socialist corruptors. The movement led to widespread mob violence in China's rural areas, including thousands of executions and suicides of those accused.[23] By 1964, the movement had reached Bao'an County's Shahe Farm. The Tangtou Village bookkeeper Chi was singled out for embezzlement and charged with giving the farm's corn feed to his own "self-retained livestock," the family pigs. With his charac-

Standing on the roof terrace of his own building, a Baishizhou villager looks out at the older tiled village row houses and high-rises of the OCT in the distance.

teristic stubbornness, Chi adamantly refused to admit to the charges even after being locked away in the county jail. Fortunately for him, he was released just after one month, along with others who were also arrested in the same movement. Chi was determined to avoid future financial or political complications. He refused to go back to his job as bookkeeper, insisting that it was not worth the trouble of being accused of embezzlement. The village leaders caved in and offered him a job teaching at the local Shahe Elementary School. Around this time, Mao announced that the Four Cleanups Movement, under the direct leadership of Liu Shaoqi, was ineffective, as it relied on a task force rather than on the masses of the people. In a January 1965 talk on the Four Cleanups Movement, Mao criticized Liu Shaoqi without naming him:

> I think if we make revolution this way, the revolution will take a hundred years. Some professors were in the task force, and they weren't as good as their assistants, while some of the assistants weren't as good as the students. The more books one reads, the more stupid one becomes, knowing almost nothing. That is all. You won't annihilate the enemy if you fight the battle of annihilation this way. It behooves you to rely on the masses and to mobilize them.[24]

In 1966, the Great Proletariat Cultural Revolution was launched. It would cripple the country for ten years, during which time Liu Shaoqi and Deng Xiaoping were persecuted. They were accused of being "capitalist-roaders," given their support for the "Three Self's and One Contract" policies and their disagreement with Mao's thoughts on the Four Cleanups Movement. The Guangzhou Military Area Command also demilitarized the Shahe Farm in 1966. However, it did not return ownership and governance to the local commune or the villages. The land was given to the Guangdong Overseas Chinese Administration Bureau. As a result, Shahe Farm—which had formerly been owned collectively by the villages—became state-owned. The transfer of land entitlement was further complicated after Shahe Farm became incorporated as the Shahe Branch of the Guangming Overseas Chinese Livestock Farm. These convoluted land transfers later proved to be the beginning of a series of decades-long complications, known as Baishizhou's "historically leftover" problems, a term often used in China for complicated issues that are related to past sensitive political events.

The Shahe Farm jurisdiction changes were also reflected in the governance changes of the Shahe Elementary School, which had been established by the Guangzhou Military Area Command in 1959 for the children of military personnel in the area. When Chi started teaching there in 1965, the school was given to the Baishizhou villages on Shahe Farm. Soon after in 1967, the Guangming Overseas Chinese Livestock Farm took over management of the school; it was returned to Shahe Farm in 1978, just prior to the establishment of the SEZ.[25] Chi continued to teach there through the early years of the Shenzhen special economic zone. Having taught at the school for nearly twenty years, he was referred to by all the young villagers of Baishizhou as "Mister Teacher." Throughout this time, Chi lived with his family in the Tangtou row-house complex. The home witnessed the birth of his brother and sister, his marriage, the passing away of his mother and father, and the arrival of his own children.

INDUSTRIALIZATION OF THE STATE FARM

The year 1978 brought major changes to the Baishizhou villages, now formally administered by the Guangming Overseas Chinese Livestock Farm. The farm introduced modern equipment and procedures to their livestock and dairy farming, in order to meet Hong Kong and British standards. Chenguang Dairy Co. Ltd. was launched to export fresh cow's milk and other dairy products to Hong Kong. Guangming Overseas Chinese Livestock Farm would become China's largest dairy product exporter. Success of the project prompted the later adoption of its dairy production procedure as the Chinese national standard.[26] The farm also benefited from the construction of China's first mechanized pork and poultry production facilities, along with other forms of modernization and industrialization.[27] Increased production and rigorous standards allowed the dairy and meat products from Guangming Farm to become nationally recognizable brands valued for decades in China and neighboring Asian countries. By 2005, fresh milk produced from Chengguang Dairy Co. Ltd. took up 90 percent of the market share in Shenzhen and 70 percent in Hong Kong.[28] These recognitions built upon, and added to, Bao'an County's historic reputation for prized aquaculture and agricultural yields such as oysters and lychees.

In addition to industrializing livestock production, Guangming Farm also experimented with other industries such as electronics. In 1978, the administrative office of the farm initiated an experimental collaboration with a Hong Kong electronics company. The products were successfully retailed through the international distribution network of the Hong Kong partner, with the first year's revenue reaching 830,000 yuan.[29] The success of the experiment attracted other investors.

In 1978, China was also approaching the breaking point in its political relationship with the Soviet Union and Vietnam. By the time that the Sino-Vietnamese War broke out in 1979, China had resettled 224,000 Chinese-Vietnamese refugees in forty-three state-operated industries around the country.[30] Guangming Farm started to receive refugees from Vietnam in 1978, and would eventually accept 4,300 refugees by 1979. The large-scale operation was facilitated by the United Nations Refugee Agency (UNRA) with a subsidy of eight hundred thousand USD.[31] Some of the refugees with factory experience were placed in newly established factories in Shahe. Fifty refugees with experience at Saigon's electronics factories were among the first assembly line workers at Guangming's newly established cassette-recorder factory.[32]

In the spring of 1979, the Beijing-based State Council Overseas Chinese Affairs Office formally gave permission to the Guangming Overseas Chinese Livestock Farm to set up Sino-foreign joint venture enterprises, although, at that time, only with overseas Chinese investors. In April 1979, the State Council Overseas Chinese Affairs Office formally announced the establishment of the Shahe Overseas Chinese Industrial Zone, to be located on the twelve-square-kilometer Shahe Farm. The land of the Baishizhou villages became an industrial zone even before the establishment of the Shenzhen SEZ.[33]

By December 1979, Guangming Overseas Chinese Electronics Factory was established as China's first Sino-foreign joint venture enterprise.[34] The factory would later become Konka Group Co. Ltd, one of the leading consumer electronics enterprises in China. Guangming Overseas Chinese Livestock Farm utilized the unique permission from the State Council to quickly establish other joint ventures such as the Shenzhen Overseas Chinese Furniture Factory, a joint venture between Taiwan and China, as well as the Guangming Automobile Repair and Assembly Plant through the transnational network of the China diaspora.[35] Chi's younger sister would become a worker in one of the electronics factories.

More than a year after the establishment of Shahe Overseas Chinese Industrial Zone, on August 26, 1980, the State Council passed the Guangdong Province Special Economic Zone Regulations. In 1981, the Guangming Overseas Chinese Livestock Farm was formally released by the Guangdong Overseas Chinese Administration Bureau and became a state-owned enterprise, renamed the Guangdong Province Shahe Overseas Chinese Enterprise Company. Owing to this latest administrative change, the Overseas Chinese Enterprise Company assumed management of the Shahe Elementary School in 1981. The company set out to modernize the curriculum and teaching staff. No longer within the social networks of Shahe's Baishizhou villages, thirty-eight-year-old Chi was let go by the school in the following year. This marked the beginning of the split between the Shahe Farm administrative team, mostly composed of Baishizhou villagers, who would continue the agricultural livelihood of the original villagers, and the Overseas Chinese Enterprise Company, which would take over all managing responsibilities for industrial developments.

By 1983, the Shahe Overseas Chinese Industrial Zone had developed 110 subsidiary enterprises in thirty different trades and industries. The Sino-overseas Chinese partnership of Shahe was deemed a success and used as a model elsewhere in China. More than ten overseas Chinese corporations were set up in the cities of Shanghai and Guangzhou, as well as in the provinces including Fujian, Guangxi, Yunnan, Sichuan, and Shandong. While the village-operated, transnational Sanlaiyibu industries were the precursor to the massive development of the Township and Village Enterprises, the Shahe Industrial Zone was one of the first precedents for Chinese state-owned industries to import capital, technology, equipment, and management skills through the transnational networks of the Chinese diaspora, a vital aspect of nationwide reform-era industrialization.

ZONE WITHIN THE ZONE: OVERSEAS CHINESE TOWN (1983–1997)

In September 1983, with Shahe Industrial Zone as a successful model for nationwide practice, the Overseas Chinese Affairs Office submitted to the State Council a "Proposal to Revert the Shenzhen Shahe Overseas Chinese Industrial Zone and to Place It under the Direct Leadership and Management of the Overseas Chinese Affairs Office of the State Council." Consequently, Shahe Industrial Zone would be under the direct administration of Beijing's State Council—and thus outside the jurisdiction of the Guangdong provincial government and the new Shenzhen municipality. In its "Report on the Discussion of Shenzhen Shahe's Organizational Structure," submitted to the State Council on December 31, 1984, the office proposed that a land parcel of 4.8 square kilometers be carved out of the Shahe Industrial Zone and developed into an independent Overseas Chinese Town Economic Development District. The district was later renamed simply Overseas Chinese Town (OCT). In August 1985, the State Council formally approved the establishment of Shenzhen Special Zone OCT, with Shekou Industrial Zone as a model, to be administered by the Hong Kong–based China Travel Service (CTS).

In November 1985, the State Council appointed Ma Zhimin, vice general manager of the Hong Kong–based CTS, to lead the construction of Overseas Chinese Town. Like Yuan Geng of the Shekou Industrial Zone, the other site in Shenzhen with similar jurisdiction, Ma was a seasoned Communist leader with Chinese PLA military experience. Born in Guangdong, Ma arrived in Bao'an in 1949. A liaison for the Chinese People's Liberation Army, Ma took over the management of Kowloon Customs, which later became Shenzhen Customs. He was sent to Hong Kong to assist the management of CTS in 1979, after serving as army commander of Bao'an County and the Shenzhen Old Town Communist Party secretary, among other leadership roles. From 1959 to 1961, he led the construction of the Shenzhen Water Reservoir, a state-funded project specifically designed to solve the dire water shortage in Hong Kong. Directing OCT from 1985 to 1995, Ma was first ridiculed and later celebrated for his two guiding principles: the first was to establish tourism as a main industry of OCT, and the second was to insist on development led by comprehensive spatial planning.[36]

Building on his five years of work at the China Travel Services, Ma Zhimin wanted to make OCT a premier destination for domestic and international tourists by creating a scenic landscaped garden district. Given the large-scale infrastructure and industrial developments of the SEZ's first five years, Ma's vision seemed counterintuitive to many. The first OCT enterprise he established after taking charge in 1985 was not a factory, but a landscape and gardening company. In the same year, Ma hired Meng Daqiang, an "overseas Chinese" architect and planner who worked for the Singaporean government. More commonly known in China as a Singaporean, Meng was born in Beijing and educated at Taiwan's Cheng Kung University. He later attended Germany's Technische Universität Darmstadt in the 1950s. His graduation coincided with Europe's post-WWII reconstructions, and Meng gained extensive experience in city planning and construction, especially in the Netherlands. Meng brought to OCT his international experience and an ecological sensitivity that was further sharpened in Singapore, where natural resources were a precious commodity, given the island's political and cultural isolation within a predominantly Muslim region. On an initial site visit to OCT, Meng saw builders engaged in the standard site preparation process of leveling a hilled slope and removing the trees. He requested that Ma Zhimin stop all such work in OCT as a condition of his taking the job. According to Meng's later recollection, Ma Zhimin immediately agreed, and "the morning of the following day, all bulldozers left."[37]

In sharp contrast to surrounding constructions at "Shenzhen Speed," the first physical construction in OCT under the new plan was the replanting of trees in areas that had been deforested. Some mocked the sluggish speed of construction, noting that "after six months of construction in the OCT, just some grass was planted."[38] Ma defended Meng's work and the annual salary of 110,000 USD that OCT offered to pay him for two days in Shenzhen each month.[39] This was a stunning salary for the Chinese market in 1985.

Ma Zhimin's support allowed Meng to develop with confidence the 1985 OCT Comprehensive Planning, a series of spatial planning and design guidelines anchored by three principles.[40] The first principle was *mobility*. OCT was to be a walkable neighborhood, featuring a system of meandering tree-lined pedestrian pathways; the vehicular roadways would be a secondary network, supported by railways, trams, and underground transport. This was twenty years ahead of the actual city-wide planning and construction of the Shenzhen metro system. The second principle was *scale*. The plan favored low- and mid-rise building complexes, with industrial factories and commercial activities in the northern region away from the main transportation arteries surrounding the residential and leisure sites. Tall buildings were discouraged near major pathways and important public spaces, with a specific prohibition of tall buildings along Shennan Boulevard. The third principle was *evolution*. All spatial planning was based on the site's topography and geography, so that the buildings and infrastructure could grow along with the natural environment. Of all urban districts within the original Shenzhen SEZ areas, OCT is most strikingly similar to the landscapes in maps of pre-1979 agricultural and environmental features. Meng's three principles run counter to the mentalities and tendencies that characterized city planning in the early years of the SEZs, which defined a modern city as car-oriented, with tall buildings and grand open spaces. Luxuriously green and picturesque, OCT under Meng's planning principles developed striking physical distinctions from the rest of the city.

Meng Daqiang's planning worked well with Ma Zhimin's vision to develop OCT into an attractive tourist site with natural beauty. In 1985, Ma Zhimin visited the Netherlands' Madurodam, a theme park of miniature Dutch landmarks, and was inspired to build a similar theme park in China with miniatures of all the country's well-known sights. He initially thought that this theme park would be a good way for foreigners to understand China's cities and culture, while also providing domestic visitors and local OCT residents with a place to unwind in bustling Shenzhen. Construction of Shenzhen Splendid China began in May 1987, and the park opened in November 1989. Although such a large-scale entertainment facility was unusual for China in the 1980s, three million tourists visited during the first year. The number of visitors was so unexpected that the first Splendid China television advertisement was to plead for Shenzhen residents to stay at home because of traffic congestion.[41] Investments in the theme park's construction were recovered within nine months of its opening. Encouraged by the success, Ma Zhimin exported Splendid China to Orlando, Florida. Surrounded by Disney World, Epcot Center, Sea World, and Universal Studios, Florida Splendid China opened in the hot summer of 1993, fulfilling Ma's vision of introducing the wonders of China to the world through miniaturized models of the Great Wall, Forbidden City, and Chinese heritage landscapes such as Three Gorges Dam, Mount Taishan, and Guilin Stone Forest. While Ma was denounced by the Communist Party in the mid-1980s for bringing capitalistic consumption to China, the Splendid China in Florida was criticized in the United States for importing communist propaganda.

Meanwhile, OCT continued constructing theme parks that only increased in popularity—the China Folk Culture Village in 1991, Window of the World in 1994, and Happy Valley in 1998. In 1999, OCT invested ninety million yuan to build the first monorail in China to link an all-encompassing entertainment district with the four sprawling theme parks, three luxury hotels, and an "eco-tourism" site at the coastal mangrove areas on the banks of Shenzhen Bay.[42] While most of the parks and associated shopping malls are obscured by carefully designed landscapes, Window of the World—the most popular and flamboyant of the four theme parks—stands out clearly. Within the 4.8-square-kilometer OCT, the 108-meter-tall Eiffel Tower and the nearby grand Saint Peter's Piazza at Window of the World are the only monuments clearly visible from the main Shennan Boulevard. Window of the World gathered famous pieces of architecture and landscape from prehistoric to contemporary times, and featured everything from ancient Egyptian pyramids to Manhattan skyscrapers. Millions of visitors each year walked through the eight sections of the park: the World Square, Asia, Oceania, Europe, Africa, America, the Sculpture Park, and the International Street. While the cultural sites were decontextualized, formalized, appropriated, and packaged to create spectacles, the theme park offered a "Window of the World" that was then still forbidden for most Chinese.

But for the first two decades of the SEZ, the theme parks of Ma Zhimin gave Shenzhen a cultural identity of leisure, commerce, consumption, and global fantasy. The success of OCT's theme parks inspired thousands of theme park constructions all over China, and Ma Zhimin came to be affectionately known as the "Father of Chinese Theme Parks." For outside observers, Shenzhen's theme parks were also a window into China's reforms. American urban historian Thomas J. Campanella wrote the following about Splendid China in 1995:

> Like Shenzhen itself, Splendid China is expressive of the renewed spirit of optimism and outlook (as well as a new emphasis on materialism and consumption) that become a leitmotif of post-Mao China. Shenzhen is the maiden city of China's Opening Up to the world, and Splendid China is its cultural ambassador. The park is not a glance through a rosy lens but, rather, an act of outreach and annexation; not shelter against change, but one of its agents, a device adopted for distributing a revamped cultural identity to the four corners of the globe.[43]

While the theme parks leveraged tourism into an economically strong industry, OCT also kept up with industrial production and developed a real estate industry. In keeping with Meng's planning principles, OCT developed low-density residential projects including the 1987 Oriental Garden, the 1988 East and West Clusters, and the 1989 Fanghua Court. These represented Ma and Meng's idealized neighborhood clusters, hidden with carefully manicured nature. However, with Hong Kong investors and buyers emerging as the largest market force in Shenzhen during the 1990s, OCT's new leadership set aside the height restrictions and developed a series of high-rise "Hong Kong–Style" apartment towers, including the 1990 Seaview Garden and the 1996 Jinxiu Garden. The commercial success of these developments inspired the creation of high-rise residential towers throughout Shenzhen. Soon OCT's identity and brand were threatened, and the company started to develop another approach to design that capitalized on the theme parks' fantasy-making power. In 2001, the company introduced the so-called tourism and real estate model, featuring high-end themed residential developments such as the medieval-Italy inspired "Portofino Riviera." The second phase of development for the Portofino properties began in 2002, and was centered around two natural lakes—the forty-thousand-square-meter Swan Lake and the seventy-thousand-square-meter Swallow Lake. The two lakes had a combined shoreline of four kilometers, and the project achieved an exceptionally low building and population density within an already highly urbanized district at the center of the SEZ. The rental rate for a bungalow on the Portofino Riviera was the highest among all real estate properties in Shenzhen.[44] To ensure a transformative experience and to protect the properties, a landscaped and well-guarded perimeter wall, two to three meters in height, was erected around Portofino.[45] On the western side of the wall was the *other* world—Tangtou Village of Baishizhou.

In 2002, the same year in which phase two of the OCT Portofino began, 569 Baishizhou villagers were dismissed from their jobs.[46] Employed by various subsidiary companies under the Shahe Industrial Group Ltd., they were given modest settlement fees and told that Shahe Group would no longer hire directly from the villages. This brought years of escalating confusion to a breaking point, and led to a series of protests, demonstrations, and, at times, violent confrontations. The source of the confusion and confrontation was the ambiguity of land rights for the originally collectively owned rural land of the Baishizhou villages, and later of the Shahe Farm. While Shahe Farm had experienced a convoluted series of ownership transfers and administration changes, its status seemed conclusively decided in July 1992. That year, Shenzhen's policy on urban villages had converted all land inside the SEZ to urban status—thus making it state-owned.[47] The first clause of the written policy, entitled "Temporary Provisions on the Urbanization of Rural Villages in the Shenzhen special economic zone," stated its purpose:

> Since the establishment of the Shenzhen special economic zone, for the agrarian villages inside the special zone, economic development, urbanizing constructions, and living conditions have undergone significant changes. In order to adapt to these changes and to further economic development, enhance living standards of the people, accelerate socialist modernization in the special zone, and achieve the strategic goal of building Shenzhen into an export-oriented, multifunctional international city, these provisions are stipulated.[48]

The second clause stated the scope of the policy, and specifically mentioned Shahe Farm: "Applicable rural villages and peasants under the provisions refer to the sixty-eight village committees in the special zone, the Shahe Overseas Chinese Farm, and all the farm-affiliated peasants, fishermen, and oyster breeders who hold permanent rural *hukou* and reside inside the special zone."[49] Subsuming sixty-eight administrative villages, 173 natural villages, and the five "special cases villages" of Shahe Farm, the policy would impact the lives of 46,000 villagers.[50] The centuries-old village organizations were formally dismantled, and the villagers legally became urbanites overnight. If there was ever a moment when the stroke of a policy "instantly" urbanized Shenzhen, it was in the summer of 1992.

For most villagers, such as Cai Zhuxiang and Zhang Lianhao of Caiwuwei Village, this conversion meant very little.[51] Leaders of village collectives, such as Zhuang Shunfu of Huanggang, were aware that their villages were losing ownership of lands that had belonged to their ancestors for centuries,[52] land that their future generations would no longer possess. The villages were allowed to maintain land use and management rights, and they were requested to set up shareholding companies. While land ownership no longer belonged to each village collective, the village corporation would still maintain control over the village-operated factories, hotels, and real estate developments. The government intended for the village corporation to maintain the economic operations of the new "Neighborhood Unit," and expected the new "Neighborhood Unit Office" to be staffed with government-appointed managers who would take over the administrative management of the village, just as in other urban districts of Chinese cities. However, the split between economic and political governance did not really happen as planned. For most villages, such as Huanggang, the village corporation led by the former village leaders remained the primary decision maker for all resolutions. In addition to collective interest, each villager was assured of his or her property right to the self-built "peasant house," even though the original homestead was then owned by the state.

The five Baishizhou villages were originally included in this 1992 policy, as they were located inside the SEZ. However, in August 1992, the Guangdong provincial government transferred the administrative power of Shahe Farm and the Shahe Overseas Chinese Enterprise Group to the Shenzhen municipal government. The overlapping of the two major operations—urbanization of rural *hukou* and the bureaucratic restructuring of administrative power from the provincial level to the city level—

together with the already complicated land occupation history, kept Baishizhou from establishing a collective shareholding company.

Unlike the original land expropriation process for villages during the first years of the SEZ, which allowed villages such as Caiwuwei and Huanggang to utilize the compensation to start up their village enterprises, this process did not provide Baishizhou villages with compensation for their land, as it was already within the state-owned Shahe Farm prior to the establishment of the SEZ. While other villagers received homesteads, designated plots of land on which to build their own family houses, the villagers of Baishizhou were never formally allocated such land. When migrant workers flocked to the factories in the Shahe Industrial Zone starting in the early 1980s, the villagers of Baishizhou emulated villagers elsewhere and started to construct similar two- to four-story buildings. As the land was not formally distributed in the form of homesteads, each of the five Baishizhou villages adopted a different process of casual allocations, usually involving individual negotiations with families and neighbors while the Shahe Farm leadership turned a blind eye. This resulted in an unusually high density of self-built "peasant houses." The size of individual plots was less uniform, there was at times hardly any space in between buildings, and some alleyways leading to the buildings were nearly unnavigable to outsiders.

The Shahe Elementary School promised to provide *Danwei,* or work unit, housing to the teaching staff, including Chi. A large plot of land next to the school was leveled, but no housing was realized for several years. By 1982, tired of waiting, Chi built a two-story house on this empty dirt lot and moved out of the collective Tangtou Village compound. When other villagers at Baishizhou started to demolish their two-story houses to build taller ones, he followed suit in 1988 and built an eight-story "house." However, like many villagers of Tangtou, he did not have the necessary funding to construct the "peasant house." So Chi, like many others, funded the construction of his own building by giving permission for a non-villager to build on the land next to his. This is how a migrant merchant from a rural village in Zhejiang Province came to be Chi's neighbor. While the land plot occupied by the "guest-villager" was certainly not Chi's to give away, neither was the land plot for his own building. Both buildings were eight stories tall, with three separate apartment units on each floor, built by a construction team of migrant workers from Sichuan Province. Chi was aware that the land technically belonged to the "country," the term commonly used in China to denote public or government ownership. However, the illegality of the matter was lost in the face of the growing necessity to provide for his own family. In addition, Chi's logic was that he was "originally a migrant into this land, so why not allow other migrants to build a home here as well?"[53]

Soon, the land next to the school was filled in by other similarly financed "peasant houses." Among them was one by Chi's brother, who had already established residency in Hong Kong since his illegal crossing over in 1979. Given the danger of arrest if he was found, Chi helped his brother to supervise the construction, collect the rent, and manage the tenants. This was common in Baishizhou, as most of Chi's generation had smuggled into Hong Kong prior to the establishment of the SEZ. The majority of the tenants living in Baishizhou's buildings, therefore, had never met their actual owners. Throughout the 1980s and into the 1990s, self-built "peasant houses" grew exponentially in number around the historical village settlements, thoroughfares, and factories. Land use, building rights, and ownership inside the Baishizhou villages came to be more complex and inscrutable than those of any other urban village in Shenzhen. This made the enforcement of the 1992 policy problematic for Baishizhou villagers. In addition, they did not have the mechanism or resources to form a collective shareholding company or receive compensation for relocation, as technically they were no longer villagers in a collectively owned village. Their land was already urban. Suddenly, it became apparent that according to Chinese land laws, the Baishizhou villagers were equivalent to rural migrants *squatting* on urban land.

In February 1993, the Shenzhen municipal government issued a document to "disband the organization of Shahe Overseas Chinese Farm and establish the Shenzhen Shahe Enterprise Co. Ltd." However, since the buildings' ownerships and land-use rights were so complex, the Shahe Group was reluctant to push the plan forward. Thus in 1994, this first attempt to establish a collective shareholding company failed.[54]

Members of the five Baishizhou villages of the Shahe Farm faced an uncertain future. Meanwhile, the number of self-built "peasant houses" rapidly continued to increase. They became taller and bigger, crowding the already narrow spaces between them. A policy-triggered rush to build more illegal constructions occurred in 1989, when Shenzhen released a decree to curb illegal construction on village land and halt the trend of raising the height of "peasant houses" on home-based land. In a race with the government, villagers living in two- or four-story "legal" buildings who had been saving up for further construction now rushed to borrow money from local or Hong Kong relatives to build more floors. Urban villages throughout the SEZ, especially those located in the more urbanized districts of Luohu and Futian, hastened to build larger and taller buildings before they were caught and stopped. Thus, the policy intended to absolve the urban villages while ending rampant building activities actually again triggered one of the biggest waves of illegal construction in Shenzhen in 1992. There were reports of most villages being lit up all through the night, as construction teams rushed to build as fast as possible.[55] The local government departments took notice and sent workers, in some cases the police, into the villages to stop construction, but these interventions were largely unsuccessful given the strong insistence of the villagers. Physical altercations were common, but a 1998 confrontation in Baishizhou led to tragic fatalities. During the forced demolition of an illegal building under construction, two Baishizhou villagers were wounded and a law enforcement worker was killed by gunfire.[56] As gun ownership was illegal and exceedingly rare in China, the incident further contributed to the sinister public image of Baishizhou.

THE LAST OF SHENZHEN'S RURAL VILLAGES (1999–2009)

The Shenzhen government issued two more decrees consecutively in 1999 and 2002, stipulating higher fines and more severe punishments for illegal building.[57] However, these decrees did little to curb the construction activities because the villagers were willing to risk fines in exchange for the lucrative rental income. Each time, the government directive triggered new waves of illegal construction farther out from the city center. The construction wave was most fierce during the 2000s in Nanshan District, and also in Longgang and Bao'an, two large and relatively underdeveloped districts to the north of the city center. While rental demands by tenants were considerably less in the suburban districts, the villagers there put up unwired empty structures just to stake a claim to the land. Between 1999 and 2011, an estimated one hundred thousand illegal self-built "peasant house" buildings were constructed in Shenzhen.[58]

In 2003, the Shenzhen government released "Instructions Regarding the Expedition of Urbanization Processes in the Two Districts of Bao'an and Longgang,"[59] which extended the 1992 rural to urban *hukou* conversion and village land urbanization to the entire city. By 2004, Shenzhen's remaining 218 villages and 270,000 rural *hukou* villagers were converted to urban status.[60] The stated purpose of this legislation was to promote more efficient comprehensive urban planning for future development, by fully integrating all land within Shenzhen's municipality. *People's Daily* triumphantly declared that "Shenzhen will become the first city in China with no villages and no peasants."[61] Hong Kong–based Chinese-language newspaper *Wenhui Po* soon followed with an article stating that "peasants in Shenzhen will become history—Shenzhen will be the first city in China without a single village by the end of the year."[62]

By 2004, all former rural villages had been officially designated urban neighborhoods, except for the five villages of Baishizhou. With the dismissal of all villages from Shahe subsidiaries, Chi was "retired" from his last employer—the Shahe Commerce Trading Company. The landless and now jobless Baishizhou villagers could no longer wait for the Nanshan District and Shenzhen municipal government to reach a solution. Leaders from the five villages started to self-organize to fight for their rights.

The 2003 "Instructions Regarding the Expedition of Urbanization Processes in the Two Districts of Bao'an and Longgang" did not even mention Shahe Farm, as the disputes over land rights between the state and the villages were nowhere to be resolved. The root of the problem was in the conflicting statuses of the Shahe Group and the Baishizhou villagers. The Shahe Group, as it was formed to manage the state-owned-and-operated Shahe Farm, was a state-owned enterprise with an urban status. Therefore, land under the management of the Shahe Group was owned by the state. But the villagers of the five Baishizhou villages argued that the land should be regarded as urbanized rural land; therefore, their rights to use the land for economic development had to be recognized, and land for the village collectives as well as homesteads for the villagers had to be allocated.

Between the years of 2003 and 2005, village leaders made eight petitions to both the Guangdong Provincial Communist Party Committee and the highest level of authority a civilian can reach—the Central Bureau for Letters and Calls, located in Beijing. Throughout these years, the villagers staged several large-scale demonstrations. The most notable was in June 2005, when two thousand Baishizhou villagers surrounded the Shahe Group office building. The Central Bureau ordered the Shenzhen Bureau for Letters and Calls to investigate as the situation in Baishizhou worsened.

While a Shahe Neighborhood Unit Office was established in 2004 to replace the former Shahe Farm's role in community administration, the government-appointed administrators could not resolve the conflicts. With the jurisdictional power of the former village community organization no longer formally recognized, public order, hygiene, and services all deteriorated even further. Crime and gang activities were frequently reported. The criminal activities posed such security threats, not only to Baishizhou but also to the city itself, that the Shenzhen government had to request assistance from the Ministry of Public Security.[63]

While Baishizhou's resolution was at a stand-still, the Shenzhen government released its first city-wide program of action on urban village redevelopment: "Master Planning Outline for the Redevelopment of Urban Villages (Old Villages) in Shenzhen (2005–2010)." The document declared that "illegal buildings and the problem of urban villages have become the most prominent, complicated, and concentrated conflicts and troubles in the economic and social development of the entire city."[64] The five-year redevelopment plan called for the demolition and reconstruction of 20 percent of the existing volume of urban villages inside the SEZ and 5 percent in the outer districts, which totaled to 11.5 million square meters of floor areas that occupied land areas of nine hundred thousand square meters.[65] The plan also expanded on the nature of the "conflicts and troubles" associated with the urban villages:

> In addition to the difficulty of improving the in-village environment and continuously enhancing the residents' quality of life, as well as the presence of serious potential safety hazards in many villages, the problems of urban villages lie also in the fact that they have hindered the progress of urban restructuring and the enhancement of land use efficiency, corroded the land value of surrounding areas, and sabotaged the city's equitable development environment and legal management order with their illegal operation measures. The urban villages with all these problems are a far cry from the mandate of building a harmonious society.[66]

Given its prime location and its status as the largest, most populous, and worst-reputed urban village, Baishizhou was easily marked as a major target for redevelopment under this particular policy. Government agencies at both the city and Nanshan District levels began researching implementation procedures for the redevelopment plan. In the first year of 2006 alone, the government planned to "completely demolish and reconstruct" forty villages and "partially demolish and renovate" seventy-three villages, with an additional seventy-six villages to implement redevelopment procedures.[67]

In August 2006, the Shahe Neighborhood Unit Office delivered its "Report on Resolving the Historical Problems Concerning the Five Shahe Villages"[68] to the District Party Committee and district government of Nanshan, Shenzhen. The report requested government approval for the establishment of a shareholding company to administrate the economic interests of the five Baishizhou villages. It was a bold move to propose rupturing the fraught relationship between the villages and the Shahe Group, which had begun with the Shahe Farm in 1959. The government approved the proposal and the Baishizhou Investment and Development Enterprise Co. Ltd. was finally established in December 2006. This mechanism granted urban status to both the land of Baishizhou and the villagers. Shenzhen, from a land use and legal organization perspective, finally became China's first city without villages.

However, negotiations on land rights still lasted for another three years. Shahe Group, as a state-owned enterprise with many subsidiary factories and commercial establishments, still claimed rights to the land. Without much financial and political power, the newly established Baishizhou Enterprise was yet a shell of a company. The villagers' economic situation did not improve. Village Head Wu, from the oldest original Baishizhou natural village on site, pleaded to the government for assistance. Speaking of the Baishizhou Enterprise, which had no land or property, Wu said, "Our company has always been a tree without roots." He added that everybody in the city thought that native villagers in Shenzhen were landlords, with a lot of money; however, Baishizhou was the poorest urban village in Shenzhen. Wu reported that Baishizhou's young and middle-aged villagers also faced employment challenges. Most of these villagers had no marketable skills; the only way they knew to make a living was to collect rents. Few young villagers performed well in school, with only around ten studying in colleges. In Wu's own words, "A large number of youngsters have nothing to do, whom the shareholding company feels obligated to absorb but cannot, for our company doesn't have many jobs to offer, nor is there sufficient funding. So what can we do? We do the so-called enclosure management, or simply put, collecting parking fees."[69]

Finally, in December 2009, the Shenzhen municipal government made the following decisions: 440,000 square meters of village residential land and 81,600 square meters of industrial-use land would be under redevelopment, to be directly administered by the Nanshan District government. The Shahe Group would retain 210,000 square meters of industrial land for its continued development.[70]

In 2011, various stakeholders began meeting to plan the urban redevelopment of Baishizhou: the Nanshan District Office, Urban Planning, Shenzhen Land and Resources Commission, the Baishizhou Enterprise, Shahe Group, and the OCT Group met and negotiated redevelopment proposals. In 2012, the district government established the Baishizhou Urban Redevelopment Office. With a land area of nearly six hundred thousand square meters and 2.4 million square meters of existing floor areas, this is the largest urban redevelopment project in Shenzhen's history.[71] Various major development companies in Shenzhen came to actively court the Redevelopment Office and the Baishizhou villages, including OCT Group. Chi, by then a respected village elder, assisted the younger Tangtou Village leaders in the negotiation process. The villagers, who possessed long-held resentments over past conflicts, chose not to work with OCT as the developer for the project and ultimately decided to hire the developer LVGEM.[72]

LVGEM is a Shenzhen-grown development company founded by Huang Kangjing in 1995.[73] By 2012, LVGEM was recognized as one of the top eight real estate enterprises in the city.[74] Coincidentally, like Chen Hua, the CEO of the Kingkey Group that redeveloped Caiwuwei Village, Huang Kangjing led his first start-up construction project in 1983: the redevelopment of Meilin Village in Shenzhen's Futian District.[75] Over the years, LVGEM came to specialize in urban village redevelopment projects in Shenzhen. The personal and corporate experience of LVGEM in dealing with village collectives and negotiating with individuals was vital to winning the trust of the Baishizhou villagers. The redevelopment, already complicated owing to the complexities surrounding land entitlement, was made even more complicated by the fact that prior to the redevelopment project, no formal survey was done and no boundary was drawn between the 416,000 square meters of Baishizhou and the eighty-two thousand square meters of Shahe Group. In addition, the density of the existing buildings to be demolished was already high, at an FAR (floor area ratio) of four. The planned new construction had to be unusually dense and tall to recoup economic investment.

A number of top architecture offices, from US-based SOM to Shenzhen-based Urbanus and CAUPD, were contracted to work with Baishizhou and LVGEM to create a satisfactory urban plan and design. In the various schemes, the majority of Baishizhou's 2,477 buildings were to be demolished and replaced with a series of luxury residential and commercial towers, the highlight of which would be a cluster of "Super Talls"—that is, towers taller than six hundred meters.[76] The proposed three-phase redevelopment scheme was projected to ultimately finish in 2022. The first phase would be conducted in 2014–2017, including prime office space facing Shennan Boulevard to the south and resettlement apartments further north. The super-tall tower to be built fronting the boulevard was to be completely owned by the village collectives, for the provision of sustained income and corporate business opportunities for the villagers. The second phase would be conducted in 2015–2019, including commercial, cultural, and public amenities. The third phase, to be completed in 2017–2022, would be primarily residential, and would focus on the land parcel of the existing Baishizhou Village to the south of the boulevard. Finally, a light rail system was proposed to connect the buildings from all three phases. The project's ambition was to outshine not only the neighboring Overseas Chinese Town, but also the Central Business District.

Baishizhou villagers such as Chi saw this as their ultimate wish coming true. Each villager would be compensated in the new development with real estate in a 1:1 ratio for their current property. Even those non-Baishizhou villagers who did not hold Shenzhen *hukou* status would be compensated in a 1:0.8 ratio. It appeared that after decades of struggle, an amicable resolution had been reached for all—all, except the nearly two hundred thousand other residents of Baishizhou who called it home.

HOME AWAY FROM HOME

While the Nanshan government's survey of the renting population inside Baishizhou obtained a total count of 110,000, other estimates placed the number closer to 150,000.[77] Much like data on the population of Shenzhen in general, data on exactly how many people lived in Baishizhou varied with every information source. Even statistics on those with registered Shenzhen *hukou* fluctuated from twenty thousand to forty thousand.[78] By the most conservative estimate, Baishizhou is the most densely populated neighborhood in Shenzhen. From poorly educated migrant workers in the

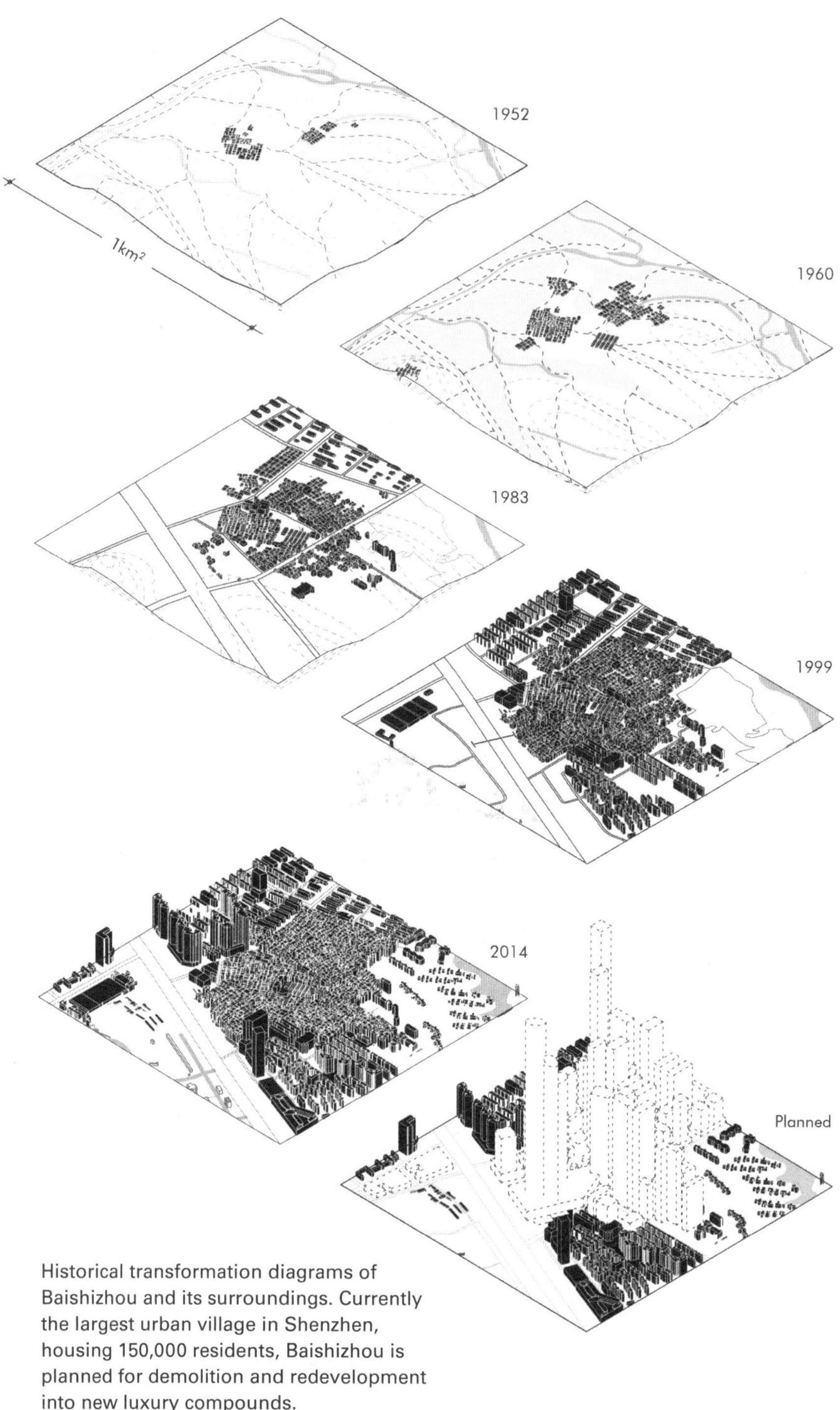

Historical transformation diagrams of Baishizhou and its surroundings. Currently the largest urban village in Shenzhen, housing 150,000 residents, Baishizhou is planned for demolition and redevelopment into new luxury compounds.

nearby factories to new PhD graduates starting up in the neighboring technology parks, diverse groups of migrants from all over China were drawn to Baishizhou thanks to its central location and cheaper rent.

In the 2013 version of the "Baishizhou Redevelopment Master Plan" prepared for LVGEM by the Shanghai Office of the American architecture firm SOM, one million square meters of the future 5.5 million square meters of new construction would be compensation housing to replace the existing "peasant houses."[79] Even that seemed not enough, for by the time the self-built housing boom finally slowed down in 2004, nearly three thousand "peasant houses" stood inside Baishizhou.[80] With an average height of eight stories, the elevator-less buildings were of varying degrees of quality in construction, but were similar in appearance and each held over ten apartment units. The total number of units was estimated to be thirty-five thousand, totaling over two million square meters of building area.[81] The villages of Baishizhou had morphed into a complex urban district with Shenzhen's highest building density.

For a new arrival in Shenzhen, Baishizhou was an easy place to start. There were beds, rooms, units with shared toilets and kitchens, or entire floors to be rented for years or just for a few hours. Colorful signage advertising rooms for rent filled every surface of the buildings fronting the streets. Most of the phone numbers led to an agent, or middleman, who would usually take a cut of the rental fee. The tasks of renting and managing the hundreds of thousands of renters in Baishizhou created jobs for thousands of middlemen. Like the buildings themselves, units for rent inside Baishizhou varied from cramped rooms with poor natural lighting and stifling air, to spacious newly renovated apartments with satellite TV and ping-pong tables. While those with resources and good prospects saw the village housing as a starting point or transitional arrangement, the low-income working population relied on this housing for survival in the city.

As poor as some of the rental facilities might be, the quality of life far exceeded the repressive workers' dormitories in Shenzhen's factory housing compounds. The difference was not so much in the physical features; rather, it was in the experience of social living. In the factory compounds, not only were the workers monitored during the work hours, but they were also constantly monitored by managers and dormitory guards when they slept, ate, and gathered for social nights in an enclosed compound.[82] In addition, the choice to quit and seek other jobs

Cheap housing in the urban village is often the first point of arrival for migrants into Shenzhen. Rental information is mostly found posted on handwritten posters, such as in this scene in Baishizhou.

was rendered difficult because the quitter would not even have a place to live. As the workers were totally dependent on the employers for not only work but housing, most had no choice but to accept the minimal wage, long working hours, and lack of company welfare. Children were strictly prohibited in the factory compound, and married workers could not even live together as most dormitories were divided by gender. The limitations to personal freedom and the extreme social control created toxic conditions that continue today. The shocking series of workers' suicides reported to have taken place in Foxconn, just kilometers north of Baishizhou, was more because of their isolated living quarters than because of their working conditions. According to 2004 statistics on Shenzhen's migrant working population, only 15 percent of the workers lived in factory dormitories, while 50 percent chose to live in the urban villages throughout the city.[83]

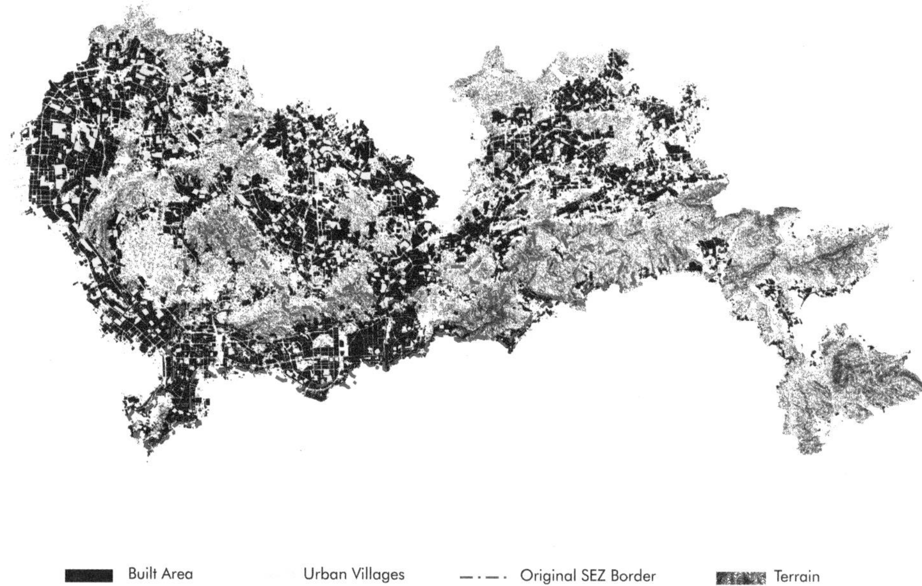

Built Area   Urban Villages   Original SEZ Border   Terrain

Shenzhen's post-1979 urbanization patterns are determined by both the natural geography and the preexisting townships and villages. The city's urbanization and economic development could not have been achieved through such speed and scope without the communities whose histories have been overlooked.

With such a large migrant population living in Baishizhou, tens of thousands of small businesses sprang up to feed, service, and entertain the residents. These businesses were run by other migrants, who brought their regional specialties to Shenzhen. Food found in the alleyways of Baishizhou—spicy Sichuan hotpots, steaming Shandong dumplings, smoky Mongolian barbecues, and sweet Guangdong dessert soups—represents the great diversity of China in a manner far exceeding the curated scenes of OCT's Splendid China. Migrants from every locale in China can find something to satisfy their cravings and find someone who speaks in their local dialect to subdue bouts of homesickness. The diverse cuisines and lower prices attracted people not only from within Baishizhou, but also from elsewhere in the city. Many residents living in the high-rise apartment towers bordering Baishizhou would visit for an easy and cheap night out. Like other urban villages in Shenzhen's city center, Baishizhou also attracted visitors seeking other types of services from iPhone shops to KTVs. However, Baishizhou hosted the most vibrant street culture and nightlife in OCT.

With an increasingly larger population and deteriorating conditions, the Shahe neighborhood unit experimented with giving incentives to building owners to self-upgrade their rental properties. In May 2012, it initiated a Quality Rental Housing licensing system in Baishizhou Village, where eligible properties could receive a partial—up to 20 percent—discount on the typical management fees owners paid to the neighborhood unit.[84] Baishizhou was the first in Shenzhen and Guangdong Province to implement such a system to encourage self-upgrade within the urban villages. By December 2012, 522 village houses were enrolled in the program. Inspections deemed 504 of those houses to have reached the standard, and they were awarded the "Quality Rental Housing" recognition. In addition, five thousand fire extinguishers, 3,600 emergency lights, sixty-six fire hoses, 1,683 emergency windows, and ninety-six rooftop escape passes were installed. Of these buildings, 80 percent were monitored by electronic security systems, and CCTV network covered the whole Baishizhou Village. According to the village officers, after the implementation of the scheme, the crime rate in Baishizhou was reduced by 29 percent, and industrial accidents decreased by 50 percent. Tenant occupancy rose from 89 percent to 98 percent, and rentals increased by 25 percent.[85] The growing economy and the physical improvements since 2012 allowed the neighborhood to attract a more diverse population.

Organic coffee shops, artist galleries, and vegetarian gourmet foods—the types of establishments usually found in the adjacent OCT—also migrated into Baishizhou. In addition to the occupied street-fronted ground floors of the "peasant houses," the former factory blocks of the Shahe Industrial Zone to the north of Tangtou Village also were adapted for commercial uses. Large space and cheaper rent, with more space and air between the buildings, allowed new restaurants and bars to turn the former factory zone into a bustling dining and entertaining area. As the restaurant businesses usually took the ground floor of the factory buildings, light industrial production still occupied the upper floors.

In 2014, Joe Finkenbinder came to Baishizhou Shahe Industrial Zone's Eastern District, rented a space, and opened the Bionic Brewery, with a bar and restaurant, selling over ten varieties of craft beer. His reason for choosing the location was simple: "I showed up in Baishizhou, just like they did. I didn't know anybody here, I hadn't been here before, I just showed up with my stuff and was like 'I'll just start in Baishizhou. That's where everyone starts. . . . Rents in this city are just so high it's going to kill growth. Nobody can open anything. I came to Baishizhou because it's cheap."[86] As Finkenbinder was the first foreigner to open a business in the industrial zone, the brewery became popular with locals and expats living in Shenzhen. Other entrepreneurial minds in Shenzhen took notice. Soon a pizzeria opened next door, and an Italian wine bar opened across the alleyway from Bionic Brewery, both run by non-Chinese nationals. On the grounds of factories that produced Walkman cassettes just twenty years ago, one can now have a glass of Prosecco with Parma ham, and go a few doors down for steamed Hainan chicken.

DISPLACEMENT AND CONTESTED REDEVELOPMENT

The Baishizhou Shahe Industrial Zone is split into an Eastern District and Western District, separated by Baishizhou's main north-south thoroughfare, Shahe Street. The industrial zone is on the land managed by the Shahe Group, and in October 2012, land rights to the Western District were transferred to the Hong Kong–registered development company Shum Yip Century for the development of a new residential area. In December 2015, the Shenzhen-based architecture firm CAPOL International and Melbourne-based Denton Coker won the international competition for best design of the overall scheme of Shum Yip Century Valley, with a proposal that included ten high-rise towers with luxury shopping malls.[87] It was around this time that business owners in the Western District of the industrial zone started to hear about the redevelopment plans. While a brick wall had been built in August 2015 to separate the shop fronts from the main street, the business owners actually received a notice to vacate the buildings in March 2016. These small business owners, who mostly rented the spaces from middlemen agents, did not have any legal rights to stay or demand compensation. As in most cases in the urban villages, the leases were not formalized and most renters allowed their lease documents to lapse without renewal for years.

Soon the plight of this group received attention from community groups such as the Baishizhou Team. Composed of architects, artists, and playwrights, the Baishizhou Team had been conducting a series of projects in the area to call attention to the importance of Shenzhen's urban villages. They had been inviting residents of Baishizhou to take photos with a sign marked "Do Not Demolish Baishizhou" since May 2016. Most of the residents approached by the activists refused to take the photos.

Some feared retribution if they resisted a government-supported redevelopment effort, but most residents simply felt that the redevelopment of all urban villages in Shenzhen was an inevitable outcome as the city continued to modernize. As Chinese laws on eviction and displacement are not currently developed, most tenant occupants of the buildings did not feel they were entitled to participate in the decision-making process. However, through the Baishizhou Team's efforts, dozens of residents did agree to be photographed with the "Do Not Demolish Baishizhou" sign. Ultimately, the team planned to send the residents' photos and accompanying comments to the Nanshan District government.

In September 2016, the Baishizhou Team actively tried to assist the tenants of the area in resisting relocation. Most tenants initially refused to move; however, when electricity and water supply were cut and demolition teams built additional barriers, nearly all settled except one. On September 11, this business owner held up the anti-demolition sign and accepted assistance from the Baishizhou Team. He was the owner of a Lanzhou Noodle shop, the ubiquitous small restaurant type that can be found everywhere in China.[88] Originally established by Ma Zilu during the late Qing period in Gansu Province's capital city of Lanzhou, this humble dish featuring a beef stock soup could be found in every city in China. According to a 2016 *Confucius Institute Journal* article, there are over fifty thousand Lanzhou Noodle shops in China and forty in other locations around the world.[89] Like McDonald's, Lanzhou Noodle can be found in nearly every district in large and small urban areas of China alike. Unlike McDonald's, Lanzhou Noodle shops are not franchise operators of the same chain. Yet there is a key similarity between the Lanzhou Noodle restaurant in Baishizhou and nearly all the others found elsewhere in Shenzhen, China, and Chinatowns in the world. While the Confucius Institute's article does not mention this, the majority of Lanzhou Noodle shop operators are Chinese Muslims, and their shared cultural and religious practice on food and hygiene has resulted in similar qualities and atmosphere across most of the shops. The Baishizhou shop was operated by Chef Ma, a Muslim migrant from Gansu Province. Gansu has the second-largest Chinese Muslim population of all the provinces in China, and the name "Ma" is the Chinese stand-in for Muhammad among Chinese Muslims. Chef Ma bought the shop from a previous owner in May 2013 and paid a transfer fee of 26,500 yuan for all the equipment. This was the main reason that Chef Ma agreed to participate in the "anti-demolition" action.

Throughout a few tense weeks, the Baishizhou Team encouraged the media to report on the case and set up crowdfunding to help Chef Ma. The effort paid off: local media covered Chef Ma's story and activists stayed with his family, including his wife and school-age son, through the long nights without electricity. By September 19, Chef Ma was offered thirty thousand yuan in relocation compensation; the crowdfunding generated a similar amount.[90] Chef Ma decided to accept the compensation and moved out. A few hours later, the entire building was demolished. Through the Baishizhou Team, Chef Ma stated that he "is not opposed to urban renewal, but he should not be the collateral damage."[91] While the effort of resisting displacement led to a predictable result, the actions mobilized others in Shenzhen to advocate for careful consideration of future redevelopment of the Baishizhou area in general.

On June 16, 2017, as per Shenzhen's regulations, the Nanshan District government posted on the official website of Shenzhen Planning and Land Bureau the document "Public Presentation of Urban Renewal Planning for the Five Shahe Villages in Shahe Neighborhood Unit, Nanshan District."[92] The two-page information sheet contained two site plans for the Baishizhou area, indicating the redevelopment boundary and revealing that the existing buildings on 459,500 square meters of land were set to be demolished. New buildings would be developed at a plot ratio of 7.2 with a series of high-rise towers to contain one million square meters of commercial space, along with 1.25 million square meters of housing and 1.12 million square meters of serviced apartments. The top of the information sheet featured a slogan in bold letters: "Enthusiastically Participate in Planning, and Create Wonderful Homes Together."[93] The slogan was coupled with the following obligatory lines in fine print: "If you have any opinion or suggestion on the draft plan during the public presentation period, please submit it to the Bureau in writing. The submission deadline is set on July 15, 2017. Late submissions will be regarded as no objection. (For mailed submissions we will use the postmark date. You may also drop your written opinion directly into the opinion box)."[94]

In late July, the Baishizhou Team reported on their website that a team member's mail delivered to the stated address via a local carrier service was rejected. While the address and recipient conformed to the public notice's instructions, the carrier service was told no such addressee was at the office. The team posted the content of the letter, which listed six reasons for the group's opposition to the Baishizhou Redevelopment

Proposal. The sixth and final point stated: "We support urban renewal, and we understand the city's pursuit of becoming newer and better. However, this kind of space-led urban redevelopment plan is not smart from an accounting perspective. It is not progressive in terms of future development. We suggest that the bureau should first change its method and mindset for renewal."[95]

The typical period for "public presentation" of development projects by the Shenzhen government is one month. For reasons unannounced by the Shenzhen Planning and Land Bureau, or the Nanshan District government, Baishizhou's "public presentation" post did not close on July 16, indicating an unusual extension of the public presentation period. The delay caused tremendous anxiety in both the developers at LVGEM and the villagers of Baishizhou. Requested by the younger village leaders to assist in the negotiation with the developers and the government, Chi made a trip to the Tangtou Village Office and stayed there for a few hours each afternoon. The office was located on the second floor of a nondescript urban village building adjacent to the Old Tangtou Village compound. The office not only paled in comparison to the Huanggang Company's office in the penthouse of the twenty-two-story Huanggang Tower, but also appeared to be more tattered than most of the offices in Guangdong's still-rural villages. Chi, however, maintained a steady countenance and an equally steady perspective on the outcome. He knew the redevelopment would happen and believed that the clamor of opposition had been stirred up by those jealous to see Baishizhou villagers finally get their payday.

Many residents as well as small enterprises started to anticipate clearance and relocation. SZDIY, or Shenzhen Do It Yourself, is a group of young engineers and programmers that have rented a workshop on the third floor of a former village-operated industrial building in Baishizhou since 2014.[96] The large space and cheap rent allowed them to experiment and exchange ideas, and to offer a low membership fee to anyone who wanted to join. The space was open every Thursday to other makers or anyone interested in their work. SZDIY was featured in a 2015 CNN article titled "Shenzhen: China's Start-up City Defies Skeptics," where the group was described as "a member's association that meets in an old industrial building and builds everything from vehicles to games. The workshop is a study of contrasts: at once dusty and hi-tech."[97] The article did not mention that the group is located in Baishizhou village. To outside observers, such specifics seem insignificant in a city full of high-tech technology parks. The relatively affordable living and working spaces in Shenzhen's urban villages have served as incubating spaces for economic and social mobility. For some who have accumulated enough capital, the constant threat of displacement is enough cause to move. By October 2017, the SZDIY Hacker Space relocated out of the Eastern District of the Baishizhou Shahe Industrial Zone. By July 2019, tenants in the urban village received eviction notices, with one month or less to move out. The hardest hit were thousands of families with children who were registered to start school after the summer break. With the eventual total clearance and demolition of Baishizhou, over 150,000 people will lose their homes, livelihood, and, for many, future opportunities to succeed in the city.

Coincidentally, an online video game inspired by the city was released in July 2019 on the US-based Steam, one of the world's largest video game distribution platforms. According to the online release, the game's setting is in Shenzhen: "Baishizhou is a well-known village in Shenzhen, China. Almost all migrant workers begin their dream journey of urban life from places like this. Now it's your turn! Yes, it's your turn. As a player, you're just coming to Baishizhou, a village in the city. You're about to start your life from this broken-down rental house." This setting of a Shenzhen-based game is perhaps fitting owing to its iconic role as the point of arrival for new migrants, with reports of more than three million people having lived in Baishizhou from the 1990s to the 2010s. More importantly, for the creator of the video game named Drill, the project is developed from his personal experience of living in Baishizhou from 2004 to 2007.[98] While currently an independent games developer living elsewhere in Shenzhen, Baishizhou gave Drill access to an affordable and "broken-down rental house" when he was starting out in the city. Drill only found out about the clearance when he was interviewed by journalists, and he stated the importance of his video game's setting in the urban village and its working-class residents: "I want to present the city's silent majority, working so hard each day. I feel they are the real heroes of the city."[99]

Baishizhou was particularly significant to many of Shenzhen's young programmers given that it is in walking distance of the nearby technology parks in the adjacent Yuehai Neighborhood, the epicenter of China's gaming industry. In addition, from Huawei to DJI and Tencent, many of China's world-leading digital technology companies are located in this area adjacent to Baishizhou. By summer 2019, "Shenzheners" proudly claimed that the raging US-China technology trade war was in fact between the United States and the Shenzhen City/Nanshan District/Yuehai Neighborhood. Shenzhen's latest round of digital revolutions, as well as the city's numerous past innovations, are part of a deep history of entrepreneurial practices. Urban villages such as Baishizhou provide an ecosystem of affordable housing, along with inexpensive services and facilities, which has allowed Shenzhen to continuously evolve and exceed predefined expectations. Shenzhen's future sustainable growth will rely on the continued existence of affordable housing available to the city's existing population and future new arrivals. Rather than a demonstration of problems, the urban villages are sources of past knowledge and future solutions to improve the city's economic vitality and social resilience. Shenzhen's success cannot be simply attributed to policies or central planning. Some of the city's most remarkable innovations are the result of local responses to top-down planning, responses that sometimes directly contradicted those plans. The story of Shenzhen did not originate from a single person or even a collective vision, but rather was born from hundreds of millions of individual aspirations as well as struggles, a handful of which are revealed in this book.

CONCLUSION

City of Critical Experimentation

From songs and novels to plays and film, Shenzhen's unique history and urban life have inspired countless creative projects. *Heaven to the Left, Shenzhen to the Right* is one of many Chinese literary works set in Shenzhen. The noir-esque nature of the book and its outspoken Beijing-based author, Murong Xuecun, make it popular with China's young working population, but not with the government.[1] Centered on the lives of a few young white-collar migrant workers, the novel portrayed the difficulties of working in Shenzhen as well as the corruptive power of the city's market mechanism. For those recently arrived in the city, the book presented the "Shenzhen Principle": "I will invite you for a meal, but will not lend you money as I don't know if I will ever see you again. And please don't beg me to find you a job; I found a job myself. But, yes, you are a friend, so stay with me for a few days."[2] The lack of sentimentality in these words is in drastic contrast to China's typical social norms of extended hospitality to out-of-town friends. The seemingly harsh words, however, also communicate an underlying prerequisite of self-reliance for anyone to succeed in the city.

For Shenzheners, as the city's residents refer to themselves, there is a common saying that puts a spin on Murong's book title: "*Heaven to the Left, Shenzhen to the Right:* make one turn and you will end up in an urban village." In between heaven and hell, the urban village is a place of temporary transitions, lasting from days to decades. For many who arrive in

Shenzhen, landing a place in a friend's home is an unattainable luxury. For the majority of the low-income workers and young migrants, the city's urban villages have become the ultimate home base. The relatively affordable home and work spaces have made it possible to earn a living and even start up a business. According to research conducted between 2009 and 2016, there were seven-to-ten million people living in Shenzhen's urban villages, accounting for a little more than half of the city's total population over that period.[3] This is especially meaningful when contextualized within Shenzhen's current housing crisis. By 2016, real estate value in Shenzhen has exceeded that in all the other Chinese cities, and housing affordability ratings were found to be worse than those of Hong Kong. Decades into rapid urbanization, the majority of Shenzhen's new arrivals cannot afford basic forms of housing in Shenzhen's formal real estate market. Urban villages have become the only possible source of housing for the low-income working population, especially within the city's central districts. After a decade of aggressive campaigns to demolish the urban villages, by 2016 Shenzhen government's positions started to change.

In November 2016, Shenzhen released a new urban planning policy, "The 13th Five-Year Plan of Shenzhen Urban Renewal," which indicated that the government no longer viewed demolition and redevelopment as the predominant treatment of urban villages. The policy stated that while most urban villages in the outer districts should still be demolished, for the urban villages inside the city's urban center that have "decent building quality," the recommendation is to consider "integrated regeneration" that upgrades basic infrastructure but "does not change the buildings' built structure or programs."[4] By March 2019, the government extended the policy to the entire city of Shenzhen through the "Shenzhen Urban Village (Old Village) Integrated Rehabilitation Master Plan (2019–2025)." The new policy recommended a flexible and changeable strategy of "integrated rehabilitation," so as to maintain the spatial distribution of urban villages and guarantee availability of low-cost residential areas in the city.[5] However, these policy releases could not prevent the demolition of preapproved redevelopment plans for urban villages such as Baishizhou. In addition, while the new policies aim to improve the existing spatial and infrastructural qualities that are specific to each urban village, the exact implementation mechanisms of such policies are yet to be developed.

While the actual impacts of these new policies are yet to be observed, they are good demonstrations of Shenzhen's continued efforts to be adaptive and flexible. Staying true to the city's history, this latest reinvention of Shenzhen's urban renewal policies is born out of a necessity to survive and thrive. With the limited physical geography preventing the city to further sprawl and expand, Shenzhen must find new economies that are no longer based on large real-estate development. The most innovative aspect of Shenzhen's latest planning policies for decentralized and small-scale renewals is not only in its experimental nature, but in the attitude of the city government to seek ways to remedy a previously mistaken policy direction. This is especially remarkable when 2018–2019 marked aggressive urban renewal efforts throughout other major Chinese cities that have resulted in the clearance of informal settlements and low-income neighborhoods. Owing to the general lack of attention to Shenzhen's complex trials and errors throughout its urbanization history, the most innovative aspects of the city are still yet to be fully appreciated. Instead, the prevalent myth of Shenzhen's central planning and economic success continues to drive national and international urban projects to duplicate the "miraculous instant city."

"SHENZHEN" ELSEWHERE

In May 2017, the state-owned China Central Television (CCTV) announced the government's plan for a new satellite urban center located one hundred kilometers from Beijing in a news special titled "The Plan of a Millennium and an Affair of National Significance: A Documentary Report of the Decision on the Planning and Construction of Xiong'an New Area in Hebei Province by the CPC Central Committee with Comrade Xi Jinping at Its Core." The presenter confidently predicted the future success of the ambitious project: "Look to Shenzhen in the 1980s, look to Pudong in the 1990s, and look to Xiong'an in the 21st century!"[6] The broadcast rounded off a month of media frenzy, initiated by an article on April 2, 2017, in the state-owned *People's Daily*. This article had announced the Xiong'an New Area proposal, which aimed to "explore new models of prioritized development for population and economic intensive areas, adjust and optimize the urban layout and spatial structure of the Beijing-Tianjin-Hebei area, and cultivate new development engines through innovation."[7] It was followed by a *People's Daily* article two days later, with an eye-catching headline: "Writing the 'Story of Spring' of Regionally Balanced Development." This article enthusiastically responded to the government's announcement, exclaiming, "It is very exciting to learn that decisions were made by the State Council to set up the Xiong'an New Area. This is another 'Story of Spring.'"[8] Within two weeks, regional and national media had excitedly published yet more articles explicitly connecting Xiong'an with Shenzhen, adopting titles such as "One Spring over Thirty Years Ago, the Shenzhen Special Economic Zone Rose from the Earth, yet in Another Spring Thirty-Something Years Later, Xiong'an New Area Blazes across the Sky."[9] The reference to Shenzhen was not merely media hype. Although the Xiong'an plan was technically called a "New Area" rather than a special economic zone, Shenzhen was clearly stated as a precedent in the subsequently released official planning documents. The land designated as the New Area is a territory of two thousand square kilometers, the same size as Shenzhen, that is currently occupied by agricultural villages and rural townships.[10] Multiple local government leaders who had been involved in Shenzhen's planning and development were transferred to the new government team heading up the Xiong'an project.

The desire to transpose the successful "Story of Spring" to a new national strategic project is not surprising. Throughout the past two decades, "The Story of Spring" has become a catchphrase for instant success, a shorthand for China's post-1979 Reform and Opening Up. Regularly appearing in newspapers, books, television, and films, the phrase evokes an instant association with market reforms, economic growth, urbanization, and the Shenzhen SEZ. So, will Xiong'an become another "Story of Spring," like, or even surpassing, Shenzhen?[11] To begin to answer this question, it is worth reflecting upon the last forty years of China's zone-based developments.

While the success of the Shenzhen SEZ has encouraged the Chinese central government to institute zonal strategies in cities across China, only a handful of those zones have been designated specifically as SEZs. Following the establishment of the first three SEZs of Sheznhen, Zhuhai, and Xiamen in 1980, China established SEZs in fourteen coastal cities in 1984, and on the southern island Hainan Province in 1988. Since that first decade of reforms, China has designated only one additional special economic zone: in 2010, the Kashgar special economic zone was established in China's Xinjiang Autonomous Region. However, the Shenzhen zonal strategy was also institutionalized and replicated across China under other names, as part of a national push for expedited urban development. Various types of development zones emerged, designated by a variety of acronyms, including the EPZ (export processing zone), FTZ (free trade zone), HIDZ (high-tech industrial development zone), and BECZ (Border Economic Cooperation Zone). While these names suggest that each development zone type had a different purpose, in each case land expropriation and development—transforming thousands of acres of farmland into land for industrial and real-estate use—emerged as the quickest method to attract investment and generate revenue. The number of development zones in China peaked in 2003, with over 6,866 covering a total area of over 38,600 square kilometers; this exceeded the total area of all China's cities combined.[12] This phenomenon was appropriately described as "Zone Fever" by a number of international observers, as well as by academics in China.[13] The resultant rapid decrease in agricultural land has since alarmed the central government, and impelled its leaders to be more cautious when authorizing exceptionalist zones.

Of all the various types of zones, the SEZ—with Shenzhen at the forefront—remains the most prominent. However, the central government has since shown more caution and deliberation with the design of SEZs than with the other acronyms in its catalogue—as evidenced by the fact that Kashgar is home to the only new SEZ established in China since the 1980s. While the previous SEZs were located in the more developed regions along China's eastern seacoast, the city of Kashgar is located in the Uygur Autonomous Region of Xinjiang at China's western border, next to other Asian countries such as Afghanistan, Kazakhstan, Pakistan, India, Mongolia, and Russia. Use of the "SEZ" nomenclature in this culturally diverse and politically sensitive region was deliberate, intended to connote economic goodwill and prosperity through its relationship to the success story of Shenzhen. During the initial days of the Kashgar SEZ in 2010, China's state media agency Xinhua reported on the announcement enthusiastically: "The city [Kashgar] has never concealed its intention to emulate the success of Shenzhen, courtesy of a pairing assistance program, which saw the Shenzhen government take a leading role in steering Kashgar's development. In 2010, the slogan 'Shenzhen in the east, Kashgar in the west' became emblematic of the city's new status as an SEZ."[14]

However, the Kashgar SEZ has not come close to meeting anticipated growth expectations based on the growth of Shenzhen.[15] It is not alone. Neither the other special economic zones nor the variety of other "zone" developments in the country has reached Shenzhen's level of success.

These results should cast some doubt on the idea that other zone developments could replicate the "Story of Spring."

Similar caution should be applied to the vast number of zone-based developments established around the world on the model of China's special economic zones. When other countries seek to replicate China's SEZs, they are mostly referencing Shenzhen—not so much the other SEZs in China. Shenzhen has become the "poster child" for the special economic zone strategy, and the rapid economic development experienced under Shenzhen's specific conditions has become inextricably associated with the concept of SEZs more generally. In economic, political, and public discourse, Shenzhen and special economic zone have become one and the same. Shenzhen is used as a shorthand for special economic zone, when in fact the two are not interchangeable. The Shenzhen experiment, as a singular successful case, has overshadowed the numerous examples of zone-based urbanization and developments which have *not* flourished in the same way—despite investments in new town developments with transportation infrastructure, innovative housing, attractive museums, and lush parks. SEZ policy initiated the Shenzhen experiment, but the success of Shenzhen has depended on many other crucial factors beyond centralized policies, infrastructure construction, and foreign investments.

China's most recent central government policies plan to continue the country's path of economic growth through urbanization and new town creation. Over the next five years, one hundred million rural residents will be urbanized. Hundreds of new cities are planned and under construction. Of the 156 major cities in China, 145 cities currently have governmental plans to extend and build new towns. The planned population of these new cities will double the country's current urban population.[16] If Shenzhen is not a formalized and easily replicable top-down model, but a complex and shifting set of bottom-up and informal negotiations, as this book has argued, the path to successfully modernizing and urbanizing these new cities may not be so straightforward. The same goes for the many governments across the world that are currently seeking to transform their own cities and economies based on the Shenzhen model.

Most of the new megacities in Asia and the Global South are struggling with complex socioeconomic problems associated with rapid industrialization and urbanization. The most visible sign of these struggles is the prevalence of variations of informal settlements referred to as favelas, barrios, and slums. With rural migrants flocking to developing regional economic centers, the municipal governments are unable to keep up with the escalating demands of affordable housing and other public amenities. According to UN-Habitat, more than thirty percent of the urban population of developing countries live in slums, and the numbers are growing exponentially.[17] The launch of China's state-backed One Belt One Road (OBOR) initiative in 2017 has paved the way for the expansion of China's zonal development model through large-scale industrial and infrastructure projects. The ambitious initiative is set to reach over sixty countries and to impact billions of people around the world. As China promotes, invests, and constructs Chinese special economic zones worldwide, it is worth reframing the questions we ask about Shenzhen. Rather than asking how quickly we can replicate Shenzhen, we should ask what previously overlooked lessons we can draw from its complex evolution.

RETHINKING SHENZHEN

What lessons, then, can we take away from the stories of Shenzhen? First and foremost, we must recognize the complex dynamic between top-down and bottom-up processes that shaped the city's developmental history. Under the pre-1979 communist ideology, the centralization of political power was absolute. The SEZ policies gave unprecedented law-making and law-breaking powers to the Guangdong provincial government. The fact that the central government delegated political power in order to permit local trial and error, at the risk of undermining central control, is both a testament to the strength of reform-minded leadership and a reflection of the urgency for change during that specific historical moment. Just as Shenzhen city planners learned to adjust master plans by accepting unplanned developments in the physical environment, Shenzhen policy makers adjusted regulations to adapt to unanticipated bottom-up transformations in the city's economic and social operations. The central government's granting of "Special Policy, Flexible Implementation" allowed Shenzhen to create its own rules and regulations. Part of the implementation of the SEZ policy was *decentralization* of power, which, in practice, meant that many of the innovations that made Shenzhen successful were not pre-formulated by the central government as part of a top-down plan. These innovations were instead formulated at the local level, in real time, as the experiment unfolded. This reform process in Shenzhen, especially during the first decade, was marked by constant oscillation, contradiction, debate, and uncertainty. Even after six years, Deng Xiaoping himself was not so sure of Shenzhen's future. In his 1985 talk with an Algerian delegation, Deng candidly stated: "The Shenzhen special economic zone is an experiment. It will be some time before we know whether we are doing the right thing there. It is something new under socialism. We hope to make it a success, but if it fails, we can learn from the experience."[18]

However, Shenzhen was more than an experiment of "something new under socialism." Shenzhen was a critical experiment. The city was an experiment to seek a path different from and, in many ways, contradictory to the fundamental operations of China at the time. The special economic zone policy was a critical experiment in reversing the status quo, and its establishment served as an admission by the central government that what was happening outside the "zone" needed to change. Policy reforms and innovations took place at the local level, enabled by the decentralization of power but also driven by the necessity of survival and the insights of local leaders and citizens. This experimentation included radical changes to the foundational operations of China's governance, such as *hukou* reforms and the decentralization of administrative powers, which reversed the pre-1979 Mao policy of restricting and blocking rural migration to cities. Control of population flow and movement, through the *hukou* system of rural and urban designations tied to specific locations, was the most fundamental governing structure of a planned socialist economy. Shenzhen eroded that rigid control structure in order to attract people, bringing a wealth of new talents—some from the most unexpected places and individuals—to bear on the future of the city as millions migrated to the SEZ.

The success of Shenzhen has, in turn, resulted in the central government's incorporation of such locally developed strategies into a national zonal development strategy. When SEZ policies were applied elsewhere, the increased competition for talent gave Shenzhen the motivation to continue *hukou* policy innovations designed to attract and retain such talent. The nationwide *hukou* reforms currently underway in China are testament to the reverberations of Shenzhen's experimentations on population flow and urban citizenship. Such dynamics of top-down and bottom-up governance—at the central (Beijing), local (Shenzhen), municipal (mayor), and individual (citizen) levels—warrant further excavation and examination.

Policy makers seeking to replicate Shenzhen's success must begin to recognize the pivotal role of the local and the plural in its development.

Shenzhen—like every city—is not a singular transferable model but a plurality, informed by local conditions and local communities. City makers must consider the specific characteristics of *time* and *place,* including local geography and local resources. They must recognize that "instant cities" do not spring up from a blank slate, and consider a long view of the past in addition to projecting the future. They must consider *people,* recognizing that local entrepreneurs, leaders, and most importantly residents—like the many individuals featured in this book—have a vital role to play in the development of any city. Shenzhen's earliest industry and economy were the result of local efforts during a highly specific time, in a very unique geography. Much of Shenzhen's industry and infrastructure resulted from the informal responsive efforts of its formerly rural population. While the city would eventually attract millions from various socioeconomic backgrounds, during its initial decade Shenzhen had to recruit talent. And when a large migrant population did arrive, planning and construction could not keep pace with demand. Shenzhen's projections have always underestimated the speed and volume of its actual population increase, and as a result its planned housing provisions and infrastructure have been able to accommodate only a fraction of its people. It was the preexisting rural population that took the opportunity to establish housing and meet other basic needs for most of the new migrants. Shenzhen's invisible and "unplanned" populations are key to understanding the complex nature of urban construction, land expropriation, property rights, and housing affordability.

In addition, there were few foreign investments in Shenzhen without local connections during the city's earliest years. While one of the main economic strategies vested in the Shenzhen SEZ involved attracting Foreign Direct Investment (FDI), far more investment came from domestic than from foreign sources during its first, and arguably most crucial, decade. Moreover, the vast majority of FDI bestowed on Shenzhen came from Hong Kong. This development might seem obvious given the two cities' geographic proximity, but it depended on the historic specificity of Hong Kong's relationship to the Pearl River Delta region through clan and village kinship ties. Hong Kong entrepreneurs were not primarily investing in large industrial parks or joint ventures with state enterprises, but rather were mostly working with the tens of thousands of small local enterprises in Shenzhen. Most of these investments were rooted in partnerships with local rural populations and village collectives. While the

Shenzhen SEZ was sharply criticized for relying so heavily on domestic and Hong Kong investment, this unique circumstance had the advantage of not only diversifying funding sources, types, and industries in the Shenzhen SEZ, but also allowing for the transfer of basic knowledge and technologies from Hong Kong investors and managers to the local population.

While the host countries of Chinese-initiated SEZs have welcomed these projects, they have faced challenges in exactly these areas—in other words, challenges associated with engaging local participation and facilitating the transfer of expertise. Observations of the recent international SEZs have noted serious problems related to local context and people:

> As for investments for instance, local entrepreneurs in African SEZ-host countries have complained about not being allowed to invest and develop their businesses in the zones. Besides, modernisation and urbanisation around the regions that host the SEZs can create social and spatial inequalities between these hubs and other parts of the country. People who were living in the areas where the zones are built have been displaced—sometimes without compensation—and lost their livelihoods. Chinese special economic zones in African countries currently do not really appear to involve local entrepreneurs and populations' needs in term of investments and employment.[19]

The displacement of "people who were living in the areas" in order to facilitate the construction of SEZs is not only happening in Chinese SEZs in African countries. Displacement and forced relocation of villagers for the construction of SEZs have been reported in India and other South Asian countries.[20] This was not the case in Shenzhen, where housing provisions and employment opportunities created by the original villagers were essential to the SEZ's survival and eventual success. The model makers, some intentionally and others unintentionally, have created a misleading image of Shenzhen that strips away much of the nuance, conflict, and ingenuity involved in its development, as well as the contributions of its original residents. This is in contrast to the actual developmental history of Shenzhen, where local residents and small grassroots businesses were crucial. Within the Shenzhen SEZ, "local entrepreneurs" were not only involved but were among the most important economic and creative driving forces. Many of Shenzhen's internationally important enterprises, from Huawei in the 1980s and to DJI in the 2000s, started out as grassroots enterprises with no state or foreign investments.

Perhaps the greatest lesson that Shenzhen has to teach for other aspiring SEZs is the lesson of *purpose*. Shenzhen is a special economic zone—this is a fundamental and irrefutable fact. But Shenzhen is not *only* a special economic zone. Rather, Shenzhen is a dynamic and complex city, whose qualities cannot be reduced to the apparatus of a single policy, or even a suite of strategies, used to establish an SEZ. One of the most problematic misconceptions about Shenzhen is calling it merely an "illustration" of the effectiveness of SEZ policies. I question the assumption that Shenzhen's success mainly results from SEZ policies. By extension, I do not subscribe to the assumption that the SEZ policy is the most effective instrument to emulate, or to learn from, in the case of Shenzhen. Shenzhen's success is founded in the efforts of local city makers to create not just a "zone," but a real city. While economic zones are invested in quick returns, cities are invested in the future, engaged in building endeavors and institutions whose rewards may not be reaped for many years. The aspirations of Shenzhen's initial leaders for Shenzhen SEZ to become a comprehensive city—in other words, more than an industrial export processing zone—were exemplified by Liang Xiang, Shenzhen's mayor from 1981 to 1985. Liang Xiang saw the value in establishing schools, universities, and technology parks—investments in future generations—alongside the factories and commercial buildings built for rapid economic returns. City makers who look to Shenzhen must understand this distinction in purpose, striving to build dynamic and sustainable cities rather than mere economic zones.

Viewed as a comprehensive city rather than a zone, Shenzhen is truly unique among China's SEZs. Most SEZs are significantly smaller in land area than Shenzhen. In 1980, the Shenzhen SEZ encompassed 327.5 square kilometers mainly south of the Second Line Border (although in 2010, it was redesignated as the two thousand square kilometers comprising the entire city). Of the other SEZs designated in the same period, Zhuhai SEZ was 6.8 square kilometers, Xiamen SEZ was 2.5 square kilometers, and Shantou SEZ was 1.6 square kilometers.[21] These SEZs were already larger than the zone development precedents from around the world prior to China's efforts in 1979. The exaggerated size of the Shenzhen SEZ was often criticized by detractors and became the most significant practical challenge for its early leaders. It is certainly true that a bigger

SEZ is *not* necessarily a better SEZ, and there are examples of failures among zone developments larger than Shenzhen. However, the scale of the Shenzhen SEZ enabled it to be more inclusive of functions, programs, industries, and communities closely associated with the concept of a comprehensive city. Shenzhen experienced difficult years during its fledgling decade, and its success was far from obvious or "instant" during this period. However, the local leadership's decisions to devote substantial proportions of limited municipal resources to schools, parks, and civic programs during these initial years enabled Shenzhen to later become a fully functioning city.

China's modernization was not initiated by the post-1979 reforms, the establishment of the PRC in 1949, or the shift from an empire to a republic in 1912. When Yuan Geng was questioned about his progressive ideas regarding democratic corporate governance of the Shekou Industrial Zone in the 1990s, he downplayed influences from Hong Kong, or the West, and emphasized the impact of historical philosophies and periods of enlightenment within the Chinese civilization. This was not a simple case of nationalism, but rather a recognition of China as a civilization with a long and evolving cultural and political history. This kind of historic and humanistic perspective is often missing from discussions of China's recent urbanization and economic development. Shenzhen may be a "one-generation city," but the success of the past forty years must be considered with a long historical perspective. Any city that attempts to apply its lessons must carefully consider its own cultural history and social communities. The lesson of Shenzhen is not an easy recipe or model for an instant city, but rather a set of guidelines and questions to carry into the future. Moving forward, city makers should seek to learn from the mechanisms of the local and the informal, combining bottom-up responsiveness with more controlled and directed top-down conditions. We must ask ourselves how we can begin to combine conventional ways of planning and space making with other methods that are more flexible and adaptable, and how we can make room for the inevitable local differences, uncertainties, and temporalities that inform the processes of modernization and urbanization.

In the decades and even centuries ahead, Shenzhen will most likely face additional challenges, including disasters both natural and man-made. Given the current accelerated urbanization and population growth, the scales of the future challenges will correspondingly escalate in China and around the world. Globalization is not selective in its progressive benefits and consequences. What can we leave behind to prepare future generations for an ever-globalizing and destabilizing world? Shenzhen holds important lessons for cultural history, community organization, informal development, flexible planning, and sustainable growth. Careless transplantation of urbanization strategies from one locality to another may result in devastating consequences, including the erasure of deep local histories as well as a mismatch between international resources and the needs of local communities. As the majority of the world's population continues to migrate into cities, the lessons of Shenzhen will only take on increasing global importance in the years to come.

I believe that the Shenzhen Experiment has not yet reached its conclusion. The transformations of individual lives, massive changes of natural ecologies, outsized constructions of physical environments, volatile political and institutional fluctuations, and rapid shifting of ethical standards and value systems all await further evolution, implementation, and eventual evaluation. The full impacts of the transformational changes from the 1979 reforms to the current times, especially pertaining to national governance and local community actions, are still being played out in Shenzhen today and elsewhere in the world.

NOTES

INTRODUCTION

1 Kairu Jiang, "Chuntian De Gushi" ("The Story of Spring"), 1993.

2 Yongtao Li, *Dadao 30: Shennan Dadao Shang De Guojia Jiyi* (Thirty years of the boulevard: National memories on Shennan Boulevard), vol. 2 (Shenzhen: Shenzhen Press Group Publishing House, 2010).

3 Juan Du, "Don't Underestimate the Rice Fields," in *Urban Transformation*, ed. Ilka Ruby and Andreas Ruby (Berlin: Ruby Press, 2008).

4 Claude Baissac, "Brief History of SEZs and Overview of Policy Debates," in *Special Economic Zones in Africa: Comparing Performance and Learning from Global Experience*, ed. Thomas Farole (Washington, DC: World Bank, 2011).

5 Michael Engman, Osamu Onoder, and Enrico Pinali, "Export Processing Zones: Past and Future Development," in *OECD Trade Policy Working Paper* (2007); J. P. S. Boyenge, "Ilo Database on Export Processing Zones, Revised," ed. International Labour Organization (Geneva: ILO, 2007).

6 X. Zhou, "North Korea Investment Zone Promoted to Chinese as Next Shenzhen," *Bloomberg*, September 13, 2012.

7 Peter Dannenberg, Yejoo Kim, and Daniel Schiller, "Chinese Special Economic Zones in Africa: A New Species of Globalization?," *African East-Asian Affairs: The China Monitor*, no. 2 (2013); Ruben Gonzalez-Vicente, "The Internationalization of the Chinese State," *Political Geography* 30 (2011).

8 Deborah Brautigam and Xiaoyang Tang, "African Shenzhen: China's Special Economic Zones in Africa," *Journal of Modern African Studies* 49, no. 1 (2011).

9 Thomas Farole, "Special Economic Zones in Africa: Comparing Performance and Learning from Global Experience," Washington, DC: International Bank for Reconstruction and Development, World Bank, xiii.

10 Xiangming Chen and Tomas de Medici, "The 'Instant City' Coming of Age: Production of Spaces in China's Shenzhen Special Economic Zone," *Urban Geography* 31, no. 8 (2010), 1141–1147.

11 Demetri Sevastopulo, "Delta Blues," *Financial Times,* January 23, 2014.

12 Clifford Coonan, "Hong Kong Border Crossing a Growth Gateway," *Irish Times,* August 5, 2014.

13 Shenzhen Statistics Bureau and NBS Survey Office in Shenzhen, eds., *Shenzhen Tongji Nianjian* (Shenzhen statistical yearbook) (Beijing: China Statistics Press, 2000). The official figure for the population of Shenzhen in 1979 was 314,100.

14 Ibid. The official figure for the population of Shenzhen SEZ in 1980 was 94,100.

15 *Shenzhen Jingji Tequ Zongti Guihua Lunpingji* (Commentary on the overall planning theory of Shenzhen's special economic zone) (Shenzhen: Haitian Publishing House, 1987).

16 Neil Fullick, "Here's What People Fear in China's 'Silicon Valley,'" *Huffington Post,* June 13, 2016.

17 Qingzhi Dong and Qiuyue Liang, "Shenzhen Chengzhongcun Nongminfang Huo Zijianfang Chao 35 Wan Dong, Zhan Zhufang Zongliang 49%" (Over 350,000 peasant and self-constructed homes in Shenzhen's urban villages account for 49% of the city's total housing), *National Business Daily,* 2018.

18 Ibid.

19 Yaping Wang, Yanglin Wang, and Jiansheng Wu, "Urbanization and Informal Development in China: Urban Villages in Shenzhen," *International Journal of Urban and Regional Research* 33, no. 4 (2009); Shenjing He et al., "Social Groups and Housing Differentiation in China's Urban Villages: An Institutional Interpretation," *Housing Studies* 25, no. 5 (2010); P. Hao et al., "What Drives the Spatial Development of Urban Villages in China?," *Urban Studies* 50, no. 16 (2013); Dror Kochan, "Placing the Urban Village: A Spatial Perspective on the Development Process of Urban Villages in Contemporary China," *International Journal of Urban and Regional Research* 39, no. 5 (2015); Peilin Li, *Cunluo de Zhongjie: Yangchengcun de Gushu* (The end of the village: The Story of the village of Yangcheng) (Beijing: Commercial Press, 2004); Yuyun Lan, *Dushili de Cunzhuang: Yi Ge "Xin Cunshe Gongtongti" de Shidi Yanjiu* (Village in the city: A field study of the "new village community") (Beijing: SDX Joint Publishing Company, 2005).

20 Mary Ann O'Donnell, Winnie Won Yin Wong, and Jonathan Bach, eds., *Learning from Shenzhen: China's Post-Mao Experiment from Special Zone to Model City* (Chicago: University of Chicago Press, 2017); Linda Vlassenrood and International New Town Institute, eds., *Shenzhen: From Factory of the World to World City* (Rotterdam: Nai010, 2016); Shen Liu, *Shuishuo Shenzhen Shi Xiaoyucun* (Who says Shenzhen is a small fishing village?) (Shenzhen: Shenzhen baoye jituan chubanshe, 2011); Zhaoxu Nan, *Shenzhen Jiyi 1949–2009* (Memory of Shenzhen, 1949–2009) (Shenzhen: Shenzhen Press Group Publishing House, 2009); Chuihua Judy Chung, Jeffrey Inaba, Rem Koolhaas, and Sze Tsung Leong, eds., *Great Leap Forward: Harvard Design School Project on the City* (Cambridge, MA: Harvard Design School, 2001).

1. SONG FOR "THE STORY OF SPRING"

1 *The People's Daily* began as an internal Communist Party newsletter in 1948 and, as the new China's state mouthpiece, eventually became the country's most authoritative newspaper. Xitian Chen, "Dongfang Fenglai Manyan Chun: Deng Xiaoping Tongzhi Zai

Shenzhen Jishi" ("Eastern Wind Brings an Eyeful of Spring": A documentary report of Comrade Deng Xiaoping's tour of Shenzhen), *People's Daily*, March 31, 1992.

2 Bingan Chen, Ge Hu, and Zhaosong Liang, *Shenzhen De Sifenkesi Zhimi* (The mystery of the Shenzhen sphinx) (Shenzhen: Haitian chubanshe, 1991).

3 Ibid.

4 Zhonggong Huizhou Shiwei Dangshi Yanjiushi Ketizu (China's Central Party Huizhou Municipal Committee Party History Research Office, Topical Section), "Shenzhen Tequ Jianli Guochengzhong Huiyang Diqu de Lishi Zuoyong" (The historical impact of Huiyang region during the construction process of SZSEZ), *Shenzhen Shizhi Bangongshi* (Shenzhen Historic Records Office), December 7, 2015.

5 Wang Wei, "Shenzhen Chengshi Guihua Fazhan Jiqi Fanxing de Lishi Yanjiu" (A historical study on the development and paradigm of Shenzhen city planning), master's thesis, Wuhan University of Technology, April 2005.

6 Shenzhen Planning Bureau, "Shenzhen Jingji Tequ Shehui Jingji Fazhan Guihua Dagang" (Shenzhen SEZ socioeconomic development plan outline) (1982); Shenzhen Planning Bureau and China Academy of Urban Planning and Design, "Shenzhen Jingji Tequ Zhongti Guihua" (Shenzhen SEZ master plan, 1986–2000) (1986); Shenzhen Statistics Bureau and NBS Survey Office in Shenzhen, eds., *Shenzhen Tongji Nianjian* (Shenzhen statistical yearbook) (Beijing: China Statistics Press, 2015).

7 Human Rights in China (HRIC), "Not Welcome at the Party: Behind the 'Clean-up' of China's Cities: A Report on Administrative Detention under 'Custody and Repatriation'" (New York: Human Rights in China, 1999).

8 Jason Young, *China's Hukou System: Markets, Migrants and Institutional Change* (Basingstoke, UK: Macmillan, 2013).

9 Jianming Wu, "1995 Nian Shenzhen Renkou Jiegou Ji Bianhua Qushi Zhaiyao" (The population structure and trend of Shenzhen in 1995), *Shenzhen Statistical Yearbook* (1996).

10 Jianfei Li, "Shehui Biange Zhongde Zhongguo Laodong Hetong Lifa" (Chinese labor contract legislation during societal reform), *Jurist*, no. 6 (2009).

11 Kairu Jiang, "Jiang Kairu: Yong Geci Jilu Jubian Shidai De Xintiao" (Kairu Jiang: Record the heartbeat of an era of dramatic change with lyrics), *Shenzhen Evening News*, July 2, 2014.

12 Xiaoli Lu, "Jiang Kairu: Xiaoping Jiuxiang Shi Wode Jiaren" (Kairu Jiang: Xiaoping was like my family), *Shenzhen Evening News*, September 19, 2014.

13 Honglei Liao, Huangyou He, and Qun Li, "Jing, Jie, Shi: Cong Shenzhenxu Dao Dongmen Shangye Qu" (Shenzhen's Old Town), *Architectural Worlds*, no. 10 (2013).

14 Shenzhen Statistics Bureau and NBS Survey Office in Shenzhen, eds., *Shenzhen Tongji Nianjian* (Shenzhen statistical yearbook) (Beijing: China Statistics Press, 2015).

15 Zhongguo Liu, "Jishi Shenzhen Jinji Tequ 25 Nian" (Records on 25 years of SZSEZ) (Shenzhen: Haitian chubanshe, 2006), 5.

16 Kairu Jiang, interview by the author, April 3, 2015.

17 Mengting Liu, "Jiang Kairu: Woshi Caocong Limian 'Zhang' Chulai De Cizuojia" (Kairu Jiang: I am a lyricist who grew up in the fields), *Shenzhen News*, March 4, 2013.

18 Kairu Jiang, interviewed by the author, April 3, 2015.

19 Yaolin Yang, *Shenzhen Jindai Jianshi* (A brief history of modern Shenzhen) (Beijing: Cultural Relic Publishing House, 1997), 52–56.

20 Yongtao Li, "Shennan Dadao: Yitiao Jiedao De Guojia Jiyi" (Shennan Boulevard: A boulevard connected to the national memory), *Jinxiu* (2010).

21 Yuefei Gu, "Chuntian De Gushi Ci Zuozhe Jiemi: Cengyin Tongsu Yin Zhengyi" (The lyricist of 'The Story of Spring' uncovered: Controversial lyrics for a demotic song), *Yangtze Evening News*, June 29, 2011.

22 "*CPC Shenzhen Municipal Committee Organ Newspaper* was the first comprehensive newspaper in China's special economic zone. It was created in Shenzhen on May 24, 1982. Its 1992 'Eastern Wind Brings an Eyeful of Spring' report on Deng's secret trip would help to change governmental and public opinion on China's reforms"; Xifen Gan, ed., *Dictionary of Journalism* (Zhengzhou: Henan People's Publishing House, 1993), 371.

23 Kairu Jiang, "Chuntian De Gushi" (lyrics to "The Story of Spring"), *Shenzhen Special Zone Daily*, March 7, 1993.

24 Kairu Jiang and Xuquan Ye, *Chuntian De Gushi* ("The Story of Spring") (Shanghai: Shanghai Audio and Video Press, 1995).

25 Lei Feng, "Xiaoping Xin Huaxiang Shenqing Ningwang Pengcheng Guaxiang Guangchang Tongshi Huanran Yixin" (New portrait of Xiaoping gazes affectionately at Shenzhen, giving the Square a new look), *Southern Metropolis Daily*, August 16, 2004.

26 Lin Fu, *20 Years of Chinese Pop Music* (Beijing: China Federation of Literary and Art Circles Publishing House, 2003).

27 The live broadcast of the Spring Festival Gala began in 1983. The earliest videotaped TV program of a similar type was in 1956. The CCTV first broadcast a videotaped version of the gala in 1979.

28 "Guinness World Records™ Presents CCTV New Record for Most Watched National Network TV Broadcast," *PRNewswire UK*, April 3, 2012.

29 "Wenhua Zhongguo: Wangri Dege 2007 Ai Meiguo Linken Zhongxin Shangyan" (China's culture: Songs of the past performed at Lincoln Center, 2007), *China Press*, April 8, 2007.

30 Zhuo Lin et al., "Deng Xiaoping Tongzhi De Qinshu Zhi Jiang Zongshuji Bing Dangzhongyang Dexin" (A letter to Chief Secretary Jiang and the Party Central Committee from Comrade Deng Xiaoping's family members), ed. State Council (Beijing: State Council, 1997).

31 "Chengqian Qihou Jiwang Kailai: Relie Zhuhe Dang De Shiwuda Kaimu" (Take over from the past and set a new course for the future: Warm congratulations on the opening of the 15th National Congress of the Communist Party of China), *People's Daily*, September 12, 1997.

32 Xiaofang Zhang, "Zhuxuanlu Gequ Zoujin Xinshidai Sanji" (Notes on the major melody: Entering a new era), *Dangshiwenyuan* (2014).

33 Jun Liu, "Zoujin Xinshidai Zuozhe: Xiezhe Shouge Chuyu Dui Lingluren De Qidai" (The lyricist enters a new era: Song written out of anticipation of a new leader), *Southern Weekly* (2013).

2. THE "SOUTHERN TOURS" THAT CHANGED CHINA

1 Huoxiong Liu, "Yong Shengming Zuo Duzhu Toudu Xianggang Zhendong Zhongyang De Dataogang Fengchao" (Betting life to escape to Hong Kong a great exodus that shook the central government), *History Reference* 2010, no. 13 (2010), 37.

2 Donglian Xiao and Jisheng Yang, "Qinli Jingji Tequ Juece Guocheng" (A personal experience in the process of establishing the special economic zone), *Yanhuangchunqiu*, no. 5 (2015).

3 Xiaoping Deng, "Jiefang Sixiang Shishi Qiushi Tuanjie Yizhi Xiangqiankan" (Emancipate the mind, seek truth from facts, unite, and look forward), in *Deng Xiaoping Wenxuan* (Selected works of Deng Xiaoping), ed. Zhonggong Zhongyang Wenxian Yanjiushi (CCCPC Party Literature Research Office) (Hong Kong: Joint Publishing, 1996 [1978]), 75–90.

4 Tianming Xu, *Chuntian De Gushi: Shenzhen Chuangyeshi* ("The Story of Spring": The start-up history of Shenzhen) (Beijing: China Citic Press, 2008), pt. 1, p. 3.

5 Father of Xi Jinping, China's current president. For the details of Xi Zhongxun's biography, see Xi zhongxun chuan bianweihui (Editorial board of the biography of Xi Zhongxun), *Xi Zhongxun Zhuan* (Biography of Xi Zhongxun) (Beijing: Zhongyang Wenxian chubanshe, 1996).

6 Xiao and Yang, "Qinli Jingji Tequ Juece Guocheng." Later in 1980, as Shenzhen's party secretary, Wu was instrumental in the start-up phase of the planning and financing of Shenzhen's infrastructure.

7 Hong Chen, *Shenzhen Zhongda Juece He Shijian Minjian Guancha* (Civil observations on the major decision making and events in Shenzhen) (Wuhan: Zhangjiang wenyi chubanshe, 2006), 9–23.

8 Di Lu, "Guangdong Jingji Tequ De Tuohuangzhe: Wu Nansheng" (The pioneer of SEZs in Guangdong: Wu Nansheng), no. 1 (2001).

9 Fangqing Cheng, "Zhongguo Huiji Gaige Chuangxin De Shiyanchang: Shenzhen Tequ 30 Nian Huiji Gaige Chuangxin De Changshi" (The experimental field of China's accounting reform) (China Financial Publishing House, 2011); Di Lu, "Guangdong Jingji Tequ De Tuohuangzhe."

10 Ezra F. Vogel, *Deng Xiaoping and the Transformation of China* (Cambridge, MA: Belknap Press of Harvard University Press, 2011), 220, 224.

11 Vogel, *Deng Xiaoping and the Transformation of China*, 219–220.

12 Mu Gu, *Gumu Huiyilu* (Memoirs of Gumu) (Beijing: Zhongyang wenxian chubanshe, 2009).

13 Nansheng Wu, "Guanyu Guangdong Jianli Jingji Tequ Jige Wenti De Huibao Tigang" (Report summary of several problems regarding the establishment of special economic zones in Guangdong) (1979).

14 Ibid.

15 "Shenzhen Shi Chengshi Jianshe Zongti Guihua" (Shenzhen city urban construction overall plan), ed. Shenzhen Urban Planning Bureau (SUPB) (Shenzhen,1980); Huida Gu, ed., *Shenzhen Chengshi Guihua De Huigu Yu Zhanwang* (Review and prospect of urban planning in Shenzhen), collection of essays by the Urban Planning and Design Institute of Shenzhen (Shenzhen: Urban Planning and Design Institute of Shenzhen, 1998).

16 Shenzhen Municipal Government, *Shenzhen Jingji Tequ Shehui Jingji Fazhan Guihua Gangyao* (Shenzhen Special Economic Zone Social and Economic Development Planning), 1982.

17 Archives Bureau of Shenzhen Municipality, "1982 Chronicle."

18 Anthony Gar On Yeh, "Physical Planning," in *Modernization in China: The Case of the Shenzhen Special Economic Zone*, ed. K. Y. Wong and D. K. Y. Chu (Hong Kong: Oxford University Press, 1985), 108–130.

19 John Zacharias and Yuanzhou Tang, "Restructuring and Repositioning Shenzhen, China's New Mega City," *Progress in Planning* 73, no. 2010 (2010).

20 Weixiang Huang and Songlin Ma, eds., *Baoan Xianzhi* (Baoan annals) (Guangzhou: Guangdong renmin chubanshe, 1997).

21 "Chule Wuxing Hongqi, Hai Youmeiyou Shehui Zhuyi" (Other than the five-star red flag, are there no signs of socialism?), *Jingji ribao*, October 23, 1987.

22 Shuo Wang, "Zhongguo Jingji Tequ Chengbai: 1980 Niandai Zhongqi De Bianlun Yu Jueze" (The success or failure of China SEZs: Debates and decisions in the mid-1980s), *Twenty-First Century* 139 (2013).

23 Chongshan Zhu and Rongguang Chen, *Shenzhen Shizhang: Liangxiang* (Mayor of Shenzhen: Liangxiang) / *Liangxiang: Zhuozhu Laoshu Bushi Haomao* (Liangxiang: Catching a rat is not a good cat) (Guangzhou / Hong Kong: Huacheng chubanshe / Gonghe chubanshe, 2007 / 2011).

24 Rong Leng and Zuoling Wang, eds., *Deng Xiaoping Nianpu* (The chronicle of Deng Xiaoping) (Beijing: Zhongyang wenxian chubanshe, 2004), 954.

25 Yunhua He, "1984 Nian Deng Xiaoping Shicha Shenzhen Qianhou" (Before and after Deng Xiaoping's 1984 inspection in Shenzhen), *Yanhuangchunqiu* 2004, no. 3 (2004).

26 Ibid.; Ezra F. Vogel, "Experiments in Guangdong and Fujian, 1979–1984," in *Deng Xiaoping and the Transformation of China* (Cambridge, MA: Belknap Press of Harvard University, 2011).

27 Yunhua He, "1984 Nian Deng Xiaoping Shicha Shenzhen Qianhou (Before and after Deng Xiaoping's 1984 Inspection in Shenzhen)," *Yanhuangchunqiu* 2004, no. 3 (2004).

28 Archives Bureau of Shenzhen Municipality, "1980 Chronicle."

29 Li Li et al., "Cong Shenzhen Nongcun De Bianhua Kan Shehui Zhuyi Zhidu De Youyuexing" (Reading the superiority of socialism from the development of Shenzhen villages), *Jinan daxue xuebao (zhexue shehui kexue ban)* 4 (1981).

30 Ibid.

31 Chongshan Zhu and Rongguang Chen, *Shenzhen Shizhang Liangxiang* (Mayor of Shenzhen: Liangxiang) (Guangzhou: Huacheng chubanshe 2011), 92.

32 "1984 Nian Deng Xiaoping Shicha Shenzhen, Kending 'Shijian Jiushi Jinqian'" (Deng Xiaoping visited Shenzhen in 1984 and agreed that "Time is money"), Takungpao.com, October 23, 2013.

33 Qiao Tu, *Yuangeng Zhuan: Gaige Xianchang* (A biography of Yuangeng: On the frontier of reform, 1978–1984) (Beijing: China Writers Publishing House, 2008).

34 Yunhua He, "1984 Nian Deng Xiaoping Shicha Shenzhen Qianhou" (Before and after Deng Xiaoping's 1984 inspection in Shenzhen), *Yanhuangchunqiu*, no. 3 (2004).

35 Zhonggong Zhongyang Wenxian Yanjiushi (CCCPC Party Literature Research Office), ed. *Deng Xiaoping Sixiang Nianpu 1975–1997* (Chronicle of Deng Xiaoping's thoughts, 1975–1997) (Beijing: Zhongyang wenxian chubanshe 1998), 277.

36 Xiaoping Deng, "Banhao Jingji Tequ Zengjia Duiwai Kaifang Chengshi" (Improve the special economic zones, increase the number of open cities) (1984), in *Deng Xiaoping*

Wenxuan (Selected works of Deng Xiaoping), ed. Zhonggong Zhongyang Wenxian Yanjiushi (CCCPC Party Literature Research Office) (Hong Kong: Joint Publishing, 1996 [1984]).

37 The CPC Central Committee, "Guanyu Jingji Tizhi Gaige De Jueding" (The Central Committee of CPC's decision on economic system reform), ed. CPC Central Committee (Beijing: CPC Central Committee, 1984).

38 Shenzhen Daily and Shenzhen Municipal Archive, "Shenzhen Gaige Kaifang Ziliao" (Information on the Reform and Opening Up policies of Shenzhen).

39 Shenzhen Development Planning Bureau, *Shiji De Kuayue: Shenzhen Shi Lici Wunian Guihua Huibian* (Crossing the century: A collection of five-year plans of Shenzhen) (Shenzhen: Haitian chubanshe, 2002).

40 Chuanfang Li, ed., *Shenzhen Chengshi Guihua* (Shenzhen urban planning and design) (Shenzhen: Haitian chubanshe, 1990), 15.

41 Luxin Huang and Yongqing Xie, *The Plan-Led Urban Form:* A Case Study of Shenzhen, 48th ISOCARP Congress 2012.

42 Shenzhen Statistics Bureau and NBS Survey Office in Shenzhen, eds., *Shenzhen Tongji Nianjian* (Shenzhen statistical yearbook) (Beijing: China Statistics Press, 2016).

43 Li, ed., *Shenzhen Chengshi Guihua*, 15.

44 Shenzhen Statistics Bureau and NBS Survey Office in Shenzhen, eds., *Shenzhen Tongji Nianjian* (Shenzhen statistical yearbook) (Beijing: China Statistics Press, 2016).

45 Rongyuan Zhu, "Tuibian: Shenzhen Fenyuan Bangong Changsuo Bianqian Sumiao" (Metamorphosis: A profile of the changing work places of the Shenzhen Branch), in *Liujiao Xiecui Caupd Shenzhen 1954–1984–2014*, ed. Rongyuan Zhu (Shenzhen: CAUPD Shenzhen, 2014).

46 Dawei Jiang, "Sanshi Nian Qian De Pianduan" (Fragments from thirty years ago), in *Liujiao Xiecui Caupd Shenzhen 1954–1984–2014*, 466–469 (Shenzhen: CAUPD Shenzhen, 2014).

47 Zhu, "Tuibian."

48 Ibid.

49 Translated from *Liujiao Xiecui Caupd Shenzhen 1954–1984–2014*, ed. Rongyuan Zhu (Shenzhen: CAUPD Shenzhen, 2014), 568.

50 Yanqing Zhao, "Shenzhen Jishi (Shenzhen Chronicle)," in *Liujiao Xiecui Caupd Shenzhen 1954–1984–2014*, ed. Rongyuan Zhu (Shenzhen: CAUPD Shenzhen, 2014).

51 Rongyuan Zhu, interview by the author, May 7, 2016, Shenzhen. To cope with the rapid increase, substantial investment was necessary in social, educational, and other urban services. In fact, the new infrastructure constructed since that time was designed to accommodate a population of 1.5 million, and the transportation system to serve a population of two million.

52 Wenhong Chen, "Shenzhen De Wenti Zaina Li?" (Where are the problems of Shenzhen?), *Wide Angle* 149 (1985); Wang, "Zhongguo Jingji Tequ Chengbai."

53 Shenzhen Statistics Bureau and NBS Survey Office in Shenzhen, *Shenzhen Tongji Nianjian* (Shenzhen statistical yearbook).

54 *Shekou Tongxun* (Shekou news), April 25, 1985; Xiwu Zhou, "Shenzhen Jingji Tequ Shikao Guojia Shuxue Huoming Dema" (Did the Shenzhen SEZ survive its early years from the nation's "blood transfusion"?), *Zhonggong dangshi ziliao* (Information on the history of the Communist Party) 3 (2007).

55 Renzhong Ding, "Lun Woguo Duiwai Kaifang De Quanmianxing" (A discussion on the all-roundedness of China's Opening Up Reform), *Finance and Economics* 1996, no. 1 (1996).

56 Ibid.

57 Yongqiang Zhang, "Chengshi Kongjian Fazhan Zizuzhi Yanjiu" (Research on self-organization of urban space development: A case study of Shenzhen) (Southeast University, 2003), 98.

58 Party chairman, 1981–1982; party general secretary, 1982–1987.

59 Vogel, "The Tiananmen Tragedy, May 17–June 14, 1989."

60 Chen Nan, "Deng Xiaoping Nanxun De Bada Neimu," *Wenshibolan* 2012, no. 4 (2012); Luoli Li, "Qinli Deng Xiaoping Nanxun" (A personal experience in Deng Xiaoping's South Tour), *Yanhuangchunqiu* 2011, no. 2 (2011).

61 Xiaoping Deng, "Zai Wuchang Shenzhen Zhuhai Shanghai Dengdi De Tanhua Yaodian" (Summary of speeches given in Wuchang Shenzhen Zhuhai Shanghai), in *Deng Xiaoping Wenxuan* (Selected works of Deng Xiaoping), ed. Zhonggong Zhongyang Wenxian Yanjiushi (CCCPC Party Literature Research Office) (Hong Kong: Joint Publishing, 1996 [1992]), 483–497.

62 "Kou'an" (Checkpoint), *Shenzhen Shi Shizhi Bangongshi* (Shenzhen Office of Records of History), 2017.

63 Liangfei Chen, "Shenzhen Xin Shiming: Shouge Tequ Ruhe Zai 'Ganchuang Gangan Yixie'" (Shenzhen's new mission: How can the first SEZ in China "act with courage and determination"), *Dongfang Zaobao* (Oriental morning post), January 18, 2012.

64 Yanqin Zhan, "Li Guangyao De Shenzhen Tequ Guan" (Lee Kuan Yew's view on Shenzhen special economic zone), *Hongguangjiao* 2015, no. 6 (2015).

65 Chao Huang, "Deng Lin Jiemi Fuqin Deng Xiaoping Nanxun Huaxu" (Deng Lin revealed her father Deng Xiaoping's highlights during the South Tour), *South Daily*, January 18, 2012.

66 Xitian Chen, "Dongfang Fenglai Manyan Chun: Deng Xiaoping Tongzhi Zai Shenzhen Jishi" ("Eastern Wind Brings an Eyeful of Spring": A documentary report of Comrade Deng Xiaoping's tour of Shenzhen), *Shenzhen Special Zone Daily*, March 26, 1992.

67 Ibid.

68 Chris Yeung, "Deng in Surprise Shenzhen Visit," *South China Morning Post*, January 22, 1992.

69 "Deng's Visit Symbolic of Southern Success," *South China Morning Post*, January 25, 1992.

70 James L. Tyson, "Deng Tour Sends Mixed Signals on Reform," *Christian Science Monitor*, February 3, 1992.

71 "China's Deng Appears on TV for 1st Time in Year," *The Gazette*, February 4, 1992.

72 Ezra F. Vogel, *Deng Xiaoping and the Transformation of China* (Cambridge, MA: Belknap Press of Harvard University Press, 2011).

73 "Asian-Pacific Brief: China: Jiang Affirms Reforms," *Asian Wall Street Journal*, February 5, 1992.

74 Ezra F. Vogel, *Deng Xiaoping and the Transformation of China* (Cambridge, MA: Belknap Press of Harvard University Press, 2011).

75 Ibid.

76 "Xiaoping Tongzhi Zai Xianke Ren Zhongjian" (Comrade Xiaoping with the people of Sast), *South Daily*, March 22, 1992; Jigang Zhou and Jun Chen, "Nanfang Tanhua Zhibi Jizhe Chen Xitian Jiangshu: 1992 Nian: Xiaoping Shenzhen Jishi" (The reporter of Southern Talks Chen Xitian narrates the year of 1992: A chronicle of Xiaoping in Shenzhen), *Chongqing Daily*, February 21, 2012.

77 Chen, "Dongfang Fenglai Manyan Chun."

78 Deng, "Zai Wuchang Shenzhen Zhuhai Shanghai Dengdi De Tanhua Yaodian" (Summary of speeches given in Wuchang Shenzhen Zhuhai Shanghai) (1992).

79 "Deng Nan Deng Rong Jiemei Huiyi Pei Deng Xiaoping Nanxun De Qingkuang" (Deng sisters recalled their experience accompanying Deng Xiaoping on the South Tour), *Huaxi dushi bao*, February 22, 2007.

80 "Yanhai Chengshi Kaifang Dashiji" (A memorabilia of the Opening Up of coastal cities).

81 Ibid.

82 Vogel, "Deng's Finale: The Southern Journey, 1992."

83 "Accelerating Economic Growth and Opening, 1982–1989."

84 Ibid.

3. GATEWAY CITY TO THE SOUTH CHINA SEA

1 Honglei Liao, "Shenzhen Mazu 'Cisha' Yu Chiwan" (Shenzhen Mazu "Cisha" ceremony and Chiwan), *Huaxia Jingwei Wang*. More recent studies argued that in 1986 and 1987 there were tens of thousands of visitors to the temple around the days of Tianhou's birth. Shan Jiang and Si Shen, "Shilun Mazu Shenhua Yu Gang Ao Shen Diqu De Yingxiang" (Impacts of the legends of Mazu on the regions of Hong Kong, Macao, and Shenzhen), in *Mazu Yanjiu Lunwenji* (Collected papers on researches on Mazu), ed. Tianshun Zhu (Xiamen: Lujiang chubanshe, 1989).

2 See Helen Siu and David Faure, eds., *Down to Earth: The Territorial Bond in South China* (Standford, CA: Stanford University Press, 1995). Several chapters discuss the relationship between deity worship in South China and the formation of local community memberships.

3 Huacao Zhong, *Taiwan Diqu Shenming De Youlai* (Origins of deities in the Taiwan region) (Taichung: Taiwan sheng wenxian weiyuanhui, 1979).

4 Yiping Zhang, *Shen Gang Ao De Tianhou Gong* (Tianhou temples in Shenzhen, Hong Kong, and Macau) (Hong Kong: Haifeng chubanshe, 1998).

5 Yan Lu, "Chiwan Tianhou Gumiao" (The ancient Tianhou temple in Chiwan), in *Xianggang Zhanggu* (Anecdotes of Hong Kong) (Hong Kong: Wide Angle Publication, 1981).

6 Zhang, *Shen Gang Ao De Tianhou Gong*, 68; Zhiwei Liu, "'Guanfang' Miaoyu De Yiyi Zhuanbian: Chiwan Tianhoumiao Beiming Jiexi" (Changes of the meanings of "official" temples: A study on the inscriptions in Chiwan Tianhoumio) in *Beiming Yanjiu* (Inscription studies), ed. Zhenman Zheng (2014).

7 Qida Liu, "Chiwan Bishui Zaifengyun" (Chiwan: A site that witnesses history), *Shenzhen Special Zone Daily*, December 16, 2015.

8 Junji Mao and Wenguang Chen, "Chiwan Mazu Miao Yu Haishang Sichou Zhilu Tanxi" (A study on the Mazu Temple in Chiwan and the Maritime Silkroad), *Practice and Theory of SEZs* 5 (2016).

9 Beizhen Qin, *Renjian Tiangong: Feifan Zaoyi De Mazu Miaoyu* (Paradise on earth: Mazu temples of exceptional crafts) (Xinbei: Songbo chubanshe, 2016).

10 Haiguan Sun, "Chongxiu Chiwan Tianhoumiao Yin" (Introduction to the refurbishment of Chiwan Tianhou temple), in *Xin'an Xianzhi: Jiaqing* (Annals of Xin'an County: Jiaqing version), ed. Maoguan Shu and Chongxi Wang (Beijing: Qing Government, 1819).

11 Yibing Zhang, *Shenzhen Gudai Jianshi* (A brief ancient history of Shenzhen), ed. Shenzhen Museum (Beijing: Wenwu chubanshe, 1997).

12 Shenzhen Museum, "The Predecessor's Footmark," in *Shenzhen Museum Permanent Exhibition: Ancient Shenzhen*, ed. Daxian Rong (Beijing: Wenwu chubanshe, 2010).

13 Mu Shan, "Nantou Gucheng Nanhai Zhi Bin De Gulao Chengshi" (Nantou Fort: An ancient city on the coast of Nanhai), *Urban and Rural Development*, no. 12 (2006). A team of three hundred people was formed by Shenzhen Cultural Heritage Office, Shenzhen Municipal Museum, and Nantou Ancient City Management Office.

14 Ibid.

15 Ling Huang, "Cong Lici Xiuzhi Kan Shenzhen Wenmingshi" (Civilization history of Shenzhen through the editing of several versions of annuals), Shenzhen Chinese people's Political Consultative Conference.

16 Weixiang Huang and Songlin Ma, *Baoan Xianzhi* (Baoan annals) (Guangzhou: Guangdong renmin chubanshe, 1997), 56.

17 Scott Wilson (Hong Kong) Ltd., Ecosystems Ltd., and Dredging Research Ltd., "Tai O Sheltered Boat Anchorage: Environmental Impact Assessment," ed. Civil Engineering Department (Hong Kong, 2000).

18 Zijin Wang, "Ocean Exploration and Marine Development of Emperor Wu of Han," *Social Sciences in Chinese Higher Education Institutions*, no. 7 (2013).

19 Zhang, *Shenzhen Gudai Jianshi.*

20 Ibid.

21 Kuan Huan, *Yan Tie Lun* (Discourses on salt and iron) (81–89 BCE); Liqi Wang, *Yantielun Jiaozhu* (Yantielun with notes) (Beijing: Zhonghua Shuju, 1992).

22 Mu Shan, "Nantou Gucheng Nanhai Zhi Bin De Gulao Chengshi."

23 Daxian Rong, "Gudai Shenzhen De Yanye Shengchan" (Salt production in ancient Shenzhen), Shenzhen Wenshi (Literature and history of Shenzhen), no. 4 (2013).

24 State Council, "Guowuyuan Guanyu Yinfa Yanye Tizhi Gaige Fangan De Tongzhi" (A notice of salt industry reform by the State Council) (Beijing, 2016); Louise Moon, "China Eases State Monopoly on Salt Market Overhauling 2,000-Year-Old System," *The Telegraph*, January 3, 2017.

25 Shenzhen Museum, "Ancient Immigration," in *Shenzhen Museum Permanent Exhibition: Ancient Shenzhen*, ed. Daxian Rong (Beijing: Wenwu chubanshe, 2010).

26 Ibid.

27 Guojian Xiao, *Shenzhen Diqu Zhi Jiazu Fazhan* (Clans development in the region of Shenzhen) (Hong Kong: Xianzhao shushi, 1992).

28 Rong, "Gudai Shenzhen De Yanye Shengchan."

29 Yibing Zhang, "Disizhang Tang Wudai Shiqi De Shenzhen Diqu" (Chapter 4: Shenzhen areas in Tang and the Five Dynasties Era), in *Shenzhen Gudai Jianshi* (A brief ancient history of Shenzhen), ed. Shenzhen Museum (Beijing: Wenwu chubanshe, 1997).

30 Yibing Zhang, "Diwuzhang Song Yuan Shiqi De Shenzhen Diqu" (Chapter 5: Shenzhen areas in Song and Yuan Era), in *Shenzhen Gudai Jianshi* (A brief ancient history of Shenzhen), ed. Shenzhen Museum (Beijing: Wenwu chubanshe, 1997).

31 Ibid.

32 Shenzhen Museum, "Ancient Immigration."

33 A poem entitled "Across the Lingding Ocean" (Guo Lingdingyang), written by Wen Tianxiang (Southern Song Dynasty), translated from *Shenzhen Jiuzhi Sanzhong* (Three ancient annuals of Shenzhen) (Shenzhen: Haitian chubanshe, 2006), 522.

34 Guojian Xiao, *Shenzhen Diqu Zhi Jiazu Fazhan* (Families development in the area of Shenzhen) (Hong Kong: Xiaozhao Shushi, 1992).

35 Shenzhen Museum, "Ancient Immigration"; Xiao, *Shenzhen Diqu Zhi Jiazu Fazhan.*

36 Zhang, *Shenzhen Gudai Jianshi.*

37 Jungpang Lo, "The Emergence of China as a Sea Power During the Late Sung and Early Yuan Periods," *Far East Quarterly* 14, no. 4 (1955); Joseph Needham, *Science and Civilization in China* (Macau: University of East Asia, 1986).

38 Chongguan Kwa, "The Maritime Silk Road: History of an Idea" (Singapore: Nalanda-Sriwijaya Centre, 2016).

39 Zhang, *Shenzhen Gudai Jianshi.*

40 Xianyong Zeng, *Songdai Chenchuan "Nanhai Yihao"* (The sunken ship from Song Dynasty: Nanhai no. 1) (Guangzhou: Guangdong renmin chubanshe, 2013).

41 Xueyuan Cai, "Chongxiu Chiwan Tianhoumiao Ji" (A record of the refurbishment of Chiwan Tianhou Temple), in *Xin'an Xianzhi: Jiaqing* (Annals of Xin'an County: Jiaqing Version), ed. Maoguan Shu and Chongxi Wang (Beijing: Qing Government, 1819).

42 Edward L. Dreyer, "Zheng He's Early Life and His Patron, Emperor Yongle," in *Zheng He: China and the Oceans in the Early Ming Dynasty, 1405–1433,* ed. Peter N. Stearns (New York: Pearson / Longman, 2007).

43 Huan Ma, *Ying-yai Sheng-lan: The Overall Survey of the Ocean's Shores* (Cambridge, MA: Cambridge University Press, 1970 [1433]).

44 Tansen Sen, "The Impact of Zheng He's Expeditions on Indian Ocean Interactions," *Bulletin of the School of Oriental and African Studies, University of London* 79, no. 3 (2016).

45 Yuanzhi Kong, "Dui Dongnanya Zhenghe Miao De Shidi Kaocha Yu Sikao" (Thoughts and field works on Zhenghe temples in Southeast Asia), in *"Mulin youhao" Zhenghe xueshu yantaohui* (Nanjing: Zhenghe yanjiu hui in Jiangsu Province, 2002).

46 Xiao, *Shenzhen Diqu Zhi Jiazu Fazhan.* During the Yuan Dynasty (1280–1368 CE), migrant clans continued to move into Shenzhen: for example, the Huang Clan moved from Fujian to Nantou; Liao from Jiangxi to Futian; and Zheng from Guangdong Nanxiong to Nantou, Xixiang.

During the Ming Dynasty (1368–1644 CE), strong economic development in Shenzhen attracted a large number of immigrants to the region: the Lin Clan moved from Fujian to Nantou; Yuan from Jiangxi to Luohu; Zhang from Fujian to Huangbeiling, Hubei, and Nantou; and Su from Fujian to Nantou and Baishi.

47 Yuan Ruan, ed., *Daoguang Guangdong Tongzhi* (Guangdong annuals: Daoguang), vol. 24 Haifang (Coastal defense) (Nanjing: Fenghuang chubanshe, 2010 [1822]).
48 "Shenzhen Lishi Zhi Gen Nantou Gucheng" (The root of Shenzhen history: The Nantou ancient walled city), *Forward Position in Economics* 12 (2005).
49 Zhang, "Diliuzhang Ming Dai De Shenzhen Diqu Ji Xin'an Xian De Sheli" (Chapter 6: Shenzhen areas in the Ming Dynasty and the establishment of Xin'an County), 138–148.
50 Ibid.
51 Zhongxiong Wang, "Shenzhen Nantou Gucheng" (The Shenzhen Nantou ancient city), *Lingnan Culture and History* (1994).
52 Xuefei Ren, *Urban China* (Cambridge: Polity, 2013), 17–19.
53 Quanmin Peng, "Woguo Zuizao Xiang Xifang 'Folangji' Xuexi Deren: Wang Hong Chuan Lue Kao" (The person who learnt Folangji from the West: A brief biography of Wang Hong), *Southeast Culture* 9, no. 137 (2000).
54 Tome Pires, *The Suma Oriental of Tome Pires: An Account of the East, from the Red Sea to China* (London: Hakluyt Society, 1944).
55 Zhang, "Diliuzhang Ming Dai De Shenzhen Diqu Ji Xin'an Xian De Sheli" (Chapter 6: Shenzhen areas in the Ming Dynasty and the establishment of Xin'an County).
56 Shenzhen Museum, "An Important Strategic Town on Coastal Defense."
57 Zhang, "Diliuzhang Ming Dai De Shenzhen Diqu Ji Xin'an Xian De Sheli" (Chapter 6: Shenzhen areas in the Ming Dynasty and the establishment of Xin'an County), 162.
58 Wang, "Shenzhen Nantou Gucheng."
59 Huijun Liu, "Qingchao Jinhailing Luelun" (A brief discussion on the forbiddance of the sea in the Qing Dynasty), *Guangming Daily*, June 23, 2009.
60 Ibid.
61 Ibid.
62 Zhang, "Diqizhang Qing Dai De Xin'an Xian" (Chapter 7: Xin'an County in the Ming Dynasty), 168–204.
63 Weibin Wang, "Li Kecheng Yu Xin'an Bajing" (Li Kecheng and the eight scenes of Xin'an), in *Shenzhen Zhanggu* (Shenzhen anecdotes) (Shenzhen: Haitian Publishing House, 2013), 100.
64 "Fuqian" (Forbiddance of the sea and the return of population), in *Xin'an Xianzhi: Kangxi* (Annals of Xin'an: Kangxi version), ed. Wenmo Jin (Beijing: Qing Government, 1688).
65 "Hukou" (Registration), in *Xin'an Xianzhi: Kangxi* (Annals of Xin'an County: Kangxi version), ed. Wenmo Jin (Beijing: Qing Government, 1688).
66 Ibid.
67 Honglei Liao and Quanmin Peng, "Li Kecheng: Zhanjie Fugeng Chengji Feiran Zhi Xin'an Xianling" (Li Kecheng: The Xin'an County magistrate who made great achievement of re-cultivation), *Shenzhen Archives Bureau*, 2014.
68 "Fuqian" (Forbiddance of the sea and the return of population), in *Xin'an Xianzhi: Kangxi* (Annals of Xin'an County: Kangxi version), ed. Wenmo Jin (Beijing: Qing Government, 1688).
69 Kecheng Li, "Bajing Shi" (Poems on the eight landscapes), in *Xin'an Xianzhi: Kangxi* (Annals of Xin'an County: Kangxi version), ed. Wenmo Jin (Beijing: Qing Government, 1688).
70 Ibid.

71 Yibing Zhang, ed., *Shenzhen Jiuzhi Sanzhong* (Three ancient annuals of Shenzhen) (Shenzhen: Haitian chubanshe, 2006). For Shenzhen (Dongguan, Bao'an, Xin'an), a major source of historical references in this text and others today is the collection of the *Three Old Records of Shenzhen,* edited and annotated by Zhang Yibing. Zhang also gave detailed accounts of sixteen historical Xianzhi titles by various authors at various times, with their current condition and archive locations. Unfortunately, most of such valuable records were lost or became incomplete over the span of time. Zhang's collection contains the only remaining first three out of twelve chapters of Dongguan Xian'zhi (1457–1464), Xin'an Xianzhi (1688), and Xin'an Xianzhi (1818), which consolidated the original and edited manuscripts by scholars from Feng'gang Academy.

72 "Zhixian Likecheng Tiaoyi Xingge Shiyi Batiao" (Eight notes on revitalization). Chap. Yiwen Zhi (Art and Culture Section), in *Xin'an Xianzhi: Kangxi* (Chronicle of Xin'an County: Kangxi version), ed. Wenmo Jin (Beijing: Qing Government, 1688).

73 "Tutian" (Agriculture), in *Xin'an Xianzhi: Kanagxi* (Chronicle of Xin'an County: Kangxi version), ed. Wenmo Jin (Beijing: Qing Government, 1688).

74 Xiao, *Shenzhen Diqu Zhi Jiazu Fazhan.*

75 Shenzhen Museum, "Ancient Immigration," in *Shenzhen Museum Permanent Exhibition: Ancient Shenzhen,* edited by Daxian Rong, 139–173, Beijing: Wenwu chubanshe, 2010.

76 Wang, "Shenzhen Nantou Gucheng."

77 Maoguan Shu and Chongxi Wang, eds., *Xin'an Xianzhi: Jiaqing* (Annals of Xin'an County: Jiaqing version) (Beijing: Qing Government, 1819).

78 Deshao Lai, "Shenzhen Shi Wenwu Baohu Danwei Gaishu" (An overview of heritage protection units in Shenzhen), in *Lingnan Kaogu Yanjiu (8)* (Archaeological research in Lingnan: Eight), ed. Zhenhong Zhang and Licheng Qiu (Hong Kong: China Review Academic Publishers Limited, 2009).

79 Li Lu and Jie Cui, "Bainian Laoxiao Nantou Zhongxue Tanyuan" (Origins of the hundred-year-old Nantou Secondary School), *Nanfang Daily,* January 13, 2011; Xianjun Xiong, "Mingqing Shiqi Xin'an Xian De Shuyuan Lunlue" (Schools in Xin'an County during the Ming and Qing Dynasties), *Journal of Shenzhen Polytechnic* 9, no. 2 (2010); Caimei Li, "Ming Qing Guangdong Xin'an Xian Chengshi Dili Ruogan Wenti Yanjiu" (Some issues on the urban geography of Xin'an County in Guangdong during Ming and Qing Dynasties) (Jinan University, 2011).

80 Shu and Wang, eds., *Xin'an Xianzhi: Jiaqing.*

81 Yibing Zhang, "Chutu Wenwu Cheng Rikou Qinzhan Shenzhen Tiezheng" (Excavated relics proved history of Japanese Occupation), *Daily Sunshine,* August 8, 2015.

82 Qilong Xia and Yongliang Tan, eds., *Xianggang Tianzhujiao Xiuhui Ji Chuanjiaohui Lishi* (History of the Catholic Church and missionary in Hong Kong) (Hong Kong: Centre for Catholic Studies, Chinese University of Hong Kong, 2011).

83 Lu and Cui, "Bainian Laoxiao Nantou Zhongxue Tanyuan."

84 Wei Qi and Bing Chen, "Rizhan Qijian Shenzhen Pingmin Shangwang 2.5 Wan Ren" (Shenzhen lost 25,000 lives during Japanese Occupation) *Shenzhen Special Zone Daily* 2014.

85 Ibid.

86 Ibid.

87 Lin Ge, "Shenzhen Nantou Gucheng Tianzhujiao Yuyingtang Tanjiu" (Investigation of Catholic Foundings' School in Nantou District, Shenzhen), in *2014 nian Zhongguo jianzhu shixuehui nianhui ji xueshu yantaohui* (The 2014 China Architectural History Association Annual Conference and Academic Seminar) (Fuzhou, 2014).

88 Shenzhen Museum, "Administrative Division and Population," in *Shenzhen Museum Permanent Exhibition: Modern Shenzhen*, ed. Huiyao Cai (Beijing: Wenwu chubanshe, 2010).

89 Huang and Ma, eds., *Baoan Xianzhi* (Baoan annals), 55–81.

90 Jie Cui, "Nantou Gucheng De Baohu Yu Fuxing" (Protection and revitalization of the Nantou ancient walled city), *Nanfang Daily*, May 14, 2009.

91 CAUPD (SZ), "Shenzhen Shi Xin'an Gucheng Baohu Guihua Yu Chengshi Sheji" (Planning and urban design for the protection of the Xin'an ancient walled city in Shenzhen), ed. Shenzhen Lands and Resources Commission (Shenzhen, 2001).

92 Hongjin Wan, "Gujing Jiangshu Nantou Lishi" (Ancient well told the history of Nantou), *Shenzhen Shengbu*, March 20, 2004.

93 Zhiwei Ye, "Huang Jinfa: He Shekou Jieyuan 74 Nian Qinli Shekou Cangsang Jubian" (Huang Jinfa: 74 years of a relationship with Shekou; a personal experience of the great changes), *Shenzhen Special Zone Daily*, October 13, 2010.

94 Ibid.

95 Shenzhen shi Chengpin dichan youxian gongsi, "Xian You Shuiwan Houyou Shekou: Jiemi Gaige Kaifang Diyicun" (Shuiwan came before Shekou: Revealing the secrets of the first village of the Reform and Opening Up), http://blog.sina.com.cn/s/blog_12b8577ec0101jsi2.html.

96 Geng Yuan, "Guanyu Chongfen Liyong Xianggang Zhaoshangju Wenti De Qingshi" (Request to maximize the use of the Hong Kong Merchants Group), ed. Ministry of Transport (Beijing, 1978).

97 Qiao Tu, *Yuan Geng Zhuan: Gaige Xianchang* (A biography of Yuan Geng: On the frontier of reform, 1978–1984) (Beijing: China Writers Publishing House, 2008).

98 Dianqing Wu, "Yefei Yu 'Shekou Moshi'" (Yefei and the "Shekou Mode"), *General Review of the Communist Party of China*, no. 2 (2013).

99 Zhongguo Liu, ed., *Jishi Shenzhen Jinjitequ 25 Nian* (Shenzhen: Haitian chubanshe, 2006); Di Lu, "Guangdong Jingji Tequ De Tuohuangzhe: Wu Nansheng" (The pioneer of SEZs in Guangdong: Wu Nansheng), *Hongguangjiao*, no. 5 (2000).

100 Tu, *Yuan Geng Zhuan: Gaige Xianchang*, 246.

101 Ibid., 246.

102 Kezhen Wang, "30 Nianqian Xiang Dou Bugan Xiang Deshi (The Unthinkable 30 Years Ago)," *Shenzhen Special Zone Daily*, 2010.

103 Ibid.

104 Said Amir Arjomand, *Turban for the Crown: The Islamic Revolution in Iran* (New York: Oxford University Press, 1988).

105 Tu, *Yuan Geng Zhuan: Gaige Xianchang*, 240.

106 Ibid., 240–242.

107 Ibid., 244.

108 "Nanshan 'Cisha' Ji Mazu Yidian Chuancheng 600 Nian Gufeng Minsu" (Nanshan Mazu worshipping ceremony: Inheriting a 600-year-old tradition), *Shekou Xiaoxi Bao,* May 31, 2016.

109 Tu, *Yuan Geng Zhuan: Gaige Xianchang,* 238–280.

110 Ibid., 252.

111 Mary Ann O'Donnell described Liang Xiang, Yuan Geng, and Luo Zhenqi as the three key leaders of the SEZ's early development; Mary Ann O'Donnell, *Learning from Shenzhen: China's Post-Mao Experiment from Special Zone to Model City,* ed. Mary Ann O'Donnell, Winnie Won Yin Wong, and Jonathan Bach (Chicago: University of Chicago Press, 2017).

112 Yujin Ke, "Nanhai Chiwan Shiyou Gongying Jidi Guihua" (Planning of the petroleum base in Chiwan, South China Sea), *Achitectural Journal,* no. 7 (1985).

113 Yi Huang, Xiong Chen, and Qiming Du, "Zhongwai Hezi Jiangang De Chenggong Tansuo—Shenzhen Chiwangang Wunian De Shijian" (A successful exploration on the China-foreign joint venture in port development; 5 years of practice in Chiwan Port), *South China Economy,* no. 4 (1987).

114 "Shenzhengang" (Shenzhen ports), *Shippers Today* 26, no. 2 (2003).

115 Shenzhen Statistics Bureau and NBS Survey Office in Shenzhen, eds., *Shenzhen Tongji Nianjian* (Shenzhen statistical yearbook) (Beijing: China Statistics Press, 2015).

116 Wang, "Shenzhen Nantou Gucheng."

117 Xiangyang Zhuang, "Shekou Tongxunbao: Shekou Gaige De Jiluzhe Ji Canyuzhe" (Shekou news: A recorder and participant in the Shekou reform), *Youth Journalist,* no. 32 (2016); Guang Jun, "Yifeng Laixin De 'Xinwen Chongjibo'" (A "shockwave" sent by an incoming letter) *Xinwen Je,* no. 4 (1986).

118 Zhuang, "Shekou Tongxunbao."

119 Geng Yuan, "Women Suo Zhouguo De Lu" (The roads we walked), in *Yuangeng Chuan: Gaige Xianchang* (A biography of Yuangeng: On the frontier of reform, 1978–1984), ed. Tu Qiao (Beijing: China Writers Publishing House, 1984).

4. OYSTERS OF THE PEARL RIVER DELTA

1 Guihong Deng and Shaoxiong Liu, eds., *Qiannian Chuanqi Shajing Hao* (A thousand years of legends of the Shajing oyster) (Shenzhen: Shajing jiedao xuanchuan wenhuaban, 2006), 83–87.

2 Ibid., 5.

3 Jingyi Chen and Songlin Wei, "Tan Haokewu De Cunliu Xianzhuang Yu Baohu" (Discussion on the current situation of the oyster-shell house and its protections), *Shanxi Architecture* 39, no. 29 (2013); Li Wen, "Ni Tingshuoguo Haozhai 'Ma?'" *Environment and Life* 2011, no. 5 (2011).

4 Susan D. Morris, "Tabby," *New Georgia Encyclopedia* (2014).

5 *Buyong Jiangshi Zupu* (A genealogy of Jiang's Clan in Buyong) (Shenzhen, 1884).

6 Erping Liang and Yuxuan Yang, "Shajing Haoke Wu, Qiannian Haoxiang Chuanqi" (Oyster house in Shajing: A thousand years of legends of the home of oysters), *Shenzhen Evening,* January 25, 2013.

7 Dajun Qu, *Guangdong Xinyu* (New writings on Guangdong) (Beijing: Zhonghua Shuju, 1985).

8 Shenzhen Museum, *Gudai Shenzhen* (Ancient Shenzhen) (Shenzhen: Shenzhen Museum, 2009).

9 For more on Shenzhen Market Town, see Chapter 6.

10 Weixiang Huang and Songlin Ma, eds., *Baoan Xianzhi* (Baoan annals) (Guangzhou: Guangdong renmin chubanshe, 1997).

11 Jingying Yang et al., "Changjiang Sanjiaozhou Yu Zhujiang Sanjiaozhou Jingji Fazhan De Bijiao" (An economic development comparison between the Yangtze and Pearl River Deltas), *China National Conditions and Strength* 2004, no. 4 (2004).

12 Project 2022, "Hong Kong and the Pearl River Delta: Expanding Horizons" (Hong Kong: Li and Fung Group, 2001).

13 Jie Chen, "Zhujiang Liuyu Zhu Shuixi De Xingcheng Yu Yanbian Jianshu" (A brief summary of the formation and transformation of the water systems in the Pearl River Delta), *Zhujiang xiandai jianshe* 145, no. 5 (2008).

14 World Bank, "East Asia's Changing Urban Landscape: Measuring a Decade of Spatial Growth," in *Urban Development Series* (Washington, DC: World Bank, 2015).

15 Xun Liu and Xun Lu, *Lingbiao Luyi* (Record of peculiarities in Lingbiao), vol. 3 (Guangzhou: Guangdong ren min chu ban she, 1983).

16 Ibid.

17 Ibid.

18 Supratidal, intertidal, and subtidal zones.

19 Yaochen Mei, *Wanling Xiansheng Ji* (Taipei: Taiwan Commercial Press, 1965).

20 Shudian Wu and Zhu Xia, "Meiyaochen Shi De Shixue Yiyi," *Journal of Chinese Studies*, no. 49 (2009).

21 Yaochen Mei, "Shihao (Eating Oysters)," in *Kangxi Dongguan Xianzhi* (Chronicle of Dongguan County in the Kangxi years), ed. Chaoling Wen and Wenbing Guo (Nanjing: Fenghuang chubanshe, 2014).

22 Huan Liu, Chaoyu Wu, and Yaju Wu, "The Energy Budget under the Influence of Topography in the Zhujiang River Estuary in China," *Acta Oceanologica Sinica* 34, no. 1 (2015); Xiaoming Wu et al., "A Super-Large Tidal Physical Model for the Pearl River Estuary," in *International Conference on Estuaries and Coasts* (Hangzhou, 2003).

23 Zhaoyin Wang, Dongsheng Cheng, and Cheng Liu, "Renlei Huodong Dui Dianxing Sanjiaozhou Yanbian De Yingxiang: Changjiang He Zhujiang Sanjiaozhou" (Impacts of human activities on the transformations of river deltas: Yangtze and Pearl River Deltas), *Journal of Sediment Research*, no. 6 (2005).

24 Pingri Li et al., *Zhujiang Sanjiaozhou Yi Wan Nian Lai Huan Jing Yan Bian* (The environment evolution of the Zhujiang Delta in the last 10,000 years) (Beijing: China Ocean Press, 1991), 78.

25 Shenzhen Museum, ed., *Shenzhen Gudai Jianshi* (A brief history of ancient Shenzhen) (Beijing: Cultural Relics Press, 1997).

26 Kaiyuan Guo and Jian Cheng, *Qiannian Chuanqi Shajing Hao* (A thousand years of legends of the Shajing Oyster) (Beijing: Haichao Press, 2006), 59.

27 Ibid., 21.

28 Ibid., 21.

29 Economic Research Unit of the Bank of Guangdong, "Guangdong Jingji Nianjian 1940" (Economic chronicle of Guangdong, 1940) (1940).

30 Guo and Cheng, *Qiannian Chuanqi Shajing Hao,* 21.

31 Chengming Wu and Zhikai Dong, *Zhonghua Renmin Gongheguo Jingji Shi* (The economic history of the PRC), vol. 1 (Beijing: China Financial and Economic Publishing House, 2001), 46.

32 Yanmei Tao, "Rethinking on the Land Reform Movement in the Beginning of New China," *Agricultural History of China,* no. 1 (2011).

33 Guo and Cheng, *Qiannian Chuanqi Shajing Hao,* 62.

34 "Danganhu" (Independent production household), in *Xinyuci Da Cidian* (Dictionary of new words), ed. Mingan Han (Harbin: Heilongjiang renmin chubanshe, 1991).

35 Guo and Cheng, *Qiannian Chuanqi Shajing Hao,* 62.

36 Jianxin Wu, "Guangdong Haichan Yangzhi De Qiyuan Ji Qi Fazhan" (The origin and development of aquaculture in Guangdong), *Ancient and Modern Agriculture,* no. 1 (1988).

37 Guo and Cheng, *Qiannian Chuanqi Shajing Hao,* 189, 223–225.

38 Ibid., 35, 59.

39 Ibid., 224.

40 Ibid., 70.

41 Ibid., 69.

42 Ibid., 230.

43 Commonly known as "Three Years of Natural Disaster" within China. For more details, see Jisheng Yang, *Tombstone: The Great Chinese Famine, 1958–1962,* trans. Stacy Mosher and Jian Guo (New York: Farrar, Straus and Giroux, 2012). See also Frank Dikotter, *Mao's Great Famine: The History of China's Most Devastating Catastrophe, 1958–62* (London: Bloomsbury, 2010).

44 Huang and Ma, eds. *Baoan Xianzhi* (Baoan annals) 66.

45 Ibid., 66.

46 Felix Wemheuer, "Sites of Horror: Mao's Great Famine," *China Journal* 66 (July 2011); Jasper Becker, *Hungry Ghosts: Mao's Secret Famine* (London: John Murray, 1996); Basil Ashton and Kenneth Hill, "Famine in China, 1958–1961," *Population and Development Review* 10, no. 4 (1984).

47 Shuhan Liu and Yujing Wang, eds., *Dangdai Zhongguo Jingji Zhengce Yu Shijian* (Economic policies and implementation in contemporary China) (Beijing: China Financial and Economic Publishing House, 2014).

48 Bingan Chen, *Dataogang* (The Great Escape to Hong Kong) (Guangzhou: Guangdong renmin chubanshe, 2010).

49 "Guanyu Jing Baoan Xian Toudu Xianggang Wenti De Diaocha Baogao" (An investigation report regarding illegal emigration to Hong Kong via Baoan County), ed. Baoan wai shi ban gong shi (External Affairs Office of Baoan County), January 28, 1959 (Shenzhen).

50 John P. Burns, "Immigration from China and Future of Hong Kong," *Asian Survey* 27, no. 6 (1987); Bingan Chen, *Dataogang* (The Great Escape to Hong Kong) (Hong Kong: Hong Kong Open Page Publishing Company, 2013), 208; Guangdong sheng difang shizhi

bianzuan weiyuanhui, ed., *Guangdong Shengzhi: Gongan Zhi* (Chronicle of Guangdong: Public security) (Guangzhou: Guangdong People's Publishing House, 2001).

51 Houxiong Liu, "Yong Shengming Zuo Duzhu Toudu Xianggang Zhendong Zhongyang De Dataogang" (Betting life to escape to Hong Kong: The great exodus that shook the central government), *History Reference,* no. 13 (2010), 38.

52 "Sent-down youths" refers to the millions of educated urban youths who were sent to live in rural China and be re-educated by peasants during the 1960s and 1970s (see Chapter 6); Kathrin Hille, "China's 'Sent-Down' Youth," *Financial Times,* September 20, 2013.

53 Kitchun Lam and Pakwai Liu, "Earnings Divergence of Immigrants," *Journal of Labor Economics* 20, no. 1 (2002); Burns, "Immigration from China and Future of Hong Kong."

54 Liu, "Yong Shengming Zuo Duzhu Toudu Xianggang Zhendong Zhongyang De Dataogang," 40.

55 Burns, "Immigration from China and Future of Hong Kong," 664.

56 Census and Statistics Department, "1981 Population Census," ed. Census and Statistics Department (Hong Kong: Census and Statistics Department, 1981).

57 Burns, "Immigration from China and Future of Hong Kong," 662.

58 Yi Zhang and Songsong Zhang, eds., *Zhongguo Xiangzhen Qiye Jianshi* (A brief history of township and village enterprise in China) (Beijing: China Agriculture Press, 2001).

59 Hongyun Wei, ed., *Guoshi Jishi Benmo (1949–1999)* (A history of national records), vol. 5 (Shenyang: Liaoning People's Publishing House, 2003), 723–740.

60 Ibid., 723–740.

61 The bottom-up, nonideological local development stories delineated by Kate Xiao Zhou credited the Chinese farmers as a key driving force behind the country's rapid economic and social reform. See Kate Xiao Zhou, *How the Farmers Changed China* (Boulder, CO: Westview Press, 1996).

62 Huang and Ma, eds., *Baoan Xianzhi* (Baoan annals), 163.

63 Barry Naughton, *The Chinese Economy: Transitions and Growth* (Cambridge, MA: MIT Press, 2007), 273–275.

64 CCCPC Party Literature Research Office, ed., *Deng Xiaoping Sixiang Nianpu: (1975–1997)* (A chronicle of Deng Xiaoping's thoughts) (Beijing: Zhongyang wenxian chubanshe, 1998), 641.

65 "Quanguo Nongcun Gongzuo Huiyi Jiyao" (National report on agricultural works), ed. CPC Central Committee (Beijing, 1982).

66 Huang and Ma, eds., *Baoan Xianzhi* (Baoan annals), 163.

67 Ibid., 67; Hang Ma and Yiaowu Wang, *Shenzhen Chengzhongcun De Kongjian Yanbian Yu Zhenghe* (The space evolvement and integration of villages in Shenzhen) (Beijing: Intellectual Property Publishing House, 2011).

68 Weijie Lai, ed., *Shajing Zhenzhi* (Chronology of Shajing Town) (Changchuan: Jilin Photography Publishing House, 2002), 242–257.

69 Ibid., 242–257.

70 Ibid., 247.

71 Qiangen Pan, "Luxian Shihang Gufenzhi Dadao Gongtong Fuyu De Wanfengcun" (Wanfeng Village: A village of shared prosperity and the pioneer of shareholding), in *Zhongguo Tongji Nianjian 1993* (Statistical yearbook of China 1993), ed. Sai Zhang (Beijing: National Bureau of Statistics of the PRC, 1993), 184–185.

72 Xianfa Liu, "Nanhai Moshi De Xingcheng Yanbian Yu Jieju" (The formation, transformation, and result of the Nanhai Model), in *Zhongguo Zhidu Bianqian De Anli Yanjiu (Tudi Juan)* (Case studies of the transformation of Chinese systems [lands]), ed. Shuguang Zhang (Beijing: China Financial and Economic Publishing House, 2011), 68–132.

73 Lai, ed., *Shajing Zhenzhi,* 242–257.

74 Pan, "Luxian Shihang Gufenzhi Dadao Gongtong Fuyu De Wanfengcun," 184–185.

75 Lai, ed., *Shajing Zhenzhi,* 242–257.

76 Xuefei Ren, *Urban China* (Cambridge: Polity, 2013); Giovanni Arrighi, *Adam Smith in Beijing: Lineages of the Twenty-First Century* (London: Verso, 2007), 5–6; Yasheng Huang, *Capitalism with Chinese Characteristics: Entrepreneurship and the State* (New York: Cambridge University Press, 2008), 6–7.

77 For more on the impact of industrialization on the urbanization process in the urban periphery in the region, see George Lin, "Evolving Spatial Form of Urban-Rural Interaction in the Pearl River Delta, China," *Professional Geographer* 53, no. 1 (2001).

78 Guo and Cheng, *Qiannian Chuanqi Shajing Hao,* 36.

79 Ibid., 231.

80 Ibid., 225–227.

81 "Chen Zhaogen: Shajing Haomin Ceng Huoping Quanguo Laomo" (Chen Zhaogen: An oyster farmer who was hailed as a national labor model), *Daily Sunshine,* May 21, 2009.

82 Weifang Wu, "Shidi Shengtai Wenhua De Jingguan Chuangzuo Zhuiqiu" (Landscape creation in a wetland ecology), *Guangdong Yuanlin* (Guangdong Landscape), no. 2 (2002).

83 Qihao Weng, "A Historical Perspective of River Basin Management in the Pearl River Delta of China," *Journal of Environmental Management* 85 (2007).

84 Ibid.

85 Gongfu Zhong, Zengqi Wang, and Houshui Wu, "Jitang Xitong De Shuilu Xianghu Zuoyong (Land-water interactions of the dike-pond system) (Beijing: Science Press, 1993).

86 Wang Zhenyu and Guizhu Chen, "Ziran Tiaojian Jiaocha Diqu Kaifa Shengtai Luyou Tantao: Yi Shenzhen Haishang Tianyuan Shidi Shengtai Luyouqu Weili" (Discussion on eco-tourism development in a bad environmental area. An example: Shenzhen Waterlands Resort), *Marine Environmental Science* 26, no. 1 (2007).

87 Ding Song, "Shenzhen Haishang Tianyuan: Doushi Shengtai Luyou De Tanlu Gongcheng" (Shenzhen Waterlands Resort: A pioneer in urban eco-tourism), *Tequ Jingji (Economics of the SEZ)* 2003, no. 5 (2003).

88 Fei Li et al., "Hongshu Zhongzhi: Yangzhi Ouhe Xitong Muli Shiyouting Hanliang Ji Hongshu Jinghua Xiaoguo" (Petroleum hydrocarbon content in oyster and purifying effect of mangrove in mangrove plantation: Aquaculture coupling systems), *Chinese Journal of Applied and Environmental Biology* 18, no. 3 (2012).

5. TOWERS BY THE HONG KONG BORDER

1 Yang Hungxiang in discussion with the author, August 17, 2015.

2 Kunya Zhang, "Jijian Gongchengbing Jianzheng Shenzhen De Huangwu Yu Fanrong" (The Infrastructure Corps who witness the development of Shenzhen), *Shenzhou* (Divineland), no. 8 (2008).

3 Zeqing Pan, "Zhongguo Renmin Jiefang Jun Lishi Shang Chexiao De Junbingzhong" (The decommission of troop categories in the history of the People's Liberation Army), *Dangshi Bocai* 8 (2007).

4 "Deng Xiaoping Caijun Baiwan" (Deng demilitarized one million soldiers), *Chuan Cheng* no. 2 (2014).

5 Zhang, "Jijian Gongchengbing Jianzheng Shenzhen De Huangwu Yu Fanrong."

6 Chengli Ma, "Zhengdang Tequ De Paitoubing" (To be the vanguard of the SEZ), in *Shenzhen Tuohuang Ren: Jijian Gongchengbing Chuangye Jishi* (The pioneers in Shenzhen: A history of the Infrastructure Corps), ed. Yabing Duan (Beijing: Renmin chubanshe, 2013), 47–57.

7 Hongxiang Yang, *Zhuji: Yang Hongxiang Jijian Gongchengbing Tuohuang Jiyi* (Building, traces: Memoir of pioneering works of Infrastructural Corps by Yang Hongxiang) (Shenzhen: Yuezhong Cultural Transmission, 2013), 91.

8 Zhaoxu Nan, *Shenzhen Jiyi, 1949–2009* (Memory of Shenzhen, 1949–2009) (Shenzhen: Shenzhen Press Group Publishing House, 2009), 295.

9 Mingtian Xu, *Chun Tian De Gu Shi: Shenzhen Chuang Ye Shi (Shang), 1979–2009* ("The Story of Spring": The start-up history of Shenzhen, 1979–2009), vol. 1 (Beijing: China Citic Press, 2008), 21–22.

10 Ibid.

11 Nanling Li, "Dapo Tiefanwan Cuisheng Laodong Hetongzhi" (Breaking the Iron Rice Bowl: Catalyzing the labor contract system), in *Cong Shenzhen Kaishi: Gaige Kaifang 30 Nian* (Beginning from Shenzhen: 30 years of open reform) (Shenzhen: Shenzhen Press Group Publishing House, 2008).

12 Shanquan, "Liu Tianjiu: 'Buyiyang' De Chuanqi Rensheng" (Liu Tianjiu: A legendary life experience), *West Canada Weekly*, February 5, 2012.

13 Li, "Dapo Tiefanwan Cuisheng Laodong Hetongzhi."

14 Ibid.

15 Ibid.

16 Lingun Guan, ed., *Shenzhen Shi Laodong He Shehui Baozhang Zhi* (A history of Shenzhen's labor and social security) (Shenzhen: Haitian chubanshe, 2005).

17 Frederick Engels, "The Housing Question" (Leipzig: Cooperative Publishing Society of Foreign Workers, 1872).

18 Shanquan, "Liu Tianjiu."

19 Xu, *Chun Tian De Gu Shi*, 22–25. For further information on the many influences of Beijing and Hong Kong on the development of the SEZ in its early stages, see Weiwen Huang, "The Tripartite Origins of Shenzhen: Beijing, Hong Kong, and Bao'an," in *Learning from Shenzhen: China's Post-Mao Experiment from Special Zone to Model City*, ed. Mary Ann O'Donnell, Winnie Won Yin Wong, and Jonathan Bach (Chicago: University of Chicago Press, 2017).

20 Fanglu Chen, "Pigan Lidan Kenhuangniu Sihuo Jiqing Jian Tequ: Zhuiji Yuan Shenzhen Shiwei Shuji Shizhang Liangxiang" (A passionate pioneer who built the special zone: Remembering the secretary and mayor of Shenzhen, Liangxiang), in *Nanyue Zhi Zi* (Sons of the Southern Guangdong), ed. Nanyue zhi zi editorial board (Hong Kong: China Socio-economy Publishing, 2004).

21 Ibid.

22 Ma, "Zhengdang Tequ De Paitoubing," 47–57.

23 Ibid.

24 Ibid.

25 Daozheng Du and Gailong Liao, "Shenzhen Tequ Jianshezhong De Liangxiang" (Liangxiang during the development of the SSEZ)," in *Zhongda Juece Muhou* (Behind the scenes of important decision making), ed. Daozheng Du and Gailong Liao (Haikou: Nanhau chubanshe, 1998).

26 Ibid.

27 Kezhen Wang, "'Santian Yiceng Lou' Dansheng Zhuiji" (The birth of "three days per floor"), *Shenzhen Special Zone Daily*, July 15, 2010.

28 Zhimin Hu, "Santian Yiceng Lou De 'Shenzhen Sudu' Shi Zenyang Dansheng De" (How did the "Shenzhen Speed" of 3 days per floor begin?), *Shenzhen Special Zone Daily*, September 8, 2008.

29 Urban Planning Land and Resources Commission of Shenzhen Municipality and Shenzhen Design Centre, *Qucheng Shenzhen Jianzhu Ditu* (Shenzhen architectural guide) (Shenzhen: Haitian Chubanshe, 2014), 71.

30 Jamie Walker, "Tight Security as Bush Stops Traffic," *SCMP*, October 19, 1985.

31 "Bush Calls on Soviet to Imitate China," *New York Times*, October 19, 1985.

32 Xiaohong Lin, "Baishi Ershiba Nian: Chengzhang Beihou De Zhongguo Liliang" (28 years of Pepsi: The power of China behind growth), *Foreign Investment in China*, no. 8 (2008); "Study 1986 (China Trip Conference Material)," H. John Heinz III Collection (Carnegie Mellon University, 1986).

33 "Bush Calls on Soviet to Imitate China," *New York Times*.

34 Yang, *Zhuji*, 131.

35 Ling Cui, "Shenzhen Gaige Kaifang Chuqi Chengshi Jianzhu Yichan Goucheng Chutan" (The research of urban architecture heritage constitution in Shenzhen in early Reform and Opening Up) (Xian University of Architecture and Technology, 2011).

36 Li Qin and Yuan Liu, "Shenzhen Gao Ceng Jian Zhu Kong Jian Zao Xing Shi Tai Diao Yan" (Field research on the space form of Shenzhen's high-rise buildings), *Urbanism and Architecture*, no. 8 (2014).

37 Aiping Chi, "Chenyun Yu Jingji Tequ: Jiantan 20 Shiji 80 Niandai Dang Dui Jingji Tequ Zhengce De Tansuo" (Chen Yun and special economic zones: On the CPC's exploration of special economic zones policy in the 1980s), *Journal of China Executive Leadership Academy Pudong* 5, no. 3 (2011).

38 Chen, "Pigan Lidan Kenhuangniu Sihuo Jiqing Jian Tequ."

39 Huida Gu, ed., "Shenzhen Chengshi Guihua De Huigu Yu Zhanwang" (Review and prospect of urban planning in Shenzhen), *Collection of Essays by the Urban Planning and Design Institute of Shenzhen* (Shenzhen: Urban Planning and Design Institute of Shenzhen, 1998), 359–371.

40 Shenzhen Statistics Bureau and NBS Survey Office in Shenzhen, *Shenzhen Tongji Nianjian* (Shenzhen statistical yearbook); Meekam Ng and Wingshing Tang, "The Politics of Urban Regeneration in Shenzhen, China: A Case Study of Shangbu Industrial District" (Hong Kong: Hong Kong Baptist University, Centre for China Urban and Regional Studies, 2002).

41 Shenzhen Urban Planning Bureau (SUPB) and China Academy of Urban Planning and Design (CAUPD), "The Master Layout Plan of the Shenzhen Special Economic Zone (in Chinese)" (Shenzhen: Shenzhen Government, 1986).

42 "Deng Xiaoping Huijian Aerjiliya Waibin Shi Zhichu: Shenzhen Shige Shiyan" (Deng Xiaoping pointed out that Shenzhen is an experiment when meeting with guests from Algeria), *Shenzhen Special Zone Daily*, June 30, 1985.

43 Wang, "'Santian Yiceng Lou' Dansheng Zhuiji."

44 Jesse Wong, "China's Modernization Woes Are Mirrored by Frustrations of Shenzhen Economic Zone," *Wall Street Journal*, July 9, 1985.

45 "Gumu Huijian Riben Pengyou Shi Shuo: Zhongguo Duiwai Kaifang Zhengce Meiyou Gaibian" (Gumu told Japanese counterparts that the Opening Up policy of China has not changed), *Shenzhen Special Zone Daily*, July 16, 1985.

46 Xiaoping Deng, *Deng Xiaoping Wenxuan (Selected Writings of Deng Xiaoping)*, vol. 3 (Beijing: Renmin chubanshe, 1993), 133.

47 Lebo Chen, "Shenzhen Shi Zenme Zouchu Kunjing De?" (How did Shenzhen get out of trouble?), *World Economic Herald*, November 16, 1987.

48 Xu, *Chun Tian De Gu Shi*, 117–118.

49 Kris Cheng, "Revealed: Why the UK did not warn Beijing's top man in HK about risky bid to save newspaper," *Hong Kong Free Press*, October 10, 2016.

50 Mu Gu, "Gumu Tongzhi Zai Jingji Tequ Gongzuo Huiyi Shang De Jianghua" (Comrade Gu Mu's speeches in the working conference on special economic zones), in *Gumu Tongzhi Guanyu Tequ Gongzuo De Tanhua Yaoji* (A collection of Comrade Gu Mu's speeches on works on the special economic zones) (1986).

51 Mu Gu, *Gu Mu Huiyilu* (Memoirs of Gu Mu) (Beijing: Central Party Literature Press, 2009), 259–371.

52 Wang, "'Santian Yiceng Lou' Dansheng Zhuiji"; "Renmin Ribao Fabiao Shenzhen Shizhang Fangwen Ji" (*People's Daily* published an interview with the mayor of Shenzhen), *Shenzhen Special Zone Daily*, February 17, 1987.

53 Chongshan Zhu and Rongguang Chen, *Shenzhen Shizhang Liangxiang* (Mayor of Shenzhen, Liangxiang) (Guangzhou: Huacheng chubanshe, 2011), 100–103.

54 Hongying Chen, "Gaoceng Jianzhu Zai Woguo De Fazhan" (Development of high-rise buildings in our country), *Journal of Qinghai University (Natural Science)*, no. 4 (1995).

55 Douxiang Zhong, ed., *Shenzhen Special Economic Zone Yearbook* (Guangzhou: Guangdong renmin chubanshe, 1991), 228–229.

56 Xu, *Chun Tian De Gu Shi*, 201–202.

57 Qitai Wu and Yabing Duan, "Shenzhen: Liangwanren De Tongku Yu Zhuanyan" (Shenzhen: Pain and Dignity of 20,000), *Tequ wenxue* (Special zone literature), no. 5 (1986).

58 Hongxiang Yang, interviewed by the author, August 17, 2015, Shenzhen.

59 Mu Gu, "Qing Bawo Maizai Wutongshan" (Please bury me at Wutong Mount), in *Shenzhen Duben: Gandong Yizuo Chengshi De Wenzi* (Shenzhen reader: Words that touch a city), ed. Wei Jiang (Shenzhen: Haitian chubanshe, 2010).

60 Gao Gao, "Kuansong Kuanhou Kuanrong" (Tolerance, generosity, and relaxation), in *Deng Xiaoping, Hu Yaobang, Zhao Ziyang Santou Mache Shidai* (Troika Era: Deng, Hu, Zhao) (Carle Place, NY: Mirror Books, 2009).

61 “Zhongguo Xinwen Renwu Tan Zhongguo ‘Mingan Wenti,’” *Shenzhen Youth Daily*, September 30, 1986.

62 Lizhi Fang, “Zhengzhi Tizhi Gaige De Guanjian Shi Yidang Zhi Haishi Duodang Zhi?” (The key to China’s political institutional reform is single party or multiple party system?), *Shenzhen Youth Daily*, October 4, 1986.

63 Chaoying Qian, “Wo Zancheng Xiaoping Tongzhi Tuixiu: Yu Weiyin Tongzhi Shangque” (I agree with Comrade Xiaoping’s retirement: In discussion with Comrade Weiying), *Shenzhen Youth Daily*, October 21, 1986.

64 Deng Xiaoping, “Interview with Mike Wallace of 60 Minutes,” September 2, 1986. As abridged in *Selected Works of Deng Xiaoping*, vol. 3; Xiaoping Deng, “Da Meiguo Jizhe Maike Hualeisi Wen” (Answering questions from Amercian reporter Mike Wallace), in *Deng Xiaoping Wenxuan* (Selected writings of Deng Xiaoping) (Hong Kong: Joint Publishing, 1996 [1986]).

65 Changqing Cao, “Benbao ‘Wo Zancheng Xiaoping Tongzhi Tuixiu’ Yiwen Yinqi Qianglie Fanxiang” (Our article “I Agree with Comrade Xiaoping’s Retirement” received strong feedback), *Shenzhen Youth Daily*, October 28, 1986; Guo Li, “Renmin Yingyou Yilun Lingxiu De Quanli” (The people should have the right to discuss the leader), *Shenzhen Youth Daily*, October 21, 1986.

66 Changqing Cao, “Bao Xilai Fuqin Huidiao «Shenzhen Qingnian Bao»” (Father of Bao Xilai destroyed *Shenzhen Youth Daily*), *Radio Free Asia*, April 12, 2012.

67 State Council, “1987 Nian Jingji Tequ Gongzuo Huiyi Jiyao” (Summary of the 1987 working conference on special economic zones), in *Zhongyang Dui Guangdong Gongzuo Zhishi Huibian 1986–1988* (Compilation of work instructions from the central government to Guangdong Province 1986–1988), ed. Zhonggong Guangdong Shengwei bangongting (Guangzhou: Zhonggong Guangdong Shengwei bangongting, 1988).

68 Dingguo Huang, “Shenzhen Nongcun Jingji Fazhan De Zhuyao Xingshi: Sanlai Yibu Qiye” (Enterprises of processing industries and compensation trade: Foundation of rural economic development in Shenzhen), *Shenzhen University Journal (Humanities & Social Sciences)*, no. 4 (1992). See the following chapter for more on the formations and economic contributions of Sanlaiyibu.

69 Zhu and Chen, *Shenzhen Shizhang Liangxiang* (Mayor of Shenzhen, Liangxiang).

70 Xu, *Chun Tian De Gu Shi*, 135.

71 Ibid.

72 Xiaoping Deng, “Gaige De Buzi Yao Jiakuai” (The steps of reform should be accelerated), in *Deng Xiaoping Wenxuan* (Selected works of Deng Xiaoping), ed. Zhonggong Zhongyang Wenxian Yanjiushi (CCCPC Party Literature Research Office) (Hong Kong: Joint Publishing, 1996 [1987]).

73 Huaming Duan, “Guangdong Gaige Kaifang 30 Nian De Licheng Yu Jingyan” (30 years of history and experience of reform in Guangdong), *Academic Search for Truth and Reality*, no. 6 (2008).

74 Lingyun Zhao, ed., *Zhongguo Gongchandang Jingji Gongzuo Shi* (A history of economic works of the Communist Party of China) (Wuhan: Hubei renmin chubanshe, 2005), 337–338.

75 Jiaojiao Xu, “Wang Haihong: Shenzhen Woba Zuihao Nianhua Xiangeini” (Wang Haihong: Shenzhen, I devoted my best years to you), *Shenzhen Evening*, August 6, 2014.

76 Huiyi Ceng, "Yang Gongxiang: Yiming Wagong De Rensheng Sanjitiao" (Yang Hongxiang: A bricklayer's triple jumps in his life journey), *Shenzhen Evening*, June 6, 2014.

77 Zhong, ed., *Shenzhen Special Economic Zone Yearbook*, 228–229.

78 Xitian Chen, "Dongfang Fenglai Manyan Chun: Deng Xiaoping Tongzhi Zai Shenzhen" (Eastern wind brings an eyeful of spring: A documentary report of comrade Deng Xiaoping's tour of Shenzhen), *People's Daily*, March 31, 1992.

79 Renzhong Ding, "Lun Woguo Duiwai Kaifang De Quanmianxing" (A discussion on the all-roundedness of China's Opening Up reform), *Finance and Economics*, no. 1 (1996), 54–56.

80 Yahui Luo, "Pengcheng Biandi Qi Gaolou: 25 Zai Shenzhen Fangdichan Licheng Huigu" (Towers everywhere in Shenzhen: 25 years of Shenzhen real estate development review), *Chinese and Foreign Real Estate Times* (2005), 4–17.

81 Ibid.

82 Falü chubanshe, ed., *Zhonghua Renmin Gongheguo Xianfa* (PRC Constitution) (Falü chubanshe, 2015).

83 "Diwang Dasha: Jiushi Niandai De Shenzhen Sudu" (Land King Tower: Shenzhen Speed in 1990s), *Guandian* (2007).

84 "Jianshe Yazhou Zuigao Lou Zaichuang Shenzhen Xinsudu: Zhongjian Sanju Yigongsi Zai Shenzhen Diwang Shangye Dasha Jianshe Zhong Lixin Gong" (Building the tallest tower in Asia, achieving the new Shenzhen Speed: The Third Bureau made new contributions in the Land King Project)," *Special Zone Economy*, no. 2 (1995).

85 "Diwang Dasha: Jiushi Niandai De Shenzhen Sudu" (Land King Tower: Shenzhen Speed in the 1990s).

86 Ibid.

87 Ibid.

88 Ibid.

89 Qin and Liu, "Shenzhen Gao Ceng Jian Zhu Kong Jian Zao Xing Shi Tai Diao Yan."

90 Guy Nordenson, *Tall Buildings* (New York: Museum of Modern Art; London: Thames & Hudson, 2003).

91 "Caiwuwei Jinrong Zhongxin Qu Xiangmu Gaikuang" (Project overview of Caiwuwei Financial Centre District), ed. Luohu District Economic Promotion Bureau (Shenzhen, 2012).

92 Jonathan Glancey, "The Tower and the Glory: Looming over the Sprawling Chinese City of Shenzhen, This Building Is the Tallest Skyscraper Ever Designed by a British Architect; Terry Farrell Tells Jonathan Glancey How He Did It," *The Guardian*, February 1, 2012.

93 Herbert Wright, "Terry Farrell KK100 Shenzhen: A Personal Tour of the Tallest Building by a UK Architect," *Blueprint* 311 (2012).

94 Ibid.

95 Ibid.

6. NAIL HOUSE ON "WALL STREET"

1 Lianhao Zhang to Nanfang diyi gaolou zhi zhengdi chaiqian lingwo gandao ruoshi, Oeeee, March 29, 2007, Blog.oeeee.com/zlh1947.

2 "I'd Rather Be a Hammer, China," *The Economist*, April 7, 2007; Howard French, "Homeowner Stares Down Wreckers, at Least for a While: One Women Is an Island," *New*

York Times, March 27, 2007; Zhiling Huang, "We Are Not Going Anywhere," *China Daily,* March 31, 2007.

3 Lei Wang and Ye Chang, "Jiexi Xinlangwang Dui Chongqing 'Dingzihu' Shijian De Wenben Jina" (An analysis on Sina's text collection strategy on the Chongqing "Nail House" Incident) (Southwest University of Political Science and Law, 2007).

4 Caruso St. John Architects and Thomas Demand, "Nagelhaus," *Venice Biennale: The 12th International Architecture Exhibition,* Venice, Italy, 2010.

5 Ying Liu, "Chengshi Gengxin Bu Tingbu 'Shenzhen Huaer Jie' Zheyang Liancheng" (Urban renewal never stops: The making of Shenzhen Wall Street), *Nanfang Metropolis Daily,* July 10, 2015.

6 Yu Zhang and Kaiwen Zhong, "Zouxiang Shendu Chengshihua De Duoyuan Lujing" (Multiple ways to achieve heightened urbanization), *China Land and Resource* 5 (2015).

7 Jie Tang, "5 Nianqian Huopei 1700 Wan Shenzhen 'Zhongguo Zuigui Dingzihu' Jin Hezai" *Daily Sunshine,* November 1, 2012; Zhang and Zhong, "Zouxiang Shendu Chengshihua De Duoyuan Lujing."

8 Lianhao Zhang to Nanfang diyi gaolou zhi zhengdi chaiqian lingwo gandao ruoshi, Oeeee, March 29, 2007.

9 Ibid.

10 Jianfeng Fu, "'Zuigui Dingzihu' Huo Buchang Yu Qianwan Quanli Huifou Bei Lanyong" ("The most expensive nail house" was compensated with ten million: Will the power be abused), *Southern Weekly,* October 18, 2007.

11 Lianhao Zhang to Nanfang diyi gaolou zhi zhengdi chaiqian lingwo gandao ruoshi, Oeeee, March 29, 2007.

12 Steve Hess, "Nail-Houses, Land Rights, and Frames of Injustice on China's Protest Landsape," *Asian Survey* 50, no. 5 (2010).

13 Fu, "'Zuigui Dingzihu' Huo Buchang Yu Qianwan Quanli Huifou Bei Lanyong."

14 Huanggang Cunmin to "Nanfang diyi gaolou zhi zhengdi chaiqian lingwo gandao ruoshi" (Forced land acquisition for the tallest tower in the South makes me feel helpless), *Shenzhen Luntan* (Shenzhen BBS), March 29, 2007.

15 Fu, "'Zuigui Dingzihu' Huo Buchang Yu Qianwan Quanli Huifou Bei Lanyong"; Bin Li et al., "Shenzhen Qidong Shishang Zuiqiang Chengzhongcun Gaizao" (Shenzhen kick-started the largest urban village redevelopment project in history), *Nanfang Metropolis Daily,* October 27, 2004.

16 Lianhao Zhang to Nanfang diyi gaolou zhi zhengdi chaiqian lingwo gandao ruoshi, Oeeee, March 29, 2007.

17 "Mao Zedong Zhishi 'Zhishi qingnian dao nongcun qu'" (Chairman Mao instructed "educated youth should go to the countryside"), *People's Daily,* December 22, 1968.

18 Michel Bonnin and Krystyna Horko, *The Lost Generation: The Rustication of China's Educated Youth (1968–1980)* (Hong Kong: Chinese University Press, 2013); Yiran Pei, "'Zhiqing Xue' Ji Dacheng Zhizhu" (A comprehensive work on educated youth), *Twenty-First Century* 121 (2010); Yizhuang Ding, *Zhongguo Zhi Qing Shi: Chu Lan, 1953–1968 Nian* (A history of Chinese educated youth: The beginning, 1953–1968) (Beijing: Zhongguo shehui kexue chubanshe, 1998); Xiaomeng Liu, *Zhongguo Zhiqing Shi: Dachao, 1966–1980 Nian* (A history of Chinese educated youth: Its peak, 1966–1980) (Beijing: Zhongguo shehui

kexue chubanshe, 1998); *Zhongguo Zhiqing Koushu Shi* (An oral history of Chinese educated youth) (Beijing: Zhongguo shehui kexue chubanshe, 2004).

19 Jisheng Yang, *Tombstone: The Great Chinese Famine, 1958–1962,* translated by Stacy Mosher and Jian Guo (New York: Farrar, Straus and Giroux, 2012); Xizhe Peng, "Demographic Consequences of the Great Leap Forward in China's Provinces," *Population and Development Review* 13, no. 4 (1987), 639–670; Ansley J. Coale, "Population Trends, Population Policy, and Population Studies in China," *Population and Development Review* 7, no. 1 (1981), 85–97; Jasper Becker, *Hungry Ghosts: Mao's Secret Famine* (London: John Murray, 1996); Penny Kane, *Famine in China, 1959–61: Demographic and Social Implications* (New York: St. Martin's Press, 1988); Basil Ashton and Kenneth Hill, "Famine in China, 1958–1961," *Population and Development Review* 10, no. 4 (1984), 613–645; Carl Riskin, "Seven Questions about the Chinese Famine of 1959–61," *China Economic Review* 9, no. 2 (1998), 111–124; Felix Wemheuer, "Sites of Horror: Mao's Great Famine," *China Journal* 66 (2011): 155–164.

20 Becker, *Hungry Ghosts,* 320–323.

21 Zewu Zhang, "Shenzhen Chengshihua Licheng Zhong De Shequ Bianqian" (Community changes during the urbanization process of Shenzhen), *Practice and Theory of SEZs* 10, no. 1 (2011).

22 Haihua Ma, "Zhishi Qingnian" (Educated youth), Zhongguo pinglun xueshu chubanshe (China Review Academic Publishers Limited).

23 Honglei Liao, "Dongmen Laojie Jianzheng Tequ Bianqian Lingnan Mingzhen Puxie Shangye Chuanqi" (Shenzhen Old Town witnessed changes of the SE: The renowned town in the South created commercial legends), *Shenzhen Economic Daily,* March 15, 2010.

24 Honglei Liao, Huangyou He, and Qun Li, "Jing, Jie, Shi: Cong Shenzhen Xu Dao Dongmen Shangye Qu (Shenzhen Old Town)," *Architectural Worlds,* no. 10 (2013): 18–20.

25 Ibid.

26 This clan genealogy was hand-copied by villager Cai Diesen. The original manuscript of the genealogy was lost; while this version can't be proven historically, it is widely accepted by local villagers.

27 Yi Song and Xiaopeng Chen, "Luohu Cunzhuang 60 Nian Zhi Caiwuwei" (60 years of villages in Luohu, Caiwuwei), *Yangcheng Evening News,* September 2, 2009; Tang, "5 Nianqian Huopei 1700 Wan Shenzhen 'Zhongguo Zuigui Dingzihu' Jin Hezai."

28 Huiyao Cai, "Caiwuwei Jishi" (Caiwuwei chronicle), *Shenzhen Wenshi* (Literature and history of Shenzhen), no. 6 (2013).

29 Song and Chen, "Luohu Cunzhuang 60 Nian Caiwuwei."

30 Song and Chen, "Luohu Cunzhuang 60 Nian Zhi Caiwuwei." For further discussion on the regional characteristics of transnational kinship network, see Alan Smart and George Chusheng Lin, "Local Capitalisms, Local Citizenship and Translocality: Rescaling from Below in the Pearl River Delta Region, China," *International Journal of Urban and Regional Research* 31, no. 2 (2007).

31 Tang, "5 Nianqian Huopei 1700 Wan Shenzhen 'Zhongguo Zuigui Dingzihu' Jin Hezai."

32 Under Mao's Household Registration System, enacted in 1958, at birth every citizen is assigned a registration *hukou* for his or her location of residence. Goods and services are collected and distributed to the registered population in each province's cities and villages.

33 Cong Cong, "'Hong' Paifang–Baiqixian Hunyin Wenti Diaocha Zhuiji" ("Red" memorial gateway: A historic study on the marriage issues of Baiqixian), *Zhongguo Funu* 8 (1987); Xiaomeng Liu, "Xiaxiang Nu Zhishi Qingnian Hunyin Pouxi" (An analysis of the marriage of educated female youth), *Twenty-First Century* 30 (1995).
34 "Xiaxiang Nu Zhishi Qingnian Hunyin Pouxi"; Cong, "'Hong' Paifang–Baiqixian Hunyin Wenti Diaocha Zhuiji."
35 Zedong Mao, *Zai Yanan Wenyi Zuotanhui Shang De Jianghua* (Speeches in the Yanan Cultural Symposium) (Shanghai: Xinhua Shudian, 1942).
36 Liu, "Xiaxiang Nu Zhishi Qingnian Hunyin Pouxi."
37 Poyee, "Bianjing Jinqu: Huoyu Jiafeng De Cunluo" (Frontier closed area: Villages that survived in the interim), *Ming Pao,* January 4, 2015.
38 Seymour Topping, *Journey between Two Chinas* (New York: Harper & Row, 1972), 208–209.
39 Chunliang You, "Shen Gang Bianjing Guanlixian Shang Xianwei Renzhi De 'Gengzuokou'" (Lesser-known farming ports along the control lines between Shenzhen and Hong Kong), *Legal Daily,* May 15, 2012.
40 Tang, "5 Nianqian Huopei 1700 Wan Shenzhen 'Zhongguo Zuigui Dingzihu' Jin Hezai."
41 Ibid.
42 Liu, *Zhongguo Zhiqing Koushu Shi.*
43 Ibid.
44 Doutian Wang, "Zai Xiwang De Tianye Shang: Caiwuwei Gufen Gongsi Ershinian Fazhan Jishi" (On a field of hopes: A chronology of the 20 years of development of the Caiwuwei Shareholding Company), *Shenzhen Economic Daily,* January 11, 2013.
45 Shenzhen Municipal Government, "Shenzhen Jingji Tequ Tudi Guanli Zanxing Guiding" (Interim provisions of land management in the Shenzhen special economic zone) (Shenzhen, 1981).
46 "Shenzhen Shi Jingji Tequ Nongcun Sheyuan Jianfang Yongdi Zanxing Guiding" (Interim provisions of village commune members housing construction land in the Shenzhen SEZ)," (Shenzhen, 1982).
47 Tang, "5 Nianqian Huopei 1700 Wan Shenzhen 'Zhongguo Zuigui Dingzihu' Jin Hezai."
48 Fu Chen, "Caiwuwei: Gu Cunluo Biancheng Jinsanjiao" (Caiwuwei: An ancient village transformed into a golden triangle), *Shenzhen Special Zone Daily,* December 23, 2008.
49 Lei Feng, "Shenzhen Huaerjie Ruhe Tuwei?" (How can Shenzhen's "Wall Street" stand out?), *Nanfang Metropolis Daily,* January 12, 2010.
50 Zhiwei Ye, "Caiwuwei Diyi Dachang Dingdan Jiedao Shouruan" (The largest factory in Caiwuwei received too many orders), *Shenzhen Special Zone Daily,* March 5, 2010.
51 Ibid.
52 Ibid.
53 Huang, "We Are Not Going Anywhere."
54 Ibid.
55 Yihua Deng and Shenghua Deng, "Shenzhen Waimao Fazhan Ruogan Wenti De Tantao" (A study of several issues regarding external trade development in Shenzhen), *Special Zone Economy,* no. 9 (1996).

56 Tang, "5 Nianqian Huopei 1700 Wan Shenzhen 'Zhongguo Zuigui Dingzihu' Jin Hezai."

57 Shenzhen Municipal Government, "Guanyu Jinyibu Jiaqiang Shenzhen Tequ Nongcun Guihua Gongzuo De Tongzhi" (Notice of further reinforcement of rural villages planning in Shenzhen SEZ) (Shenzhen, 1986).

58 "Guanyu Shenzhen Jingji Tequ Nongcun Chengshihua De Zanxing Guiding" (Interim regulations of village urbanization in the Shenzhen SEZ) (Shenzhen, 1992).

59 Shuxiong Zhuang and Lina Xu, "Shenzhen Chengzhongcun Gaige Mouqiu Poti" (Searching for a breakthrough for the reform in urban villages in Shenzhen), *Nanfang Metropolis Daily,* February 13, 2014.

60 Defa Pu and Bin Li, "Shenzhen Chengshihua Quanmian Tisu Jiang Chengwei Quanguo Shouge Wunongcun Chengshi" (Acceleration of the urbanization process), *Nanfang Metropolis Daily,* October 31, 2003.

61 Feng, "Shenzhen Huaerjie Ruhe Tuwei?"

62 Ibid.

63 Shenzhen Municipal Government, "Shenzhen Jingji Tequ Fangwu Zulin Tiaoli" (Bylaws of rental housing in the Shenzhen special economic zone) (Shenzhen, 1992).

64 "Guanyu Chuli Shenzhen Jingji Tequ Fangdichan Quanshu Yiliu Wenti De Ruogan Guiding" (Management of problems caused by property rights of real estate in the Shenzhen special economic zone) (Shenzhen, 1993).

65 "Shenzhen Shi Renmin Daibiao Dahui Changwu Weiyuanhui Guanyu Jianjue Chachu Weifa Jianzhu De Jueding" (Decisions by the Standing Committee of the Shenzhen People's Congress on inspection and punishment of illegal constructions) (Shenzhen, 1999).

66 "Shenzhen Jingji Tequ Chuli Lishi Yiliu Weifa Sifang Ruogan Guiding" (Provisions for dealing with remaining illegal private houses) (Shenzhen, 2002); "Shenzhen Jingji Tequ Chuli Lishi Yiliu Shengchan Jingyingxing Weifa Jianzhu Ruogan Guiding" (Shenzhen, 2002).

67 Feng, "Shenzhen Huaerjie Ruhe Tuwei?"

68 Rong Wang, Shaoqiang Jia, and Doutian Wang, "Shenzhen Chengzhongcun Gaizao Xingcheng Duozhong Moshi" (Various ways of redeveloping urban villages in Shenzhen), *Shenzhen Economic Daily,* July 28, 2006.

69 Fu, "'Zuigui Dingzihu' Huo Buchang Yu Qianwan Quanli Huifou Bei Lanyong."

70 Ibid.

71 Fu, "'Zuigui Dingzihu' Huo Buchang Yu Qianwan Quanli Huifou Bei Lanyong."

72 Lianhao Zhang to Nanfang diyi gaolou zhi zhengdi chaiqian lingwo gandao ruoshi, Oeeee, March 29, 2007, Blog.oeeee.com/zlh1947.

73 Mo Zhang, "From Public to Private: The Newly Enacted Chinese Property Law and the Protection of Property Rights in China," *Berkeley Business Law Journal* 5, no. 2 (2008).

74 Fu, "'Zuigui Dingzihu' Huo Buchang Yu Qianwan Quanli Huifou Bei Lanyong."

75 Chen, "Caiwuwei: Gu Cunluo Biancheng Jinsanjiao."

76 Doutian Wang, "Luohu Yuanzhumin Gongxiang Gaige Kaifang Chengguo" (Luohu indigenous villagers share the fruits of Opening Up reform), *Shenzhen Economics Daily,* June 23, 2011.

77 Zhiwang Deng, "Chengshi Gengxin Dui Renkou De Yingxiang: Jiyu Shenzhen Yangben De Fenxi," *China Opening Journal* 180, no. 3 (2015).

78 Wang, "Luohu Yuanzhumin Gongxiang Gaige Kaifang Chengguo."

79 Qfang, "Jingji Caiwuwei Laowei Huayuan, KK100" (Kingkey Caiwuwei Old Village Garden, KK100); Fang Tian Xia, "Caiwuwei Ershoufang Fangjia Zoushi" (Property price trend of second-hand flats in Caiwuwei).

80 Herbert Wright, "A Personal Tour of the Tallest Building by a UK Architect," *Blueprint Magazine* 311 (2012).

81 Lianhao Zhang to Nanfang diyi gaolou zhi zhengdi chaiqian lingwo gandao ruoshi, Oeee, March 29, 2007.

82 Shenzhen Channel China United TV, "Caiwuwei Huiqianfang Zhengshi Ruhuo" (Resettlement of Caiwuwei started moving in).

83 Tang, "5 Nianqian Huopei 1700 Wan Shenzhen 'Zhongguo Zuigui Dingzihu' Jin Hezai."

84 Doutian Wang, "Shenzhen Caiwuwei Jiang Zhengti Gaizao Jingji Zaicheng Kaifa Zhuti" (Kingkey will be lead developer again of the overall redevelopment of Caiwuwei), *Shenzhen Economic Daily*, July 9, 2012.

85 "Luohu Tianjie + Dijie Caiwuwei Nijian 666m Shenzhen Diyi Gaolou" (Sky and earth streets of Luohu, a 666m is proposed to become Shenzhen's tallest tower), *Shenzhen Economic Daily*, March 19, 2012.

86 Ibid.

87 Ibid.

7. CORPORATE VILLAGE IN THE CENTRAL BUSINESS DISTRICT

1 Rupert Hoogewerf, "China Business Aviation Special Report" (Shanghai: Hurun Report, Minsheng Financial Leasing, 2016).

2 John Gittings, "Rambling Clinton Strolls Off with $250,000," *The Guardian*, May 25, 2002.

3 "Jingji Jiugai Xiangmu Huizong" (An overview of Kingkey's redevelopment projects), *Read01*, April 13, 2017.

4 "'Wei Chengshi Jianshe He Renju Shengji Gongxian De Sanshi Da Jianshizhe' Rongyubang" (Thirty practitioners contributing to the city's development and habitats upgrade), *Shenzhen Special Zone Daily*, May 25, 2012.

5 Yangpeng Zheng, "Real Estate Giants Toast Debut Listing in Fortune 500," *South China Morning Post*, July 20, 2016.

6 "'Wei Chengshi Jianshe He Renju Shengji Gongxian De Sanshi Da Jianshizhe' Rongyubang."

7 Shi Wang and Chuan Miao, *Wang Shi: Twenty Years with Vanke* (Beijing: China Citic Press, 2006), 6–12.

8 Ibid., 6–12.

9 Ibid., 8.

10 Nanling Li, "Gongtong Fuyu Shi Genben 'Deng Xiaoping De Hua Wo Mingji Yi Beizi'" (I will remember Deng's words for a lifetime: "Becoming wealthy together is the core principle"), *CCTV International* (2004).

11 Wang and Miao, *Wang Shi*, 8.

12 Ibid., 10.

13 "Wangning Tongzhi Shengping" (A biography of Wangning: A eulogy), *Communist Party of China*, September 5, 2013.

14 Ibid.

15 Musheng Dai and Yanzi, *Jinxiu Huanggang* (Splendid Huanggang) (Guangzhou: Huacheng chubanshe, 1999), 13–14.

16 Ibid., 14; *Zhuangshi Zupu: Huanggang Xiang* (Geneaology of Zhang: Huanggang Village) (Shenzhen).

17 Wenmo Jin, ed., *Xin'an Xianzhi: Kangxi* (Chronicle of Xin'an County: Kangxi version) (Beijing: Qing Government, 1688).

18 Yanting Tong, "Cong Yucun Dao CBD Hou Huayuan Zuimei Huanggangcun" (From fishing village to the backyard of CBD, the most beautiful Huanggang village), *Shenzhen Evening News*, March 19, 2013; Dai and Yanzi, *Jinxiu Huanggang*, 14.

19 Tong, "Cong Yucun Dao CBD Hou Huayuan Zuimei Huanggangcun."

20 James L. Watson's ethnographic study on a village in Hong Kong showed that the agrarian history of the community had prevented the community from dissolving amid large-scale emigration trends. See James L. Watson, "Saltwater Margin: A Common-Fields System in South China," *Past & Present* 224, no. 1 (2014).

21 Tong, "Cong Yucun Dao CBD Hou Huayuan Zuimei Huanggangcun"; Zhonggui Shan, "Huanggangcun Sanshinian Jingli San Da Jubian" (Three major changes during the past thirty years of Huanggang), *Shenzhen Economic Daily*, July 2, 2011.

22 Buyun Yang, "Hongse Shengmingxian" (The red lifeline) (2013); Zhonggong Shenzhen shiwei dangshi bangongshi" (Office for party history of the Shenzhen Municipal Communist Party), *Shenzhen Dangshi Ziliao Huibian* (A compilation of information on the Shenzhen Municipal Communist Party), vol. 1 (Shenzhen: Zhonggong Shenzhen shiwei dangshi bangongshi [Office for party history of the Shenzhen Municipal Communist Party], 1985).

23 Shimou Sun, "Aiguo Rexue Zhangliutang Gaige Kaifang Huanxinzhuang" (Patriotic blood flows during the Reform and Opening Up), epub, March 22, 2010.

24 Xiaohong Yi, Tianli Jiang, and Xiaodan Cui, "74 Nian Qian Dongjiang Zongdui Bannian Yingjiu 800 Duo Wenhua Mingren Chuang Kangzhan Qiji" (The Dongjiang column rescued 800 cultural celebrities in half a year 74 years ago: A defense war miracle), *Shenzhen Evening*, August 10, 2015.

25 Sun, "Aiguo Rexue Zhangliutang Gaige Kaifang Huanxinzhuang."

26 Hui Lei, "Huanggang Taogang Zhongzaiqu Bian Guoji CBD" (Huanggang: From the base of the Great Escape to an international CBD), *Nanfang Daily*, May 24, 2012.

27 Li Li and Nan Mei, "Yige Pingfanren Puxie Chu De Bupingfan Yuezhang" (A normal person writes an exceptional Song), *China Outlook* 30 (2007).

28 Ibid.

29 Wang and Miao, *Wang Shi*, 19–23.

30 Tong, "Cong Yucun Dao CBD Hou Huayuan Zuimei Huanggangcun."

31 Li and Mei, "Yige Pingfanren Puxie Chu De Bupingfan Yuezhang."

32 Dai and Yanzi, *Jinxiu Huanggang*, 285–296.

33 Li and Mei, "Yige Pingfanren Puxie Chu De Bupingfan Yuezhang."

34 Ibid.

35 "Huanggang Dai 'Huangguan' De Quanguo Wenmingcun" (Huanggang: A national cultural village with a crown), *Shenzhen Economic Daily,* February 16, 2011.

36 Dai and Yanzi, *Jinxiu Huanggang,* 198.

37 Zhuang's Clan Association, *Huanggang Village Shenzhen China* (Shenzhen, 2002); Dai and Yanzi, *Jinxiu Huanggang,* 231.

38 Qingshan Huang and Keren He, "Sanshinian Sanda Zhuanxing" (Three major changes in thirty years), *Shenzhen Economic Daily,* August 23, 2010.

39 "Gaizao Chengzhongcun: Huanggang Xinxincun Huocheng Yangban" (Urban village redevelopment: Huanggang's new village can serve as an example), *Hong Kong Commercial Daily,* July 19, 2001.

40 Dai and Yanzi, *Jinxiu Huanggang,* 230.

41 Li and Mei, "Yige Pingfanren Puxie Chu De Bupingfan Yuezhang."

42 "Zhuang Shaobo: Fubei Kaichuang Le Meihao De Jintian" (Zhuang Shaobo: Fathers have created our great present), *Shenzhen Economic Daily,* June 29, 2008.

43 Excellence Group, "Shenzhen CBD Diyi Gaodu Dansheng" (The birth of Shenzhen CBD's greatest height).

44 Zhuang's Clan Association, *Huanggang Village Shenzhen China.*

45 Ibid.

46 Ibid.

47 Ibid.

48 Futian District Redevelopment Bureau, "Zoujin Chengzhongcun: Xianzhuang Diaocha Baogao" (Step in an "urban village": Current conditions report), in *Futian qu chengzhongcun gaizao yanjiu baogao* (Reconstruction research of the "urban village" in Futian District) (Shenzhen: Futian District Redevelopment Bureau, 2005).

49 Richard Y. C. Wong and Y. S. Joseph Cheng, "Cross Border Traffic," in *The Other Hong Kong Report* (Hong Kong: Chinese University of Hong Kong, 1990).

50 Legislative Council Secretariat, "Background Brief on the Operation of Boundary Control Points" (2001).

51 Ibid.

52 Haibo Wei and Shuang Gao, "Xianchang Zhiji Tongguan" (Live broadcast on the Opening of the new border control), *Southern Metropolis Daily,* January 27, 2003.

53 Qiao Tu, "'Ernai' Shenghuo Quan Jilu: Jizhe Wodi Kuishi 'Jinwu Cangjiao'" (Life record of the "second wives": One undercover reporter unveils the "hidden mistresses in golden homes"), *Hong Kong Commercial Daily,* 2001 (April 7–May 4 daily serial).

54 Ibid.

55 Xingsheng Lu, "Kuhun: Tanfang 'Ernaicun'" (Bitter marriages: Visiting a "concubine village"), *Tribune of Villages and Townships* 1 (2005).

56 Qiao Tu, "Wozai Shenzhen Ernaicun De 60 Ge Riri Yeye" (My 60 days and nights in Shenzhen's second wives village), *Beijing Literature,* no. 4 (2004).

57 *Kuhun: "Wodi Nuxia" 60 Tian Yinxing Caifang Shilu* (Bitter marriages: An undercover heroine's 60 days of covert coverage) (Beijing: Writers Publishing House, 2004), 3.

58 Jianfeng and Beifang, "Zouchu 'Ernai Cun'" (Leaving the "second wife villages"), *Woman's Life,* no. 6 (2008).

59 "Shenzhen Huanggang Diqu Juju Shuqian Ming Ernai" (A few thousand second wives live in Shenzhen Huanggang areas), *Xinhua News Agency & China Review News,* June 22, 2011; "Ernai Cun Xian Shenzhen Tequ" (Second wife villages were found in the Shenzhen special zone), *Apple Daily,* September 27, 2009.

60 M. Pablo Diez, "La Ciudad De Las Segundas Esposas" (The city of the second wives), *ABC,* June 19, 2011.

61 Meetings and discussions between author and village leaders in 2007–2009.

62 Qiao Tu, Hao Chen, and Lin Gu, "Bao Ernai Sandi Laogong Gehuai Guitai: Gangren Caikun Jian Qingkuang" (Husbands of second wives each with his own ax to grind: Hong Kong husbands became less frivolous under financial pressure), *Wenhui Po,* September 14, 2002.

63 "Guannei Chengzhongcun Zufang Gonglue" (Tips for renting rooms in villages in inner Shenzhen), *Shenzhen News,* October 17, 2016.

64 Qingshan Huang and Di Qiu, "Gaige Kaifang Zhujiu Huanggang Zhi Hun" (Opening and Reformation forged the spirit of Huanggang), *Shenzhen Commercial Daily,* January 12, 2009.

65 "Shenzhen Shizhongxin Shuijingdao Sheji Fangan Guoji Jingsai Jiexiao" (International competititon results of the Shenzhen City Center Crystal Island Design Proposal announced), *Shenzhen News,* June 17, 2009.

66 Shenzhen Municipal Government, "2007 Shenzhen Shi Chengzhongcun (Jiucun) Gaizao Niandu Jihua" (2007 Shenzhen urban villages [old villages] annual redevelopment plan) (Shenzhen, 2007).

67 Jie Tang, "Chengzhongcun Gaizao Yuanzhumin Cong Dizhi Dao Zhichi" (Urban village redevelopment: Indigenous villagers converted from resistance to support), *Southern Metropolis Daily,* August 23, 2007.

68 "Futian Qu 15 Ge Chengzhongcun Dongshizhang Tan Zhuanxing Mou Fazhan (Zhaiyao)" (Fifteen chairpersons of the urban villages in Futian District discuss restructuring for development [excerpt]), *Shenzhen Commercial Daily,* April 6, 2010.

69 The author is the founding principal of IDU and the lead designer on the Huanggang Project.

70 Shenzhen Municipal Government, "Zhonggong Shenzhen Shiwei, Shenzhenshi Renmin Zhengfu Guanyu Biaozhang Jingshen Wenming Jianshe Xianjin Jiti He Xianjin Geren De Jueding" (Decisions of the Shenzhen Municipal Committee of the CPC and Shenzhen Municipal Government regarding recognition to Pioneering Civilized Unit and Pioneering Personnel) (Shenzhen, 2004).

71 "Guangdong Sheng Chuangjian 'Liuhao' Pingan Hexie Shequ Wenjian Ziliao Huibian" (Compiled information of Guangdong Province's creation of "six goods" safe and harmonious communities), ed. Guangdong sheng shequ jianshe gongzuo lingdao xiaozu bangongshi (Guangdong Province Community Building Leading Group Office) (Guangzhou, 2006).

72 Li and Mei, "Yige Pingfanren Puxie Chu De Bupingfan Yuezhang."

73 Bin Li, "Kaichuang Jingji Tequ De Meihao Mingtian: Wen Jiabao Zongli Zai Shenzhen Kaocha Jishi" (Creating a bright future for the SEZ: A record of Premier Wen Jiabao's visit in Shenzhen), *People's Daily,* August 22, 2010.

74 Ibid.

75 Xiaobin Ye, "Zhanzai Xin De Lishi Qidian Shang: Wen Jiabao Zongli Kaocha Shenzhen Jishi" (Standing on a new historical starting point: A Record of Premier Wen Jiabao's visit in Shenzhen), *Shenzhen Special Zone Daily*, August 23, 2010.

76 Tong, "Cong Yucun Dao CBD Hou Huayuan Zuimei Huanggangcun."

77 Ibid.

78 Liangjun Zhu, "Huanggang Zhuangshi Jiu Zongci Quliu Liangnan" (The dilemma of whether to keep or demolish Zhuang's Clan's ancestral hall in Huanggang), *Shenzhen Special Zone Daily*, April 24, 2011.

8. "SLUM" IN THE HIGH-TECH GARDEN CITY

1 John Zacharias and Yuanzhou Tang, "Restructuring and Repositioning Shenzhen: China's New Mega City," *Progress in Planning* 73, no. 4 (2010): 209–249.

2 The majority of information related to Chi and Tangtou Village history was gathered through multiple interviews by the author from 2006 to 2016. Owing to the controversial nature of the village history as well as the status of the indigenous villagers, only Chi's last name is used to protect his privacy.

3 Shenzhen Academy of Social Sciences, "Shenzhen Chengzhongcun De Xianzhuan Wenti Yu Duice Yanjiu" (Research on the existing conditions, problems, and solutions to the vices in Shenzhen), *Southern Forum*, September 3, 2004.

4 Christopher Balding, "One Chinese City Has Figured Out the Future," *Bloomberg LP*, June 13, 2016.

5 Tom Whitwell, "Inside Shenzhen: China's Silicon Valley," *The Guardian*, June 13, 2014.

6 Paul Mozur, "The World's Biggest Tech Companies Are No Longer Just American," *New York Times*, August 17, 2017.

7 State Council, *Zhonghua Renmin Gonghe Guo Guowuyuan Xinwen Bangongshi Xinwen Fabu Huiji* (A compilation of press releases from the news bureau of the State Council, PRC) (Beijing: China International Communication Center, 2003).

8 Hui Shen and Yangteng Yang, "Shenzhen Gaoxinqu: 'Chuntian Gushi' Li De Chuangxin Yinji" (Shenzhen Science and Technology Industrial Park: Innovation in the "Story of Spring"), *Economic Daily*, July 25, 2016.

9 Ibid.

10 Guochuan Ma, "Luo Zhengqi: Daxue Li Buneng Meiyou Gushi" (Luo Zhengqi: There is no university without a story), *Economic Observer*, August 7, 2012.

11 Kezhen Wang, "Shahe Jiedao Hexie Jianshe Yuchu Jiucun Gaizao Jingyan" (Shahe Jiedao harmoniously nurtured the experience of old village redevelopment), *Shenzhen Special Zone Daily* (2010).

12 Eli MacKinnon, "The Twilight of Shenzhen's Great Urban Village," *Foreign Policy* (2016).

13 Julia Carneiro, "Favela Life: Rio's City within a City," *BBC News*, June 9, 2014.

14 Shenzhen Wanshi Tong 0755, "Baishizhou, Zuihou De Chengzhongcun, Ceng Anfang Le Wushu Shenzhen Ren De Qingchun" (Baishizou, the last urban village, housed the youth of numerous Shenzheners), *KK News*, July 9, 2017; Jingjiao Ceng,

"Shizhi 2500 Yi De Shenzhen Chengzhongcun Yao Chai Le, Duoshao Fuweng Jiang Dansheng?" (A 250 billion yuan–worth urban village in Shenzhen is going to be demolished, how many billionaires will it make?), *Caijing Wang* (Finance online), June 23, 2017.

15 Ping Hu, May 29, http://home.51.com/dengdeyon/diary/item/10052514.html.

16 "Baishizhou: Zai Chuntian Li Chonghuo Xinsheng" (Baishizhou: Rebirth in spring), in *Urban Planning, Land & Resource Commission of Shenzhen Municipality*, ed. Pengcheng Jiehua Diyi Juan (Stories of Pengcheng 1) (Guangzhou: Lingnan Art Publishing House, 2014).

17 A map of "Yanhai Quantu" (Full coastal map), in *Haiguo Wenjian Lu* (The chronicle of oceans and state), ed. Lunjiong Chen (Beijing: Qing Government, 1730); Ping Chen and Chanjuan Deng, "Dongguan Gudai Yanye Yu Yanhai Chengzhen De Xingqi" (Dongguan's salt industry in ancient times and the development of coastal towns), *Salt Industry History Research*, no. 4 (2010): 59–67.

18 Hong Chen, *Shenzhen Yuanzhumin Jiapu Baishizhou De Chuntian (Shang)* (Geneaology of Shenzhen's aboriginals: The spring of Baishizhou 1) (Shenzhen: Shenzhen baoye chubanshe, 2011).

19 Chi, interview by the author, 2006–2016.

20 Li, "Bajing Shi" (Poems on the eight landscapes).

21 Defu Li, *Jiusi Bu Hui : Yige Heiwulei De Huiyilu* (Unregretful after 9 deaths: A memoir of a Black Five Group) (Taipei: Showwe Information Co., 2012).

22 Chen, *Shenzhen Yuanzhumin Jiapu Baishizhou De Chuntian (Shang)*.

23 Yantai Zhang, "Siqing Yundong Yanjiu Zongshu" (A summary of the Four Clean-Ups Movement), *Social Sciences Perspectives in Higher Education*, no. 3 (2009).

24 Mao Zedong, "Talk on the Four Clean-Ups Movement," in *Mao Zedong Sixiang Wansui* (Long live the thought of Mao Zedong) (Beijing: Red Guard Publication, 1965).

25 Shahe Primary School, *Shahe Xiaoxue Fazhan Nianjian* (Annual of the development of Shahe Primary School) (Shenzhen).

26 Guanghan Peng et al., "Xianxingzhe" (Pioneer), *Qiaowu gongzuo yanjiu* (Study on overseas Chinese Affairs), no. 3 (2005).

27 Chen, *Shenzhen Yuanzhumin Jiapu Baishizhou De Chuntian (Shang)*.

28 Xiaowo Liu and Shi Tang, "Chenguang Ruye: Zuida Xiannai Chukou Qiye De Jingying Zhidao" (Chengguan dairy: The operation method of the largest fresh milk exporter), *China Economic Daily*, no. 328 (2005).

29 Xiaomin Li and Yihuai Chen, "Zhuzai Shenzhen De Yuenan Guiqiao: Mianmu Mohu De Qunti" (Vietnam returnees in Shenzhen: A group with an unclear identity), *Southern Metropolis Daily*, May 4, 2011.

30 Ibid.

31 Ibid.

32 Peng et al., "Xianxingzhe" (Pioneer).

33 August 26, 1980, is regarded as the birthday of the Shenzhen SEZ. On this day, the regulations on special economic zones in Guangdong Province were passed by the National People's Congress.

34 Peng et al., "Xianxingzhe" (Pioneer).

35 Hsing You-tien's empirical study on the social and political linkages of Taiwan businesses in Southern China provides further insights; See You-tien Hsing, *Making Capitalism in China: The Taiwan Connection* (New York: Oxford University Press, 1998).

36 "Huaqiaocheng Guihua Yu Shishi (1986–1995)," *Guihuashi (Planner);* Yongtao Li, "1986 Huaqiaocheng: Shenzhen Yuansheng Dimao Yichan" (October 1986: The heritage of Shenzhen's aboriginal landscape), in *Dadao 30: Shennan Dadao Shang De Guojia Jiyi* (Thirty years of the boulevard: National memories on Shennan Boulevard) (Shenzhen: Shenzhen Press Group Publishing House, 2010).

37 Li, "1986 Huaqiaocheng: Shenzhen Yuansheng Dimao Yichan."

38 Laoheng, "Ma Zhimin: Zhongguo Weisuo Jingguan Zhi Fu, Shenshang Huaqiao-cheng Paixi De Xianfeng" (Ma Zhimin: The father of China's miniature landscape, the pioneer of Overseas Chinese Town faction of Shenzhen merchants), in *Shenshang De Jingshen* (Spirit of Shenzhen Merchants) (Shenzhen: Haitian Publishing House, 2007).

39 Jinxiu, "'Zhongguo Xiandai Zhuti Gongyuan Zhifu' Ma Zhimin" (The father of China's modern theme parks: Ma Zhimin)," *Golden Age*, no. 6 (2011).

40 Jun Chen, "Jujue 'Laotaolu' De Huaqiaocheng" (OCT rejects old tricks)," *Chongqing Daily*, April 24, 2017.

41 Ibid.

42 Ling Lei, "Shahe: Chengfeng Polang Hongse Laoqu Zouxiang Xin Yuezhang" (Shahe: An old communist district is playing new songs), *Shekou News*, August 26, 2010.

43 Thomas J. Campanella, "China's Gardens of Time and Space," *Places* 10, no. 1 (1995). Campanella revisited this topic more than a decade later in "Theme Parks and the Landscape of Consumption," in *The Concrete Dragon : China's Urban Revolution and What It Means for the World* (New York: Princeton Architectural Press, 2008).

44 Shenzhen Rental Housing Management Office, "Shenzhen Shi 2007 Nian Fangwu Zulin Zhidao Zujin" (Shenzhen city's 2007 rental housing guiding rent levels) (Shenzhen, 2007).

45 Joshua Bolchover and John Lin, "Urban Village: Enclave Urbanism," in *Rural Urban Framework: Transforming the Chinese Countryside* (Basel: Birkhauser, 2014).

46 Jie Cui and Fentian Chang, "Shahe Jiedao 'Yiren Weiben' Chuang Hexie Fazhan Xin Jingyan" (Shahe Street Office emphasizes "human-oriented" and aims to explore new path for a harmonious development), *Nanfang Daily*, September 20, 2011.

47 Government, "Guanyu Shenzhen Jingji Tequ Nongcun Chengshihua De Zanxing Guiding" (Interim regulations of village urbanization in Shenzhen SEZ).

48 Ibid.

49 Ibid.

50 Zhang, "Siqing Yundong Yanjiu Zongshu."

51 See Chapter 6.

52 See Chapter 7.

53 Chi, interview by the author, 2006–2016.

54 Chen, *Shenzhen Yuanzhumin Jiapu Baishizhou De Chuntian (Shang);* Hongtai Chen, "Tigong Liangge Gean, Kan Nengfou Jiejue Wukan Cun Wenti" (Providing 2 cases to see if these can resolve the Wukan problems), *Zhongguo Zhengzhi Fazhan* (2011).

55 Anna Du, "Shenzhen Xian Qiangjian Weifa Jianzhu Rechao Zuikuai Yiye Jian Yidonglou" (A wave of illegal construction emerged in Shenzhen, where a tower could be built over the span of a night), *Guangzhou Daily*, Novermber 24, 2009.

56 Chen, *Shenzhen Yuanzhumin Jiapu Baishizhou De Chuntian (Shang)*.

57 Shenzhen Municipal Government, "Guanyu Jianjue Chachu Weifa Jianzhu De Jueding" (Decisions regarding the strengthening of law enforcement on illegal buildings) (Shenzhen, 1999); "Shenzhen Jingji Tequ Chuli Lishi Yiliu Weifa Sifang Ruogan Guiding" (Provisions for the Shenzhen special economic zone regarding historically illegal peasant houses) (2001).

58 Wending Chen, *Weilai Meiyou Chengzhongcun* (There will be no villages in the city) (Beijing: China Democracy and Legality Publishing House, 2011).

59 Shenzhen Municipal Government, "Guanyu Jiakuai Baoan Longgang Liangqu Chengshihua Jincheng De Yijian" (Opinions regarding the expedition of the urbanization processes in the two districts of Baoan and Longgang) (Shenzhen, 2003).

60 Zhang, "Siqing Yundong Yanjiu Zongshu."

61 "Shenzhen Jiang Chengwei Quanguo Shouge Wu Nongcun Wu Nongmin Chengshi" (Shenzhen will become the first city in China with no villages and no peasants), *Earth Biweekly, People's Daily*, no. 13 (2004).

62 Mingshan Yu, "Shenzhen Nongmin Jiang Chengwei Lishi" (Peasants in Shenzhen will become history), *Wenhui Po*, January 10, 2004.

63 Chen, *Shenzhen Yuanzhumin Jiapu Baishizhou De Chuntian (Shang)*.

64 Shenzhen Municipal Government, "Shenzhen Shi Chengzhongcun (Jiucun) Gaizao Zongti Guihua Gangyao (2005–2010)" (Planning outline for the redevelopment of urban villages [old villages] in Shenzhen [2005–2010]), (Shenzhen, 2005).

65 Ibid.

66 Ibid.

67 "2006 Shenzhen Shi Chengzhongcun (Jiucun) Gaizao Niandu Jihua" (2006 annual plan for the redevelopment of urban villages [old villages] in Shenzhen) (2006); Dawei Fu and Qiujin Luo, "Shenzhen 2006 Nian Jihua Quanmian Gaizao 40 Ge Chengzhongcun" (Forty urban villages are to be completely redeveloped in Shenzhen's 2006 plan), *Shenzhen News*, July 4, 2006.

68 Shahe Neighborhood Unit Office, "Guanyu Jiejue Shahe Wucun Lishi Wenti De Baogao" (A report regarding solutions to the historic problem in the Shahe 5 villages) (2006).

69 Shuxiong Zhuang, "Baishizhou Maizang Duoshao Dagong Chuanqi" (Hidden legends of the working class in Baishizhou), *Southern Metropolis Daily*, November 11, 2009.

70 Wang, "Shahe Jiedao Hexie Jianshe Yuchu Jiucun Gaizao Jingyan."

71 LVGEM, *Baishizhou Shahe Wucun Jiugai Zhuanxiang Guihua* (Planning for the redevelopment of Baishizhou Shahe Five Villages) (2012).

72 Chi, interview by the author, 2006–2016.

73 LVGEM, "Corporate Profile."

74 "Gaibian Chengshi: Sanshi Nian De Lingchuang, Sanshi Ren De Fengyun. 'Wei Chengshi Jianshe He Renju Shengji Gongxian De Sanshi Da Jianshizhe' Rong Yu Bang" (Changing the city: Thirty years of vanguard, thirty years of influence; "Thirty practitioners

contributing to the city's development and habitats upgrade"—An honor roll), *Shenzhen Special Zone Daily*, May 25, 2012.

75 Yongtao Li, *Dadao 30: Shennan Dadao Shang De Guojia Jiyi* (Thirty years of the boulevard: National memories on Shennan Boulevard), vol. 1 (Shenzhen: Shenzhen Press Group Publishing House, 2010), 184–188.

76 "Baishizhou Wangzha!" (Great explosion in Baishizhou!), *Shenzhen First Real Estate*, October 11, 2016.

77 Chen, *Shenzhen Yuanzhumin Jiapu Baishizhou De Chuntian (Shang)*; Wang, "Shahe Jiedao Hexie Jianshe Yuchu Jiucun Gaizao Jingyan."

78 Maurice Veeken, "Decisions of Migrants in Their Choice of Residence: A Case Study in Baishizhou Village in Shenzhen" (University of Amsterdam, 2013).

79 LVGEM, *Baishizhou Shahe Wucun Jiugai Zhuanxiang Guihua*.

80 Wang, "Shahe Jiedao Hexie Jianshe Yuchu Jiucun Gaizao Jingyan."

81 Veeken, "Decisions of Migrants in Their Choice of Residence"; Oeeee, "Summary: Baishizhou District"; Wang, "Shahe Jiedao Hexie Jianshe Yuchu Jiucun Gaizao Jingyan."

82 Chris Smith and Ngai Pun, "The Dormitory Labour Regime in China as a Site for Control and Resistance," *International Journal of Human Resource Management* 17 (2006).

83 Urban Planning Land and Resources Commission of Shenzhen Municipality, "Shenzhen Zanzhu Renyuan Zhufang Wenti Yanjiu" (Housing issues research on Shenzhen's temporary residents), in *Shenzhen Lanpi Shu, Zhongguo Shenzhen Fazhan Baogao* (Blue book of Shenzhen, development report of Shenzhen, China) (Beijing: Social Sciences Academic Press, 2005).

84 "Chengshi Huikeshi Di 13 Qi: Yiju Chuzuwu, Chengzhongcun Xinchulu?" (City meeting room no. 13: Livable rental flats: A new way out for urban villages?), *Southern Metropolis Daily*, October 25, 2012.

85 Guangning Qu, "Shenzhen Nanshan Shidian 'Yiju Chuzuwu' Nongminfang Bianshen Chengshi Gongyu" (Shenzhen Nanshan tests "livable rental flats," peasant houses become urban hostels), *Nanfang Daily*, December 20, 2012.

86 Interview by Van Het Wout Ricki-Lee Martina with Joe Finkenbinder, December 20, 2016.

87 Shum Yip Shahe Group, "Nanshan Qu Shahe Jiedao Shenye Shiji Shangu Chengshi Gengxin Danyuan Zhengti Fangan Ji Yiqi Gongcheng Jishu Sheji Zhaobiao Pingshen Jieguo Gonggao" (Announcement of the result of tendering for the overall scheme for Sham Yip Century Valley and phase 1 technical design in Nanshan Shahe Jiedao), news release, December 29, 2015.

88 Peng Duan and Baishizhou Group, November 1, 2016.

89 "Lanzhou Niurou Mian: Lanzhou De Yizhang Mingpian" (Lanzhou beef noodles: A name card for Lanzhou), *Confucius Institute Journal (Chinese Japanese Bilingual Version)* 3 (2016); Ruilong Qi, "40 Duo Jia Lanzhou Niurou Lamiandian Luohu Shijie Gedi" (More than 40 Lanzhou ramen shops are around the world), *Western Economic Daily*, July 5, 2017.

90 Pangniao, "Xuran Mianguan Beichai Dan Haozai Yuguo Tianqing" (Although the noodle shop was demolished, nonetheless everything is fine)."

91 Recorded by Baishizhou Team (*Baishizhou Xiaozu*), September 15, 2016.

92 Shenzhen Urban Planning Bureau (SUPB), "Guanyu Nanshan Qu Shahe Jiedao Shahe Wucun Chengshi Gengxin Danyuan Guihua (Caoan) De Gongshi" (Public presentation on urban renewal planning for the Shahe Five Villages in Shae Jiedao, Nanshan District) (Shenzhen, 2017).

93 Ibid.

94 Ibid.

95 Lengjing and Baishizhou Group, "Shixiao De Baishizhou Chengshi Gengxin Gongshi Shuilai Fuze" (Who is responsible for the ineffective Baishizhou urban renewal public review?); Weixin, https://mp.weixin.qq.com/s?__biz=MzI2ODMwODExNw==&mid =2247484609&idx=l&sn=c693ea206daf66ccc35aeb13c5120754&chksm=eaf0df3.

96 SZDIY, "Introduction."

97 Joseph Chaney, "Shenzhen: China's Start-up City Defies Skeptics," *CNN*, June 24, 2015.

98 Leo, "Ta Zuole Yikuan Dazhongzhe Baishizhou Zhumeng Youxi, Cai Zhidao Baishizhou Yao Beichai Le" (After creating a digital game of migrant workers chasing their dreams in Baishizhou, he found that Baishizhou was going to be demolished), *Shenhuxi*, July 18, 2019.

99 Ibid.

CONCLUSION

1 Xuecun Murong, "Chinese Internet: 'A New Censorship Campaign Has Commenced,'" *The Guardian*, May 15, 2013.

2 Xuecun Murong, *Tiantang Xiangzuo Shenzhen Wangyou* (Heaven to the left, Shenzhen to the right, or Another way to heaven) (Beijing: Writers Publishing House, 2004).

3 National School of Development, "Shenzhen Tudi Zhidu Gaige Yanjiu Baogao" (A report study on land policy reform in Shenzhen) (Beijing: Peking University, 2013); Ruichuan Guo, "Chengzhongcun Buyinggai Chengwei Wuye Guanli Mangqu" (Urban villages should not become a blind spot of property management), *Southern Metropolis Daily*, August 23, 2016.

4 Urban Planning, Land & Resource Commission of Shenzhen Municipality, *The 13th Five-Year Plan of Shenzhen Urban Renewal, Shenguitu*, no. 824 (2016).

5 Shenzhen Bureau of Planning and Natural Resources, *Shenzhen Urban Village (Old Village) Integrated Rehabilitation Master Plan* (2019–2025), *Shen Guihua Ziyuan*, no. 104 (2019).

6 CCTV News, *"Jiaodian Fangtan" Qiannian Daji Guojia Dashi: Yi Xi Jinping Tongzhi Wei Hexin De Dang Zhongyang Juece Hebei Xiongan Xinqu Guihua Jianshe Jishi* (Millennium plan and state affairs: A documentary of planning and construction of Xiong'an new area in Hebei Province with General Secretary Xi Jinping as the core) (Beijing: CCTV, 2017).

7 "Banhao Jianshe Xiongan Xinqu Zhejian Dashi" (Completing the important project of constructing the new district of Xiongan with high standards), *People's Daily*, April 2, 2017.

8 "Puxie Quyu Xiediao Fazhan 'Chuntian De Gushi'" (Writing the "Story of Spring" of regionally balanced development), *People's Daily*, April 4, 2017.

9 Shujuan Bi, "Xiong'an Youwang Chengwei Lingyige Shenzhen" (Xiong'an could be another Shenzhen), *China United Business News*, April 17, 2017.

10 The People's Government of Hebei Province, "Hebei Xiongan Xinqu Guihua Gangyao" (Principles of new area planning for Xiongan) (Hebei: The People's Government of Hebei Province, 2018).

11 While this is perhaps an obvious question, I think that with so much direct state-involvement in Xiong'an, the comparison of Xiong'an to Shenzhen is perhaps not very useful in terms of policy.

12 Junfu Zhang, "Interjurisdictional Competition for FDI: The Case of China's 'Development Zone Fever,'" *Regional Science and Urban Economics* 41 (2011).

13 Carolyn Cartier, "'Zone Fever,' the Arable Land Debate, and Real Estate Speculation: China's Evolving Land Use Regime and Its Geographical Contradictions," *Journal of Contemporary China* 10, no. 28 (2001).

14 "Across China: Kashgar's Silk Road Ambitions: From Backwater to Bridgehead," *Xinhua News*, August 1, 2015.

15 Bill Chou and Xuejie Ding, "A Comparative Analysis of Shenzhen and Kashgar in Development as Special Economic Zones," *East Asia* 32, no. 2 (2015).

16 Tie Li and Yi Fan, "Xincheng Xinqu Jianshe Xianzhuang Diaocha He Sikao" (Investigation and thought on the current situation of new city and new district construction in China), *Chengxiang Yanjiu Dongtai* (Study trend of urban and rural areas) 229 (2013).

17 UN-Habitat, *Slum Almanac 2015/2016: Tracking Improvement in the Lives of Slum Dwellers* (UNON, Publishing Services Section, Nairobi, 2016).

18 Xiaoping Deng, "Gaige Kaifang Shi Henda De Shiyan" (Reform and Opening to the outside world are a great experiment), in *Deng Xiaoping Wenxuan* (Selected works of Deng Xiaoping), ed. Zhonggong Zhongyang Wenxian Yanjiushi (CCCPC Party Literature Research Office) (Hong Kong: Joint Publishing, 1996 [1985]).

19 Daouda Cisse, "South Africa's Special Economic Zones: Inspiration from China?," Centre for Chinese Studies, February 3, 2012.

20 Physicians for Human Rights, "A Foreseeable Disaster in Burma: Forced Displacement in the Thilawa Special Economic Zone" (New York: Physicians for Human Rights, 2014); Chinmoy Banerjee, "Tea Garden Workers in Bangladesh Resist Displacement by the SEZ" (New Westminster, BC: South Asian Network for Secularism and Democracy, 2016).

21 Zemin Jiang, "Shezhi Jingji Tequ, Jiakuai Jingji Fazhan" (Setting up the SEZ, accelerating economic development), in *Jiang Zemin Wenxuan* (An anthology of Jiang Zemin) (Beijing: Renmin chubanshe, 1980); "Chuangban Jingji Tequ" (Establishing the SEZ), in *Xi Zhongxun Zhuzheng Guangdong* (Xi Zhongxun leading Guangdong) (Beijing: Zhonggong dangshi chubanshe, 2008).

ACKNOWLEDGMENTS

I wish to thank all of those who facilitated this book's writing and production, a process that spanned a decade, evolved through several iterations, and took place in multiple countries.

I first thank Sharmila Sen, editorial director at Harvard University Press, whose generous patience and support were surpassed only by her exacting insistence that the book should address a broad intellectual audience rather than a narrow academic discipline. I am additionally grateful for the entire HUP team, especially Heather Hughes for editorial assistance, Stephanie Vyce for permissions assistance, Louise Robbins for production help, and Susan Karani for copyediting. I also would like to thank the anonymous reviewers, whose critical comments revealed ambiguities in the drafts and helped to further clarify the central arguments. I give my sincere thanks to Anna Koor, Emily Silk, and Alan Zhang for judiciously reading and editing different versions of the manuscript, which provided much needed improvements to the writing. Many thanks to the individuals and institutions who gave permission to use the photographic works, maps, and other images that appear in the book.

I am indebted to millions of Shenzhen residents who built the city, and hundreds of people I have come to learn from over the past decade. Where individual privacy is not a concern, I listed names of people whom I interviewed in the notes. Here I would like to especially thank Jiang Kairu, Yang Hongxiang, and a number of residents of Shenzhen whose voices and personal stories helped to give human dimension to the complex and often abstract process of urbanization. I am grateful to Huang Weiwen for over a decade of collaboration and dialogue on Shenzhen's past and future, which provided a sustaining source of knowledge and inspiration. Multiple discussions spanning years with Yung Ho Chang, Li Jinkui, Liu Xiaodu, Meng Yan, Nan Zhaoxu, Mary Ann O'Donnell, Wang Peng, Yan Xiaopei, Zhu Rongyuan, and many others have provided constantly evolving and deepening perspectives on the city. My knowledge of Shenzhen also benefited from long-term collaborations with various institutions, including the Shenzhen Urban Planning, Land & Resource Commission, the Shenzhen Center for Design, Future Plus, China Academy of Urban Planning and Design Shenzhen Branch, and UABB, as well as numerous village corporations.

Research on Shenzhen's urban villages was further developed through my work with the Swiss Federal Institute of Technology in Zurich (ETH). I am extremely grateful to Kees Christiaanse for his years of constructive advice and generous support. Special thanks also to Hubert Klumpner at the ETH. I also benefited greatly from guidance and encouragement from Nezar Alsayyad and Margaret Crawford at the University of California, Berkeley, as well as Christine Boyer and Esther da Costa Meyer at Princeton University.

The majority of my writing took place in Hong Kong. I am grateful to the colleagues and students of the Faculty of Architecture at the University of Hong Kong, where I have spent more waking hours than at my residential address. The community and resources at HKU provided a stimulating and supportive environment for teaching and research. I thank Chad McKee for in-depth discussions and encouragement throughout the duration of this project. Special thanks to Nasrine Seraji, Guibo Sun, Dorothy Tang, and Chris Webster, who gave invaluable advice on the research. I gratefully acknowledge research assistants and former students Sam Cheng, Cherry Cheung, Wen Fan, Joseph Guo, Clarissa Lim, and Wenjian Pan, who provided a great amount of assistance through literature reviews, graphic mapping, lively discussions, and school cafeteria meals. I would like to acknowledge funding support from HKU's Seed Fund for Basic Research and the Architecture Department's publication fund.

I commemorate three individuals whose departures and arrival were pivotal for the book. First is the late Ralph Lerner, whose invitation to teach at HKU in 2006 gave me the opportunity to make the school, the city, and the region my adopted home for the past fifteen years. I began writing about Shenzhen in 2010, following enthusiastic encouragement from the late Peter Hall, who shared a love of cities and the appreciation of personal narrative to convey complex urban processes. I regret not being able to share this book with them. My son's birth in 2013 allowed me to view the world through the eyes of a new life, which gave a renewed sense of responsibility to delve deeper and disseminate further the knowledge of our remarkable shared humanity.

Finally, I offer my deepest gratitude to my impossibly patient and loving husband, and my impossibly supportive and caring mothers and fathers. Without them, this book would have been impossible.

ILLUSTRATION CREDITS

ii First Historical Archives of China, Guangzhou Archives Bureau.

3 Wpcpey / Wikimedia Commons, Licensed by CC BY-SA 4.0.

6 Photograph © Juan Du.

7 Map © Juan Du.

34 Gwulo.com.

39 Courtesy of China Merchants Shekou Industrial Zone Holdings Company.

44 Courtesy of Nan Zhaoxu.

58 Map © Juan Du.

61 *Upper and lower:* McMaster University Library Digital Archive. Licensed by CC BY-NC 2.5 CA. Overlay by Juan Du. *Middle:* Shenzhen Planning and Natural Resources Bureau.

63 McMaster University Library Digital Archive. Licensed by CC BY-NC 2.5 CA. Overlay by Juan Du.

73 *Upper and middle:* Shenzhen Planning and Natural Resources Bureau. *Lower:* McMaster University Library Digital Archive. Licensed by CC BY-NC 2.5 CA. Overlay by Juan Du.

93 Reproduced from *Shen Gang Ao De Tianhou Gong* (Tianhou Temples in Shenzhen, Hong Kong, and Macau) (Hong Kong: Haifeng chubanshe, 1998).

105 *Above:* Reproduced from *Shenzhen Jiuzhi Sanzhong* (Three ancient annuals of Shenzhen) (Shenzhen: Haitian Publishing House, 2006). *Below:* Reproduced from *Shen Gang Ao De Tianhou Gong* (Tianhou Temples in Shenzhen, Hong Kong, and Macau) (Hong Kong: Haifeng chubanshe, 1998).

108 *Left:* McMaster University Library Digital Archive. Licensed by CC BY-NC 2.5 CA. *Right:* Satellite imagery © 2017 DigitalGlobe, Inc. Overlay by Juan Du.

111 Reproduced from *Shenzhen Jiuzhi Sanzhong* (Three ancient annuals of Shenzhen) (Shenzhen: Haitian Publishing House, 2006).

117 Courtesy of National Library of Australia.

121 Illustration © Juan Du.

124 Satellite imagery © 2016 DigitalGlobe, Inc. Overlay by Juan Du.

125 Photograph © Juan Du.

133 Photograph © Juan Du.

137 Library of Congress, Geography and Map Division.

138 NASA Earth Observatory images by Joshua Stevens, using Landsat data from the US Geological Survey. Overlay by Juan Du.

140 *Left:* Reproduced from Baoan, Furong, 1938, Sanbo Honbu, National Australian Library. Overlay by Juan Du. *Right:* NASA Earth Observatory images by Joshua Stevens, using Landsat data from the US Geological Survey. Overlay by Juan Du.

149 Courtesy of Nan Zhaoxu.

164 Photograph by and courtesy of Yang Hongxiang.

167 Photograph by and courtesy of Yang Hongxiang.

172 Photograph by Liu Tingfang, courtesy of Shenzhen Newspaper Group Publishing House.

190 Illustration © Juan Du.

199 Photograph © Juan Du.

203 *Left:* McMaster University Library Digital Archive. Licensed by CC BY-NC 2.5 CA. *Right:* Satellite imagery © 2017 DigitalGlobe, Inc. Overlay by Juan Du.

205 Photograph by He Huangyou. Courtesy of Shenzhen Newspaper Group Publishing House.

209 *Top:* McMaster University Library Digital Archive. Licensed by CC BY-NC 2.5 CA. Overlay by Juan Du. *Bottom:* Satellite imagery © 2018 DigitalGlobe, Inc. Overlay by Juan Du.

213 Illustration © Juan Du.

215 Map © Juan Du.

223 Illustration © Juan Du.

241 *Left:* McMaster University Library Digital Archive. Licensed by CC BY-NC 2.5 CA. *Right:* Satellite imagery © 2017 DigitalGlobe, Inc. Overlay by Juan Du.

248 Photograph © Juan Du.

249 Photograph © Juan Du.

253 Illustration © Juan Du.

270 *Left:* McMaster University Library Digital Archive. Licensed by CC BY-NC 2.5 CA. *Right:* Satellite imagery © 2017 DigitalGlobe, Inc. Overlay by Juan Du.

275 Photograph © Juan Du.

294 Illustration © Juan Du.

296 Photograph © Juan Du.

297 Illustration © Juan Du.

INDEX